Exploring the
New
Management

Exploring the New Management

Third Edition

A Study Guide with Cases, Readings, Incidents, and Exercises

Robert M. Fulmer

Emory University

Theodore T. Herbert

Concordia University

MACMILLAN PUBLISHING CO., INC.
New York

Collier Macmillan Publishers
London

Macmillan Publishing Co., Inc.
866 Third Avenue, New York, New York 10022

Collier Macmillan Canada, Inc.

ISBN: 0-02-340080-3

Printing: 1 2 3 4 5 6 7 8   Year: 2 3 4 5 6 7 8 9 0

ISBN   0-02-340080-3

Preface

The critical factors that often determine whether a course is successful or less successful are the nature of instructional support given to those teaching the course and the structure of materials provided to students for reinforcing text concepts. For this third edition of *Exploring the New Management*, we've made extensive changes and additions — not substantive changes nor changes in format, for the substance and format of the previous editions were gratifyingly well accepted.

In this edition we have provided twenty new readings, while retaining three from the second edition. Twenty-nine new cases encourage the student to explore the new management in even more depth and with greater breadth than before. Fourteen new exercises have been added to stimulate the student through in-class or out-of-class projects, problems, and activities.

A format change of some importance is the Self-Review Questions on the content of the chapters in Fulmer's third edition of *The New Management*. Our intent was to allow more immediate and relevant feedback of mastery of the text material, directly to the student. At the end of each section of material are furnished the answers to the Review Questions for that chapter, for student use.

These extensive changes are intended to help make the introductory management course as effective and exciting as we think it should be. After all, would you expect a management book to claim the discipline of management to be intrinsically dull and pedantic? Or to teach that workers can best be motivated by forcing them to plod through layers of monotonous labor, sustained only by management's insistence that one day all of their effort will pay off? There often seems to be a wide gap between what a textbook promises and what it does itself.

If, as most texts claim, management is so exciting, why aren't more students excited by it? If managers ought to motivate workers creatively, why shouldn't management texts be expected to "turn on" their readers? We often asked ourselves these questions while conducting principles of management classes. They were a major stimulus to writing this manual. Being decidedly biased in favor of our field, we concluded that the problem lay not with the material being covered but with the manner in which it is traditionally presented. The usual dry approaches to presenting what is (to us, anyway) a dynamic and intriguing discipline seemed to be neither pedagogically necessary nor representative of the field's excitement. After all, does learning have to be painful to be effective?

We think not. We believe that the first step to learning is interest.

We realize that, however concerned about their students, instructors often simply don't have the time to gather all the materials they would like to have to insure that students are both stimulated and taught the basic knowledge that should be provided by the course. Coordinating such materials to the basic text is an added difficulty. We have therefore brought together in this manual a wide variety of materials that we have found to be useful in intro-ductory management courses. When selecting the materials, our major con-cern was that they be engaging while being informative. All provide the stu-dent with opportunities to practice and explore the substance of the new management; most allow the instructor assurance that students understand the essential concepts of management.

The organization of *Exploring the New Management* parallels that of Robert M. Fulmer's *The New Management*, but we believe it to be flexible enought to supplement virtually any principles of management text. Each chapter in this manual contains a number of questions to help students direct their study toward the essential knowledge being covered. Readings were chosen for their pertinence, educational value, *and readability*. It would take too much space here to elaborate on the exercises, but their variety is considerable, and we believe the exercises will be the most interest-ing, perhaps even the most educational, part of this manual for both students and instructors. The exercises are, we believe, the unique feature of this man-ual; most were originated by the authors, but some were adapted from stu-dents' ideas and other diverse sources.

We express our appreciation for the outstandingly good and timely typing services provided by the members of the Commerce Academic Sup-port Services group at Concordia University, particularly Mary Mullins, Kris Singh, and Sherri Rufh, who were directly involved in the project.

The following former students provided able assistance in researching cases, for which we thank them: Carol Ann Smith (Designkraft); Elio Bafile, Bill Cuming, Jim Mikula, and Jeff Speaks (Contingency System); Joseph J. Barret (Bank's Tanks); Andrew Daniels (State Univ. Physical Plant); Sandra J. Gladden (Mama Parker); David P. Globig (Pete's Big Decision); Irving E. Abcug (Poor Ralph); Larry R. Brown (Tunnel Optical); L. Fraser (Brown Construction Co.): Wilber F. Conley, Jr. (Tinkering Engineering Co.); James Coller (Control Control); Terrill J. Thompson (Super Wheel); John B. Kitto (Lana Dourman); Ken Lehmann (National Artcard); Patrick DeMarco (Mol-son's Bonus Boner); and R. W. McPherson (Overtime). Michael D. Gay, Jerry R. Clevenger, Paul A. Stamates, and Kevin P. Kelley assisted with some of the other materials; we thank them, too.

To our families, too, we extend our thanks for their support.

Contents

4 DECISION MAKING AND PROBLEM SOLVING

5 THE PLANNING PROCESS

6 ORGANIZATION FOR ACTION

15 TRAINING AND DEVELOPMENT FOR TOMORROW

16 COPING WITH THE CHALLENGE OF CHANGE

17 MANAGING PRODUCTION AND OPERATIONS

18 THE MODERN MANAGER'S QUANTITATIVE TOOL KIT

SO MANAGE!

Exploring the New Management

Chapter 1

The Intellectual Heritage of Management

CHAPTER OBJECTIVES

1. To show how management has been used throughout history in human attempts to progress

2. To let you see how the application of management requires a commitment to the idea of doing something better, which, in turn, requires individual creativity and curiosity

3. To trace the development of America's business system by looking at the changing patterns of problems and responses of business

SELF-REVIEW QUESTIONS

For each chapter in *The New Management*, this manual provides a selection of Self-Review Questions. The questions are intended to assist you in reviewing text materials and to serve as a check on how well you have mastered chapter content.

We recommend that you review completely the text chapter. Then answer the Self-Review Questions. Finally, refer to the answers provided on the last page of this (and every other) chapter material.

Matching

A. efficiency, production, competition   ____ 1. Adam Smith

B. deemphasized production, devoted attention to money matters   ____ 2. financial capitalism

C. rise of government influence to balance business abuses   ____ 3. Herbert Spencer

1

D. rise of the professional as the head
of large organizations   _____ 4. industrial capitalism

E. father of classical economics   _____ 5. laissez faire

F. no governmental interference in the
affairs of business   _____ 6. managerial capitalism

G. social Darwinism   _____ 7. national capitalism

True—False

T F   1. The businessperson has always been held in high regard because of the direct and indirect benefits brought and the needs met.

T F   2. The need for control by managers may have prompted the development of early writing.

T F   3. The early Egyptians excelled in the managerial skills of directing their human resources toward the accomplishment of huge tasks.

T F   4. Plato recognized the need for merchants to fill the day-to-day needs of the citizens.

T F   5. Aristotle was the first real champion of the role of profit in business dealings.

T F   6. One of the primary characteristics of petty capitalism was the principle of extending one's market beyond present boundaries.

T F   7. If America had had a long history of its own, it would not have been able to develop or respond to new ways of doing things as well as it has.

T F   8. The typical industrial capitalist excelled in the business skill of planning but was weak in merchandising and problem solving.

T F   9. In Smith's idea of a business system, competition would serve as a natural check to the abuses of unlimited self-interest.

T F 10. Adam Smith believed that increased productivity could be attained by increasing the degree of specialization.

T F 11. Industrial capitalists were usually no match for petty and mercantile capitalists when competition pitted them against each other; the industrial capitalists were far too slow in responding to the marketplace and were undercapitalized.

T F 12. A fundamental characteristic of financial capitalism was the cutthroat competition among competitors.

T F 13. Darwin stated that the weaker social institutions and businesses might have to be sacrificed to develop the stronger movements.

T F 14. National capitalism emerged as a solution to the problems created by the excesses (known as the Depression) of financial capitalism.

T   F   15. A danger in the system of managerial capitalism is the tendency of the large organization to swallow up and lose its human components.

Multiple Choice

1. One of the great eras of practicality in the history of mankind was

   (a) between 3000 B.C. and A.D. 1500, (b) between A.D. 1492 and A.D. 1650, (c) between A.D. 1700 and today, (d) none of the above.

2. Which of the following did *not* have a high regard for work and business?

   (a) ancient Greeks, (b) ancient Romans, (c) ancient Hebrews, (d) early Christians

3. Effective management practice is

   (a) widespread, (b) known only to the elite, (c) mostly common sense, (d) none of the above.

4. Accounting was invented by

   (a) bankers in Florence, (b) priests in Sumer, (c) misanthropes in Bulgaria, (d) gnomes in Switzerland.

5. The early Egyptians, in their pyramid-building endeavors, were just as concerned then as management is today with

   (a) time, (b) money, (c) worker satisfaction, (d) none of the above.

6. The production of goods for exchange as well as consumption

   (a) characterized pre-business capitalism, (b) led to the establishment of the stock exchange, (c) was known as petty capitalism, (d) did not take place until the Industrial Revolution.

7. Adam Smith's *The Wealth of Nations* was a landmark book because it

   (a) led the way in recognizing that true wealth sprang from the human resource, (b) foresaw the advent of a cashless society, (c) proposed an economic nation made up of kingdoms that had common trade interests, (d) none of the above.

8. Industrial capitalists' strong suit was

   (a) production technology, (b) finance, (c) marketing, (d) all of the above.

9. Under managerial capitalism, big business is run

   (a) by professionals who do not own their firms, (b) to the detriment of the consumer, (c) in strict accord with profit rules, (d) by a series of decisions on the firm's assets.

10. The philosophy of social Darwinism fits in best with the predominating beliefs of

    (a) industrial capitalism, (b) managerial capitalism, (c) national capitalism, (d) financial capitalism.

COMPLETION

1. With the birth of the nation came the period of _____ capitalism in the emerging American business system.

2. A _____ was a device for business combination in which previously competing companies transferred their stock to a central body, allowing unified action and great economic power of all the companies against their enemies.

3. Governmental reaction against business abuses by tightening controls on business and enacting legislation protective of labor and petty capitalists is a characteristic of _____ capitalism.

4. We are currently living in the era of _____ capitalism.

READING

MANAGEMENT: ITS ROOTS AND ITS EMERGENCE

Peter F. Drucker

During the last fifty years, society in every developed country has become a society of institutions. Every major social task, whether economic perform-ance or health care, education or the protection of the environment, the pur-suit of new knowledge or defense is today being entrusted to big organiza-tions, designed for perpetuity and managed by their own managements. The performance of modern society — if not the survival of each individual — increasingly depends on the performance of these institutions.

Only seventy-five years ago such a society would have been inconceivable. In the society of 1900 the family still served in every single country as the agent of, and organ for, most social tasks. Institutions were few and small. The society of 1900, even in the most highly institutionalized countries, still resembled the Kansas prairie. There was one eminence, the central govern-ment. It loomed very large on the horizon — not because it was large but because there was nothing else around it. The rest of society was diffused in countless molecules: small workshops, small schools, the individual profes-sionals — whether doctors or lawyers — practicing by themselves, the farmers, the craftsmen, the neighborhood retail stores, and so on. There were the be-ginnings of big business — but only the beginnings. And what was then con-sidered a giant business would strike us today as very small indeed.

The octopus which so frightened the grandparents of today's Americans, Rockefeller's giant Standard Oil Trust, was split into fourteen parts by the U.S. Supreme Court in 1911. Thirty years later, on the eve of America's entry into World War II, every single one of these fourteen Standard Oil daughters had become at least four times as large as the octopus when the

Supreme Court divided it — in employment, in capital, in sales, and in every other aspect. Yet, among those fourteen there were only three major oil companies—Jersey Standard, Mobil, and Standard of California. The other eleven were small to fair-sized, playing little or no role in the world economy and only a limited role in the U.S. economy.

While business has grown in these seventy years, other institutions have grown much faster. There was no university in the world before 1914 that had much more than 6,000 students — and only a handful that had more than 5,000. Today the university of 6,000 students is a pygmy; there are even some who doubt that it is viable. The hospital, similarly, has grown from a marginal institution to which the poor went to die into the center of health care and a giant in its own right — and also into one of the most complex social institutions around. Labor unions, research institutes, and many others have similarly grown to giant size and complexity.

In the early 1900s the citizens of Zurich built themselves a splendid City Hall, which they confidently believed would serve the needs of the city for all time to come. Indeed, it was bitterly attacked as gross extravagance, if not as megalomania. Government in Switzerland has grown far less than in any other country in the world. Yet the Zurich City Hall long ago ceased to be adequate to house all the offices of the city administration. By now, these offices occupy ten times or more the space that seventy-five years ago seemed so splendid — if not extravagant.

THE EMPLOYEE SOCIETY
The citizens of today in every developed country are typically employees. They work for one of the institutions. They look to the institutions for their livelihood. They look to the institutions for their opportunities. They look to the institutions for access to status and function in society, as well as for personal fulfillment and achievement.

The citizens of 1900, if employed, worked for a small family-type operation; the small pop-and-mom store employing a helper or two; the family household; and so on. And of course, the great majority of people in those days, except in the most highly industrialized countries — such as Britain or Belgium — worked on the farm.

Our society has become an employee society. In the early 1900s people asked, "What do you do?" Today they tend to ask, "Whom do you work for?"

And management is the specific organ of the new institution, whether business enterprise or university, hospital or armed service, research lab or government agency. If institutions are to function, managements must perform.

The word "management" is a singularly difficult one. It is, in the first place, specifically American and can hardly be translated into any other language, not even into British English. It denotes a function but also the people who discharge it. It denotes a social position and rank but also a discipline and field of study.

But even within the American usage, management is not adequate as a term, for institutions other than business do not speak of management or managers, as a rule. Universities or government agencies have administrators, as have hospitals. Armed services have commanders. Other institutions speak of executives, and so on.

Yet all these institutions have in common the management function, the management task, and the management work. In all of these there is a group of people whose function it is to "manage," and who have legal power and responsibility as managers. In all of them there is the same task: making the institution perform. And in all of them this requires doing specific work: setting objectives, goals and priorities; organizing; staffing; measuring results; communicating and decision making; and so on. All these institutions require management. And in all of them, management is the effective, the active, organ.

The institution itself is, in effect, a fiction. It is an accounting reality, but not a social reality. When this or that government agency makes this ruling or this decision, we know perfectly well that it is some people within the agency who make the ruling or the decision and who act for the agency and as the effective organ of the agency. When we speak of General Electric closing a plant, it is not, of course, General Electric that is deciding and acting, it is a group of managers within the company.

Georg Siemens, who built the Deutsche Bank into the European continent's leading financial institution in the decade between 1870 and 1880, once said, "Without management, a bank is so much scrap, fit only to be liquidated." Without institution there is no management. But without management there is no institution. Management is the specific organ of the modern institution. It is the organ whose performance determines the performance and even the survival of the institution.

MANAGEMENT IS PROFESSIONAL
We further know that management is independent of ownership, rank, or power. It is objective function and ought to be grounded in the responsibility for performance. It is professional — management is a function, a discipline, a task to be done; and managers are the professionals who practice this discipline, carry out the functions, and discharge these tasks. It is no longer relevant whether the manager is also an owner; ownership is incidental to the main job which is to manage.

FROM BUSINESS SOCIETY TO PLURALIST SOCIETY
Society in the Western world *was* a business society — seventy-five years ago. Then business was, indeed, the most powerful of all institutions — more powerful even than some governments. Since the turn of the century, however, the importance of business has gone down steadily — not because business has become smaller or weaker, but because the other institutions have grown so much faster. Business is no longer the singularly important institution in society; the other institutions have grown to be equally, or more, important. Society has become pluralist.

In the United States in the 1970s, no businessman compares in power or visibility with the tycoons of 1900, such as J. P. Morgan, John D. Rockefeller, or — a little later — Henry Ford. Few people today even know the names of the chief executive officers of America's biggest corporations; the names of the tycoons were household words. Not even the largest corporation today can compare in power and even in relative wealth with those tycoons who could hold the U.S. government for ransom.

The power of business has been displaced. No business today — in fact, no business in American history — has a fraction of the power that today's big university has. By granting or denying admission or the college degree, the university grants or denies access to jobs and livelihoods. Such power no business — and no other institution — ever had before in American history. Indeed, no earlier institution would ever have been permitted such power.

In the United States of 1900, almost the only career opportunity open to the young and ambitious was business. Today there are untold others, each promising as much (or more) income, and advancement as rapid, as a career in business.

Around the turn of the century, whatever of the gross national product did not go to the farmer went in and through the private business economy. The nonbusiness service institutions, beginning with government, accounted probably for no more than 10 per cent of the nonfarm gross national product of the United States at the turn of the century and up till World War I. Today, while farming has largely become a business, more than half of the gross national product goes to or through service institutions which are not businesses and which are not held accountable for economic performance.

Well over a third of the gross national product in the United States today goes directly to governments, federal, state, and local. Another 3 to 5 per cent goes to nongovernmental schools, that is, private and parochial, including the nongovernmental colleges and universities. Another 5 per cent of GNP, that is, two-thirds of the total health-care bill, is also nongovernmental, but also nonbusiness. On top of this, there is a great variety of not-for-profit activities, accounting maybe for another 2 to 5 per cent of gross national product. This adds up to 50 or perhaps as much as 60 per cent of the GNP which does not go to the business sector but to, or through, public-service institutions.

Indeed, while the current crop of radicals may talk of the big-business society, their actions show a keen awareness that business is not the dominant institution. Every period of public unrest since the end of the Napoleonic Wars began with uprisings against business. But the revolt against authority that swept the developed countries in the sixties centered in the institutions — especially the university — which were most esteemed by yesterday's radicals and which were, so to speak, the good guys of organization thirty or forty years ago.

The nonbusiness, public-service institutions do not need management less than business. They may need it more.

There is a growing concern with management in nonbusiness institutions.

Among the best clients of the large American management consulting firms these last ten or fifteen years have been government agencies such as the Department of Defense, the City of New York, or the Bank of England. When Canada in the late sixties first created a unified military service, with army, navy, and air force all combined, the first conference of Canadian generals and admirals was not on strategy; it was on management. The venerable orders of the Catholic Church are engaged in organization studies and in management development, with the Jesuits in the lead.

An increasing number of students in advanced management courses are not business executives but executives from hospitals, from the armed services, from city and state governments, and from school administrations. The Harvard Business School even runs an increasingly popular advanced management course for university presidents.

The management of the nonbusiness institutions will indeed be a growing concern from now on. Their management may well become the central management problem — simply because the lack of management of the public-service institution is such a glaring weakness, whether municipal water department or graduate university.

And yet, *business management is the exemplar.* And any book on management, such as this one, has to put management in the center.

WHY BUSINESS MANAGEMENT HAS TO BE THE FOCUS

One reason is history. Business enterprise was the first of the modern institutions to emerge. From the beginning, that is, from the emergence of the railroads as large businesses in the late nineteenth century, business enterprise was unmistakably a new and different institution rather than an outgrowth of older ones, as were apparently government agency, university, hospital, and armed service. There was, of course, concern about management in these institutions. But until recently it was sporadic and undertaken usually in connection with an acute problem and confined to it. But the work on management in business and industry was from the beginning meant to be generic and continuous.

Another reason why the study of management to this day has primarily been a study of business management is that so far the economic sphere alone has measurements both for the allocation of resources and for the results of decisions. Profitability is not a perfect measurement; no one has even been able to define it, and yet it is a measurement, despite all its imperfections. None of the other institutions has measurements so far. All they have are opinions — which are hardly an adequate foundation for a discipline.

The most important reason for focusing on business management is that it is the success story of this century. It has performed within its own sphere. It has provided economic goods and services to an extent that would have been unimaginable to the generation of 1900. And it has performed despite world wars, depressions, and dictatorships.

The achievement of business management enables us today to promise — perhaps prematurely (and certainly rashly) — the abolition of the grinding poverty that has been mankind's lot through the ages. It is largely the achievement of business management that advanced societies today can afford mass higher education. Business both produces the economic means to support this expensive undertaking and offers the jobs in which knowledge can become productive and can be paid for. That we today consider it a social flaw and an imperfection of society for people to be fixed in their opportunities and jobs by class and birth — where only yesterday there was the natural and apparently inescapable condition of mankind — is a result of our economic performance, that is, of the performance of business management. In a world that is politically increasingly fragmented and obsessed by nationalism, business management is one of the very few institutions capable of transcending national boundaries.

The multinational corporation brings together in a common venture management people from a great many countries with different languages, cultures, traditions, and values, and unites them in a common purpose. It is one of the very few institutions of our world that is not nationalistic in its world view, its values, and its decisions; but truly a common organ of a world economy that, so far, lacks a world polity, that is, a transnational political community or transnational political institutions.

It is also business management to which our society increasingly looks for leadership in respect to the quality of life. Indeed, what sounds like harsh criticism of business management tends often to be the result of high, perhaps unrealistically high, expectations based on the past performance of business management. "If you can do so well, why don't you do better?" is the underlying note.

This book will discuss performance in the nonbusiness service institution and I will stress again and again that managing the service institution is likely to be the frontier of management for the rest of this century. But the foundation of any work on management has to be business management.

The emergence of management may be the pivotal event of our time, far more important than all the events that make the headlines. Rarely, if ever, has a new basic institution, a new leading group, a new central function, emerged as fast as has management since the turn of the century. Rarely in human history has a new institution proven indispensable so quickly. Even less often has a new institution arrived with so little opposition, so little disturbance, so little controversy. And never before has a new institution encompassed the globe as management has, sweeping across boundaries of race and creed, language and traditions, within the lifetime of many men still living and at work.

Today's developed society, without aristocracy, without large landowners, even without capitalists and tycoons, depends for leadership on the managers of its major institutions. It depends on their knowledge, on their vision, and on their responsibility. In this society, management — its tasks, its responsibilities, its practices — is central: as a need, as an essential contribution, and as a subject of study and knowledge.

THE ROOTS AND EARLY HISTORY OF MANAGEMENT

Some writers seem to believe that the "management boom" of the post-World-War-II years invented, or at least discovered, management. Management, both as a practice and as a field of thought and study, has a long history. Its roots go back almost two hundred years.

Management, one might say, was discovered before there was any management to speak of. The great English economists from Adam Smith (1723–

1790) to David Ricardo (1772–1823) to John Stuart Mill (1806–1873), including their successor and antagonist, Karl Marx (1818–1883), knew no management. To them the economy was impersonal and objective. As a modern exponent of the classical tradition, the Anglo-American Kenneth Boulding (b. 1910) phrases it, "Economics deals with the behavior of commodities, rather than with the behavior of men." Or, as with Marx, impersonal laws of history were seen to dominate. Man can only adapt. Man can, at best, optimize what the economy makes possible; at worst, he impedes the forces of the economy and wastes resources. The last of the great English classical economists, Alfred Marshall (1842–1924), did indeed add management to the factors of production, land, labor, and capital. But this was a half-hearted concession. Management was still, even to Marshall, an extraneous factor, rather than central.

From the beginning there was a different approach which put the manager into the center of the economy and which stressed the managerial task of making resources productive. J. B. Say (1767–1832), perhaps the most brilliant economist produced by France—or for that matter by continental Europe — was an early follower of Adam Smith and the propagandist for *The Wealth of Nations* in France. But in his own works the pivot is not the factors of production. It is the entrepreneur — a word Say coined — who directs resources from less productive into more productive investments and who thereby creates wealth. Say was followed by the "utopian socialists" of the French tradition, especially François Fourier (1772–1837) and the eccentric genius, the Comte de Saint-Simon (1760–1825). At that time there were no large organizations and no managers, but both Fourier and Saint-Simon anticipated developments and "discovered" management before it actually came into being. Saint-Simon in particular saw the emergence of organization. And he saw the task of making resources productive and of building social structures. He saw managerial tasks.

It is for their stress on management as a separate and distinct force, and one which can act independently of the factors of production as well as of the laws of history, that Marx vehemently denounced the French and gave them the derisory name of "utopians." But it is the French — and above all, Saint-Simon — who, in effect, laid down the basic approaches and the basic concepts on which every socialist economy has actually been designed. No matter how much the Russians today invoke the name of Marx, their spiritual ancestor is Saint-Simon.

In America too management was early seen as central. Alexander Hamilton's (1757–1804) famous "Report on Manufactures" starts out with Adam Smith, but then Hamilton gave emphasis to the constructive, purposeful, and systematic role of management. He saw in management, rather than in economic forces, the engine of economic and social development; and in organization, the carrier of economic advance. Following him, Henry Claey (1777–1852) with his famous "American system" produced what might be called the first blueprint for systematic economic development.

A little later, a Scottish industrialist, Robert Owen (1771–1858), actually became the first manager. In his textile mill in Lanark, Owen, in the 1820s, first tackled the problems of productivity and motivation, of the relationship of worker to work, of worker to enterprise, and of worker to management — to this day key questions in management. With Owen, the manager emerges as a real person, rather than as an abstraction, as in Say, Fourier, Saint-Simon, Hamilton, and Clay. But it was a long time before Owen had successors.

THE EMERGENCE OF LARGE-SCALE ORGANIZATION

What had to happen first was the rise of large-scale organization. This occurred simultaneously — around 1870 — in two places. In North America the transcontinental railroad emerged as a managerial problem. On the continent of Europe, the "universal bank" — entrepreneurial in aim, national in scope, and with multiple headquarters —made traditional structures and concepts obsolete, and required management.

One response was given by Henry Towne (1844-1924) in the United States, especially in his paper *"The Engineer as Economist."* Towne outlined what might be called the first program for management. He raised basic questions: effectiveness as against efficiency; organization of the work as against the organization of the plant community, that is, of the workers; value set in the marketplace and by the customer as against technical accomplishment. With Towne begins the systematic concern with the relationship between the tasks of management and the work of management.

At roughly the same time, in Germany, Georg Siemens (1839-1901), in building the Deutsche Bank into the leading financial institution of continental Europe, first designed an effective top management, first thought through the top-management tasks, and first tackled the basic problems of communications and information in the large organization.

In Japan, Eiichi Shibusawa (1840-1931), the Meiji statesman turned business leader, in the seventies and eighties first raised fundamental questions regarding the relationship between business enterprise and national purpose, and between business needs and individual ethics. He tackled management education systematically. Shibusawa envisioned the professional manager first. The rise of Japan in this century to economic leadership is largely founded on Shibusawa's thought and work.

A few decades later, in the years before and after the turn of the century, all the major approaches to modern management were fashioned. Again the developments occurred independently in many countries.

In the 1880s Frederick W. Taylor (1856-1915), the self-taught American engineer, began the study of work. It is fashionable today to look down on Taylor and to decry his outmoded psychology, but Taylor was the first man in the known history of mankind who did not take work for granted, but looked at it and studied it. His approach to work is still the basic foundation. And, while Taylor in his approach to the worker was clearly a man of the nineteenth century, he started out with social rather than engineering or profit objectives. What led Taylor to his work and provided his motivation throughout was first the desire to free the worker from the burden of heavy toil, destructive of body and soul. And then it was the hope to break the Iron Law of wages of the classical economists (including Marx) which condemned the worker to economic insecurity and to enduring poverty. Taylor's hope — and it has largely been fulfilled in the developed countries — was to make it possible to give the laborer a decent livelihood through increasing productivity of work.

Around the same time in France, Henri Fayol (1841–1925), head of a coal mine which for its time was a very large company, first thought through organization structure and developed the first rational approach to the organization of enterprise: the functional principle. In Germany, Walther Rathenau (1867–1922), whose early training had been in a large company (the German equivalent of the General Electric Company, AEG, founded by his father, Emil [1838–1915], but developed in large part under the supervision of Georg Siemens), asked: "What is the place of the large enterprise in a modern society and in a modern nation? What impact does it have on both? And, what are its fundamental contributions and its fundamental responsibilities?" Most present questions of the social responsibilities of business were first raised and thought through by Rathenau in the years before World War I. Also in Germany, at the same time, the new discipline of *Betriebswissenschaft*, literally the "science of enterprise," was developed by such men as Eugen Schmalenbach (1873–1955). The management sciences developed since — managerial accounting, operations research, decision theory, and so on — are largely extensions, though in the main, unconscious ones, of the *Betriebswissenschaft* of those years before World War I. And in America, German-born Hugo Muensterberg (1863–1916) first tried to apply the social and behavioral sciences, and especially psychology, to modern organization and management.

Questions for Discussion

1. What comparisons can be made between 1900 and today in the importance of organizations?

2. As organizations grew in size, complexity, and importance, management became essential to success. Why has this happened? What is the role of the manager in affecting the functioning of an organization?

3. Did the famous economists and others cited by Drucker agree on the importance or function of management? Why or why not?

EXERCISE

MANAGING HISTORICALLY

In the text, management is defined as "the concepts, techniques, and processes that enable goals to be achieved efficiently and effectively." How important do you think that management was in each of the following eras? Be specific in identifying the reasons for your evaluation of the importance of management in the era.

A. Egypt between 4000 B.C. and 525 B.C.

B. Prebusiness capitalism (A.D. 500–1100)

C. Petty capitalism (A.D. 1100–1400)

D. Mercantilism (1400–1776)

E. Industrial capitalism (1776–1890)

F. Financial capitalism (1890–1933)

G. National capitalism (1933–1950)

H. Managerial capitalism (1950–now)

EXERCISE

THE AMERICAN BUSINESS LEADER'S BIOGRAPHICAL SKETCH

Those in business tend to reflect prevalent opportunities and system; to succeed, after all, customer needs must be recognized and met *through* methods generally approved by the current economic system. How does the businessperson reflect this environment? Why are particular types of business managers more successful under one particular economic form of business then under another? This exercise is intended to show how economic form and the business leader's "style" are so tightly related by contrasting the requirements imposed by the four periods upon how those in business operated and succeeded.

You are writing a biography of a great, nationally known business leader. He or she is distinguished as a spokesperson for industry, and as one intimately familiar enough with the workings of the American business system to have accumulated the laurels associated with complete success.

You plan on writing a chapter on that person's (1) personal traits and personality; one on (2) methods for success, one on (3) strengths (both personal and business); and one on (4) weaknesses (both personal and business).

FOR THE STUDENT

Write a one-paragraph summary on *each* of the chapter topics listed above for the subject of your book; do this for what you think a *typical* business leader would be like for each of the four periods discussed in the text (industrial, financial, national, and managerial capitalism eras).

1. A business leader during the era of industrial capitalism

2. A business leader during the era of financial capitalism

3. A business leader during the era of national capitalism

4. A business leader during the era of managerial capitalism

ANSWERS TO SELF-REVIEW QUESTIONS, CHAPTER 1

Matching

A-4, B-2, C-7, D-6, E-1, F-5, G-3

True - False

1-F, 2-T, 3-T, 4-T, 5-F, 6-F, 7-T, 8-F, 9-T, 10-T, 11-F, 12-F, 13-F, 14-T, 15-T

Multiple Choice

1-C, 2-D, 3-C, 4-B, 5-D, 6-C, 7-D, 8-A, 9-A, 10-D

Completion

1-industrial, 2-trust, 3-national, 4-managerial

Chapter 2

The Emergence of American Business and Management Thought

CHAPTER OBJECTIVES

1. To show the changing emphasis in management thought as new problems or techniques develop over time

2. To relate the contributions of some of the major luminaries of management thought and to show how they advanced the state of the discipline

3. To give you the opportunity of viewing management as a constantly changing body of knowledge, dynamically responding to its environment

SELF-REVIEW QUESTIONS

Matching

I. *Place the letter of the phrase associated with each person in the blank provided.*

A. motion study   _____ 1. Fayol

B. humanized scientific management   _____ 2. Follett

C. scientific approach to lower management problems   _____ 3. Gantt

D. employees are vital machines   _____ 4. Gilbreths

E. father of human relations   _____ 5. Mayo

F. analyzed the problems of top management   _____ 6. Owen

G. political and managerial philosopher   _____ 7. Taylor

15

II. *Match each of the people below with the letter of the "link" in the management chain with which they may be classified (each "link" may be used more than one time).*

link person

A. administration ____ 1. Babbage ____ 8. Koontz

B. human relations ____ 2. Barnard ____ 9. Mayo

C. scientific manage- ____ 3. Davis ____ 10. Munsterberg
ment

____ 4. Fayol ____ 11. Owen

____ 5. Follett ____ 12. Taylor

____ 6. Gantt ____ 13. Urwick

____ 7. Gilbreths

True–False

T F 1. A major benefit of examining the history of and contributors to management thought is that one then can answer current questions or solve today's problems using the solutions of pioneering experts.

T F 2. Charles Babbage is widely acclaimed as the "father of scientific management."

T F 3. Under Taylor's idea of functional management, a single supervisor would be replaced by eight different people, each a specialist in a particular duty.

T F 4. Gantt was one of the first to pioneer in the humanizing of the science of management.

T F 5. Gantt insisted that efficiency demanded the worker adapt to the work and work methods.

T F 6. Mayo discovered that worker productivity is related most to the tools and machines provided for workers to do their jobs.

T F 7. Robert Owen was one of the first industrialists to replace slower workers with machines.

T F 8. The Gilbreths felt that industrial productivity was pursued best through the motivation of the worker, rather than work methods.

T F 9. The "direct incentives" designated by the Gilbreths consist of promotion, pay, shorter hours, and so forth.

T F 10. The French engineer who contributed greatly to European management practice was Follett.

T F 11. Scientific management, while it was a much-needed analytical approach to management problems, nevertheless failed to provide anything but meager cost savings.

T   F   12. The Hawthorne studies showed conclusively that workers recognize the value of their work and will not be good producers unless their work is paid roughly equal to its value.

Multiple Choice

1. Which of the following is *not* a link in the management process?

   (a) administration, (b) scientific management, (c) human relations, (d) analysis

2. Charles Babbage

   (a) was a pioneer in computer principles, (b) was one of the first to scientifically study production problems, (c) believed in the benefits and efficiency of using division of labor, (d) pioneered cost studies, (e) all of the above.

3. Frederick W. Taylor felt that

   (a) labor and management have basically common interests and should work together, (b) a rational investigation to obtain information and determine correct procedures was needed in business, (c) there is only one best way to do a job, (d) none of the above.

4. In his pig-iron handling study, Taylor

   (a) increased workers' wages, (b) reduced labor cost per ton, (c) scientifically selected workers most suited to the specific job, (d) all of the above.

5. When Taylor investigated the best way to shovel, he found that the most important things to consider were _____ and _____ .

   (a) strength . . . stamina, (b) worker motivation . . . pay, (c) allowance for fatigue . . . work hours per day, (d) density of material . . . shovel load size, (e) none of the above

6. According to Chester Barnard, the first step in understanding the nature of organizations and what they do, is to

   (a) examine their output, both goods and services, (b) understand individuals and how they behave in organizations, (c) look at organization charts, (d) know managers and their theories of management, (e) none of the above.

7. The Hawthorne experiments were originally intended to investigate

   (a) productivity of workers under different conditions, (b) how special treatment of workers increases productivity, (c) how morale influences productivity, (d) the Hawthorne effect, (e) none of the above.

8. Which of the following were *not* demonstrated through the Hawthorne studies?

   (a) human social and psychological needs are just as effective motivators as is money, (b) the human factor cannot be ignored in any accurate management planning, (c) the social interaction of the work group is as influential as the way the actual work task is organized, (d) none of the above

9. The Gilbreths used motion study techniques to do all of the following except

(a) establish more accurate pay and production standards for the job,
(b) eliminate motions and effort that were nonproductive or wasted,
(c) determine the effects of fatigue on how well workers did their jobs,
(d) none of the above.

10. Which of the following were general administrative principles listed by Fayol?

(a) initiative, (b) navigational change, (c) flexibility of planning,
(d) social responsibility of business

READING

THE MASTERMINDS OF MANAGEMENT

Paula Smith

Corporate management did not spring from theorists in ivory towers. It was created out of necessity. By the mid-nineteenth century, the enterprises put together by the early tycoons had grown so big and posed so many new problems that new methods of control and communication had to be found. The railroads — more capital hungry, expensive to run and spread out than any other industry — were the first to grapple with new ideas for operating on a vast scale. From that beginning, as corporations became increasingly complex, innovative management techniques spread to one growth industry after another — from steel to chemicals to automobiles.

Over the years, scores of idea men have come up with new management concepts and techniques. But five major innovators have proven to be the most influential in determining the form and function of the American corporation: J. Edgar Thomson, Andrew Carnegie, Frederick W. Taylor, Pierre du Pont and Alfred P. Sloan.

J. Edgar Thomson, who became the first president of the Pennsylvania Railroad, developed the world's biggest and first truly modern business organization. When Thomson took over the newly formed Pennsy in 1852, a theory of large-scale administration had been worked out by Daniel McCallum, general superintendent of the Erie Railroad. Taking McCallum's principles, Thomson was the first to apply them in a major way — testing and developing them into a cohesive management structure during the two decades he guided the Pennsy.

Thomson formulated an advanced information system for management decision making. He defined lines of authority and communications, created detailed job descriptions and accountability for employees at all levels and set up an extensive recordkeeping system. Executives in every department had to keep track of revenues and expenses in great detail — providing, Thomson claimed, a checking system that virtually eliminated the possibility of fraud.

All this minute data gave the central office a precise picture of the railroad's strengths and weaknesses. Statistics such as train mileage, the number of passengers and the amount of time a locomotive spent in service or repair each day were collected at the lowest level, combined at the divisional level and presented to the general superintendent — who could then see which division and which services were profitable and efficient and which needed to be restructured or eliminated. This in turn allowed management to better determine the most profitable use of resources — whether, for instance, to make a repair or postpone it, whether to raise or lower rates. So effective was the system that the Pennsy came to be known as the "standard railroad of the world."

Thomson's techniques were carried into other fields by men who would also build huge organizations. Theodore Vail, for one, used the methods he had learned operating the U.S. Post Office's railroad mail service to create the world's most efficient and biggest privately owned communications system — American Telephone & Telegraph Co.

Thomson's most notable disciple, however, was Andrew Carnegie, former superintendent of the Pennsy's Western division. Carnegie transferred Thomson's accounting and information system to manufacturing — and added ideas of his own. Starting out in the iron and steel industry in the 1860s when it was an assortment of small producers, Carnegie built a company so large and so efficient that his competitors were forced to imitate his methods. Carnegie was obsessed with costs. At Carnegie Steel Corp., not only was every bit of material kept track of, small slivers that accumulated in the rolling of steel were collected and recycled, and the blast-furnace flue-cinder, which other steelmakers threw away, was saved to be reused as fuel.

Carnegie systematized cost analysis by setting up a detailed unit system for tracking the company's labor and material costs; the cost data were then applied in making marketing, investment and personnel decisions. Knowing his costs so precisely enabled Carnegie to price his products precisely — and undersell his competitors. His fanaticism about costs also led him to constantly seek more efficient and technologically advanced machinery, and Carnegie plowed back profits into new equipment on a scale that no one in manufacturing had ever done before. He was even known to tear down half-built new furnaces and start over if somebody came up with an idea for better cost efficiency.

Carnegie was also one of the earliest chief executives to use profit-sharing as an incentive — if in his own tightfisted way. He kept management salaries at a minimum, with a top annual salary of about $5,000 at a time the railroads were paying $100,000. Instead, he offered his managers partnership shares. But he held down the book value of the company by not allowing the capitalization to reflect true assets so that the partners' shares would not rise in value. Believing that one day their shares would be worth a great deal of money — which they were — the partners felt they could not afford to leave Carnegie.

While Carnegie started industry on a new way of thinking about production and costs in the overall manufacturing operation, it was Frederick W. Taylor who first systematically sought ways to get the most out of every man and machine on the factory floor. By the last decades of the nineteenth century, mass-production techniques were spreading, and methods for controlling and administering the factory floor were badly needed. Building on a number of ideas already known, Taylor, an engineer, formulated his concept of "scientific management," aimed at reorganizing the production line for maximum efficiency.

Taylor started developing his theories in the 1880s with time-and-motion experiments at Midvale Steel Works and Bethelehem Steel Co. Armed with a stopwatch, he tried to determine how much time and physical movement it took for workers to perform their tasks. From this knowledge, he felt that a high degree of standardization could be achieved, which would lower labor costs and increase profits. Each job was broken into as many elementary movements as possible. By observing the most skilled workmen at their jobs, the best and quickest methods were selected. Each movement was timed and recorded, and additional time was added to cover such things as unavoidable delays, a new worker's lack of familiarity with the job and rest periods. A file of these elementary movements and times could then be built for use in other jobs or types of work. Taylor conducted experiments on everything from lighting to the less tangible aspects of the working environment, such as social hierarchies in the plant and the suitability of workers to their jobs.

Needless to say, labor was not enchanted with Taylor's experiments and interpreted them as ways to push workers harder for bigger profits. Workers also balked at Taylor's incentive wage system, which penalized substandard performance. But Taylor, who always denied charges that his ideas were "inhuman," believed that maximum efficiency and output were not possible unless workers were reasonably content in their jobs.

Scientific management was promoted and publicized by Louis D. Brandeis. A lawyer for customers of Eastern railroads, Brandeis used Taylor's theories as an argument against proposed increases in freight rates. Taylor's ideas were further popularized in the press, and in 1911 more than 300 educators, consultants and businessmen gathered at Dartmouth College for the world's first Scientific Management Conference. That same year Taylor published his major treatise, *The Principles of Scientific Management.* Through the work of his many followers, Taylor's methods became standard practice throughout industry and the foundation for modern industrial psychology and personnel management.

Pierre du Pont knew the work of both Carnegie and Taylor. He had hired Taylor as a consultant when he was in the steel business. Du Pont, though, was particularly concerned about higher-echelon management problems. While Carnegie and Taylor worked out ideas at the factory level, it was with du Pont that modern top management came into being.

When du Pont took over the family firm, E. I. du Pont de Nemours & Co., already a century old, most industrial companies were still run from a central office that was basically a one-man show. Du Pont revolutionized the general office, setting up the procedures for forecasting, long-range planning, budgeting and allocating resources that executives today take for granted. Charles A. Coffin was building a general office along the same lines at General Electric, but du Pont's creation was more systematic. And while some students of management consider John D. Rockefeller the founder of top management, the committee system he had established at Standard Oil some thirty years before was eventually scrapped and replaced almost entirely with the du Pont system.

Du Pont built functional departments for manufacturing, sales, purchasing, capital expenditures planning and traffic. On top of the departments he set up a tightly centralized general office to control sales, purchasing, manufacturing, personnel and so forth for the entire organization. The company's governing body was the executive committee, composed of the president and the heads of the major departments.

To enable the executive committee to allocate resources, du Pont set up a system to provide it with information about departmental capital expenditures — data on costs, anticipated rate of return on proposed spending, and so forth. Departmental expenditure requests were also checked by purchasing, engineering and traffic specialists. Plant managers and department heads were allowed to authorize smaller capital expenditures, but a senior executive reviewed the big ones.

Besides being judged on their likely rate of return, capital spending proposals were evaluated as part of the company's long-term growth plans. That, in turn, was based on estimates of market demand, for which du Pont developed advanced forecasting techniques. The executive committee also coordinated the flow of materials through the corporate empire, attempting to control inventory at all stages, the physical movement of goods and the fluctuating demands for working capital.

But this functional, highly centralized structure broke down after World War I, when du Pont diversified into paints, dyes, chemicals and fibers. The complexities created by diversification, coupled with a severe postwar recession, brought about an inventory crisis, and du Pont suffered big losses. In a major administrative reorganization, the central office that du Pont had created was altered to become the banker and resource allocator for decentralized divisions. In effect, the company separated top management and the allocation of resources from the day-to-day operations of the divisions.

Controlled decentralization, though, really came into its own at General Motors Corp. The du Pont family had a $25 million investment in GM and Pierre du Pont became president in 1920. What he found was a company trembling on the edge of collapse, a corporate shambles. Its founder and former president William Durant, a collector of automobile and parts manufacturing companies and one of the greatest business promoters the country has ever known, had not set up any central financial or policy control. The division presidents set prices independently of each other, had complete authority over inventories and income, and very often made their own financial arrangements with banks. Durant put little stock in data and seldom bothered to tell anyone, even his executive committee, what he was up to.

One of Durant's top managers was Alfred Pritchard Sloan Jr., who headed a group of supply companies that Durant had acquired. Sloan had evolved a detailed plan for reorganizing the company. But it was ignored by Durant, and Sloan was on the verge of quitting when du Pont stepped in. Du Pont recognized and endorsed the management concepts set down in Sloan's now-famous 1920 Organization Study. Together, du Pont and Sloan, who succeeded him as president and chief executive in 1923, instituted a formula for "decentralized operations with centralized policy control." Similar to the one that was simultaneously emerging at du Pont, Sloan's system became the model for most industrial corporations.

Essentially, the system enabled top management to control the various parts of the business in a rational way. Each division was basically an individual operating company, with its own manufacturing, sales, purchasing departments and so on. But it would have to operate according to guidelines — on everything from basic organization to reporting procedures — established by top management. Under the system, the divisions were required to come up with very detailed figures on costs, sales, purchases, profits and the like so that top management could authorize production levels. And while the divisions had the responsibility of developing their own operating plans and proposals, it was ultimately headquarters that made the big decisions on how the company's resources would be deployed.

Sloan's devotion to controls, measurements and forecasts, and an organizational mechanism that made them work, was responsible for much of GM's success. It was Sloan who recognized at the right moment, after World War I, that Americans' taste in automobiles was changing. In the early 1920s, he saw, as Henry Ford did not, that consumers were no longer being adequately served by a single car that would provide reliable transportation at the lowest cost. They wanted variety — a car for every taste and every purse — with style, not engineering, as the dominant consideration. By 1926–27, GM was offering a line of cars that covered the price and range from Chevrolet to Cadillac. Needless to say, GM's flexible marketing strategy would prove to be correct.

Questions for Discussion

1. Who made the greatest contribution to the practice of management — Taylor, du Pont, or Sloan? Why?

2. Classify each of the management masterminds in the article by their orientation — scientific management, human relations, or administration.

2. If Taylor had led General Motors instead of Sloan, would GM have been as successful as it was? Why or why not?

EXERCISE

DESIGNKRAFT AND THE MANAGEMENT LINKS

The way that the manager thinks — the system of management thought used — has a direct effect on how he or she relates to people, how a management problem is analyzed, and how a management problem is solved. We can see this more clearly by investigating how a manager would "see" the same problem differently, depending on which link in the evolution of management thought is characteristically used.

Designkraft Inc. is a firm specializing in producing and marketing pressure-sensitive tape and labels. Designkraft has its own manufacturing plant, located in the same complex as the office personnel.

Designkraft has expanded rapidly in the last twenty years by building a solid reputation for excellent quality and quick delivery. Three years ago, the production workers unionized. Several production supervisors who had been with the company for years quit in a dispute over salary. Around the same time, a relative of the company's owners was hired as assistant production manager. Considered quite abrasive, this manager is in constant conflict with the workers. He has fired several employees over what they see as personal reasons and is disliked by the workers.

Designkraft's sales are increasing dramatically; the firm appears on the verge of becoming one of the major competitors in its field. Yet profits have decreased sharply. Merchandise is being returned for poor printing quality or failure to meet customer specifications. Orders are becoming backlogged, and delivery time has lengthened. The plant workers' enthusiasm seems to have slackened and their performance level has dropped. Material waste has reached an all-time high. Office personnel have been making more mistakes in completing purchase-order requisitions, and the production employees feel they are being unjustly blamed for office mistakes. Turnover and absenteeism are high. The top management recently employed your services to help determine where the problem is and to offer solutions.

FOR THE STUDENT

The text points out that management thought has shifted in its emphasis over the years; the scientific management link in management has been thought to be paramount in importance. So too, human relations and administration have their proponents.

Analyze the incident as you think a person representative of each of the three link areas would: That is, try to look at the situation from the point of view of each of the three link areas and find the problems and solutions each would likely find and propose. Which is "best"?

The following format is provided for you to write your observations. The first analysis will be for your observations as a scientific management emphasizer (perhaps like Taylor); the second with emphasis on human relations (perhaps like Mayo); the third emphasizing administration (perhaps like Fayol).

Scientific Management Link Analysis

1. What problems related to scientific management do you see in this situation?

2. How would you, an adherent to scientific management principles, solve these problems?

Human Relations Link Analysis

1. What problems related to human relations do you see in this situation?

2. How would you, an adherent to human relations principles, solve these problems?

Administration Link Analysis

1. What problems related to administration do you see in this situation?

2. How would you, an adherent to administration principles, solve these problems?

CASE

THE CONTINGENCY SYSTEM

U.S. Fastener Corporation (USFC) is a vertically integrated manufacturer of nuts, bolts, and specialized fasteners. It has eight plants in the United States and an equal number operating in Europe and Central America. Its operation begins with the purchase of iron ore and other raw materials and ends with the distribution of finished products to its customers, typically manufacturers of assembled products such as automobiles and household appliances. USFC is respected worldwide as a leader in its field. For years it has enjoyed a dominant market share in the Western Hemisphere and has supplied approximately 20 per cent of the European market.

Up until 1973, USFC and the fastener industry enjoyed a steady growth rate of about 7 per cent per year. However, in 1973 record sales of many durable goods, especially autos, caused an unexpected growth spurt of 15 per cent in the fastener industry. As a result of this unprecedented demand, USFC was forced to increase product lead times to its customers (i.e., the time required to fill an order after it was received) and fill orders on a first come, first served basis. Soon it became apparent that some major customers had not responded quickly enough to the longer lead times imposed and that these customers' production schedules would be severely disrupted if USFC adhered to its shipping policy. To prevent shorting major customers, USFC's Sales Department entered "dummy" orders for these customers, which had the desired effect of reserving fastener production for the major customers until their actual orders were received.

This case was prepared by Elio Bafile, Bill Cuming, Jim Mikula, and Jeff Speaks under the supervision of Theodore T. Herbert, to serve as the basis for class discussion.

Establishing dummy orders aggravated the problems already caused by the need for tight scheduling. In addition, a psychology of scarcity set in among all USFC customers, which resulted in each of them submitting inflated quantities on their orders.

By carefully juggling inventories and production schedules, USFC was able to avoid any serious inventory shortfalls among its customers. It even was able to supply the fastener needs of new customers who had been disappointed by USFC competitors. During 1975 demand for fasteners slackened; customers refrained from submitting inflated order quantities, and USFC lead times returned to normal.

In 1975 Jim McKay became vice-president of sales for USFC. Jim was sixty-two and had worked his way up the corporation, starting as a stock boy in the fettling department in 1936. His experience included the duties of stock attendant, fettler, foreman fettler, World War II marine sergeant, assistant to the vice-president of sales, general sales manager, and now vice-president of sales.

Jim became quite concerned about the operational problems that had developed in the sales department during the recent period when demand appeared to exceed supply. The sales department had been frustrated by not having all the products it would have liked to have to satisfy the market demand; its efficiency had suffered because of the amount of time spent in providing information to customers about availability of product, shipping information, and changes in requirements. During the period of high demand, customers were placing orders to cover their upcoming two-year requirements; this meant that each time a customer made a forecast change, 24 monthly records had to be updated at USFC to accommodate the change in delivery schedule. In periods of normal demand, in which the lead time is 13 weeks, very few records have to be changed for a given customer schedule change. During the high-demand period, the field sales representatives had also become preoccupied with solving delivery problems for their respective customers rather than carrying out their normal functions of designing USFC's products to custom applications and selling USFC products.

In examining the historical demand for USFC products, the vice-president of sales found that demand was highly irregular, following both business cycles and domestic and international economic cycles. Demand in any one quarter could swing anywhere between plus or minus 25 per cent of the long-term trend plotted for any of the USFC products. In the past, USFC had tried to optimize its production capacity and inventories to offset the effect of these peaks in demand, without having to have a large excess of capacity during the downturns in demand. McKay could see that, due to the large swing potential in demand, USFC should develop a system to predict future demand and regulate inventories. Such a system would enable proper rationing of scarce products during a market upturn and prevent USFC customers from experiencing severe shortages.

In addition, because of the downturn in the economies of the developed countries around the world in 1974 and 1975 and currency fluctuations around the U.S. dollar, the competitive situation for USFC products had worsened. USFC found itself in a situation in which the profits generated from operations were becoming insufficient to finance all of its current plant replacement and expansion plans. Capital restraints would prevent the scale of expansion needed to meet the full demand in all situations. Therefore, again it became imperative that USFC develop a plan to utilize its available capacity in the most efficient manner during both upswings and downturns in demand.

Jim decided to initiate a program to develop the required system. He issued a letter (Figure 1) designating John Cross as executive assistant to the vice-president, with responsibility for coordinating the efforts of the various planning, pricing, and systems areas within the company to come up with a computer-based contingency system that would allow USFC to make this allocation of products during the upswing in demand. The system he developed would also have to satisfy various legal restraints concerning refusal to deal, evidence of market power, and the favoring of one customer over another when both customers were mutual competitors. In order to meet legal constraints, the contingency system had to be developed and implemented on a unilateral basis. No connotation of "mutual planning" with customers would be permitted.

After carefully reviewing the system's requirements, John came to the conclusion that, for the contingency system to be effective, it had to be able to forecast, with a high degree of accuracy, both future plant capacity and future customer demand for any given product. The ratio of the forecast customer demand for a given product divided by the total forecast of available capacity for that product would then become the customer's allocation.

Because of the extremely large range of USFC products and the wide geographical dispersion of USFC plants, a complex market research model had to be developed that would accurately predict worldwide demand. The development of the system required considerable input from the marketing, production, and market research areas of the corporation. In addition, each field sales representative supplied a market forecast and a summary of current conditions for each of his or her customers. This vast amount of accumulated data had to be incorporated into the research model; nearly 15,000 person hours of systems analyst time and approximately the same number of programming hours were required to complete the program.

Through the continued efforts of John Cross, the contingency system was developed and implemented on time, which was considered a rare feat by many at USFC, considering the corporation's austerity program in effect at the time. During the 1975 downturn in demand for USFC products, the pressure was on throughout the corporation to hold costs down. One major factor in the fixed and variable costs of the corporation that came under close scrutiny was staffing levels. Because labor was becoming more and more like a fixed cost, both in the plants and in the offices, to hire new personnel required the final approval of the president of the corporation. Retirees and terminated employees were not replaced; gaps were filled in the organization by transferring personnel from less important to more important areas.

When the contingency system became operational, demand for USFC products returned to more normal levels, lead time shrank to the normal 13 weeks, and plants were working a normal five-day week.

Figure 1

U. S. FASTENER CORPORATION

Headquarters, U.S.A.

To: General Managers

From: Jim P. McKay
V.P. Sales

Gentlemen:

The following is a summary of the sequence of events which caused the inventory debacle the Fastener Industry experienced during 1973–1974:

1. Manufacturers were hardpressed to keep up with total demand.

2. Customer service was stressed so that a material shortage was intolerable and excessive inventory was accepted.

3. Customers feared that supplier capacity was limited, so double ordering was common. Receipt of the double order was acceptable in view of the inflation spiral at the time.

4. Manufacturers witnessed order backlogs growing faster than capacity, so longer delivery lead times were quoted.

5. When lead time increased, more orders were placed by users and larger backlogs became apparent. Step 4 was repeated again and again.

I am determined to henceforth control lead times and I have, therefore, appointed John Cross as my executive assistant to develop and implement a control system to avoid a repeat of these problems. Please provide him your cooperation and assistance.

cc: Corporate Services
Manufacturing Administration

As the contingency system was used, it became apparent that many daily inputs would be required to keep it current. Such variables as changes in plant capacity, industry demand, and forecast demand had to be considered for each customer. Corrections had to be made for any developments that could not have been anticipated in the original forecast.

A continual analysis would also have to be made between the contingency allocation for a given customer and the customer's level of demand in both up and down markets. In this way, unusual trends or activities by a given customer could be identified and the appropriate action taken by the field sales representatives. All this activity required continuing input from various functional areas within the sales department.

Once the contingency system was working satisfactorily, Jim decided that it was time to transfer the operation to the sales department. Each field salesperson would update the system whenever conditions changed for one of his or her customers. About this time, John Cross was transferred to another department.

Twelve months after transferring the operational responsibility to the sales department, the contingency data was reviewed by the industrial sales manager, Jack Straap, because he was concerned about a forecast upswing in market demand. Jack found that many of the basic records had not been updated in several months. He held informal discussions with the various managers and supervisors involved with the system. In particular, he talked with people who were supposed to be supplying inputs to the system or would be using the outputs during periods of high demand. In discussing the contingency system with several field salespeople, he found there to be some confusion among them about its importance. Jack learned that the salespeople had been called into a meeting shortly before the system was implemented and given instructions on how it was to be updated. At this time, they were told that continuous updating of the system was essential and that the printouts would be of great assistance to the production manager. Most of the sales representatives had submitted their (input) forms for the initial run of the contingency system and had submitted several update forms since that time. Because they had not received any feedback about their use of the forms, they had stopped submitting them. Most felt they had plenty of other things to do without worrying about additional forms sent from the head office.

The manager of market research stated that the complex market research model appeared to be working quite well, but that minor changes were required. He hoped to finalize the improvements in the system when some of his more senior people were freed from their current day-to-day activities.

The production manager pointed out that he had received the printouts from the contingency system, but felt that he really had no need for them; supply exceeded demand and he was not limited on capacity. He felt, of course, that the system would be a great benefit if and when demand exceeded supply. Therefore, he was merely filing his copy of the report. He had intended to provide updated information on plant capacity but felt that this should be done on an annual basis because current capacity far exceeded demand. When demand started to increase, he would try to update it on a more regular basis.

The people in order control had a similar reaction. They had envisioned the system being used to monitor the flow of incoming orders and allocate production to the various customers. But, because supply exceeded demand, they saw no need to monitor incoming orders. They also reviewed the first few reports and just filed the balance.

Jack Straap felt there was a real need to get the system operating satisfactorily while demand was still down, in readiness for the forecast upswing in product demand. Therefore, he was faced with decisions as to whether he should bring this matter to the attention of the vice-president of sales and, if he did, what recommendations he should offer for getting the contingency system operating properly.

Questions for Discussion

1. Analyze the case as you think a representative of each of the three link areas would: That is, try to look at the situation from the point of view of each of the three link areas and find the problems and solutions each would likely find and propose. The first analysis will be your observations as a scientific management emphasizer (perhaps like Taylor); the second with emphasis on human relations (perhaps like Mayo); and the the third emphasizing administration (perhaps like Fayol).

2. After defining the problems as the different link adherents would, prepare three sets of recommendations to Mr. Straap for getting the system operating properly, one set for each management link.

3. Finally, what conclusions can you draw about the validity or usefulness of the different links? That is, which is the "real" or "best" way to analyze management problems?

ANSWERS TO SELF-REVIEW QUESTIONS, CHAPTER 2

Matching

I. A-4, B-3, C-7, D-6, E-5, F-1, G-2.

II. A-3, 4, 5, 8, 13
   B-2, 9, 10, 11
   C-1, 6, 12
   7 (Gilbreths) could be classified either B or C.

True–False

1-F, 2-F, 3-T, 4-T, 5-F, 6-F, 7-F, 8-T, 9-F, 10-F, 11-F, 12-F.

Multiple-Choice

1-D, 2-E, 3-A, 4-D, 5-D, 6-B, 7-A, 8-D, 9-C, 10-A.

Chapter 3

Paths Through the Management Maze

CHAPTER OBJECTIVES

1. To emphasize the necessity for the complete manager to absorb and use the relevant portions of many different fields of study

2. To show that, although management can be analyzed from various points of view, there are basic things that each manager must do to accomplish his or her overall job

SELF-REVIEW QUESTIONS

Matching

A. We must study the past or be doomed to repeat it.

_____ 1. controlling

B. The complete manager understands and studies people.

_____ 2. coordination

C. The worker is part of a group and a group behaves differently from its members.

_____ 3. decision-theory approach to management

D. Every managerial activity is one of decision making.

_____ 4. directing

E. systematic approach to problem solution

_____ 5. empirical approach to management

F. setting objectives and determining how to take action

_____ 6. human behavior approach to management

G. arranging the necessary jobs so
they will be done most efficiently   ____   7. mathematical approach
to management

H. making sure that events go as
intended   ____   8. organizing

I. manpower considerations   ____   9. planning

J. guiding employees as they do
their jobs   ____ 10. social sciences approach
to management

K. any collection of things that
work together for a common
purpose   ____ 11. staffing

L. the essence of management   ____ 12. system

True–False

T   F   1. Management closely resembles law or medicine in that it is a science based on precedent.

T   F   2. If you faced a situation in the past and solved it, then by using the same solution you should be able to solve that problem again.

T   F   3. By using the results of psychological studies, the manager can make workers do just what he or she wants.

T   F   4. Leaders are usually managers.

T   F   5. The social sciences approach to management stresses the importance of the individual as the primary orientation of the manager.

T   F   6. Decision theorists are weakest where managers must be strongest — in dealing with the human factor.

T   F   7. All major decisions to be made by the manager can be solved through the decision theory approach.

T   F   8. The problem with adopting a strictly mathematical approach to management is that life itself does not follow mathematical prescriptions — nor do people.

T   F   9. The complete manager is increasingly required to be competent in the quantitative techniques.

T   F 10. The job of the manager is common to all types of organizations, whether they be educational, manufacturing, or governmental.

T   F 11. Planning involves the making of many decisions.

T   F 12. Planning is complete when a single alternative has been selected that states what action will be taken.

T   F   13. Organization is complete when there exists an orderly explanation and description of the things that must be done in order to accomplish the overall objective.

T   F   14. Coordination is the difficult managerial task of synchronizing individual and group efforts in each of the basic functions of management.

T   F   15. A heating system with a thermostat has open-loop control.

Multiple Choice

1. Which of the following is *not* one of the well-known approaches to management discussed in the text?

   (a) human relations, (b) administration, (c) central system, (d) empirical

2. The major benefit to be realized from studying historical management incidents is that one can draw generalizations from them to

   (a) serve as guides to present actions, (b) give tried-and-true answers to current problems, (c) think about, (d) none of the above.

3. The complete manager

   (a) is a student of the history of management, (b) draws historical generalizations, (c) acts independently according to what is demanded by her or his own situation, (d) all of the above.

4. To which approach to management did Chester Barnard subscribe?

   (a) human behavior,(b) operational, (c) empirical, (d) decision theory, (e) none of the above

5. To Barnard, the factor common to and causing all organizations is

   (a) physical facilities, (b) planning, (c) control, (d) cooperation.

6. The overall job of the manager is to create within the enterprise an _____ , which will facilitate the _____ of its _____ .

   (a) advantage . . . making . . . profit, (b) operation . . . use . . . resources, (c) economy . . . lowering . . . costs, (d) environment . . . accomplishment . . . objective

7. When the manager checks on how workers' work is progressing, he or she is

   (a) planning, (b) organizing, (c) staffing, (d) directing, (e) controlling.

8. Which of the following comes closest to summarizing what management is?

   (a) planning, (b) decision making, (c) controlling, (d) coordinating, (e) none of the above

9. A system that is static or does not change in response to changes in its surroundings is

   (a) no system at all, (b) closed, (c) homeostatic, (d) stagnant, (e) none of the above.

10. A system which is influenced by and responds to changes in its surroundings is

    (a) dynamic, (b) a loop, (c) realistic, (d) closed, (e) none of the above.

Completion

1. The analysis of the ways in which groups work and their effects on the manager and worker is of interest in the _____ approach to management.

2. When the manager has decided what to do and determined exactly how to do it, the manager has _____ .

3. When the manager has broken down the method to reach a goal into its component jobs, grouped together related jobs, assigned managers to coordinate these groups' activities, and decided on the relationships between these managers, the manager has _____ .

4. The manager has _____ when making sure that things are going as desired, making the necessary changes when they are not.

5. The function of _____ involves getting and keeping the employees necessary to help reach the organization's goals.

READING

PUTTING EXCELLENCE INTO MANAGEMENT

Thomas J. Peters

What makes for excellence in the management of a company? Is it the use of sophisticated management techniques such as zero-based budgeting, management by objectives, matrix organization, and sector, group, or portfolio management? Is it greater use of computers to control companies that continue to grow even larger in size and more diverse in activities? Is it a battalion of specialized MBAS, well-versed in the techniques of strategic planning?

Probably not. Although most well-run companies use a fair sampling of all of these tools, they do not use them as substitutes for the basics of good management. Indeed, McKinsey & Co., a management consultant concern, has studied management practices at 37 companies that are often used as examples of well-run organizations and has found that they have eight common attributes. None of those attributes depends on "modern" management tools or gimmicks. In fact, none of them requires high technology, and none of them costs a cent to implement. All that is needed is time, energy, and a willingness on the part of management to think rather than to make use of management formulas.

The outstanding performers work hard to keep things simple. They rely on simple organizational structures, simple strategies, simple goals, and simple communications. The eight attributes that characterize their management are:

- A bias toward action.

- Simple form and lean staff.

- Continued contact with customers.

- Productivity improvement via people.

- Operational autonomy to encourage entrepreneurship.

- Stress on one key business value.

- Emphasis on doing what they know best.

- Simultaneous loose-tight controls.

Although none of these sounds startling or new, most are conspicuously absent in many companies today. Far too many managers have lost sight of the basics — service to customers, low-cost manufacturing, productivity improvement, innovation, and risk-taking. In many cases, they have been seduced by the availability of MBAS, armed with the "latest" in strategic planning techniques. MBAS who specialize in strategy are bright, but they often cannot implement their ideas, and their companies wind up losing the capacity to act. At Standard Brands Inc., for example, Chairman F. Ross Johnson discovered this the hard way when he brought a handful of planning specialists into his consumer products company. "The guys who were bright [the strategic planners] were not the kinds of people who could implement programs," he lamented to BUSINESS WEEK. Two years later, he removed the planners.

Another consumer products company followed a similar route, hiring a large band of young MBAS for the staffs of senior vice-presidents. The new people were assigned to build computer models for designing new products. Yet none of the products could be manufactured or brought to market. Complained one line executive: "The models incorporated 83 variables in product planning, but we were being killed by just one — cost."

Companies are being stymied not only by their own staffs but often by their structure. McKinsey studied one company where the new-product process required 223 separate committees to approve an idea before it could be put into production. Another company was restructured recently into 200 strategic business units — only to discover that it was impossible to implement 200 strategies. And even at General Electric Co., which is usually cited for its ability to structure itself according to its management needs, an executive recently complained: "Things become bureaucratic with astonishing speed. Inevitably when we wire things up, we lose vitality." Emerson Electric Co., with a much simpler structure than GE, consistently beats its huge competitor on costs — manufacturing its products in plants with fewer than 600 employees.

McKinsey's study focused on 10 well-managed companies: International Business Machines, Texas Instruments, Hewlett-Packard, 3M, Digital Equipment, Procter & Gamble, Johnson & Johnson, McDonald's, Dana, and

Emerson Electric. On the surface, they have nothing in common. There is no universality of product line: Five are in high technology, one is in packaged goods, one makes medical products, one operates fast-food restaurants, and two are relatively mundane manufacturers of mechanical and electrical products. But each is a hands-on operator, not a holding company or a conglomerate. And while not every plan succeeds, in the day-to-day pursuit of their businesses these companies succeed far more often than they fail. And they succeed because of their management's almost instinctive adherence to the eight attributes.

BIAS TOWARD ACTION
In each of these companies, the key instructions are *do it, fix it, try it.* They avoid analyzing and questioning products to death, and they avoid complicated procedures for developing new ideas. Controlled experiments abound in these companies. The attitude of management is to "get some data, do it, then adjust it," rather than to wait for a perfect overall plan. The companies tend to be tinkerers rather than inventors, making small steps of progress rather than conceiving sweeping new concepts. At McDonald's Corp., for example, the objective is to do the little things regularly and well.

Ideas are solicited regularly and tested quickly. Those that work are pushed fast; those that don't are discarded just as quickly. At 3M Co., the management never kills an idea without trying it out; it just goes on the back burner.

These managements avoid long, complicated business plans for new projects. At 3M, for example, new product ideas must be proposed in less than five pages. At Procter & Gamble Co., one-page memos are the rule, but every figure in a P&G memo can be relied on unfailingly.

To ensure that they achieve results, these companies set a few well-defined goals for their managers. At Texas Instruments Inc., for one, a typical goal would be a set date for having a new plant operating or for having a designated percent of a sales force call on customers in a new market. A TI executive explained: "We've experimented a lot, but the bottom line for any senior manager is the maxim that more than two objectives is no objective."

These companies have learned to focus quickly on problems. One method is to appoint a "czar" who has responsibility for one problem across the company. At Digital Equipment Corp. and Hewlett-Packard Co., for example, there are software czars, because customer demand for programming has become the key issue for the future growth of those companies. Du Pont Co., when it discovered it was spending $800 million a year on transportation, set up a logistics czar. Other companies have productivity czars or energy czars with the power to override a manufacturing division's autonomy.

Another tool is the task force. But these companies tend to use the task force in an unusual way. Task forces are authorized to fix things, not to generate reports and paper. At Digital Equipment, TI, HP, and 3M, task forces have a short duration, seldom more than 90 days. Says a Digital Equipment executive: "When we've got a big problem here, we grab 10 senior guys and stick them in a room for a week. They come up with an

How 10 well-run companies performed in 1979

	Sales	Profits	Return on Sales	Return on Equity
	Millions of dollars		Percent	
IBM	$22,862.8	$3,011.3	14.8%	21.6%
Procter & Gamble	10,080.6	615.7	5.6	19.3
3M	5,440.3	655.2	12.2	24.4
Johnson & Johnson ...	4,211.6	352.1	6.5	19.6
Texas Instruments.....	3,224.1	172.9	5.1	19.2
Dana	2,789.0	165.8	6.1	19.3
Emerson Electric	2,749.9	208.8	7.5	21.5
Hewlett-Packard	2,361.0	203.0	8.2	18.1
Digital Equipment	2,031.6	207.5	9.7	19.7
McDonald's	1,937.9	188.6	8.7	22.5
BW composite of 1,200 companies			5.1	16.6

answer and implement it." All members are volunteers, and they tend to be senior managers rather than junior people ordered to serve. Management espouses the busy-member theory: "We don't want people on task forces who want to become permanent task force members. We only put people on them who are so busy that their major objective is to get the problem solved and to get back to their main jobs." Every task force at TI is disbanded after its work is done, but within three months the senior operations committee formally reviews and assesses the results. TI demands that the managers who requested and ran the task force justify the time spent on it. If the task force turns out to have been useless, the manager is chided publicly, a painful penalty in TI's peer-conscious culture.

SIMPLE FORM AND LEAN STAFF
Although all ten of these companies are big — the smallest, McDonald's, has sales in excess of $1.9 billion — they are structured along "small is beautiful" lines. Emerson Electric, 3M, J&J, and HP are divided into small entrepreneurial units that — although smaller than economies of scale might suggest — manage to get things done. No HP division, for example, ever employs more than 1,200 people. TI, with 90 product customer centers, keeps each notably autonomous.

Within the units themselves, activities are kept to small, manageable groups. At Dana Corp., small teams work on productivity improvement. At the high-technology companies, small autonomous teams, headed by a product "champion," shepherd ideas through the corporate bureaucracy to ensure that they quickly receive attention from the top.

Staffs are also kept small to avoid bureaucracies. Fewer than 100 people help run Dana, a $3 billion corporation. Digital Equipment and Emerson are also noted for small staffs.

CLOSENESS TO THE CUSTOMER

The well-managed companies are customer driven — not technology driven, not product driven, not strategy driven. Constant contact with the customer provides insights that direct the company. Says one executive: "Where do you start? Not by poring over abstract market research. You start by getting out there with the customer." In a study of two fast-paced industries (scientific instruments and component manufacturing), Eric Von Hippel, associate professor at Massachusetts Institute of Technology, found that 100 per cent of the major new product ideas — and 80 per cent of the minor new product variations — came directly from customers.

At both IBM and Digital Equipment, top management spends at least 30 days a year conferring with top customers. No manager at IBM holds a staff job for more than three years, except in the legal, finance, and personnel departments. The reason: IBM believes that staff people are out of the mainstream because they do not meet with customers regularly.

Both companies use customer-satisfaction surveys to help determine management's compensation. Another company spends 12 per cent of its research and development budget on sending engineers and scientists out to visit customers. One R&D chief spends two months each year with customers. At Lanier Business Products Inc., another fast growing company, the 20 most senior executives make sales calls every month.

Staying close to the customer means sales and service overkill. "Assistants to" at IBM are assigned to senior executives with the sole function of processing customer complaints within 24 hours. At Digital Equipment, J&J, IBM, and 3M, immense effort is expended to field an extraordinarily well-trained sales force. Caterpillar Tractor Co., another company considered to have excellent management, spends much of its managerial talent on efforts to make a reality of its motto, "24-hour parts delivery anywhere in the world."

These companies view the customer as an integral element of their businesses. A bank officer who started his career as a J&J accountant recalls that he was required to make customer calls even though he was in a financial department. The reason: to ensure that he understood the customer's perspective and could handle a proposal with empathy.

PRODUCTIVITY IMPROVEMENT VIA CONSENSUS

One way to get productivity increases is to install new capital equipment. But another method is often overlooked. Productivity can be improved by motivating and stimulating employees. One way to do that is to give them autonomy. At TI, shop floor teams set their own targets for production. In the years since the company has used this approach, executives say, workers have set goals that require them to stretch but that are reasonable and attainable.

The key is to motivate all of the people involved in each process. At 3M, for example, a team that includes technologists, marketers, production people, and financial types is formed early in a new product venture. It is self-sufficient and stays together from the inception to the national introduction. Although 3M is aware that this approach can lead to redundancy, it feels that the team spirit and motivation make it worthwhile.

Almost all of these companies use "corny" but effective methods to reward their workers. Badges, pins, and medals are all part of such recognition programs. Outstanding production teams at TI are invited to describe their successes to the board, as a form of recognition. Significantly, the emphasis is never only on monetary awards.

AUTONOMY TO ENCOURAGE ENTREPRENEURSHIP

A company cannot encourage entrepreneurship if it holds its managers on so tight a leash that they cannot make decisions. Well-managed companies authorize their managers to act like entrepreneurs. Dana, for one, calls this method the "store manager" concept. Plant managers are free to make purchasing decisions and to start productivity programs on their own. As a result, these managers develop unusual programs with results that far exceed those of a division or corporate staff. And the company has a grievance rate that is a fraction of the average reported by the United Auto Workers for all the plants it represents.

The successful companies rarely will force their managers to go against their own judgment. At 3M, TI, IBM, and J&J, decisions on product promotion are not based solely on market potential. An important factor in the decision is the zeal and drive of the volunteer who champions a product. Explains one executive at TI: "In every instance of a new product failure, we had forced someone into championing it involuntarily."

The divisional management is generally responsible for replenishing its new product array. In these well-managed companies, headquarters staff may not cut off funds for divisional products arbitrarily. What is more, the divisions are allowed to reinvest most of their earnings in their own operations. Although this flies in the face of the product-portfolio concept, which dictates that a corporate chief milk mature divisions to feed these with apparently greater growth potential, these companies recognize that entrepreneurs will not be developed in corporations that give the fruits of managers' labor to someone else.

Almost all these companies strive to place new products into separate startup divisions. A manager is more likely to be recognized — and promoted — for pushing a hot new product out of his division to enable it to stand on its own than he is for simply letting his own division get overgrown.

Possibly most important at these companies, entrepreneurs are both encouraged and honored at all staff levels. TI, for one, has created a special group of "listeners" — 138 senior technical people called "individual contributors" — to assess new ideas. Junior staff members are particularly encouraged to bring their ideas to one of these individuals for a one-on-one evaluation. Each "contributor" has the authority to approve substantial startup funds ($20,000 to $30,000) for product experimentation. TI's successful Speak'n'Spell device was developed this way.

IBM's Fellows Program serves a similar purpose, although it is intended to permit proven senior performers to explore their ideas rather than to open communications lines for bright comers. Such scientists have at their beck and call thousands of IBM's technical people. The Fellows tend to be highly skilled gadflies, people who can shake things up— almost invariably for the good of the company.

The operating principle at well-managed companies is to do one thing well. At IBM, the all-pervasive value is customer service. At Dana, it is productivity improvement. At 3M and HP, it is new product development. At P&G it is product quality. At McDonald's it is customer service — quality, cleanliness, and value.

STRESS ON A KEY BUSINESS VALUE

At all these companies, the values are pursued with an almost religious zeal by the chief executive officers. Rene McPherson, now dean of Stanford University's Graduate School of Business but until recently Dana's CEO, incessantly preached cost reduction and productivity improvement — and the company doubled its productivity in seven years. Almost to the day when Thomas Watson Jr. retired from IBM he wrote memos to the staff on the subject of calling on customers — even stressing the proper dress for the call. IT's ex-chairman Patrick Haggerty made it a point to drop in at a development laboratory on his way home each night when he was in Dallas. And in another company, where competitive position was the prime focus, one division manager wrote 700 memos to his subordinates one year, analyzing competitors.

Such single-minded focus on a value becomes a culture for the company. Nearly every IBM employee has stories about how he or she took great pains to solve a customer's problem. New product themes even dominate 3M and HP lunchroom conversations. Every operational review at HP focuses on new products, with a minimum amount of time devoted to financial results or projections — because President John Young has made it clear that he believes that proper implementation of new-product plans automatically creates the right numbers. In fact, Young makes it a point to start new employees in the new-product process and keep them there for a few years as part of a "socialization" pattern. "I don't care if they do come from the Stanford Business School," he says. "For a few years they get their hands dirty, or we are not interested." At McDonald's the company's values are drummed into employees at Hamburger U., a training program every employee goes through.

As the employees who are steeped in the corporate culture move up the ladder, they become role models for newcomers, and the process continues. It is possibly best exemplified by contrast. American Telephone & Telegraph Co., which recently began to develop a marketing orientation, has been hamstrung in its efforts because of a lack of career telephone executives with marketing successes. When Archie J. McGill was hired from IBM to head AT&T's marketing, some long-term employees balked at his leadership because he "wasn't one of them," and so was not regarded as a model.

Another common pitfall for companies is the sending of mixed signals to line managers. One company has had real problems introducing new products despite top management's constant public stress on innovation — simply because line managers perceived the real emphasis to be on cost-cutting. They viewed top management as accountants who refused to invest or to take risks, and they consistently proposed imitative products. At another company, where the CEO insisted that his major thrust was new products, an analysis of how he spent his time over a three-month period showed that no more than 5 per cent of his efforts were directed to new products. His stated emphasis therefore was not credible. Not surprisingly, his employees never picked up the espoused standard.

Too many messages, even when sincerely meant, can cause the same problem. One CEO complained that no matter how he tried to raise what he regarded as an unsatisfactory quality level he was unsuccessful. But when McKinsey questioned his subordinates, they said, "Of course he's for quality, but he's for everything else, too. We have a theme a month here." The outstanding companies, in contrast, have one theme and stick to it.

STICKING TO WHAT THEY KNOW BEST
Robert W. Johnson, the former chairman of J&J, put it this way: "Never acquire any business you don't know how to run." Edward G. Harness, CEO at P&G, says, "This company has never left its base." All of the successful companies have been able to define their strengths — marketing, customer contact, new product innovation, low-cost manufacturing — and then build on them. They have resisted the temptation to move into new businesses that look attractive but require corporate skills they do not have.

SIMULTANEOUS LOOSE-TIGHT CONTROLS
While this may sound like a contradiction, it is not. The successful companies control a few variables tightly, but allow flexibility and looseness in others. 3M uses return on sales and number of employees as yardsticks for control. Yet it gives management lots of leeway in day-to-day operations. When McPherson became president of Dana, he threw out all of the company's policy manuals and substituted a one-page philosophy statement and a control system that required divisions to report costs and revenues on a daily basis.

IBM probably has the classic story about flexible controls. After the company suffered well-publicized and costly problems with its System 360 computer several years ago — problems that cost hundreds of millions of dollars to fix — Watson ordered Frank T. Cary, then a vice-president, to incorporate a system of checks and balances in new-product testing. The system made IBM people so cautious that they stopped taking risks. When Cary became president of IBM, one of the first things he did to reverse that attitude was to loosen some of the controls. He recognized that the new system would indeed prevent such an expensive problem from every happening again, but its rigidity would also keep IBM from ever developing another major system.

By sticking to these eight basics, the successful companies have achieved better-than-average growth. Their managements are able not only to change but also to change quickly. They keep their sights aimed externally at their customers and competitors, and not on their own financial reports.

Excellence in management takes brute perseverance — time, repetition, and simplicity. The tools include plant visits, internal memos, and focused systems. Ignoring these rules may mean that the company slowly loses its vitality, its growth flattens, and its competitiveness is lost.

Questions for Discussion

1. This article is about the practices of very well-managed companies. Review those practices and identify those that are related to the management tools of (a) planning, (b) organizing, (c) staffing, (d) controlling, (e) directing, and (f) coordinating.

2. What do you think it takes for a company to *be* well managed, as these ten are?

EXERCISE

SAFETY PROGRAM

If there are specific things that a manager does, how are they done? What does it "look" like when one manages? This exercise describes a typical situation in which a manager performs managerial functions.

As production manager of the Vamp Stamping Company, you've become quite concerned over the metal stamping shop's safety record. Accidents that resulted in operators' missing time on the job have increased quite rapidly in the past year. These more serious accidents have jumped from 3 per cent of all accidents reported to a current level of 10 per cent.

Since you're concerned about your workers' safety as well as the company's ability to meet its customers' orders, you want to reduce this down-time accident rate to its previous level or lower within the next six months.

You call the accident trend to the attention of your production supervisors, pointing out the seriousness of the situation and their continuing responsibility to enforce the gloves and safety goggles rules.

Effective immediately, every supervisor will review his or her accident reports for the past year, file a report summarizing these accidents with you, and state their intended actions to correct recurring causes of the accidents. They will make out weekly safety reports as well as meet with you every Friday to discuss what is being done and any problems they are running into.

You request the union steward's cooperation in helping the safety supervisor set up a short program on shop safety practices.

Since the machine operators are having the accidents, you encourage your supervisors to talk to their workers and find out what they think can be done to reduce the down-time accident rate to its previous level.

While the program is going on, you review the weekly reports, looking for patterns that will tell you how effective the program is and where the trouble spots are. If a supervisor's operators are not decreasing their accident rate, you discuss the matter in considerable detail with the supervisor and his or her key workers.

FOR THE STUDENT

Briefly describe the steps you went through as production manager in trying to solve your safety problem. Be sure to specifically relate your answer to the activities of planning, organizing, controlling, staffing, and directing.

CASE

BANK'S TANKS

Bank's Tanks is a local manufacturer of metal septic tanks, a company started some thirty years ago. The company's primary source of income is selling residential septic tanks to building contractors.

Mr. Banks is an entrepreneur who started out poor; his privately owned corporation is relatively small, yet it provides a very comfortable living for him and his family. He has two sons, both in their late twenties; one serves as vice-president and the other as secretary-treasurer. The two sons have had life relatively easy, especially when compared to their father. Their lives have included sports cars and generous allowances since they were teenagers. Both sons attended college but neither earned a degree. They have been working in their father's business since they left college, but not with the discipline or consistency of good employees.

To compensate for their shortcomings, Mr. Banks hired a competent general manager, Charlie Harrow. Charlie does an excellent job of coordinating the company's activities. At times, however, the load gets to be too much even for Charlie, and things fall apart.

The elder Banks son is Everett, who is aggressive and ambitious and who often acts first and thinks later. When he is at the plant, he works very hard supervising the manufacturing process. However, he is also an avid outdoorsperson and often takes off on hunting or fishing trips at will. Martin is the other son; he is more oriented toward managing the office. He borders on being an overly active participant in civil activities. Many times he attends to such affairs on company time and at company expense. Their father spends much of his own time on the road, calling on customers.

On one typical day, Mr. Banks left town on a three-day business trip. Charlie arrived at work at 7:00 A.M. After checking the agenda for the plant operations that day, he began figuring costs for several of the new orders. Everett came in at 8:30 A.M. Without checking in at the office, he rearranged the activities in the plant. He had the work crews stop work on job 506 and start on jobs 510, 604, and 607. Then he headed to the office, leaving behind chaos and a dismayed plant superintendent. The superintendent had to start informing employees at one end of the plant of the changes. Immediately he ran into problems in getting the machinery settings readjusted. All the while the news of Everett's latest hit-and-run attack was traveling through the plant via the grapevine. By the time the story got to the lower end of the plant, the information had been altered so many times that no one knew for sure what was going on.

It was 10:00 A.M. and Martin had not yet shown up for work nor bothered to call in. Everett was griping to his secretary about his brother's lack of concern for the business. The plant superintendent called Charlie Harrow on the intercom to inform him of the havoc Everett created in the plant. Charlie exclaimed, "What? Mr. Smith called last Friday about job 506 and said he needed his tanks ASAP (As Soon As Possible)! Get back to work on 506. I'll talk to Everett."

After being informed of the situation, Everett was miffed that no one had told him about Smith's call. "Just because I took off at noon on Friday! I felt like it, and every other time I've taken off no one's complained — and besides, it's my business!" he thought to himself.

The superintendent had the machines readjusted and instructed the workers to go back to work on job 506 without offering much explanation. They became angry, feeling management to be intentionally trying to aggravate them and create problems.

Another customer, Mr. Willoughby, called not long thereafter. He got Everett on the telephone and increased his order by two more tanks; he mentioned that he felt that the price Martin quoted to him on Thursday on the original order was more reasonable than anyone else's. Everett was pleased and promised the two additional tanks.

At 11:30 A.M. Martin appeared for work. Everett questioned him about where he had been and why he had not let anyone know that he would be out. Martin replied that he was attending a brunch sponsored by a local civic group. Everett dropped the matter and mentioned the addition to Thursday's order; out of curiosity Everett asked what price had been quoted Willoughy. Martin replied, $515 per tank.

Charlie Harrow had been listening to the conversation. He looked at that job's cost sheet, which had been prepared on the previous Wednesday. Bank's direct cost to make the tanks was a little over $530 per tank. Charlie showed the figures to the boys. Martin shrugged and turned red, realizing (although he did not admit it) that he should have checked with Harrow on the costs before making a quote.

At 12:15 P.M. Everett left for lunch, after which he was to go hunting for the rest of the afternoon. Martin told Charlie that he had to take his daughter to the dentist and would not be in until the next day. Charlie was left with the secretary in the office. Working feverishly he continued to take phone calls, place orders, and contend with the problems brought to him by the plant superintendent.

At 3:00 P.M. the phone rang; it was John Grimaldi, an old and valued customer.

"Hello, Charlie," Grimaldi said. "Is Martin there?"

"Why, no, he's not," Charlie replied.

"Well, I talked to him last Tuesday, and told him I was flying in today. He said he would pick me up at the airport, take me to my motel, and buy me a couple of drinks."

"He had to leave, John," Charlie said. "But hang on; I'll be there in twenty minutes."

Questions for Discussion

1. The managerial tools are planning, organizing, staffing, directing, controlling, and coordinating. Which of these are *mis*applied at Bank's Tanks?

2. How would you, as the president of the company, remedy the difficulties you identified in the first question?

CASE

STATE UNIVERSITY PHYSICAL PLANT

The physical plant crew of State University services 25 major buildings and 5 athletic fields. The Physical Plant Operations Center (PPOC) is headed by Jeremy Bolton, who reports to the vice-president for finance (see Exhibit 1). Craft crews are made up of painters, plumbers, electricians, carpenters, or maintenance specialists. Although referred to as craft crews, not all of these trades are classified and paid as if they were indeed a craft in the real sense of the word by the State, under whose civil service jurisdiction they fall; the groups not included in the craft pay scales are the painters and the maintenance people. A union exists, but it is of limited effectiveness and is disregarded by most hourly employees — especially because wage scales are determined by the State and not by the University.

Exhibit 1

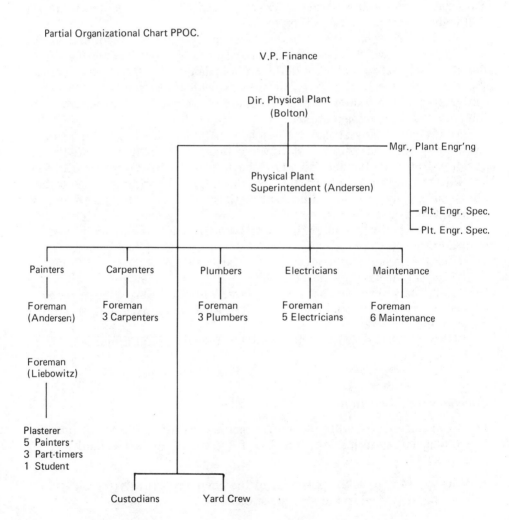

Partial Organizational Chart PPOC.

Rudy Andersen is a painter by training. He still holds the title of paint foreman even though the paint shop has another formally designated, full-time foreman, Jake Liebowitz. Andersen has a unique arrangement in the PPOC operations; he runs his job from the paint shop, even though he has an office located in the PPOC administration wing of the building. He also actually runs the day-to-day operations of the paint shop while serving as superintendent over the other "crafts," whose shops are run by their own foremen.

The role of the other paint foreman, Liebowitz, has never been defined either to him or to the other members of the crew. It is his belief that he was given the title of foreman to effect a pay raise because he had been at the highest wage classification as a painter.

Andersen is viewed by the painters as a perfectionist, as very demanding on the paint crew, and as displaying negligible interest in the performance of the other crews. The painters complain that there is rarely any feedback from Andersen regarding their job performance, unless they have "goofed" up. When there is any praise, there is always a qualifier attached, such as, "Good work but, oh, so little."

It was not uncommon for painters to be sent on jobs before the carpenters or plumbers. This led to the painters having to do the job twice, much to their irritation. Furthermore, painters often were sent to do jobs that were not within their classification, such as cleaning up after the electricians and carpenters; this led to the other crews coming to expect this of the painters. The various crews found it very difficult to discuss any problems or offer suggestions on how to accomplish a task with Andersen; discussions seemed always to end with Andersen's not having heard what was said or choosing to ignore it.

In the months of June and July 1981, Andersen was required to attend a course dealing with worker motivation and productivity. He summed up the materials on motivation as being a bunch of "bunk"; furthermore, it was obvious to him that motivation and productivity were not related, because not all individuals could be motivated — so why waste time? He then applied this as a general rule and regarded the classes as a two-hour break every Wednesday. From this course, however, he did find one thing that appealed to him, and so he brought it along for the benefit of the craft crews: It was a tape that was played at 7:00 A.M. one Monday to all members of the craft crews. The gist of the tape was that a worker will be paid what he or she is worth, and that management will see to it; all the employee has to do is work hard and rewards will be increased according to the value of the work to the organization. In addition, all one had to do was decide where in the organization he or she wanted to be and then work hard once again to be rewarded accordingly. The crews regarded this tape as an affront to their intelligence, because the State determined their wages and not productivity. They also thought the tape was an attempt by Andersen to trick them to do more work for the same pay.

Work was to be performed in response to job requisitions issued by campus department heads to the director of physical plant, who forwarded them to Andersen. In turn, Andersen informed the appropriate foremen of the work to be done, with no priority assigned except first come, first served. What actually happened, more often than not, however, was that someone with political clout or status would call on the VP for finance, requesting that a job be performed. When this happened, the VP would call Bolton who, in turn, would tell Andersen. The necessary employees would be pulled off whatever jobs they were doing at the time to go on the new job. This situation had led to resentment on the part of the crews, and especially the painters; there seemed to be no continuity in their jobs. One painter might have three incomplete jobs going at the same time. Those whose jobs were dropped in favor of another job were frustrated by the inconvenience and length of time it took to finish their jobs.

Questions for Discussion

1. Evaluate Andersen's performance as a manager.

2. In which functions (planning, organizing, staffing, directing, controlling, coordinating) was he most proficient? Most deficient? Why do you think so?

3. What effect did Andersen's managerial performance have on other PPOC members? Clients?

ANSWERS TO SELF-REVIEW QUESTIONS, CHAPTER 3

Matching

A-5, B-6, C-10, D-3, E-7, F-9, G-8, H-1, I-11, J-4, K-12, L-2.

True–False

1-F, 2-F, 3-F, 4-F, 5-F, 6-T, 7-F, 8-T, 9-T, 10-T, 11-T, 12-F, 13-F, 14-T 15-F.

Multiple-Choice

1-C, 2-A, 3-D, 4-E, 5-D, 6-D, 7-E, 8-D, 9-B, 10-E

Completion

1. Social Sciences. 2. Planned. 3. Organized. 4. Controlled. 5. Staffing.

Chapter 4

Decision Making and Problem Solving

CHAPTER OBJECTIVES

1. To show how decisions must be made in virtually all human activities, especially by managers

2. To introduce you to several successful approaches to and techniques of decision making

3. To underscore the too-often-ignored impact on the decision-making process of decision makers and to examine how their psychological make-up and personal goals influence the process

SELF-REVIEW QUESTIONS

Matching

A. decision method similar to brainstorming, although calling for silent writing of ideas

_____ 1. decision making

B. Consensus decision method using anonymous questionnaires and summaries of answers

_____ 2. problem solving

C. logical process through which the manager recognizes and isolates the nature of the crisis to be resolved

_____ 3. Japanese approach

D. technique that allows the manager to take into account the results — and the odds — of alternatives.

_____ 4. satisficing

E. process of considering alternatives until one is found that (although not the best) meets a minimum standard

_____ 5. NGT

F. decision method that relies on gaining
    wide consensus   _____ 6. Delphi

True–False

T   F   1. Decision making occurs in each of the management functions of planning, organizing, staffing, directing, and controlling.

T   F   2. Planning for the worst is a sound way to head off impending crises.

T   F   3. One often can solve a problem by taking action to remove or remedy its symptoms.

T   F   4. One should never make a decision until the necessary facts are available.

T   F   5. Foreseeing problems through forecasting has no effect on decision making and is used only to plan the future.

T   F   6. In comparison with the Japanese procedure, American decision making is extremely participative.

T   F   7. Japanese managers are much more concerned than are their American counterparts with finding an answer quickly.

T   F   8. American managers are much more likely to be able to implement a decision quickly and effectively than are the Japanese.

T   F   9. The Delphi method is a sophisticated format in which an interacting group solves a problem.

T   F   10. The initials NGT, which identify an approach to decision making, stand for nongeometric thinking.

T   F   11. In the Delphi method, expert consensus is reached by each expert's answering several sequential questionnaires, then receiving a summary of others' answers before responding again.

T   F   12. Committee decisions are slower but more accurate than those of most individuals working alone.

T   F   13. The first step in recognizing crisis situations is knowing how things should be so that when things are wrong they will be recognized.

T   F   14. Problem solving and decision making are different terms for the same process.

T   F   15. According to Chris Argyris, group decision making greatly diminishes the risk-taking abilities of executives, even makes them indecisive.

Completion

1. Murphy's Law of Management states, "If anything can go wrong, _____ _____ ."

2. A deviation between what should be happening and what actually is happening is known as a _____ .

3. The _____ process begins with identifying the problem.

4. According to Professor Chris Argyris, the biggest single barrier to effective _____ is the interpersonal relationships between executives that eliminate the taking of risks.

5. Participatory decision making is characteristic of _____ management methods.

READING

HOW TO MAKE AN INTELLIGENT DECISION

Robert L. Heilbroner

There is nothing in the world so common and ordinary and yet so agonizingly difficult as a tough decision. Most of us have marched up to some crossroad in our lives — whether or not to get married, to change jobs, to choose this or that career — and experienced the awful feeling of not knowing which route to choose. Worse yet, many of us have known what it is like, after a paralyzing wait, to start down one road with the sinking sensation that we've picked the wrong one.

Ever since Adam and Eve made the wrong one, decisions have been bedeviling people. Damn-fool decisions and half-cocked decisions lie behind much of the unhappiness of life. More pathetic yet is the misery caused by no-decision. "Everything comes to him who waits," writes Bill Gibson, in *The Seesaw Log*, "— too late."

What makes us decide things badly, when we "know better"? What is it that sometimes stalls our decision-making machinery entirely? There is no single or simple reason why decisions are the pitfall of our lives. A high school senior who sits with his pencil wavering between the True and False answers on an examination may be baffled by the difficulty of the questions or may simply be reduced to a blue funk by the pressure of taking an exam. A young woman in the throes of indecision over a marriage proposal may be trying to weigh the pros and cons of a tangled life situation or may be panicked by the thought of marriage itself. Foolish decisions and indecision are the consequence not only of the complexity of the world about us but the complicated crosscurrents of the world within us.

Reprinted by permission of the author and *Think* Magazine (December 1968, pp. 2–4), published by IBM, copyright 1968 by International Business Machines Corporation.

Whatever their causes, the agonies of decision making are often magnified because we go about making up our minds so ineffectively. Faced with a hard choice, we allow our thoughts to fly around, our emotional generators to get overheated, rather than try to bring our energies to bear as systematically as we can.

There is no ABC for decision making. But, there are a few guidelines that have helped others, and we can use them to help ourselves.

MARSHAL THE FACTS

A lot of the mental anguish of decision making comes because we often worry in a factual vacuum. An endless amount of stewing can be avoided if we do what all good executives do with a problem that can't be settled: send it back for more data. Dale Carnegie once quoted a distinguished university dean as saying, "If I have a problem that has to be faced at three o'clock next Tuesday, I refuse to try to make a decision about it until Tuesday arrives. In the meantime I concentrate on getting all the facts that bear on the problem. And by Tuesday, if I've got all the facts, the problem usually solves itself."

But just gathering facts won't solve hard problems. "The problem in coming to a firm and clear-sighted decision," says Lt. General Thomas L. Harrold, veteran infantry commander and now Commandant of the National War College, "is not only to corral the facts, but to marshal them in good order. In the Army," General Harrold explains, "we train our leaders to draw up what we call an Estimate of the Situation. First, they must know their objective. Unless you know what you want, you can't possibly decide how to get it. Second, we teach them to consider *alternative* means of attaining that objective. It's very rarely that a goal, military or any other, can be realized in only one way. Next we line up the pros and cons of each alternative, as far as we can see them. Then we choose the course that appears most likely to achieve the results we want. That doesn't guarantee success. But at least it allows us to decide as intelligently as the situation permits. It prevents us from going off on a half-baked hunch that may turn out to be disastrous."

Some people, however, *misuse* the idea of fact-collecting. They go on and on getting advice, gathering data, and never seem to be able to clinch the case. When we find ourselves assembling more and more facts without coming to any clear conclusions, without acting, it's time to be suspicious. Frequently we are merely waiting for the "right" fact which will rationalize a decision we have already made.

An executive of a New York placement agency tells of a young man who couldn't make up his mind whether or not to take a job that involved a move out of town. He kept coming back for more and more information until one day he learned that the company had had tough sledding during the '30's and nearly closed down. That clinched it. With obvious relief the young man "reluctantly" turned the job down.

"Actually," the placement official comments, "it was clear that he didn't want to move. But he had to find a 'fact' to make this decision respectable in his own eyes."

When we reach this point, it is time to stop fact-collecting.

CONSULT YOUR FEELINGS

The psychiatrist Theodore Reik, when still a young man, once asked Sigmund Freud about an important decision he had to make. "I can only tell you of my personal experience," Freud replied. "When making a decision of minor importance I have always found it advantageous to consider all the pros and cons. In vital matters, however, such as the choice of a mate or a profession, the decision should come from the unconscious, from somewhere within ourselves. In the important decisions of our personal life, we should be governed, I think, by the deep inner needs of our nature."

We can usually tell when a decision accords with our inner nature by the enormous sense of relief that it brings. Good decisions are the best tranquillizers ever invented; bad ones often increase our mental tension. When we have decided something against the grain, there is a nagging sense of incompletion, a feeling that the last knot has not been pulled out of the string.

TIMING

We must learn to distinguish between our deep-running characters and our transient moods. There is an old rule that we should sleep on big decisions, and contemporary psychological research has established that the rule is sound.

Data from questionnaires answered by some 500 persons at Columbia University's Bureau of Applied Social Research show that our behavior is affected by our passing moods. When we are blue, low, our actions tend to be aggressive and destructive; when we are in good spirits, all fired up, our behavior swings toward tolerance and balance. Everyone knows that the boss is more apt to make lenient decisions when he's in a good mood, and that it's no time to ask him for a raise when he comes into the office glowering. We do well to take account of our emotional temperatures before we put important decision on our *own* desks. On paydays, for example, we are all apt to be a little happy-go-lucky, especially about money decisions; on days when we've had a run-in with our wife or the day's work has gone all wrong, we are apt to decide things harshly, pessimistically, sourly.

A sense of timing also requires that we know when *not* to make a decision. "In surgery," says Dr. Abram Abeloff, surgeon at New York's Lenox Hill Hospital, "a doctor often studies a situation for days or even weeks until he feels reasonably confident to go ahead. Time itself is an essential component of many decisions. It brings uncertain situations to a head. Premature decisions are the most dangerous a person can make."

Consciously postponing a decision — deciding not to decide — is not the same as indecision. As Chester I. Barnard, first president of the New Jersey Bell Telephone Company, has put it in a famous book on business leadership, *The Functions of the Executive:* "The fine art of executive decision consists in not deciding questions that are not now pertinent, in not deciding prematurely, in not making decisions that others should make."

In ordinary life, as well as in business and medicine, many of the most involved and difficult decisions are best not "made," but allowed to ripen. Facts accumulate, feelings gradually jell and, as Barnard says, other people take a hand in the situation. By holding ourselves back — refusing to plunge in the moment our adolescents ask us, "Should I go to college?" "Should I enlist in the Army now, or should I wait?" — we give complicated situations a chance to work themselves out, and sometimes save ourselves a great deal of exhausting and useless brain-cudgeling.

FOLLOW-THROUGH

We all know that decisions do not mean much unless we back them with the will to carry them out. The alcoholic decides a thousand times to give up drink; the smoker vows again and again that this is his last cigarette. Many times an inability to make up our minds reflects just such an unwillingness to *go through* with a decision. "Thinking," wrote the great Swiss psychiatrist, Otto Fenichel, "is preparation for action. People who are afraid of actions increase the preparation."

Thus, indecision can sometimes help us *clarify* our minds. It can be the signal flag that forces us to look beyond the immediate point at issue into the follow-through that a decision demands of us. Frequently, when we make fools of ourselves at a retail counter, trying to decide which gift to buy, we are really wrestling with a quite different problem — such as our unconscious feelings about the person for whom we're selecting the gift. At a more serious level, an unhappily married woman, endlessly debating with herself whether or not to ask for a divorce, may in fact be avoiding the more difficult question of what she would do with her life if she were divorced.

FLEXIBILITY

Part of the worrisomeness of decision making comes from a natural tendency to overstress the *finality*, the once-for-allness of our choices. There is much more "give" in most decisions than we are aware. Franklin D. Roosevelt, for example, was a great believer in making flexible decisions. "He rarely got himself sewed tight to a program from which there was no turning back," his Secretary of Labor, Frances Perkins, once observed.

"We have to do the best we know how at the moment," he told one of his aides. "If it doesn't turn out all right, we can modify it as we go along."

Too many of us find decisions painful because we regard them as final and irrevocable. "Half the difficulties of man," Somerset Maugham has written, "lie in his desire to answer every question with yes or no. Yes or no may neither of them be the answer; each side may have in it some yes and some no."

Sometimes, naturally, we have to answer a question with a firm yes or no. But even then it is often possible to modify our answer later. That's why some advisers counsel: "When in doubt, say no. It's a lot easier to change a no to a yes, than vice versa."

THE FINAL INGREDIENT

Finally, there is one last consideration to bear in mind. In making genuinely big decisions we have to be prepared to stand a sense of loss, as well as gain. A student who hestitates between a lifetime as a teacher or a businessman, a talented young girl trying to make up her mind between marriage and a career, face choices in which sacrifice is involved, *no matter what they do.*

That's one reason why big decisions, in contrast to little ones, do not leave us exhilarated and charged with confidence, but humble and prayerful.

It helps to talk big decisions over with others — not only because another's opinion may illuminate aspects of the dilemma that we may have missed, but because in the process of talking we sort out and clarify our own thoughts and feelings. Talk, as a clergyman and the psychiatrist both know, has a cathartic effect; it gives vent to feelings which may otherwise be expressed, not always wisely, in actions.

After this, meditation, reflection — letting the problem stew in its own juice — can also help. But in the end, after talk and thought, one ingredient is still essential. It is courage.

"One man with courage makes a majority," said Andrew Jackson; and this was never more true than in the election of our minds where the one vote we cast is the deciding one.

Questions for Discussion

1. What are five major factors that keep us from making good decisions?

2. Freud suggests that major personal decisions should be made by our inner feelings. Doesn't this process of placing intuition over rationality in seeking the best possible solution contradict the value of a logical and systematic attack via the decision-making process?

3. Think back to the last time you couldn't decide whether to do something. What were some of the reasons, as suggested in the article, for your decision? Did the problem resolve itself on its own or did you force yourself to take an action? With what result?

4. Most problems do not have clear-cut solutions; that is, an alternative rarely exists which is clearly superior in all aspects to the other possible courses of action. How does this complicate the process of arriving at a decision?

EXERCISE

LOST AT SEA

Under what circumstances are group decisions better than individual decisions? Does it help to gather information from others before making your decision? This problem offers the opportunity to compare the quality of individual and group answers. What conclusions can you draw from such a comparison?

Source: Based on "Lost At Sea: A Consensus-Seeking Task," by Paul M. Nemiroff and William A. Pasmore in *The 1975 Annual Handbook for Group Facilitators* (La Jolla, Calif.: University Associates Publishers, Inc., 1975), edited by J. William Pfeiffer and John E. Jones, pp. 28–34.

INSTRUCTIONS

You are adrift on a private yacht in the South Pacific. As a consequence of a fire of unknown origin, much of the yacht and its contents have been destroyed. The yacht is now slowly sinking. Your location is unclear because of the destruction of critical navigational equipment and because you and the crew were distracted trying to bring the fire under control. Your best estimate is that you are approximately one thousand miles south-southwest of the nearest land.

Below is a list of 15 items that are intact and undamaged after the fire. In addition to these articles, you have a serviceable rubber life raft, with oars, large enough to carry yourself, the crew, and all the items listed here. The total contents of all survivors' pockets are a package of cigarettes, several books of matches, and five one-dollar bills.

	(1) Individual ranking	(2) Group ranking	(3) Ranking key
Sextant	____	____	____
Shaving mirror	____	____	____
Five-gallon can of water	____	____	____
Mosquito netting	____	____	____
One case of U.S. Army C rations	____	____	____
Maps of the Pacific Ocean	____	____	____
Seat cushion (flotation device approved by the Coast Guard)	____	____	____
Two-gallon can of oil-gas mixture	____	____	____
Small transistor radio	____	____	____
Shark repellent	____	____	____
Twenty square feet of opaque plastic	____	____	____
One quart of 160-proof Puerto Rican rum	____	____	____
Fifteen feet of nylon rope	____	____	____
Two boxes of chocolate bars	____	____	____
Fishing kit	____	____	____

Step 1:

Working independently and without discussing the problem or the merits of any of the items, your task is to rank the 15 items in terms of their importance to your survival. Under the column headed "Individual Ranking," place the number 1 by the most important item, the number 2 by the second most important and so on through number 15, the least important.

When you are through, do not discuss the problem or rankings of items with anyone.

Step 2:

Your instructor will assign you to a team. The task for your team is to rank the 15 items according to the group's consensus on order of importance to your survival. Do not vote or average team members' rankings; try to reach agreement on each item. Base your decision on knowledge, logic, or the experiences of group members. Try to avoid basing the decision on personal preference. Enter the group's ranking in the column headed "Group Ranking." This should take between 20 and 30 minutes, or as the instructor requires.

Step 3:

When everyone is through, your instructor will read the correct ranking, provided by officers of the U.S. Merchant Marines. Enter the correct ranks in the column headed "Ranking Key."

Step 4:

Compute the accuracy of your Individual Ranking. For each item, use the absolute value (ignore plus and minus signs) of the difference between Column 1 and Column 3. Add up these absolute values to get your *Individual Accuracy Index.* Enter it here: _____ .

Step 5:

Perform the same operations as in Step 4, but for your group ranking; use Columns 2 and 3. Adding up the absolute values yields your *Group Accuracy Index.* Enter it here: _____ .

Step 6:

Compute the *average* of your group's Individual Accuracy Indexes. Do this by adding up each member's Individual Accuracy Index and dividing the result by the number of group members. Enter it here: _____ .

Step 7:

Identify the *lowest* Individual Accuracy Index in your group. This is the most correct ranking in your group. Enter it here: _____ .

EXERCISE

MINI-DELPHI FOR 1990

SITUATION

Your organization has decided to make some major changes in its product lines. To prepare for this great undertaking, you have been asked to participate in strategic planning sessions aimed at making accurate, knowledgeable assessments of future conditions in the United States. Part of this experience involves predicting some critical statistics for 1990. Your group has met to develop these important forecasts.

YOUR TASK

Step I:

   Below is a list of 10 issues that must be answered. Each member of your team is to *individually* fill in the blank with your individual prediction. When you have finished, transfer your answers to the next page under Step I. Do not discuss the issues until each of you has finished this step.

ISSUES FOR 1990

1. The population of the USA will be _____ .

2. The probability of any type of nuclear war is _____ per cent.

3. The number of teen-agers in the USA will change by _____ per cent.

4. The labor force participation rate of women will be _____ per cent.

5. The GNP growth among the advanced capitalist nations will average _____ per cent per year.

6. If current trends continue, the average cost of government will be _____ per family.

7. _____ per cent of the labor force will be members of a union.

8. The percentage of the U.S. population living in central cities will be _____ per cent.

9. The number of nonwhites in the work force will change by _____ per cent.

10. The average age in the USA will be _____ .

(Read ahead, but do not begin discussion until instructed by session leader.)

Step II:

   This is an exercise in group decision making. Your group must employ the group-consensus method in reaching its decision on each item. This means that, as a group, you must try to arrive at an answer on which *all* group members can at least *partially* agree. The prediction for each of the 10 items must be agreed on by each group member before it becomes a part of the group decision. Once you have reached consensus, record your team's answers on the next page under Step II.

Here are some guides to use during your discussion:
1. Use logic and knowledge about the present as you approach the task. Try not to argue for your own individual judgments.
2. You may be tempted to change your mind simply to reach agreement and avoid conflict. However, only support answers with which you are able to agree at least somewhat.
3. You may not use techniques to reduce conflict, such as voting, averaging, or trading to reach a decision.
4. Try to look upon differences of opinion as a help rather than as a hindrance in decision making.

You have _____ minutes to complete Step II. You will then be given further instructions.

Table I

Mini-Delphi for 1990

	Step I Your answer		Step II Team answer		Step III Futurist's answer
		Points		*Points*	
1. Population of USA					
2. Nuclear war probability					
3. Per cent change, teen-agers					
4. Per cent women working					
5. GNP growth rate (per cent)					
6. Cost of government per family					
7. Per cent of workforce in union					
8. Per cent of people living in cities					
9. Per cent change of nonwhites in workforce					
10. Average age in USA					
TOTALS:					

(The lower the score the better)

Please complete the following steps and insert the scores under your team's number.

		TEAM NUMBER						
		1	*2*	*3*	*4*	*5*	*6*	*7*
Step IV —	AVERAGE AND INDIVIDUAL SCORE: Add up all the individual points (Step I) on the team and divide by the number on the team.							
Step V —	TEAM SCORE: Points in Step II							
Step VI —	GAIN SCORE: The difference between the team points and the individual points. If the team score is lower than the average individual score, then gain is "+." If team score is higher than average individual score, then gain is "—."							
Step VII —	LOWEST INDIVIDUAL SCORE							
	TOTAL SCORES							

CASE

MAMA PARKER

Mama Parker has been a long-time favorite of the children of her community. As her hobby, Mama Parker has designed and sewn a number of stuffed animals; because she has priced the toys so reasonably (usually charging for materials only), she is also a favorite among the adults.

Recently, Mama Parker had been taking her creations to local arts and crafts fairs and had met with much approval. Soon she was selling so many of her toys that she only had a few samples left and had to start taking orders from customers.

Her niece had also been quite fond of the stuffed toys and for several years had made them for her own children. Mama Parker had commented on how her niece's toys were almost identical to her own. Mama Parker discussed with her niece the recent orders for toys she had received, a quantity so large that she was afraid she might not be able to make them in time for Christmas.

Her niece mentioned that she had been interested in selling a few of her own stuffed toys, and also that her husband's woodworking hobby had included making wooden toys. "Perhaps," suggested the niece, "We could help you out and maybe open a little shop."

Mama Parker was dubious about the idea; she had started making the stuffed toys for her children and later as just a relaxing hobby. She was concerned that a toy shop would require long hours if the toys were hand-made by the proprietor.

The niece offered to do most of the shop management; all Mama Parker need to do is make her toys and let the niece build on her excellent reputation.

Mama Parker thought a minute and said that it might not be such a bad idea to put a little more money in the bank, especially since poor Papa Parker had passed away.

Mama Parker said she would go to the bank the next day to discuss financial concerns — after all, she said, because it would be her shop she should bear the financial responsibilities.

Questions for Discussion

1. In the text, the first guideline for decision making is identified as "marshall the facts." What facts does Mama Parker *need*? What information does she currently *have*?

2. What are some potential problems that might affect Mama Parker's decision — or the success of her venture?

3. Should Mama Parker set up the shop?

CASE

PETE'S BIG DECISION

Pete Smith had graduated from college with a bachelor's degree in sales, but he had no definite plans for the future. All that he knew was that he wanted to find a job in sales. His primary desire was to support himself working in sales so that he could spend time in his first love, working with young people. He felt that there was a great void in the area of youth workers in contemporary society, and because of this he wanted to do his part to fill the gap.

Shortly after graduation he received a phone call from a minister in the Detroit area who had heard of Pete's desire to work with young people and wanted him to consider his church as a possible base for his efforts. Pete traveled to Detroit, where he spent two weeks in deep consideration and prayer before making his final decision to locate in that area. He then began looking for a job in the sales field that would provide him the necessary income to cover his living expenses. Three weeks later he received and accepted a job offer as a Sales Trainee for a large regional department store.

The first six months on the job proved to be very enjoyable for Pete, with many new things to learn and a great bunch of people to work with. The job required a large amount of effort, but he still had plenty of time for his youth work and relaxation.

At his six-month review, John Wilson, the store manager, suggested that Pete should consider further education on a part-time basis to help him realize his full potential in the retailing field. After a month of prayerful consideration Pete applied to the local state university. He was accepted and promptly made plans to begin working on his MBA the following fall.

Pete's youth work also began to require more of his time as the group grew and required additional attention. He was pleased with the suggestions that the young people had made that the group branch out into other areas. He realized, however, that he was not going to have as much time to devote to his schooling as he had originally hoped. He changed his plans from two courses per term to one to relieve some of the pressure on his time.

It was about this time that Pete began dating Sue, one of the girls that he had met at church. He found that between his job, his involvement with the young people, his schooling, and dating his free time was fast becoming all but extinct. As Pete began graduate school in the fall he soon found it necessary to budget his time still more effectively, leaving less time for his personal relaxation.

In his review about a year later, Pete was promoted to manager of his department. He was told that his ability to work with people — not only leading them, but drawing out their full potential — was very instrumental in his promotion. Pete was quite surprised when these factors were mentioned as being important in his promotion. He had always known that he

Source: This case was prepared by David P. Globig under the supervision of Theodore T. Herbert. The case is not intended to reflect either effective or ineffective administrative or technical practices; it was prepared as a basis for class discussion.

had the ability to motivate others in particular endeavors, but he had assumed that his possible promotions would come more as a result of his honesty and hard work than from his ability to motivate others.

Shortly after Pete's promotion, John Wilson was transferred to another store; a new store manager, Dick Allison, was transferred in to replace him. In the three short years that Dick had been with the company he had been promoted three times, from sales trainee to department manager, to assistant store manager, and now to store manager. Dick's explosive rise to store manager had come at the expense of anyone who dared to stand in his way. His long hours and quick temper had resulted in the breakup of his marriage just four months prior to his promotion into Pete's store.

Almost immediately after he assumed command of the store Dick began suggesting that the department heads could reduce their total costs by working longer hours themselves. Any hours that they worked would reduce the total number of hours that the hourly personnel would be needed and therefore reduce the department's payroll. Although the departmental managers realized that the only one who really gained from their increased workload was Dick, many of them grudgingly increased their hours. Pete tried to increase the number of hours that he was putting in but soon discovered that his numerous outside activities just did not leave much flexibility for extra hours.

When the other managers saw that Pete was not giving in to the pressure that Dick was applying on him, they began pressuring him themselves. Instead of yielding to the pressure, Pete chose to spend less time with his peers and more time with his own personnel. His subordinates responded immediately to Pete, accepting him as one of the gang. As the communication between Pete and his department became more open, he found that they had many valuable suggestions to offer for his consideration.

When Dick realized that Pete was not following his initial suggestions he began applying increased pressure for longer hours and Sunday work. When this didn't work, Dick began dropping subtle hints that the extra hours would be more important at review time than the fact that his departmental sales had doubled and that his department was one of the bright spots in the store. When Pete mentioned the time required for his coursework he was told that that was his problem and not Dick's.

Pete was in a real dilemma; his graduate schooling was taking 15 to 20 hours per week plus the time spent in class, his youth work took a couple of evenings a week plus all day Sunday, and Sue reminded him that she would like to see him occasionally as well. Pete also had a personal belief that it was wrong for the store to be open on Sunday and this made it very difficult for him to consider Sunday as a normal workday. He decided to sit down and calculate the total number of hours that would be required of him if he were to fulfill all of the obligations that were his. He found that there were several times when his job conflicted with his schooling and his youth work. He decided that his best bet for the time being was to sift through the conflicts and see if the problems wouldn't resolve themselves.

It was shortly after this that Pete was called into Dick's office for a conference. Dick informed him that he had just received word that his assistant store manager was being transferred and he had been asked if he had any recommendations for a replacement. He had mentioned Pete to the district manager but had stated that he wasn't sure that Pete could handle the responsibilities that went along with the job. He went on to ask Pete if he would be interested in the job, including the obligation of working every other Sunday and closing the store at least three evenings a week. He told Pete that he had very little question that he could handle the job responsibilities, but he wasn't sure that Pete would be willing to give up his "outside" activities. Pete would have three days to make his decision. An affirmative answer would open the door to a promotion with a large pay increase; a negative answer would close the door to future promotions with the company regardless of his performance. Dick asked him to give the matter careful consideration before making what might be the biggest decision of Pete's life.

Question for Discussion

Show how you would apply the steps in the decision-making process, if you were Pete.

ANSWERS TO SELF-REVIEW QUESTIONS, CHAPTER 4

Matching

A-5, B-6, C-2, D-1, E-4, F-3.

True–False

1-T, 2-T, 3-F, 4-T, 5-F, 6-F, 7-F, 8-F, 9-F, 10-F, 11-T, 12-T, 13-T, 14-F, 15-T.

Completion

1. It will. 2. Problem. 3. Problem solving. 4. Decision making.
5. Japanese.

Chapter 5

The Planning Process

CHAPTER OBJECTIVES

1. To help you see planning and goal setting as processes that chart the course an organization and its people will sail

2. To show how planning and goal setting depend on effective analysis and appraisal of the firm's environment, coupled with the cooperation and participation of the members of the organization

3. To point out ways in which plans and objectives can be met by setting up stages of implementation and standards of performance

SELF-REVIEW QUESTIONS

Matching

A. assumptions

B. the end results planning attempts to reach

C. broad guides to thinking and action

D. general plans that give overall direction to company efforts

E. sequences of alternative actions and outcomes

F. sequences of steps, taken in a certain order, to accomplish a task

G. inflexible statements of what will be done

H. measure and evaluate progress toward the plan's goals

_____ 1. algorithms

_____ 2. objectives

_____ 3. policies

_____ 4. premises

_____ 5. procedures

_____ 6. rules

_____ 7. standards

_____ 8. strategies

True–False

T F   1. Because things will always occur that cannot be fully expected, one should not devote a lot of time to planning.

T F   2. Objectives are needed in every area where performance and results directly and vitally affect the survival and prosperity of the business.

T F   3. Management by objectives is an approach that requires that one's subordinates have prescribed goals to work toward.

T F   4. When making a premise, the manager should consider factors that can be influenced as well as those over which he or she has no control.

T F   5. In planning, one must first survey the resources available so that the objective chosen is one capable of being reached.

T F   6. The only way to forecast the future is to project the past.

T F   7. The manager is not faced with the task of planning unless a choice must be made among alternative choices.

T F   8. When all possible courses of action have been identified, the manager should examine each alternative for its effects on the plan's objectives.

T F   9. Procedures allow considerable leeway in solving problem situations by providing general statements of end results.

T F 10. A rule sets out a particular sequence of events that must be followed.

T F 11. To be effective, a budget must be expressed in monetary units for the period of time under consideration.

T F 12. In regard to plans to be met, it is vital that budgets be followed without exception.

T F 13. One of the most common causes of failure is the lack of a clear-cut and carefully considered statement of objective.

T F 14. The purpose of the Delphi technique of forecasting is to crystalize the reasoning process while identifying and clarifying the major alternatives.

T F 15. In the end, plans become the standards by which performance is measured, and that fact needs to be taken into consideration in the plans themselves.

Multiple Choice

1. All planning, whether it be for the next 24 hours or the next century, should include

(a) a careful budget, (b) preparation of statistical evaluations, (c) prediction and evaluation of the future, (d) mathematical analysis.

2. Management by objectives emphasizes

(a) accomplishments, (b) putting in an eight-hour day, (c) objectivity in analyzing personality, (d) working hard.

3. The management by objectives concept includes the idea that a worker's goals should be established by

(a) the worker, (b) a goals committee, (c) the personnel department, (d) the work group.

4. Planning does *not* necessarily involve which of these:

(a) choosing an objective, (b) establishing a course of action, (c) taking predetermined actions until the desired end is reached, (d) making charts and budgets.

5. The Delphi technique does *not* encourage its participants to

(a) clarify the major alternatives to the issue under consideration, (b) conform to group pressure, (c) pool knowledge on a particular problem, (d) all of the above.

6. The effective manager

(a) gives detailed attention to every alternative in the planning situation, (b) focuses attention only on those alternatives in the planning situation which are felt to be capable of being carried out, (c) limits attention only to those alternatives in the planning situation which are felt to be easiest to put into effect, (d) restricts the number of alternatives in the planning process to a maximum of five so each can be considered in great detail.

7. If your company had a task of rather routine nature that was performed again and again and for which it was important that the same types of results be attained each time, you would probably establish a

(a) policy, (b) rule, (c) procedure, (d) plan.

8. Which of the following is useful in measuring progress toward the meeting of objectives?

(a) milepost budgeting, (b) Delphi technique, (c) forecasting, (d) decision tree.

Completion

1. One of the most common causes of failure in managerial planning is the lack of a clear-cut and carefully considered statement of _____ .

2. The forecasting method which brings together the opinions of experts is known as the _____ technique.

3. The strategy that sketches the outlines of the nature of the business and policies of the firm is called a _____ strategy.

4. The strategy that details the reaction of the firm to its rival's actions is known as a _____ strategy.

5. _____ _____ defined "prevoyance" as assessing the future and making allowance for it.

6. Goals or end points of planning are known as _____ .

7. The concept of _____ _____ _____ is ensuring that everyone understands what is being worked toward and knows what the objectives are.

8. _____ are the assumptions about the future on which plans are based.

9. A company's _____ is its general plan, or the plan for a major project of the company.

10. _____ differ from procedures in that they usually stand alone rather than as part of a sequence.

READING

OLIN'S SHIFT TO STRATEGY PLANNING

A few years ago, Olin Corp. was awash in aggressive marketing plans for goosedown sleeping bags, propane stoves, tents, and other camping products. At the same time, Olin was pushing industrial mainstays such as polyester film and polyvinyl chloride. But profits were still lackluster at best. Today, however, the $1.5 billion Stamford (Conn.) conglomerate has jettisoned all these products and is putting its capital into such areas as brass sheeting and hydrazine chemicals — products that fit in much better with its established corporate expertise. Reason: Olin has turned to a planning method that stresses overall corporate goals above individual product potentials.

The concept, known variously as strategy planning or strategy management, enables a company to spot — and capitalize on — its strengths in certain markets, and to sacrifice those market areas where growth is marginal. Although its cutthroat nature can make individual product managers unhappy at times, "it shows you how to drop your dogs and pick up stars," explains one veteran corporate planner.

THE STRATEGIC MOVES

The concept is by no means unique to Olin, a company that this year is struggling just to match its record 1977 profits. In fact, most management consultants — many of whom are pushing a form of strategy planning to their clients — credit General Electric Co. with pioneering the rudiments of

MAKING THE CONCEPT FIT A COMPANY'S NEEDS

Olin Corp. is just one of an estimated 100 U.S. companies that have taken strategy planning concepts and modified them to suit their existing markets and management style. Here are some ways they try to make the systems work:

Mead Corp., the Dayton papermaker, credits its six-year-old system with lifting return on total capital to 12 per cent in 1977 from 5 per cent in 1972, and jumping its industrywide rank among forest-product companies to No. 2 of 15 (tied with three others) from No. 12 in 1972. Mead's method: rejuggle 24 former profit centers into that number of strategic business units, and move 24 top executives into new slots so that their expertise matches the businesses they would run. "If you have a business you want a lot of cash out of instead of growth, you don't put a high-powered marketing man in charge, and if you want growth, don't put a conservative accountant in charge," explains William W. Wommack, Mead's vice-chairman. Mead also is allocating money differently: Instead of funding projects with "fair share" allocations, it now funds strategies, a method that lets the company weed out "dog" products, milk its mature cash producers, and concentrate investment on potential growth lines.

Gulf Oil Corp. has one of the weightiest systems around, with 35 planners at corporate headquarters and 73 planners at seven strategy centers. The system has helped Gulf steer clear of the solar energy field, for instance, an area that an energy company might have felt compelled to enter, but one in which Gulf found it would not have competed profitably. Nonetheless, chief planner Juergen Ladendorf says the system, now in its fourth cycle, may take six years to improve bottom-line results.

Daylin Inc., a $300 million Los Angeles retailer that was in deep financial trouble two years ago, asks each product-area manager to draw up a five-year plan to assess his unit's competitive position and spell out a set of actions to enhance it. William M. Duke, planning director, credits the two-year-old system with substantially boosting profits at Daylin's Handy Dan Home Improvement Centers, for one, and with bolster-

the concept more than a decade ago. And today any number of companies, still reeling from the recession of 1974–75, are using variations of the theme in hopes of surviving in a continuing climate of declining capital resources and heightened foreign competition.

But Olin, which introduces fresh thinking to its units' strategy planning sessions by having an "outsider" sit in, claims the system, among other things, has helped it weed out such ailing businesses as a polyester film plant in Greenville, S.C., sold in 1974 for $22 million, followed by the sale of its Statesville (N.C.) tent business to National Canvas Products Corp. of Toledo, its Seattle Quilt Co. to Raven Industries Inc. in Sioux Falls, S.D., and its Turner Co. (propane camping appliances) to Cleanweld Co. in Los Angeles — all for a total of $9 million.

At the same time, the system has helped pinpoint the need for investments: more than $100 million to build a chlorine-caustic soda plant in McIntosh, Ala., which will boost the line's production 60 per cent; $75 million to $80 million to expand its polyols, hydrazine, and swimming-pool chemical operations; and $80 million to boost growth in its copper-based alloy markets.

ing Daylin's fortunes as a whole. Success has come at a price, however. At the company's Diana Fashion Stores division — a group of about 150 women's specialty shops — Daylin President Sanford C. Sigoloff called for an assessment of lifestyle changes to determine a proper merchandise mix over the next five years. "We wanted to gear store openings accordingly," Duke notes, but the division's managers were reluctant to comply. He says Sigoloff had to recruit "a whole new [management] team that was responsive" to the idea.

Fairchild Camera & Instrument Corp., faced with accelerating changes in technology and reversals in key markets, jumped into strategy planning just last fall by realigning top management and naming Vice-Chairman C. Lester Hogan director of strategy planning. Hogan concedes that Fairchild planning has not always been successful. For example, the company was badly burned by last year's price war in the digital watch industry. So the company has now augmented its product planning staff with a corporate team of six planning specialists to map out orderly entries into new markets. For example, industry processing techniques may make it possible to put as many as 10 million transistors on a single chip of silicon in 1985, says Hogan, adding. "You don't sell [high-technology] components the way you sell simple diodes."

Eaton Corp., a $2.1 billion automotive and industrial parts maker, began its form of strategy planning four years ago by creating 400 "product market segments" within its 26 divisions. Eaton's system identifies two primary factors that affect strategy planning — "push" and "pull." The pull factors, which are largely uncontrollable, include inflation, exchange rates, and the growth rate of one business as compared with others. All operating divisions monitor the impact of such factors on their businesses, then contribute data on them to a 10-year benchmark report. The push factors are actions the company can take to control operations: increase R&D, build a new plant, or aggressively pursue market share growth. To influence the push factors, explains corporate development chief Robert C. Brown, each division and market segment unit creates a five-year plan, as does the corporation. To date, Eaton attributes rapid growth in its automatic cruise control product line to the planning system.

'ENLIGHTENED OBJECTIVITY'

The key to Olin's system is the process in which plans are formulated. In a traditional planning approach, managers of a business unit would sit down by themselves once a year to hammer out a five-year plan. But at Olin, managers from each of 30-odd strategic planning units (components for which the company can define specific goals) meet with two or three managers from other areas of the company who generally know very little about that unit's operation. Such outside managers are called profilers, and it is their job to lend perspective and to help the planning unit's managers communicate better. "We act as a catalyst to stimulate discussion," explains Joseph R. Rindler, a profiler whose main job is director of financial analysis. "We're there to offer planning unit managers enlightened objectivity."

Profilers, who number about 35 to 40, come from both staff and line jobs that range from personnel executive to product manager. But because they are not professional planners — they spend only 3 to 5 per cent of their time in the profiler role— each must go through a brief training program to prepare for the annual planning sessions, which last one or two days. The planning sessions focus on reaching a consensus on the business unit's optimum strategy. The resulting profile is outlined in a standard two-page format and, in turn, is passed up the line to top management.

From this profile, management prepares a yearly "action document" for each of Olin's five groups — a kind of nonfinancial budget of actions that should be taken to meet long-range goals. Actions prescribed involve moving into new geographic markets or phasing out of existing ones, seeking acquisitions, or unloading properties. "Recent decisions have mostly been to improve our position in existing markets," notes James F. Towey, Olin's chairman and chief executive officer. "We think there are enough opportunities in the businesses we're now in."

'OLINIZING'

Although Olin's corporate staff has two full-time planners and the five operating groups have one each, the meat of the planning analysis is done in the profiler sessions. The benefits, according to Olin executives, are that each unit is forced to think through its ideas carefully; the profilers gain knowledge of the unit's activities, which helps them work with or serve the unit better in their primary jobs; the process is a good management development tool; and top management gets a clear picture of where each unit stands and where it should be headed. For example, Rindler says a recent shift in marketing of Olin's pool chemicals, HTH and Pace, came directly from a profiling session. Under profiler questioning, unit managers discovered that one product made from an inorganic compound was more effective in certain densities of sunlight than another product made from an organic compound. Thus, the company decided to concentrate domestic sales of one product in the Sunbelt region and the other product elsewhere.

The profiler concept originated at Arthur D. Little Inc., the Boston-based consulting firm that helped Olin get its system off the ground in 1972. At that time, ADL staffers assumed the role of profilers. Since then, however, Olin has used its own personnel. "We 'Olinized' the ADL system," says James M. Sheridan, manager of corporate planning analysis. Adds Gilbert C. Mott, vice-president of planning: "It's been considerably [changed] since. And it has the side benefit of improving communications throughout the company.

THE PITFALLS

Still, company officials agree, the system is far from perfect. "We have to introduce some new questions and new reviews each year to make sure that people rethink their situations," observes Mott. "We are constantly alert to ensure that the process, by repetition, doesn't become too mechanical." Mott also cautions that there are other dangers built into strategy planning, such as a temptation to "develop a lot of sophisticated concepts like futurology," an attempt to project trends 10 years into the future and beyond. "But we try to keep ours on a practical level," Mott adds. Moreover, friction occasionally occurs between profilers and unit planners who feel the profilers are meddling or spying. "But this is a natural part of constructive dialogue," explains Sheridan.

Nonetheless, says William L. Wallace, who was one of the prime movers in setting up Olin's system before he left the company in 1974, the system has brought a beneficial change in outlook. In the past, he says, "we never asked ourselves how we could win." Though Olin started five-year planning as early as 1963, it was not until 1971, after the company experienced four consecutive years of falling profits, and a drop in return on equity to 4.1 per cent from 12.5 per cent in 1966, that the company decided to rethink its controls on its diverse operations. This led management to ADL and its system of strategy planning. "We needed somebody to give us structure from which to start," says Towey. Since then, Olin's net income has fluctuated on rising sales, but net income from continuing operations has tripled, to $78.1 million in 1977.

No one at Olin credits all of the company's major moves to strategy planning. For example, the spinoffs of its aluminum business to Consolidated Aluminum Corp. for $126 million in 1974 and its Olinkraft subsidiary to Olin shareholders as a separate company in 1974 were in progress before the system was instituted. Nonetheless, says Wallace, "the thing the planning process did was keep us from reneging [on the aluminum business sale] when the market turned up."

Despite an expected profit decline in the first quarter, resulting from rising costs, work stoppages, and bad weather, and despite uncertain prospects for the remainder of 1978, Olin executives think the system has proven itself. The acid test, according to former Olin planner Wallace, was what happened to strategy planning at Olinkraft. "We weren't sure if the new venture would continue using the system, because the former president had only accepted it grudgingly," he recalls. "Once they got spun off that would have been a perfect time to ditch it, but they didn't.

Questions for Discussion

1. The text identifies 10 steps in the planning process. Which steps are part of Olin's strategy-planning system? How are they used?

2. What role does strategy play in Olin's total way of managing? Why is strategy planning thought to be so important at Olin?

3. From the descriptions of strategy planning at Mead, Gulf, Daylin, Fairchild, and Eaton, what problems — and benefits — seem to be associated with such a system?

INCIDENT

DECLINE AND FALL OF SANTA

Managerial planning is only as good as the information on which it is based; the company in this incident discovered this important principle the hard way.

The Calico Candy Company has manufactured salt water taffy for over 100 years and began a sideline of chocolate candy in 1970. Last year the company advertised heavily for the Christmas season, concentrating on a new salt water taffy Santa Claus. The campaign was such a success that the advertising budget for the Santa Claus taffy was tripled. Encouraged by the Christmas campaign results, the company allocated the other half of its advertising budget to this year's salt water taffy Easter Bunny campaign. Production was immediately put into full swing to meet the anticipated heavy demand.

Meanwhile, George King, a young sales representative calling on candy and drug stores, became increasingly dismayed by store managers' reports. These managers had ordered heavily from Calico but had been unable to sell the taffy; their inventories were therefore overstocked and the managers were pessimistic about selling the taffy, even on sale. The consensus seemed to be that taffy was no longer in demand, and that chocolate candy was sweeping the tastebuds of the nation.

George reported this immediately to the advertising manager, who expressed polite interest. The advertising manager did mention George's findings to the production manager later that week over a cup of coffee. After which they had a good laugh at the thought of a decline in the popularity of their company's mainstay.

The Christmas campaign lost over $200,000; a staggering amount of candy was in stock, consisting of salt water taffy Santa Clauses and Easter Bunnies. Production was cut; but nonetheless much money had already been spent on the Easter Bunny campaign.

The Calico president was shocked about all the taffy stockpiled and the near-bankruptcy of the company. He was warned by the board of directors to correct the situation immediately. The Calico president had only to figure out how to do this.

Incident Analysis

1. How would you, as Calico president, prevent this situation from happening again?

2. What information would you require, and from whom?

3. What planning techniques would you use to put the information to best use?

EXERCISE

QUIKI-BURGER

Management by objectives is a technique widely used to develop participation in goal setting and planning. It is extremely important in developing concrete measures of how well plans are carried out, not to mention in deciding what plans should be put into effect to achieve one's goals. How would you plan with an MBO system? In this exercise we are faced with such a problem.

Tom Boyle looked proudly around the almost-completed Quiki-Burger building. He'd had to cut corners and float a bank loan to come up with the rather substantial frachise fee, but now the town Quiki-Burger franchise was his.

National headquarters had, of course, given him careful instruction in the delicate art of creating the famous Quiki-Burger as well as in keeping his account books in order. He even had down pat the way to use all the various order forms with which to replenish his inventory from the national larder.

But now the grand opening was but two weeks away, and Tom felt vaguely ill at ease about the actual managing of his franchise. He desperately wanted to do the best possible job, not only because of the comfortable income he wanted for his family but also for the personal satisfaction of delivering a quality product to his townspeople.

But how could he keep track of how well he was doing? Who was to tell him where he could do a better job? In what ways could he instill his sense of dedication and pride into his three employees?

FOR THE STUDENT

1. Assume you are Tom Boyle and National Headquarters has sent you some literature on management by objectives. How would this technique help you in the areas of concern indicated in the last paragraph above?

2. Set up a management-by-objectives system for Tom's use, listing his major objectives, the measurement used to check accomplishment of these goals, review dates and possible ways to accomplish each goal.

INCIDENT

QUICK FIGURING

The cost of health claims at Computechnics, Inc., had reached the point where the system needed to be computerized to reduce cost per claim, speed processing, and (particularly) gain better statistical data to allow better management of the steadily increasing costs. Steve Timmons, of the management information systems department, was appointed project manager and began to organize the project.

A week later, Ben Terrison, Steve's manager, came into Steve's office. "Steve," he said, "the departmental five-year plans are due this week, and I need to know what resources to allocate to your benefits project." Steve thought, "Oh, boy!" but said, "OK, I'll try to have it for you tomorrow."

Doing some quick figuring, Steve thought to himself, "Eighteen months is a reasonable time to complete the project, and the most likely guys to work on it are Johnson and Michaels because they've worked in the personnel area before. Now, 2 times 18 is 36 person–months. At $15 an hour, 150 hours a month, that's $81,000 for staff costs. Computer charges have been averaging around $2,500 a month, so with a little fudge factor, that's $50,000 for computer charges."

Steve's estimates were incorporated into the departmental plan and were also used as the basis for the project plan that was presented soon afterward to the benefits department. After some initial misgivings about the length of the project, the benefits department decided that the project was cost-effective, accepted it, and based their next year's budget on the cost figures contained in it.

When Timmons outlined the project to Johnson and Michaels, Michaels became upset. "How can you say that the project will be completed on May 1 a year and a half from now," he objected, "when we don't even know what's involved! For all we know, it could be a three-year project! Besides, I'm spending half of my time working on personnel's skills inventory system now. I can't just drop that. And another thing, I just read a directive this morning that MIS will charge out staff costs at $18.50 an hour, starting next month. We'll never be able to meet your commitments on this project!"

Questions for Discussion

1. How did planning premises affect the quality of the plan developed?

2. Evaluate the manner in which the plan was developed. (Hint: How well was each step performed in the planning process?)

3. Develop a management-by-objectives system for planning and evaluating performance on the project.

CASE

BARKSDALE METAL PRODUCTS COMPANY

The Barksdale Metal Products Company is a sheet metal manufacturer, the primary product of which is metal utility tool boxes used in pick-up trucks. Barksdale employs some 75 persons. Approximately 30 of the total employees work directly in manufacturing, in a job-shop situation; they turn out the boxes on a piecework basis, using metal-forming and electric-welding machinery. Barksdale has enjoyed much success over its 15 years of existence and has always experienced good demand for its product. The company has been able to hold its own against competition over the years, mainly because of its product quality and ability to keep highly competent sheet metal-workers in the shop.

Frank Barksdale, founder and president of the company, believes in rewarding hard work on the part of his employees; he is particularly proud of Donald Hughes, who advanced himself from an apprentice in the shop to his present position as supervisor of production. Donald knows the sheet metal business inside and out and has been a key force in the company's success.

Allen Gregory is a college graduate with a background in marketing. Allen's knowledge of manufacturing processes is limited, but sales have increased by 12 per cent each year during his two years as director of marketing for the firm.

Recently, Gregory informed Barksdale that a competitor had modified its operations to include a product line of utility boxes made of fiberglass, at a price comparable to the Barksdale product. Gregory fears that the new product could cut deeply into Barksdale's share of the market. He contends that the fiberglass boxes offer a substantial advantage over Barksdale's steel products, in durability, resistance to corrosion, and light weight. The competitor's product line will put the company in a very unfavorable marketing position unless immediate steps are taken to counter these advantages.

As a result of this information, Barksdale has called a meeting with Hughes and Gregory to discuss the situation. Gregory feels that the Barksdale Company should make an immediate effort to acquire the manufacturing equipment necessary to initiate the production of its own line of fiberglass tool boxes. Hughes, however, contends that such drastic action would be unfounded, and that the company should continue to produce high-quality steel products without further consideration. Barksdale agrees with Hughes and the matter is settled. His opinion is that the company has faced adversity before and has always managed to satisfy consumer needs with quality products. "If it works, don't fix it."

Besides, Gregory is relatively new to the industry and may have overreacted.

Questions for Discussion

1. Evaluate the validity of the "If it works, don't fix it" attitude in comparison with the purpose of planning.

2. Should Barksdale Metal produce fiberglass tool boxes? Why or why not?

3. How can good planning help a company avoid a crisis? How does this apply to Barksdale Metal?

CASE

UNITED STAINLESS STEEL COMPANY

United Stainless Steel Company (USSC) was experiencing a very slowly expanding market. Fierce competition existed from other producers battling for steel tonnage and market share. USSC was barely maintaining profitability.

Over the past two years market share had decreased by one percentage point, down from 10 to 9 per cent of the market. Quality rejects had increased 8 per cent and claims were up by 4 per cent within the same period. In addition, delivery performance had decreased from 75 per cent on-time delivery to 58 per cent.

At present several major battles are being fought among USSC management. Bob Stark, manager of sales, has charged that both the production planning and the operations departments are acting irresponsibly. He claims the loss in market share to be because the quality of steel being produced is becoming inferior to that of United's competitors. Also, delivery performance has dropped off considerably, even as he has been telling his customers that United is working toward 80 per cent on-time delivery. Stark has maintained that it is the responsibility of operations to reduce costs and cut down on quality rejects; the Production Planning Department must reduce downtime and meet delivery schedules.

The operations manager, Ron Macklin, spoke out at the last general meeting. According to Macklin, unit costs were being reduced because productivity and incentive performance were constantly increasing in the plant. He said productivity could be even better if there weren't so many breakdown-caused delays incurred on the equipment. Some of the old rolling mills couldn't withstand the much higher weight and increased hydraulic pressure called for on many of the new products that Sales was pushing — and for which it was booking sales. Ron said that Operations could not produce many of the new finishes being ordered; the old equipment was inadequate and inefficient for those applications. In addition, he protested that Production Planning wasn't using the most efficient schedules; they were incurring unnecessary delays for setup times because of the type of products they were scheduling.

Production Planning's response to the decrease in delivery performance was that not only were breakdown delays contributing to poor performance, but that they had to reschedule orders on many occasions. The steel that was being prepared for orders often was rejected for quality defects and had to be remade, thus adding an additional week onto promised delivery dates. They also defended themselves on the grounds that Sales was quoting unreasonable delivery times on many products.

Chuck Treeter had recently been hired to replace the suddenly retiring general manager, Joe Williams. Chuck brought with him a wealth of steelmaking knowledge and industry experience. He had been relatively softspoken in the several general operating meetings held so far; he appears to be just absorbing all the comments being made.

Before Williams left, Chuck got to spend one day with him, obtaining background information on past policies and procedures. Chuck had asked Williams for a copy of the profit plan; Joe replied that it was in the final stages of completion. His goal for the year had been to improve profits by 7 per cent without losing market share. He had held each manager (including Sales, Operations, and Production Planning) responsible for this goal. He commented to Chuck that in a formal letter sent to all the managers recently, he told them that they should all know how to contribute to the goal. Because he hadn't received any letters back regarding his letter, it was apparent that everybody understood the situation.

When Chuck asked about the declining market share, Joe replied that he knew it would get better; he had seen Bob Stark putting in long hours the last few months, although he wasn't quite sure what Bob had accomplished.

On that note, Chuck sat back in his chair and wished Williams a good retirement.

Questions for Discussion

1. What was the matter with the way in which Williams set goals for his managers?

2. Would better planning have helped reduce the interdepartmental fault finding? How?

3. How would a management-by-objectives system have helped?

CASE

POOR RALPH

Ralph Thompson was an only child. The small town in which he grew up had a population of 1,500 people, and the closest large town was 50 miles away. His father owned a small grocery store that serviced the town and local farm community.

When Ralph graduated from high school, his father was very pleased that Ralph wanted to work fulltime at the store. The name of the store was changed to B. Thompson and Son Grocery the day Ralph started. The work was long and hard; both Mr. Thompson and Ralph worked seven days a week, from six in the morning until seven at night, serving customers, stocking shelves, and delivering grocery orders. Ralph enjoyed the work; he didn't mind hard work and liked to talk to the customers. Ralph was basically shy but he had known their customers all his life and felt comfortable talking to them. Being located in a small farming community, the store extended credit to practically all its customers as a normal business practice.

Life moved on at a slow pace at the store; when Ralph was twenty-nine, his father became ill and was forced to retire. Ralph operated the entire business by himself. He hired two high school students, one to make the deliveries, while the other helped him in the store after school and on weekends.

Three years ago a major appliance manufacturer decided to buy land and build a large manufacturing facility just outside town. Two years ago the facility was completed and people started to move into the area from the large city 50 miles away. This spurred an enormous home-building boom for the town; the population jumped from 1,500 to 5,000 practically overnight.

Source: This case was prepared by Irving E. Abcug under the supervision of Theodore T. Herbert, to serve as the basis for class discussion.

At first Ralph tried to handle the new business in the same way he had dealt with customers in the past, but the number of customers was too large to handle from his small store. He was having trouble paying his own and the store's bills because of all the credit he was extending. He also found himself spending longer hours at the store just to keep the shelves stocked and to keep up on his bookkeeping and accounts.

Ralph decided he could not operate this way anymore. He borrowed money from the bank to expand his store, hired more help, and stopped giving credit to his customers. When his older customers complained, he explained that he could not pay his bills or mortgage on the new larger grocery store by extending credit. His old customers were unhappy but paid in cash.

Last year two large supermarket chains each opened a store in town and started a price war to compete for customers. Ralph started to lose customers. The first customers he lost were the new people who moved into town and the older customers who were disgruntled by the loss of extended credit. In order to try to compete, Ralph cut his prices to match those of the new supermarkets, but he couldn't meet his larger payroll or mortgage payments on the expanded store out of the profits the lower prices generated. Besides, Ralph could not buy goods as cheaply as could the large supermarket chains that buy in large quantities. Ralph could not meet his payments and was forced to close his business. Last week he started working on the assembly line at the appliance factory.

Questions for Discussion

1. An important part of the planning process is keeping track of the impact of the "outside world" — or reality — on plans and premises. Evaluate how well Ralph identified and accommodated his changing environment.

2. How would a formal strategy have helped Ralph? What strategy would you have recommended Ralph follow? Why?

3. Why — from a planning or strategy point of view — did Ralph's business fail?

ANSWERS TO SELF-REVIEW QUESTIONS, CHAPTER 5

Matching

A-4, B-2, C-3, D-8, E-1, F-5, G-6, H-7

True–False

1-F, 2-T, 3-T, 4-T, 5-F, 6-T, 7-T, 8-T, 9-F, 10-F, 11-F, 12-F, 13-T, 14-T, 15-T.

Multiple Choice

1-C, 2-A, 3-A, 4-D, 5-B, 6-B, 7-C, 8-A

Completion

1. Objectives. 2. Delphi. 3. Grand. 4. Competitive. 5. Henri Fayol.
6. Objectives. 7. Management by objectives. 8. Premises. 9. Strategy.
10. Rules.

Chapter 6

Organization for Action

1. To familiarize you with the basic ideas involved in structuring or preparing the ways in which people and activities relate to each other in order to achieve a goal

2. To point out the advantages and drawbacks associated with the organizational forms in widest use today

3. To show the ways in which groups of people can logically attack a task too large for any individual — and do the task easily within an organization

SELF-REVIEW QUESTIONS

Matching

A. people working together toward a common goal

B. the breaking down of a process into individual jobs, none of which in itself turns out a complete product

C. structuring of varied tasks that gives each employee more different operations to perform

D. the process of moving an individual from one job assignment to another

_____ 1. participation approach

_____ 2. job enlargement

_____ 3. A. V. Graicunas

_____ 4. job rotation

78

E. the strategy of giving workers the
opportunity to participate in the mak-
ing of the decisions that will affect them _____ 5. organization

F. a delimited form of line authority that
cuts across organizational lines in a
particular area _____ 6. departmentation

G. associated with determining the number
of relationships inherent in a given span
of management. _____ 7. span of control

H. refers to the number of persons a manager directly manages _____ 8. functional authority

True–False

T F 1. Division of labor increases productivity.

T F 2. Job enlargement is the opposite of division of labor.

T F 3. After job enlargement, a person who had only operated equipment might have a job that consists of the following: setting
up the job, sharpening the tools, inspecting the work, and
operating the equipment.

T F 4. A well-designed job should let the worker see a definite output
or result of personal effort.

T F 5. A well-designed job should demand as little individual skill or
judgment as possible, because the expense of training new workers
increases greatly with the skill level required.

T F 6. Responsibility gives the worker power to act officially within
the scope of the duties delegated.

T F 7. When a job is delegated, the manager is accepting the chance that
the worker will make a mistake.

T F 8. The Fayol Bridge is an organizational arrangement to enable
individuals to have access to their respective managers.

T F 9. When departmentation by function is used, the manager should
beware of the built-in tendency of a worker to shift loyalty
from the entire company to his or her own department.

T F 10. The manager who delegates is no longer responsible for the task;
the responsibility for the outcome now rests entirely with the
subordinate to whom the task was delegated.

T F 11. A worker who holds a staff position is responsible for issuing
orders to line workers.

T F 12. The hierarchy or chain of command is a direct result of the
application of the functional process.

T F 13. The primary value of organizational levels is in determining power relationships.

T F 14. Supervisors are the last managers in the chain of command who can delegate work.

T F 15. Organizations with a wide span of management tend to be conducive to improved employee morale.

Multiple Choice

1. Weber felt the three main factors to be considered when attempting to understand the behavior of any organization were

   (a) product, personnel, and management, (b) structure, strategy, and standards, (c) taboos, leadership, and bureaucracy, (d) society, structure, and management.

2. To Weber, the idea of a bureaucracy was

   (a) as now, full of negative connotations, (b) more distasteful than today, (c) a positive good since it removed human weaknesses and failings and substituted rational and systematic ways of accomplishing duties, (d) unknown since large bureaucratic corporations developed in the United States at a later date.

3. Red tape is

   (a) characteristic only of governmental organizations, (b) caused by there being too many steps involved in getting things done, (c) necessary for making sure that errors are minimized, (d) an important reason for the organization to exist.

4. Organization is primarily concerned with the way _____ and _____ relate to each other in pursuit of _____.

   (a) money . . . buildings . . . profits, (b) people . . . activities . . . goals, (c) rules . . . people . . . conformity, (d) labor . . . management . . . productivity

5. Organization may be defined as

   (a) the management process of setting up the ways in which people, work, and resources relate to each other, (b) a group of people working together in pursuit of a common goal, (c) the pattern of ways in which people, work, and resources relate to each other, (d) all of the above.

6. The idea of division of labor is based upon the process of

   (a) creating dissent in the union's ranks, (b) splitting a job into several distinct pieces, (c) organizing the work force so that workers performing the same job are grouped together, (d) none of the above.

7. After a certain point is reached, continued division of labor

   (a) gives continually increasing gains in productivity, (b) has no effect on productivity, (c) lowers productivity, (d) increases morale.

8. Job enlargement attempts to decrease boredom on the job by

   (a) giving the worker more and different operations to perform, (b) paying the worker more for increased productivity, (c) telling the worker how his effort contributes to the final product, (d) raising the fringe benefits of the job.

9. The participation approach requires that management be willing to give up some of its _____ in order to gain _____ for its workers.

   (a) profits . . . raises, (b) rights . . . respect, (c) demands . . . work, (d) authority . . . satisfaction

10. The manager who turns over tasks to subordinates has

    (a) shirked, (b) passed the buck, (c) delegated, (d) participated.

11. What departmentation strategy has been used to establish the position of sales manager?

    (a) function, (b) geographical area, (c) customer, (d) none of the above

12. Responsibilities should be delegated as far down the organization structure as possible.

    (a) in this way, cheaper labor can be applied to these tasks, (b) only in this way is the type of competence and information most suitable to doing the task likely to be applied, (c) this gives workers additional tasks and keeps them busy, (d) the statement is false

13. One who functions as a member of the board of directors, providing policy and making decisions that will be carried out by all levels below, is at the

    (a) trustee management level, (b) general management level, (c) departmental management level, (d) supervisory management level.

14. One who has responsibility for direction of the operations of the entire organization is at the

    (a) trustee management level, (b) general management level, (c) departmental management level, (d) supervisory management level.

15. Through a mathematical investigation of the relationships involved between supervisor and subordinates, Graicunas was able to offer convincing evidence that the span of management of the effective manager is

    (a) less than five, (b) between three and six, (c) more than five, (d) none of the above.

Completion

1. Job _____ is the process of moving an individual from one job assignment to another.

2. To increase job satisfaction, the _____ approach has proved effective by giving workers the opportunity to take part in the making of decisions which will affect them.

3. _____ is the obligation incurred by the worker to perform the delegated task satisfactorily.

4. _____ deals with the basic problem of grouping units of workers.

5. Organizational levels of authority are established by the applications of the _____ process.

6. The _____ of management is the number of persons a manager directly manages.

READING

ESB RAY-O-VAC: DECENTRALIZING TO RECHARGE ITS INNOVATIVE SPIRIT

The problems of ESB Ray-O-Vac Corp. have been a pressing concern to David C. Dawson ever since he became president of the country's second largest battery maker almost a year ago. But only recently has the forty-six-year-old executive begun addressing ESB's troubles, partly because just three months after Dawson arrived he suffered a mild heart attack.

Dawson was plucked from the vice-presidential ranks of the Philadelphia company's parent, Inco Ltd., and sent to ESB to arrest the erosion of the subsidiary's battery business, as well as to untangle a management setup one close observer termed "an organizational Gordian knot."

Recovering quickly from his heart attack, Dawson spent his early months at ESB talking with some 300 managers, getting a sense of the company, its weak spots, and what corrective measures were needed. After mulling things over, Dawson last month began a massive corporate reorganization aimed at solving the problem that is at the root of the company's declining share of the battery market — its failure to develop and market new products fast enough to keep pace with more aggressive competitors such as Union Carbide Corp., whose Eveready division is the nation's largest battery maker, as well as Gould Inc. and P. R. Mallory & Co.

To do that, Dawson is eliminating a major layer of corporate supervision that he believes stifled the marketing of new battery products. His reorganization calls for wholesale decentralization. It divides ESB into four clearly defined and fairly autonomous operating companies and places much greater responsibility for performance on managers in the field. Among other things, each company will now conduct its own research and product-development work, a reversal of the previous arrangement under which most R&D projects were clustered at a corporate technology center in Philadelphia.

BATTERY EMPHASIS
Dawson's program also signals the first major attempt by Inco to influence the direction of the big battery company it acquired nearly five years ago. Dawson,

who took over the CEO spot at ESB following the death of then-Chairman Frederick J. Port, is the first Inco executive to be installed in the top management ranks of the battery subsidiary. Now it is clear that, under Dawson, ESB will rely in a major way on Inco's enormous financial resources for the first time to help solve its problems. Aided by $50 million annually from Inco, ESB will now double its capital spending to an estimated $40 million, with most of the money going to modernize run-down plants and to build a few new facilities as part of an effort to reduce the company's above-average production costs. R&D spending, too, will be increased, by about 50 per cent to roughly $8 million.

The guiding purpose behind all these initiatives, Dawson stresses, is "to concentrate our efforts on the things that make money for the company and to organize for clearer accountability." More than anything else, that translates into concentrating on improving the company's position in battery markets, where it garnered 83 per cent of its revenues last year. And in recent months it has collected about $12 million by selling off various non-battery operations — including a specialty chemical producer, a fishing tackle business, and a molded plastics division.

ESB is by no means in desperate shape. Although the company has not grown as impressively as some counterparts in the industry, its pretax earnings increased by 44 per cent last year to an estimated $49 million on an 11 per cent rise in sales to $785 million. When ESB was acquired in 1974, it reported pretax profits of $24.8 million on sales of $436 million. The company still makes more types of batteries than any other producer in the world, ranging from the button-sized dry cells used in digital watches to the huge stationary storage systems designed for telephone exchanges.

SMOTHERING INNOVATION

In recent years, however, ESB has steadily lost market share to competitors. In the automotive battery business, these rivals have included Gould, Globe-Union, and General Battery, while Union Carbide and Mallory have been the winners in the dry cell field.

The most important shortcoming at ESB has been its inability to bring new products rapidly to market. The popular long-life alkaline dry cells and maintenance-free automobile batteries are symptomatic examples of this problem. Both became widely marketed in the mid-1970s, and in both cases, ESB's scientists had mastered the new technology early enough to make the company one of the market leaders with the new products.

But each time, the yen for innovation was smothered either by the Byzantine bureaucracy or the overly cautious attitude at ESB's corporate headquarters. "Their technical people came up with ideas, but management didn't come out with the product," says Jerome T. Lawrie, a vice-president at Chloride Inc., a Tampa (Fla.) battery company. "They maintained status quo, and now they are in the follower's position." Thus, ESB finds itself a laggard in a couple of the industry's hottest product categories — the high-profit items whose sales are growing by up to 20 per cent annually.

This pattern, repeated for years, seems to be the primary cause of ESB's lackluster profitability. If Dawson's overhaul works, he expects ESB's profits to climb roughly 50 per cent within three years.

'BARROOM BRAWL'

Until now, Inco has done little to correct matters. Ever since it moved to buy ESB, the two have had an unsettled, sometimes contentious relationship. The $230 million acquisition was the first of the unfriendly takeover deals involving blue-chip adversaries; the Inco-ESB deal is generally pointed out as a watershed event that legitimized the "hostile" takeover. "It was the first time we saw a barroom brawl in a Fifth Avenue duplex, " says Felix G. Rohatyn of Lazard Freres & Co., the dean of investment banking's takeover specialists.

Moreover, it was not until last year that a consent order was approved in a federal court, permitting the Toronto mining company to hold onto the battery manufacturer. In that settlement, ending an antitrust suit by the Justice Dept., Inco agreed to grant royalty-free licenses on certain battery-related patents and to not acquire another battery maker for at least 10 years. The litigation prevented Inco from moving sooner than it did in addressing ESB's troubles. "We couldn't run ESB like one of our businesses," says Charles F. Baird, president of Inco. Just three months after the court ruling, Dawson became president of ESB.

In Dawson, Inco selected a seasoned executive who joined the company's New York sales office in 1958. Within industry circles, Dawson has a reputation for being a man with top-notch credentials in marketing, international finance, and planning and development. "I know so little about batteries it's laughable," he observes, "but I feel I have the capacities in planning and organization which are precisely the things required here."

This is not the first time ESB has attacked its problems with an organization chart. In 1977, Port decided that closer ties between headquarters and the company's operating units would enhance the use of product and technological knowhow. So he installed a layer of four executive vice-presidents, each responsible for an assortment of products, corporate functions, and geographical areas.

"I helped implement that system and then had to try and live with it," recalls Richard T. Nalle Jr., a former executive vice-president, who is now senior vice-president for long-term planning. "The decision-making process was very cluttered."

THE NEW TEAM

Dawson has eliminated that extra corporate layer and divvied up ESB solely according to four product groupings. Folded into three major operating companies are the products that account for more than 90 per cent of ESB's business: Ray-O-Vac Co. for dry cells (the so-called primary batteries) used in flashlights, radios, calculators, and the like; Exide Co. for auto batteries and industrial models; and Systems & Electronics Co. for a potpourri of products, including emergency lighting, power conversion systems, and heart pacemakers. A fourth company, ESB's Universal Electric Co., makes small electric motors, sold to original-equipment manufacturers, that power household appliances.

The heads of these companies now have more complete control over their operations, and each one reports directly to Dawson. The new formation at

ESB represents mostly a change in structure, not content. In the decentralization, the company's top executives may have moved to different offices, but most are still around. As one analyst puts it: "It's the same old team, just a different batting order."

REEMPHASIS ON R&D

The big test for ESB now will be how quickly it can catch up after several years of slow-motion management. The company can no longer afford the sort of competitive slippage it suffered in dry cells when it moved much more slowly than Mallory in marketing long-life alkaline batteries. In 1974, ESB's dry cell sales were almost twice those of Mallory: $167 million for ESB, compared with $94 million for Mallory. By 1977, Mallory had nearly caught up, with sales of $215 million to ESB's $220 million, estimates James Bartlett, an analyst for Maison Placements Canada Inc. Bartlett notes that both companies still trail Union Carbide, which in 1977 had dry cell sales of $810 million.

Playing catch-up will not be cheap. "Over the next five years," Dawson admits, "we won't generate the cash flow we need internally. We will require support from our corporate parent to meet our objectives." But that support may be in doubt, since Inco itself is in financial warm water, according to some analysts. Inco's earnings dropped 22 per cent to $77.8 million on sales of $2.1 billion because of a still-unsettled miners' strike in Canada, depressed nickel prices throughout much of last year, and huge recent investments in overseas properties. Yet Dawson is confident that the corporate parent's commitment of roughly $50 million a year is assured. "It's large for us," he says, "but it's small for Inco."

Questions for Discussion

1. In the article, the major problem to be solved at ESB Ray-O-Vac is slow product development and marketing. The changes, however, deal with delegation, decentralization, and organization structure. How could these have created the slow product development and marketing problem?

2. How could the delegation, decentralization, and organization structure changes made at ESB Ray-O-Vac resolve the slow product development and marketing problem? Why?

INCIDENT

CHECK-OUT LINE

By organizing, the manager sets up the activities to achieve his or her goals. Sometimes, however, even the most astute manager can set up an organization that detracts from goal attainment! How does the organization of the check-out stand affect the objectives of the grocery store in this incident?

James Jones, a new graduate from one of the better business schools, had taken a job with a chain grocery store. Mr. Kelly, the regional vice-president, took him on a survey tour of several of the stores in the metropolitan area of a large midwestern town. They went into the last store — a large, modern, well-lit, spacious suburban store.

Jones inquisitively remarked, "You know, one thing I've noticed about all of our stores is that there always seem to be people standing in line to get checked out."

Kelly answered, "Yes, we do seem to have that a little bit; after all though, our surveys show that our customers typically spend anywhere from 20 to 45 minutes shopping. Certainly they don't mind spending, oh, an additional 5 to 10 minutes standing in a line, do they?"

Jones thought about it for a while, watching the check-out procedures. After a while, he asked, "Do you mind if I talk to the store manager for a few minutes?" Kelly assented and Jones walked over to Yancy, the store manager.

"Mr. Yancy, do you have any ideas about why in the world we have so many people standing in lines here? Don't you think that cuts down on their willingness to come back and spend money in our stores?"

"No, sir," said Yancy, "after all, they do keep coming back. I really think," he continued, "that what they come here for is the service, anyway. See, we have a companywide policy emphasizing service. Our bag boys must ask if the customer wants help to his car with his groceries and should help unasked if the customer has over two bags of groceries."

Jones watched for a time, and finally said, "What are these bag boys supposed to be doing, then? Are they being paid to take groceries out to the cars? I thought the checkers get paid to check groceries. Instead, I guess that a good three fourths of the time taken on each order is spent by the checkers' bagging the groceries because the bag boys are outside. Why is this? Isn't the bag boy supposed to be helping the checker get the food out of the way?"

Yancy slowly said, "Well, that's just part of the hazards of the game. We want to give the best service possible to our customers, and in order to do that sometimes the checkers have to take up some of the slack themselves."

Incident Analysis

1. Describe the organization of the check-out stand.

2. Did the policies of the store help — or hinder — the way in which the check-out stands were organized?

3. Given the policies of the store, how would you reorganize the check-out stands? Or would you prefer to change store policy?

EXERCISE

DISORGANIZATION CHART

This is an organization chart. (1) Identify what you think is wrong with it, if anything. (2) If there are some deficiencies, redraw the chart in a way that reflects a more correct way of organizing this manufacturing company. (3) Explain each change you made, if any.

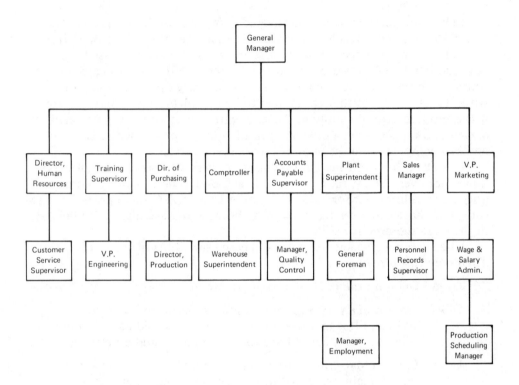

CASE

THE MAN IN THE MIDDLE

"One more year and then I'll have vested interest in the company pension plan and when that time arrives I can tender my resignation," thought Jason as he drove to work that morning.

Jason Matthews is thirty-two years old and married with two children. Jason is the manager of accounting for the southwestern district of the Bailey Company.

During his first years with Bailey he went through the training program and was assigned to the position of general accountant, from which he advanced to manager of the general ledger in his fifth year. He held that position until last year when he was promoted to his present position.

His immediate supervisor is Raymond Gillis, controller, whose chief concern is controlling cost. Gillis has a reputation of being hard-nosed, opinionated, and insistent that his orders be carried out to the letter. Jason had worked under Gillis when Gillis was manager of the general ledger and found that he could tolerate Gillis even though his demands seemed unreasonable at times.

In his new position, Jason discovered he would also have to report to David Jackson, vice-president and area director of southwestern operations. Jackson's primary concern is to maximize profit. He has requested that Jason supply him with various reports to determine the performance of the southwestern district. These requests were not very difficult to comply with. In fact, most of the reports had to be completed for Gillis; therefore, it was just a matter of supplying Jackson with a copy of the report. Jackson always allowed Jason an ample amount of time to comply with his requests and had complimented Jason on his work several times.

However, the profit margin for the southwestern district went down by 2 per cent over the last six months and Jackson has been making more requests for additional information. In order to complete the reports for Jackson, Jason has been working many extra hours and is starting to fall behind in the work required for Gillis.

When Jason arrived at work yesterday, he saw Gillis sitting in his office. Their conversation went as follows:

Jason: Good morning, Mr. Gillis. How are you today?

Gillis: I'm not in a very good mood since I discovered that you're late again this month on your reports. I would like to know when do you plan to have them completed and on my desk.

Jason: I plan to have them completed today, Mr. Gillis. I'm sorry that I'm late, but I had several reports to complete for Mr. Jackson.

Gillis: That's no excuse! Jackson's reports require very little of your time.

Jason: I agree, Mr. Gillis, but lately Mr. Jackson has requested many more reports because of the reduced profit margin in the southwestern district.

Gillis became very upset and told Jason that he was not to do any additional work for Jackson without Gillis' approval.

Later that afternoon Jackson's secretary stopped by Jason's office to show him the note Jackson had left for him. It was another request for a very detailed report; Jackson had stated, in his request, that it was of utmost importance that the report be completed by the time he returned from Dallas. Jason knew that Gillis would not approve the request and because Jackson wouldn't be back for another week he could wait a couple of days before telling Gillis.

Case Analysis

1. What does this case suggest about the difficulties of delegation?

2. Classical authors have argued that the principle of "unity of command" should not be violated by having a subordinate report to two or more superiors. What does this case suggest about the reasons for not violating this principle?

3. What do you think that Jason can do to get out of his problem situation?

CASE

TUNNEL OPTICAL

Rick Baker, a production foreman at Tunnel Optical, was dumbfounded. Mr. Brown, his boss and production manager, had just called him on the phone and told him, "Rick, the high-ups want to get rid of you! They say your department is costing the company money. I hope this warning will straighten you out, but if another complaint comes my way I will have to fire you. Understand?" Rick thought back over his four years at Tunnel and couldn't think of one thing he had done wrong. In fact, top management must have flipped out, because Rick's department had the highest production rate in the plant.

BACKGROUND
Rick started at Tunnel Optical right out of high school as a clean-up person. He was smart and, probably more important, ambitious and hard working. Production was "where the money was." And the company had three incentive plans: profit sharing, over-quota bonuses, and advancement for the hard-working production-minded person.

In three months he was promoted to production from clean-up because of his drive to do things right. After two years in the plant, Rick was promoted again, to production foreman, because month after month he produced the most lenses over quota. After having been foreman for two years, Rick's department produced the most of any in the plant. Mr. Brown was planning to promote Rick to be his assistant and Rick knew it. All the workers liked Rick; their bonuses got bigger and bigger because of him. But black clouds were building over Rick's head from outside the production department.

Source: This case was prepared by Larry R. Brown under the supervision of Theodore T. Herbert, to serve as the basis for class discussion.

A TYPICAL DAY

Rick was at his desk when Paul Dunn, the quality control manager at Tunnel, came in to see him.

Paul: "Hey, Rick, Sears accepted that batch of oversized lenses I wanted to reject last Friday."

Rick: "I told you they would! They weren't that bad. I have to get so many units out a week or they'll be after me. Production is the most important thing. Would you excuse me? I have to call maintenance."

[*Telephoning*] "Say, Bob, I have to have machines three and four worked on and done before my people get back from lunch."

Bob: "It can't be done, Rick. All my people are on lunch and those old machines will take longer than a half hour to fix. Maybe tomorrow morning?"

Rick: "Listen, Bob, you owe me a favor. Get those machines fixed in one hour."

Bob: "Okay, Rick, but I'll have to pull two or three extra men to get the job done that quickly. The cost will be high including overtime."

Rick: "Charge it to my department, old buddy."

Paul: "Rick, I just wanted you to understand that Sears wasn't happy with another shipment of faulty lenses. Next time they threatened to cancel their account, and their account makes the money around here."

Rick: "Listen, Paul, I told you everything would be all right. You worry too much. You take care of quality control and I'll take care of production."

Later that day, Paul was about to reject some deficient parts produced on machines three and four when Rick walked up.

Rick: "Paul, you can't reject those parts. We've been having trouble with those machines for weeks. My operators will have production running smoothly in just a few minutes."

Paul: "But, Rick, these parts are bad."

Rick: "The heck they are! I'll take the responsibility for these parts. Now let us run production and you do your inspecting where the parts are really bad."

Paul: "Okay, Rick, but this goes to the Plant Manager. You know I have the right to pull parts off the line."

Rick: "I don't care who you tell! You aren't stopping production as long as I am here."

CASE

BROWN CONSTRUCTION COMPANY

In the fall of 1976, George R. Brown organized the Brown Construction Company. Brown had worked for the previous four years as a field supervisor for Monroe Construction Corporation. Mr. Brown had a B.Sc. degree in civil engineering, as well as excellent technical abilities. He had distinguished himself as a doer at Monroe and knew he could establish a successful money-making business.

Brown's initial job contracts were small and filled easily. He quickly hired approximately 10 employees, who included a secretary-bookkeeper, carpenter, foreman, and unskilled laborers. Besides being sole owner and chief executive, Brown served as yard supervisor, crane operator, welder, salesman, bidding estimator, quality controller, purchaser, and organizer of all transportation for products.

Brown Construction Company remained small for the first few years, and earnings and sales rose slowly. Brown was a hard worker and oversaw all facets of his business. Gradually, however, things began to change. As contracts increased, minor problems surfaced. Planning was often incomplete. Turnover was high. Top-level talent was sometimes hard to attract and keep. There was no "esprit de corps."

Because of the new demands placed on his time from the growing business, Brown needed a person to take over the responsibilities of yard superintendent. He tried to train several men, but none of them worked out because they lacked engineering skills, quality control know-how, or the ability to direct men. (He did have one excellent crew foreman who remained until 1981 and a carpenter who is still employed by him.)

During 1978 and 1979 the organization did an excellent volume of business and posted good earnings. Although Brown spread himself very thinly, he was able to supervise all the jobs and all projects were completed satisfactorily. His improved financial position enabled him to hire a salesperson, who doubled as the head of purchasing.

In the spring of 1981, two very large jobs were awarded simultaneously to the company. Together these contracts doubled the past year's sales. Brown hired a supervisor who was technically capable, but who proved unable to do the job because of an inability to organize. When this person was released, both jobs were in progress. The salesperson took over production control of one of the jobs, with Mr. Brown directly supervising the other and checking up on the former periodically. However, both jobs were in trouble. Production planning was ineffectual, materials purchasing haphazard, turnover very high, and the internal office unorganized; everyone turned to Brown for help. Quality control fell and Brown had problems with architects and inspectors.

Brown completed both jobs, although not on schedule. The company's reputation was tarnished because of product quality. Employee morale was very low. When accused of inadequacy in managing one of the jobs, the salesperson quit. Earnings fell substantially.

Brown Construction Company is still in business. Production has reverted to 1978 levels. Brown is again supervising all operations and the organization is running relatively smoothly. But because of the difficulties Brown faced just when he thought his company was ready to take off, and because of the long hours and continual disappointments, Brown is burned out and discouraged.

Question for Discussion

Identify and discuss the reasons behind Mr. Brown's lack of success.

CASE

TINKERING ENGINEERING COMPANY

The Tinkering Engineering Company is a medium-sized partnership specializing in consulting services in the civil, mechanical, and electrical engineering fields. The partnership consists of four men, of which one serves as managing partner; the other three serve as department heads for the various engineering disciplines.

The managing partner is Henry Colby, who also is the chief marketing representative for the company and the overseer of the general office personnel (typists, clerks, printers, and so on). The other three partners are Carl Overstreet, Les King, and Hal Brenner, department heads for the civil, mechanical, and electrical departments, respectively. All three partners also assist in the marketing efforts. Overstreet also serves as the comptroller; King, in addition, administers the quality-control function for the entire company; and Brenner is in charge of the computer section.

When the partnership was formed, the total employment of the company was 15; most of these employees were experienced in their respective fields, requiring little or no supervision. In fewer than five years, however, the number of employees has increased to 125. The breakdown of the employees is as follows:

	Engineers	Draftmen/ technicians	Surveyors/ field inspectors	Office
Civil department (44)	20	10	14	
Mechanical department (26)	15	5	6	
Electrical department (41)	20	6	15	
Office staff (12)				12
Computer section (2)		2		
	55	23	35	12

Source: This case was prepared by Wilber F. Conley, Jr., under the supervision of Theodore T. Herbert, as the basis for class discussion.

Only four of the original 15 employees are still with the company. The average experience levels of the engineers are four-and-one-half years, three years, and two-and-one-half years in the civil, mechanical, and electrical departments, respectively.

The primary duties of the department heads are supervising and training their personnel. Training is especially critical, because the types of projects handled by the company are highly technical and require a working liaison between the production or design personnel and the clients.

The rapid growth of the company was accomplished by major marketing effort by the four partners, spearheaded by Colby. During the rapid growth period, the experienced personnel had taken up the slack by supervising and training the younger, inexperienced personnel. However, the departure of 11 experienced engineers in a single year-and-a-half period had created a crisis situation; the four partners had been devoting most of their time to business development, but were faced now with a major decision regarding the company's future.

The partners met to discuss the possibility of restructuring the company. After a week of conferences, no consensus had been reached. Each partner had his own view of what should be done.

Colby wanted to create a separate marketing section and hire new, full-time marketing personnel. This would release the other partners to function primarily as department heads, along with the other duties assigned to them. He posed this as an interim measure and proposed that the firm retain a management consultant to aid in the company reorganization.

Overstreet agreed that there should be a separate marketing department but contended that the company had grown to be large so quickly that it should be restructured to include some more managerial-supervisory positions.

King also agreed with the marketing idea, but in addition wanted to hire more experienced personnel to head the departments.

Brenner felt that the partners should continue as the marketing force, reasoning that the business had grown to the present stage as a result of their efforts. He advocated promoting "in-house" personnel to department heads whenever possible and hiring experienced department heads where required.

Colby also stated that they should consider some way to maintain a closer liaison with clients, because approximately 40 per cent of the firm's revenues was derived from repeat work. His concern was that the use of young, inexperienced personnel could result in a laxness in this area. King agreed with this logic, whereas Overstreet and Brenner contended that this area was not one of immediate concern.

Questions for Discussion

1. What is wrong or correct about each partner's viewpoint?

2. What course of action should the partners take?

ANSWERS TO SELF-REVIEW QUESTIONS, CHAPTER 6

Matching

A-5, B-6, C-2, D-4, E-1, F-8, G-3, H-7

True–False

1-T, 2-T, 3-T, 4-T, 5-F, 6-F, 7-T, 8-F, 9-T, 10-F, 11-F, 12-F, 13-T, 14-T, 15-T.

Multiple Choice

1-C, 2-C, 3-B, 4-B, 5-D, 6-B, 7-C, 8-A, 9-D, 10-C, 11-A, 12-B, 13-A, 14-B, 15-D.

Completion

1. Rotation. 2. Participation. 3. Responsibility. 4. Departmentation. 5. Scalar. 6. Span.

Chapter 7

Concepts of Control

CHAPTER OBJECTIVES

1. To review the manager's role in making sure that plans are going as intended
2. To introduce the tools available to the manager in fulfilling the control function

SELF-REVIEW QUESTIONS

True–False

T F 1. Control techniques have only been recently developed, mainly in response to common business problems.

T F 2. Measuring performance is a vital step in the control process.

T F 3. After one evaluates how well the plan is being carried out, standards should be established.

T F 4. Statistical standards are sometimes called historical standards.

T F 5. If the manager's control information is "timely," corrections can be made very shortly after a deviation has occurred.

T F 6. Because the future is so uncertain, seemingly bad trends should be dismissed, because they only confuse the issue and make more work for the manager.

T F 7. To fulfill its purpose, control data must be specific about amounts and sources of difficulties.

T F 8. A budget is a control device.

T F 9. Typically, staying within the budget's boundaries should take precedence over meeting one's performance goals.

T F 10. The break-even chart and the variable budget chart are the same.

T F 11. The return-on-investment concept emphasizes that it is necessary to invest time, money, or effort in order to make a profit.

T F 12. The direct-control philosophy embraces the idea that administrative charts and timetables can more effectively and directly monitor ongoing process than can fallible people.

T F 13. In key-area evaluation, the company closely watches its major competitors and sales areas for clues as to how well the company is meeting its goals.

T F 14. Control can occur before the manager has put a plan into effect.

T F 15. Feedback control is forward looking and exists for the improvement of the next attempt.

Multiple Choice

1. To which of these are control techniques applicable?

   (a) body temperature, (b) cash flow, (c) office procedures, (d) morale, (e) all of the above

2. The ultimate purpose of control is to

   (a) find out what's going wrong, (b) measure the performance of the manager's employees, (c) keep things going according to plan, (d) keep people from tasting freedom.

3. Standards must be

   (a) established in dollars for ready comparison, (b) kept as high as possible, (c) set so that they represent the very best performance possible, (d) able to be measured.

4. One of the more common methods of standard setting is the use of

   (a) judgment, (b) engineered standards, (c) statistical standards, (d) scientific determinism.

5. The measurement of performance is important because

   (a) it gives engineers something to do, (b) it keeps employees on their toes, (c) it is the method of pointing out where discrepancies exist between plan and performance, (d) it lets the manager know when the project or job is finished.

6. For a control system to be termed "adequate," the controls should reflect

   (a) the nature of the activity, (b) a "tough" stance on performance, (c) on the honesty of the employees, (d) none of the above.

7. The break-even chart differs from the variable budget chart in that

   (a) the variable budget chart sets out percentages to keep amounts flexible, (b) the break-even chart sets out percentages to show profitability ratios, (c) the statement is false, (d) none of the above.

8. A management audit is

   (a) a self-appraisal to discover and correct management mistakes, (b) an in-depth appraisal by a management team of a randomly selected department, (c) an outgrowth of human resource accounting, (d) a report done by an independent consulting firm on a company's financial strength.

9. Which of the following are *not* phases in the control activity?

   (a) post controls, (b) precontrols, (c) concurrent controls, (d) all of the above, (e) none of the above.

10. Drucker has suggested that some additional performance areas should be measured in evaluating management competence, those of performance in

    (a) appropriating capital, people decisions, innovation, and planning, (b) planning, organizing, staffing, directing, and controlling, (c) programming, planning, and budgeting, (d) social responsibility, employee welfare, and derivation of appropriate standards.

Completion

1. The first step in the control process is to establish _____ .

2. The last step in the control process is to _____ deviations from _____ and plans.

3. The manager who sets up a control system so that only nonstandard or unusual situations are brought to his or her attention for action has "managed by _____ ."

4. Controls that monitor the activity while it is going on are called _____ controls.

5. A method of _____ management control called organizational _____ is the process of uniting the whole "team" behind the organization's objectives and methodology.

6. One method of evaluating various control areas, known as _____ - _____ evaluation, measures each area according to the way it is accomplishing its stated goals in profitability, market position, public responsibility and five other key areas.

7. _____ control through _____ audit is similar to a form of financial control and can be carried out either internally or externally.

8. _____ focus on preventing problems from happening.

9. An integral part of the overall control process is the correction of _____ from standards and plans.

10. _____ controls consist of reviews of mistakes already made.

READING

HOW NORTHROP KEEPS TO BUDGET

David Clutterbuck

Few industries have such an unenviable record for cost over-runs as defence manufacturing. The industry's performance is often so bad that many developed countries include a safety net of cash in their defence budgets to bail out companies that cannot produce contracted equipment to the price agreed.

However, one company in the U.S. defence industry makes great play of the fact that it always delivers within budget. California-based aircraft manufacturer Northrop Corp. recently delivered the 3,000th of its tactical T38 and F5 aircraft all on time, within budget and to the promised performance.

"We would go to extreme ends not to over-run our budget," says Northrop's Chairman Thomas Jones. "We make adherence to a customer commitment a conviction. It is not even debated."

Northrop bases its recipe for coping with high technology mass production on two ingredients. The first is a tight production control system that involves everyone, including the operators on the shop floor. The second is the company's insistence on continually developing its own technology for simplifying production methods.

Reliability of delivery is probably one of the main reasons for Northrop's consistent profitability. Last year the 24,000-employee company had sales of nearly $1.3 billion, 28 per cent up on 1975. Profits rose 47 per cent over the same period, to some $36 million. The company currently has orders worth nearly $2.4 billion.

Production control starts when the senior production managers meet their colleagues in the marketing department at a weekly planning session. The meeting takes place in a special room in which the marketing plan is displayed on magnetized walls.

The managers have in front of them a fully current picture and can make speedy decisions on how the production department should react to changes in the market place. "We don't believe in having a staff planning group," says Jones. "Our line managers are our planners."

The charts on the magnetized walls indicate the status of each marketing project around the world. For the F5 fighter aircraft, for example, the managers can see at a glance the progress of any bills passing through countries' legislatures that will affect defence budgets. Information on key people, such as the head of the air force and the US ambassador in each country is also recorded. When, for example, the commander-in-chief of the Iranian air force, General Fazayel Tadayon, died recently in a helicopter crash, details of his successor and the likelihood of his favouring the purchase of F5s were quickly recorded on the wall display.

Armed with precise knowledge of the company's sales prospects, the departmental managers are better able to plan their own operations. Marketing and production co-operate, for example, to provide a chart, matching potential orders with production capacity for the next two years or more. From this chart, marketing executives can detect times when there will not be enough orders to maintain full production and can concentrate on finding business to fill the gaps.

The next step in the process is the regular meeting between a production head and his line managers. On the vast F5 assembly line, for example, production Vice-president B. T. Moser meets some 30 production managers and assistant managers once a week. Over the space of an hour, each manager explains to his colleagues how his section has performed in terms of keeping to schedule, number of defects, overtime and safety.

He also has to show his section's performance in terms of "equivalent unit cost" — the cost in terms of man-hours spent, overhead rates and materials to produce one unit. The company is able to add up all the equivalent unit costs to gain a picture of how much a complete aeroplane theoretically is costing to build. If the cost is over budget, it can investigate those sections whose equivalent unit costs are too high.

Quality control is also monitored in a room at the side of the 329-metre long production hall. In the room, quality control charts are displayed for every one of the 78 production sections. The supervisor in charge of each section can see clearly how it is performing compared to others. If his section is letting too many defects pass, says Moser, "it is the supervisor's responsibility to identify what went wrong and to state when he can get the problem fixed. If he does not solve it by then he has to explain again and we will determine if he needs help."

Safety is monitored by a team of supervisors and operators who tour the shop floor unannounced about once a week. Every unsafe act or condition, such as a welder not using glasses or a pile of metal tubes left lying on the floor, is reported. The pressure involved in reporting to his colleagues at the weekly meeting that his section is not working safely, embarrasses the supervisors so much that they usually take steps to remedy the situation quickly.

Each station's man-hour, materials and overhead costs are reported to Moser every two or three days. A station that is over-running budget may have to report twice a day or even hourly.

At a production meeting earlier this year, general foreman Kent Smith correctly forecast he would manufacture wings in the next week in 475 man-hours each. This was the lowest time, and hence the lowest equivalent unit cost, that part of the assembly line had yet achieved.

In the production life of every aircraft, the manufacturing time falls considerably as the operators gain experience. On the F5, which has been in production for four years, the wings originally required 1,200 man-hours each to construct.

Every few weeks the amount of time for each task is reduced on the planning schedules. The supervisors have the opportunity to protest if they think the new schedule is too demanding. A supervisor may say: "This job needs nine hours not eight," says Moser. "Usually we will accept that. Thereafter he breaks his back to get it done in nine hours. As he gets used to that, we start to discuss with him again whether it can be reduced to eight."

The supervisor uses the same tactics on his operators, getting agreement from them that they can do the job faster. Explains Roy Lindgren, supervisor of the aft fuselage fabrication section: "Every month I reduce the time a little. The first week the operators don't make it. Then they gradually do." Each operator is responsible for recording and monitoring his own performance against time. He has a bar chart in which each task has a number of spaces, according to the time it should take. As he completes the task, he pencils in the spaces alloted.

If he fails to do all the work assigned to him, there will be blank spaces left. In this case, the operator has to provide a brief report explaining why he did not achieve his target. Often the reason is a minor breakdown in equipment or supplies. When the supervisor gets the operator's report he can check whether the situation has been remedied and approach the appropriate service department if it has not.

One of the most common comments in operators' reports, however, is that the bar charts give them too little time. The bar charts are then sent to the industrial engineer for that area of the shop. If he is not satisfied with the excuse, he briefs the supervisor to investigate and report his findings the next morning. "Usually," says Lindren, "the excuses people give are justified."

Hydraulics installer Wayne Pullol maintains he likes the system. "It bothers me if I don't complete a space on the bar chart," he says.

"You don't really notice much pressure on you," adds lead mechanic Randy Newton.

The company also attempts to give the employees all the information they feel necessary to do their job. Each supervisor holds daily briefing meetings with his subordinates, where they can ask anything they want. Questions the supervisor cannot answer himself are sent to a special department which does nothing but answer employee queries.

Because the employees have free access to information, they respond well when the company does run into production difficulties, maintains M. G. Gonzales, senior vice-president of business operations. Two years ago, the company was having difficulty keeping to the gradual reduction in manufacturing time for the F5 tail. The managers asked the operators to explain what was preventing them from achieving the targets. Then the managers, operators and engineers worked together to remove as many of the constraints as possible. Where better tools were required, for example, the company provided them.

"Then we asked the employees, 'What do you think you can do?'" says Moser. "They set — and met — their own goals, which were higher than we had originally expected."

Last year, Moser found that cost estimates for some units were much too low. "I told the employees that, if we didn't accelerate the rate of production, we would have a cost over-run," he says. "In the end they exceeded their cost objectives for 1976 by more than $2.5 million." The assembly stations concerned received a plaque to congratulate them on their performance.

Information and encouragement to the employees make up only one half of Northrop's approach to ever-increasing productivity, however. At the same time the company is constantly on the look-out for technical solutions that will simplify production.

Part of this approach involves introducing small technical refinements from day to day. But the biggest gains come from the initial design of the manufacturing and assembly area. Unlike most of its US competitors in the defence industry, which lease an average of 53 per cent of their production equipment from the government, Northrop insists on owning its own tailor-made facilities. Only 3 per cent of its plant and equipment are leased.

The company also ensures that the tooling engineers work alongside the draughtsmen who design new aeroplanes. The tooling engineers can quickly spot when a design is going to be expensive to produce and suggest modifications that will make manufacture cheaper and easier.

As a result, Northrop has been able to help operators work more easily and quickly. Traditionally, for example, a mechanic who wished to put a bolt on the underside of an aircraft engine had to kneel down to it. "He was working very inefficiently," says Gonzales. "Now he has a rotating jig, which he can turn to any position. It is three times as productive as a fixed jig."

Similarly, the large metal sheets that form the skin of an aircraft can easily be damaged when handled. Under normal construction methods they are transported by fork-lift trucks and wrapped in layers of protective packaging. On the F5 line, however, the metal sections now hang unwrapped from overhead rails. One man can push or pull the piece he requires all the way from the stores to his assembly station.

At the construction plant for 747 jumbo jet fuselages, seven miles of overhead rail take the sheets from a specially constructed railway car into and around the plant. "Compared to when we used trucks for transport," says Gonzalez, "we think we have increased productivity by four times." The arrangement saves the company about 28,000-square metres of storing and manoeuvring space and some $1.2 million a year in labour costs. Damage to sheets has been reduced by around 40 per cent.

"Over the past 15 years, the U.S. defence industry has increased its productivity by 4.5 per cent a year, on average," says Gonzalez. "Northrop has an average increase of 5.8 per cent."

Questions for Discussion

1. It is often said that planning and controlling are but two different sides of the same coin. How are planning and controlling related at Northrop?

2. The three steps in the control processes are (a) establishing standards, (b) measuring performance against standards, and (c) correcting deviations. Describe the ways in which Northrop performs each of these three steps.

3. Identify what specific activities, functions, or processes are controlled at Northrop. Why does Northrop bother controlling so many activities?

4. Northrop also employs a "direct management control" system. Describe the ways in which it functions. How effective do you think such a system is?

INCIDENT

DEMAND SCHEDULING

The critical link in the control process is the correction of whatever deviations occur between what is planned and what actually occurs. The correction may consist of junking the old plan in favor of a new one. How is the control process illustrated in this incident?

"There — that looks great! Neat, tidy, real efficient. We can really be proud of our departmental course offering, eh, Bill?"

"Sure, Professor Fielder; it *looks* good, what with all courses being offered between 10 A.M. and noon and an equal number of sections for each course. I'm sure the faculty members will love it, but . . . ."

"But what? We've certainly planned our course offering to be as efficient as possible. This way we can have each professor teach two sections of two different courses; since each will only have two different preparations, we can up the number of students per class and keep from hiring new professors. That's just good management!" Professor Fielder, the department chairman, beamed as he contemplated his handiwork.

Bill, the assistant to the chairman, wasn't quite convinced, however, even though he'd drawn up the schedule according to the chairman's instructions. "Don't you remember that we tried the same sort of thing last year? And had to scrap it because our students filled up some courses, stayed away from others, and . . . ."

"Yes, yes, I remember," he said impatiently. "We had to 'kill' some undemanded courses, add new sections of overdemanded courses, add temporary instructors, and all that. But *this* is the best possible class offering."

Bill, knowing he was treading on dangerous ground, softly suggested, "Why don't we take the pattern of courses and times the students wanted last year and base this term's schedule on that? Wouldn't that let us come closer to the schedule students *actually* want, based on past experience?"

Fielder had been turning redder and redder, and by now was an unreal persimmon color. Bill snatched the schedule sheets and almost ran to the door; over his shoulders he said, "I'm on my way! Printing office will have this official course offering out in plenty of time for registration . . . ."

Incident Analysis

1. Describe the control process used in this incident.

2. How does this incident show the relationship between planning and control?

3. What control system would you recommend to Professor Fielder? Why?

CASE
_____

Q & R RAILROAD

The Q & R Railroad Company employs approximately 25,000 people and services approximately eight states. Within the past two years, this company has installed a computer center at its headquarters and is in the process of computerizing all the company's possible production and control functions. This has resulted in the hiring of 300 employees at the center and the abolishment of approximately the same number of employees in various repair facilities throughout the system. Prior to this centralizing effort, there were three regional offices. At the present time all production cost decisions are made at headquarters and disseminated to the various repairing facilities.

Under the regional system, each repair facility had a payroll clerk who kept track of the production workers' time by specific labor function codes. The office workers and foremen were not required to fill out time cards because they were on monthly rated jobs and overtime was rare. At the completion of each two-week period the labor function code hours and the payroll hours were balanced; then the payroll was closed out and sent to the regional office for issuance of paychecks. Each day the payroll clerk would post the appropriate labor hours to the daily program production cost sheets and correlate this with the materials used for that particular freight car repair program.

The computer system initiated a new process. Each repair facility was issued a two-piece time card for each employee, whether production, foreman, or office. The original was sent in daily to the computer center at headquarters after it had been signed by the employee and countersigned by the supervisor or line foreman. A carbon copy was kept on file locally. Time cards from all over the system were gathered at the computer center and keypunched. Computer printouts were sent out every two weeks to each repair facility. The printout consisted of labor function codes for each class of employee (foreman, production, office) on a daily basis. Each printout approached thirty pages in length. Due to the lack of a payroll clerk to summarize this information, the responsibility was given to the foremen and managers to sort through the information and approximate their production-cost positions for each repair program. Numerous attempts were made by various managers to obtain printouts in a form that could be easily understood by the local managers. Each attempt was refused on the basis of the extra cost associated with reprogramming the computer. Consequently, local management was at a loss to pinpoint possible future or present problems. Headquarters sent out numerous letters to each facility showing how far over budget it was running, but little other communication was received.

When production-cost overruns became numerous, headquarters sent out a time study team to determine what the problems were.

Questions for Discussion

1. Is the problem a time-study (efficiency) problem?

2. Evaluate the control process used by the Q & R Railroad Company.

3. What would you recommend be changed in the current procedure? Why?

CASE

COST CONTROL

In 1980 the Baylor Corporation began a cost-reduction incentive program. An annual bonus fund was created, from which awards were made based on each manager's ability to remain within or below budget. The manager with the best budget performance, compared with the other managers' performances, would receive the largest share of the bonus pot.

Each manager was responsible for preparing his or her budget, using guidelines established by a budget committee; this committee consisted of the vice-president of finance, the controller, and the vice-president of analysis and control. Guidelines included such items as the hourly labor rates for each classification of worker, material prices, production schedules, and expected inflation rates.

Upon being completed, each department's budget went through a series of reviews, beginning with the budget committee. After acceptance by the committee, the budgets were reviewed by the company president and finally by the board of directors.

Some costs (such as the hourly labor rates and material rates) were transferred to manufacturing departments at a standard cost rate, because these managers had no control over the prices. However, the department heads were responsible for any labor and material usage variances occurring in their departments. The purchasing department was responsible for any material price variance. Upper management assumed responsibility for labor price variance, because they were responsible for negotiations with the union.

When the program was first established, it was made quite clear by top management that managers able to reduce costs below their budget would not be penalized with lower standards the next year. If a suggestion resulted in a long-term cost savings, the department could be given a three-year grace period during which the cost savings would not lower the budget. Management was concerned that managers would try only to stay within their budget ranges, and not below, for fear of lowering standards for the next year's budget. The encouragement of long-term cost savings was consistent with a Baylor goal of improving long-term operating efficiency. The budget committee was responsible for determining if the grace period was warranted.

Baylor was very pleased with the first year's results. Overall costs were almost 10 per cent under budget; the best results.were in the repair and maintenance department and the purchasing department. Even though

Baylor paid out a record bonus amount, with the largest bonuses going to the managers of the purchasing department and the repairs and maintenance department, the added expense was more than offset by the cost savings from the program. Management was happy with the reduced costs and higher profits. The managers were happy with the largest bonuses ever received.

In the July 1981 semiannual review, the budget committee noticed that the reverse trend of the 1980 results had begun during March. Manufacturing department costs had begun to increase due to increased labor-usage variances. Also the repairs and maintenance department was 20 per cent over its budget.

By the September review meeting, many complaints had been received by the budget committee. The production managers were upset because of increased machine downtime; they complained the downtime was due to factors outside their control. It seemed as if every time a manager called the repair and maintenance department for assistance, the manager would be told to wait for assistance. Often the wait was as long as 12 hours. Within a few weeks after a repair job, the same problem would reoccur, claimed manager after manager. Overtime had increased to allow operating departments to meet production requirements with producing equipment idled for repair. The repairs and maintenance department was 36 per cent over budget, and total labor costs were 62 per cent over budget. The purchasing department was the only department under budget, being 15 per cent under budget from a favorable price variance.

The repairs and maintenance department manager stated that his department was over budget because of an increased workload, caused in turn by inferior repair material. Some replacement parts were often unusable when received, and others lasted only a short time. The committee also discovered that normal maintenance during 1980 had been reduced to a minimum, in some cases below the guidelines established by the equipment manufacturers. The company president had gone on the record as being in favor of discontinuing the cost-reduction incentive program; "The program has been worse than ineffective, it has actually been counterproductive!"

Questions for Discussion

1. A control system should use proper standards to accomplish its goals. Which standards were used in Baylor's control system?

2. Is it legitimate to try to control costs in an organization when those costs represent services supplied to other organizational units? If so, what should be considered when designing the system? If not, does this mean that internal control systems are useless?

3. What would you recommend Baylor do about its cost-control incentive system? What changes would you recommend?

CASE

CONTROL CONTROL

When Joe Casey was hired as production manager, plant manager Carl Hughes pointed out to him the negative spending variances all of the production units were experiencing. Casey agreed that there was a serious problem and that spending had to be brought under control. Hughes stated that he would like Casey to make getting cost under control one of his primary objectives. Casey understood the reasoning for this. The tight money market and high interest rates made acquisition of the unbudgeted money very expensive.

In a short period of time, he was settled into his new position and was ready to begin work on his cost-control objective. Casey had become acquainted with the two area superintendents who reported to him and with the six department supervisors who reported, three each, to each superintendent. They all appeared fully capable, but morale appeared to be a little low. Casey had also become familiar with the production operations, both processes and equipment. Casey did not think that the cost problem was due to obsolete or outmoded processes or equipment or to incompetent supervision. He decided to focus his attention on the control system itself.

The instrument used for reporting and comparing cost was a computerized monthly cost report. The report was very efficient and meaningful. For each production department, the report showed the previous month's spending and year-to-date spending and compared them to the budgeted amounts. The spending in each department was shown by each type of account and by the total. One problem that Casey did see, however, was that he did not receive his spending report until the fifteenth of the month. If the others in production supervision did not receive their reports until the middle of the month, he did not see how timely cost review meetings could be held. When Casey questioned the area superintendents about this, he was startled to find that there were no cost-review meetings. Casey asked the superintendents what they used the cost reports for.

Ray Newman answered, "We usually get the cost reports about the middle of the month. The first thing that I do is to look at the totals for each of my departments and see how far over budget they are. If any of them are over by much more than normal, I'll look to see which account or accounts caused the increase, and I'll ask the supervisor why so much was spent."

Jay Turner, the other area superintendent, agreed that he did pretty much the same thing. He also added, "We're almost always over budget in every department; but if they want the production, they're going to have to pay for it."

Casey thought these to be interesting comments and decided to have a meeting with the department supervisors to find out what they thought about the cost reports. He intentionally did not include the area superintendents in the meeting so that they could not influence or inhibit comments. Because it was nearing time to begin preparing the next year's budget, Casey let it be thought that the meeting was to discuss budget preparations. Before the meeting, Casey talked with Stan Green, the plant's accounting manager, in order to become familiar with the instruments and procedures used in last year's budget preparation.

Joe Casey walked into the meeting with the supervisors and asked lightly, "Well, are you guys about ready to start on next year's budget?" The responses by the supervisors ranged from apathy to complaints. Casey had brought with him the company's standard budget preparation sheets; he passed these out to the supervisors, who would be the ones to complete them. Each supervisor received the set of sheets that listed all of the accounts in which spending was allowed for the department. Spaces were provided to fill in the estimated amount to be spent in each account by month and totals.

Casey asked if everyone was familiar with the forms, and they answered affirmatively. Joe then asked what the supervisors thought about this type of form. One supervisor answered, "They're as good as anything else. The numbers we put down don't mean anything anyway. The budget ends up being what they want it to be."

This comment was met with nods from around the table. This was the second person to blame "they" in regard to cost control, and Casey asked who "they" were. The supervisor paused for a few seconds, then replied, "Hughes and Green, I guess." Casey did not pursue this any further at the time and the meeting continued.

Later, Casey reflected on what he had heard in the meeting with the supervisors and what Newman and Turner had told him. Combining this with his other observations of the cost-control system, he began to formulate what he thought were the problems with cost control.

Casey was sure that monthly cost-review meetings were needed. He could institute these with the superintendents and supervisors with no problem. The way in which the supervisors and superintendents viewed these review meetings would be very important. Joe knew that he would have to be very careful with the impressions that he would be projecting to them. The supervisors would have to feel that the review meetings were beneficial and useful in bringing costs within the budget and not just an opportunity for Casey to criticize them for being over the budget. Joe was also sure that these meetings had to be held by the tenth of each month. This would be impossible if the cost reports were not available until the fifteenth. The supervisors would need to have the reports by the seventh of each month to give them time to prepare for the review meetings.

Casey would have to discuss this problem with Stan Green and see if Green could be of assistance in getting the reports out earlier. Casey also wanted to invite Green to attend the cost-review meetings. Joe felt that accounting department representation at the meetings would convey that accounting was available to assist production in its cost-control efforts. Joe also hoped to use Stan's presence to help familiarize the production people with the plant's accounting procedures.

In addition, Casey thought that there might be a problem with the way in which the budget was set. To confirm this suspicion would require a meeting with Carl Hughes. A meeting was arranged the following week.

Casey began the meeting by telling Hughes that he was instituting the monthly cost-review meeting and explained why he thought that it was necessary. Hughes agreed that the meeting sounded like a good idea. Casey also aked for Hughes' backing in his efforts to receive the monthly cost reports by the seventh. Hughes stated that he did no know if it would be possible to get the cost reports out by the seventh, but that if it were important to get cost down, he would use his influence if Casey ran into a cooperation problem with Stan Green.

Joe Casey then asked some general questions about budget preparation. One of the questions related to how reductions in the amounts that the departments requested were handled.

Carl Hughes' answer was, "After the supervisors have completed their budgets, they are reviewed by the superintendents. If a superintendent notices anything that looks out of line, he or she gets with the supervisor and they discuss it. After the superintendent is satisfied with a department's budget, it is sent up to Stan Green. When Stan has all of the individual budgets, he gets with me and we review them as a whole. Stan will already have the sales and revenue estimates for the next year, and we will know at the gross margins at which we want to operate. I will also have objectives for the plant, such as reducing overtime pay by 10 per cent. Stan works up the numbers and lets me know if we can hit the gross margins and objectives with the budgets that were submitted. If we cannot, he shows me the general areas that need to be reduced, and I look at the present year-to-date spending and budget for each type of account and decide where to make cuts."

This was the answer that Joe had anticipated, and it confirmed his suspicion. Joe thought that more participation by the supervisors and superintendents was needed in the preparation of the final budgets. He thought that it was detrimental to the morale of the supervisors and to the cost-control system to have the numbers that the supervisors submitted act only as a starting point for making cuts without input from the supervisors. The supervisors were closest to the processes and the actual spending of the money, and they should have the best knowledge as to where necessary cuts should and should not be made. Casey explained his ideas and reasoning to Hughes, and told Hughes that he felt that this change in budget preparation would be necessary for him to accomplish his objective of effective cost control.

Questions for Discussion

1. Evaluate the budget system currently used (Hint: Refer to Figure 7.1).

2. Do you agree with Casey's identification of the problems? Why or why not?

3. Are his proposed solutions appropriate? Why or why not?

4. If his proposed solutions are implemented, what effects will there be on the effectiveness of the budget system?

ANSWERS TO SELF-REVIEW QUESTIONS, CHAPTER 7

True–False

1-F, 2-T, 3-F, 4-T, 5-T, 6-F, 7-T, 8-T, 9-F, 10-F, 11- T, 12-F, 13-F, 14-T, 15-T.

Multiple Choice

1-E, 2-C, 3-D, 4-A, 5-C, 6-A, 7-A, 8-A, 9-E, 10-A.

Completion

1. Standards. 2. Correct . . . standards. 3. Exception. 4. Concurrent.
5. Indirect. . . conditioning. 6. Key-area. 7. Direct. . . management.
8. Precontrols. 9. Deviations. 10. Post.

Chapter 8

The People Problem: Personnel and Staffing

CHAPTER OBJECTIVES

1. To show some of the ways for the manager to stay abreast — or ahead of — the changing manpower needs of the company

2. To point out the dangers involved in *not* planning and putting into action an effective system of manpower management

SELF-REVIEW QUESTIONS

True–False

T F 1. Very little attention is given to the staffing function, relative to the manager's other functions.

T F 2. With a little investment of effort, the manager can soon reduce the problem of evaluating people and the job they are capable of doing to a set of simple steps.

T F 3. Most staffing decisions are firmly based on the quantitative results of tests and interviews, which can validly substitute for the manager's judgment.

T F 4. Rensis Likert is most often associated with the computer program he designed to determine when the manager should replace subordinates with machines.

T F 5. Management should always promote from within, unless an outsider of substantially greater qualifications or potential is available.

T F 6. The use of detailed minimum qualifications for a job is beneficial because it allows the manager to evaluate candidates according to specific and observable criteria rather than on some subjective feeling.

T　F　7. Using detailed minimum qualifications may prove costly to the firm if the manager uses the qualifications as rules rather than guidelines and thereby dismisses an applicant who could fill the job well.

T　F　8. An outline of the duties and expectations associated with a particular job should not be provided to the person in the job.

T　F　9. It is wise for a company to set up and stick to a regular recruiting program regardless of economic or political fluctuations.

T　F　10. The résumé should list completely all of the candidate's characteristics and experience so that the interviewer may be impressed by his or her potential.

T　F　11. The performance appraisal is a valuable opportunity to openly discuss work progress and improvement opportunities with the employee.

T　F　12. MBO encourages the manager to appraise performance rather than personality traits.

T　F　13. Our system of private enterprise is based on the idea that pay should be in accord with performance.

T　F　14. The historic role of unions was to balance the economic power of the employer.

T　F　15. The Norris-La Guardia Act of 1932 gave employees the right to organize and bargain collectively.

Multiple Choice

1. The idea that people are more valuable than the company's physical assets and should therefore be carried on the balance sheet is

    (a) nonsense, (b) called human resource accounting, (c) called a social audit, (d) part of the process of setting up a manager inventory chart.

2. Managers are typically very busy people who, when faced with a staffing problem, should

    (a) delegate the task of filling a vacant position to the specialists in the personnel department, (b) conduct all personnel and personnel-related matters themselves, (c) lay down guidelines within which the personnel department can pick the person to fill the vacancy, (d) none of the above.

3. Which of the following is one of the steps or areas to which managers with a staffing opportunity should pay attention?

    (a) termination, (b) recruiting, (c) performance appraisal, (d) promotion, (e) all of the above

4. Each position shown on the organizational chart

    (a) should be undeniably necessary for the organization to reach its goal, (b) should have some overlap with other positions to ensure coordination,

(c) should provide some degree of duplication or reserve should problems arise in another position, (d) must not be so important that the firm is crippled if the position is removed.

5. To simplify the procedure and increase the chances of choosing the right person for the job, managers should first

    (a) establish a minimum and maximum pay scale, (b) list the duties and requirements of the position, (c) select candidates from within the company, (d) contact the personnel department specialists.

6. If managers do not consciously think through the methods of selection to be utilized,

    (a) they might depend only on their feelings or personal judgment of the candidate, (b) they may make no provision at all for selection, ignoring a developing problem until too late, (c) they might feel that they can pick a manager when the need arises, (d) all of the above.

7. To the effective manager, performance appraisal is necessary

    (a) as a basis for proper rewards to employees, (b) to provide feedback to workers on how well they're doing, (c) to establish for employees what is expected of them, (d) to remove the opportunity for subjectivity and personal biases, (e) all of the above.

8. U.S. union membership is currently about

    (a) one quarter of the working force, (b) one tenth of the working force, (c) three fifths of the working force, (d) none of the above.

Completion

1. _____ argued that firms should reduce their inventories and sell their machinery rather than dismiss their people in an economic recession.

2. _____ from _____ is the policy of filling vacancies only from the pool of people already working for the organization who presently fill a position lower than the vacancy.

3. The first step in an orderly approach to staffing consists of determining one's staffing _____ .

4. The skills, training, or characteristics required of the people who will fill a job are called the job _____ .

5. The process of eliminating candidates who do not fulfill the minimum requirements for the company or the job is called _____ .

6. The period of introduction in which the newly hired person is familiarized with the company is called _____ .

7. _____ _____ is the process by which employers and employee representatives try to arrive at agreements governing the conditions under which employees will contribute and be compensated for their services.

8. In the _____ by _____ approach, the manager establishes
   an objective, clearly communicates it to the subordinate, and judges
   performance on the achievement or failure of the objective.

READING

HUMAN RESOURCE DEVELOPMENT

John C. O'Callaghan, Jr.

One way of anticipating future developments in human resources is to measure the strength of present trends and to extrapolate their direction for the
years ahead. But this approach is unlikely to produce accurate forecasts,
for what will happen to benefits, wages, and labor conditions depends on
forces that influence the economic environment in which we will conduct
business in the decade ahead.

Examining the forces themselves and their impact on us may yield more
accurate results. Hence, this review concentrates on the environment in the
1980's and attempts some logical deductions about specific human resource
developments.

In examining the forces or factors likely to influence us, it seems necessary to separate them into two distinct categories. First, the forces that are
already evident and whose future course is relatively clear. Second, those
forces just beginning to emerge which seem to have important potential but
whose impact is less clearly discernible.

THE FACTORS OF THE 1980s
Let's take a look at the discernible factors. The ones that will have a material
impact on us in the 1980s are demographic changes, economic trends, and
government policy.

The Impact of Changing Demographics
Within the demographic area, perhaps the most significant change is the
dramatic shift in the age composition of the population and the work force.

Contrary to popular opinion, the 1980s will not be the era of the gray-
haired revolution. The number of people over age sixty-five will grow only
gradually from slightly under 25 million today to 30 million in 1990. Only
after the year 2010 will the number of over age sixty-five-year-olds begin to
climb — to 45 million in 2020 and 55 million in 2030.

Similarly, those age forty-five to sixty-four will be a static-sized group
in the 1980s. They number 44 million today and will increase in number only
slightly to 46 million in 1990. As a proportion of the population and of the
labor force, this group is shrinking.

The proportion of people under age twenty-five will also remain stable.
This group numbers 91 million today and will decline slightly to 90 million

Reprinted by permission from the July/August, 1981 issue of *Managerial Planning*,
pp. 38–42.

in 1990. By the year 2030, they will represent an even smaller proportion of the population than today.

Where will the burgeoning growth for the 1980's be found? In the group age twenty-five to forty-four. This age group has increased from 48 million in 1970 to 62 million in 1980. By 1990, they will number 78 million or nearly one third of the total population.

But it is as members of the work force that they will have the most impact. In 1970, those age twenty-five to forty-four represented 40% of all workers. Today, they represent about 45%. By 1990, however, they will represent well over half of the total civilian labor force. This is where change is the most dramatic. It is this group in the 1980s that will have more say about the shape of employee benefit programs, compensation forms and personnel policies.

Another factor within the demographic area is labor force participation. Older men are working less. In 1960, 34% of males age sixty to sixty-five held jobs. That proportion has declined to 22% today and is expected to drop to 20% by 1990. Similarly, the proportion of those holding jobs between ages sixty and sixty-four has declined. In 1960, 81% of males in this age bracket held jobs versus 71% today and a projected 70% by 1990. At least for the next several decades, those over age sixty will be a declining group in terms of size and influence within the labor force.

But while fewer older men are working, women of all ages are more likely to work outside the home than ever before. The "traditional" household —with working father, non-working mother and dependent children — today represents only 15% of households. Moreover, only 64% of households even have two adults. And in these, there are more likely to be two workers than one.

A final factor within the demographic area is the shift from unemployment to under-employment. With the "baby boom" of the 1950s already absorbed, growth in the labor force is dropping abruptly — from 2% per year in the 1970s to about 1% in the 1980s. This suggests that unemployment will be a smaller problem in the decade ahead.

But *under*employment will be a bigger problem. Daniel Yankelovich reports a survey showing 24 million people who would work if the right job were available — most often part-time work. Many of those willing to work are women, for whom the symbol of a paid job is increasingly important, or who would like to supplement family income; others willing to work include older persons no longer able to find or hold full time jobs. Thus, the emphasis on job *needs* has shifted.

The Impact on Human Resource Planning

How will demographics affect human resource planning? Here are some guesses:

1. Although the strategy may vary from company to company and from industry to industry, we will have to look to increased automation of routine, repetitive work in order to attract the younger workers who will be in shorter supply. We will have to make our jobs as interesting as possible. We will need to look at restructuring jobs to make them more attractive and more

challenging to older workers; not only those that we are going to the market place to find, but also for those people who are already employed. We will have to offer more opportunities for self-improvement, not only in areas directly tied to the work place and the employee's chosen line of work, but also in those areas that might tend to enrich their lives outside the work place and offer them an opportunity to grow as individuals.

Finally, I see greater flexibility in our benefit and compensation programs. We will need to be able to address the various needs of the rapidly changing work force in the area of benefit and total compensation packages.

2. What *will* be new in the 1980s? Pressure from the baby boom generation. This is the group that will press for more "now" programs versus "later" ones. They will press for capital accumulation devices that can be used during employment for such purposes as educating children and purchasing homes. The baby boom worker will want these benefits and more, but will be unwilling to settle for a trade off that involves lower cash compensation gains because of their need to keep pace with inflation.

Will any group have *no* voice in the 1980s? Yes . . . the "baby bust" bunch. The baby bust generation, those now under age twenty-five, should have relatively little say both because of their small numbers and because this is the group traditionally less interested in benefits, sophisticated compensation programs and so forth.

3. One other result of the demographic changes will be greater flexibility in work arrangements. Because of the increased number of working women and two-paycheck families, part-time work, four-day work weeks, flextime and job sharing, to name a few possibilities, may become more prevalent. This means that the traditional pattern of human resource programs geared to full time employees and not to others will require radical changes. Benefit plans, compensation programs and personnel policies need to be modified to accommodate the variety that will develop in working arrangements.

The Impact of the Economy

The next discernible factor affecting human resources is the economic environment.

The dominant fact of economic life in the United States today is inflation. The consumer price index is now rising at 13% per year. The wholesale index trails only slightly. If prices rise at 12% per year, the value of the dollar is halved in six years. On coming out of each recession since World War II, the core level of inflation has been somewhat higher. An expectation for the 1980s is that inflation will be on the order of 8% to 10% for the first half of the decade and somewhat less later. The implications are clear.

The low rate of productivity growth is another economic fact of life with many causes:

• First, the United States has experienced a decreasing level of investment in plant and equipment. Our rate of financial saving and investment is among the lowest in the industrial world.

- Second, much new investment has been diverted to pollution control. In some industries, compliance has taken up a large share of internally-generated capital without increasing output per person.

- Third, capital resources have been allocated to conserve energy. As oil prices rise, money that could finance plant improvements will be diverted to methods of using less energy and creating alternative energy sources.

- Fourth, and most significant, attitudes among workers have shifted. As will be examined later, workers today are less interested in accepting work as the center of their lives. Disinterest and even disaffection have negative effects on productivity.

The relative weight of these causes of declining productivity will shift in the 1980s. But the same net effect will continue. Former President Carter's *Economic Report* contained the discouraging projection that average productivity growth will be only 1.5% per year through 1983.

Further on in the decade, however, the outlook for productivity growth is better. The "immature" labor force will have more experience which should translate into more output per hour. Environmental protection should take less new investment. Financial savings will likely be spurred by tax incentives. And management will have productivity as a top goal. But for the early 1980s, the outlook for sizable real economic growth is bleak.

What is the impact of high inflation and low productivity growth?

Wage rates will keep rising, perhaps at a rate almost paralleling the inflation rate, but real spending power will be almost static. For many, purchasing power will actually decline. It will be difficult in the 1980s for people to improve standards of living, with the heaviest burden falling on the younger worker who will find it increasingly difficult to buy a home and accumulate physical assets.

The impact on human resources of these economic developments will be great. Some of the major results may be:

1. An increasing percentage of payroll will be needed simply to pay for today's level of benefits. Even without "improvements," the cost of some plans will rise because certain benefits are tied directly to compensation levels. Life insurance and disability insurance benefits, for instance, rise as pay increases, pension costs rise even faster because amounts paid at retirement are related to final pay. Medical plan costs will continue to accelerate because of their direct link to the cost of services. This is a source of frustration for management who find it difficult to accept that costs rise even when plans remain unchanged.

2. There will be heavy pressure on take-home pay; so much so that benefits may grow at a lesser rate than in the past. With pension and medical costs rising faster than direct wages and salaries, room for adding new benefits will be limited.

3. There will be tremendous pressure for cost-of-living clauses attached to pensions. At Samaritan we were already involved in indexing in our alternate plan.

4. There will be a bottoming out of interest in early retirement. Instead, interest should focus on keeping qualified older workers on the job longer.

The Impact of Government Policy

Government influence is the last of the discernible factors that will affect human resources.

What forms will Government influence take during the 1980s? Consider the following: EEO, ADEA, ERISA, OSHA — a veritable alphabet soup of Government intervention in how we deal with our people. The manner in which we deal with all these agencies to bring about positive results is paramount. For instance:

• There will be major changes in the Social Security system in the coming years. Benefit levels, funding mechanisms and levels will be twisted by tremendous economic and political pressures. At Samaritan we took a major step in insulating our employees from these forces by withdrawing from Social Security. We could not deal so effectively with other areas of intervention. In some cases, you simply have to make the best of it.

• The pension legislation passed in 1974 may not be the end of laws regulating private pensions. It is likely that further restrictive legislation for private pensions will be enacted in the form of ERISA II. Possible additional areas of legislative action include faster vesting, mandated vesting in the event of death, and strengthening of plan termination insurance to protect workers covered by plans in trouble, especially multi-employer programs.

Other Influencing Factors

Other factors will influence human resources in the 1980s but their impact is less easily predictable. Two important factors beginning to emerge full force are the drive for equality and the new value system of young workers.

The movement toward greater equality is readily apparent. In the 1970s the equality issue surfaced primarily in hiring and promotion practices, and in securing equal pay for equal work. In the 1980s, the equality issue will have an even larger influence in the fields of compensation and benefits.

The battle for equality in pay practices has just begun. So far, the issue has centered on equal pay for equal work. In the 1980s another principle will be addressed: equal pay for work of comparable worth. This seemingly slight shift in emphasis threatens considerably broader ramifications.

The reasoning underlying the new principle, the Blumrosen theory, is that if pay scales are set by market studies, then discrimination becomes self-perpetuating because each company copies the patterns of others. The market simply reflects *the status quo* — that jobs held primarily by men (i.e., sales, engineering, maintenance) are worth more than jobs held primarily by women (i.e., secretarial, clerical and electronics assembly).

The Blumrosen theory assumes that women or minorities can buttress their comparable worth argument with evidence of discrimination in employment policies and practices that could include:

A. Evidence that the job in question is segregated not only by the defendant employer but also by other employers in the same labor market.

B. Testimony that the jobs in question are viewed as "women's jobs" or "black jobs," or that they were so viewed at some relevant point in history.

C. Evidence of formal segregation of jobs at the time of the establishment of the wage pattern. This would strengthen the inference that the wage structure was itself influenced by segregation.

D. Evidence of past deliberate discrimination.

E. Past overt maintenance of a dual wage structure with lower female or minority rates.

F. Past intentional job segregation on the part of the employer or the relevant employment community may suggest that the overall pattern of discrimination influences the present day setting of wages as well as other aspects of the employment relationship.

G. Paying less to women or minorities than to men or whites for the same job.

H. Application by the employer of one rule, policy or practice to men's jobs and another to women's jobs.

I. That the employer determined women's pay by a woman's standard, and men's pay by a man's standard.

J. That the employer set pay rates for jobs predominantly employing blacks by reference only to other black jobs while white pay rates are similarly keyed to each other.

K. That choice of factors or the operation of an evaluation plan results in an increased evaluation of the worth of jobs held by majority males.

The impact of this new challenge to pay systems is not yet clear. But if "work content" is to be replaced by "worth" as the basis for pay differentials, substantial modification of pay systems will result. Quinn Mills of the Harvard Business School succinctly described the ramifications: "Putting it bluntly, the potential cost to many employers of such a reordering of compensation scales could be so great as to leave virtually no room for the use of compensation as a device to reward or motivate employees in the next decade."

The Drive for Equality in Benefits

The battle for equality in benefits is also just beginning. So far, it has appeared in only a few skirmishes.

The drive for equality can be expected to have increasing impact on us in the 1980s:

1. Perhaps one of the most troubling aspects will be the use of unisex factors. The movement to "equity" creates inequities along the way. Depending on the plan or program, one sex "wins" and the other "loses" in the shift toward uniformity.

2. Women likely will demand equality either in the form of comparable pay or identical benefit value for both single and married individuals. The provision of company-paid medical coverages for dependents, for example, will likely be recognized as a compensation expense primarily favoring male employees. The proportion of males with dependents is usually greater than the proportion of females with family members to support.

3. While less recognizable, spouse's benefits in pension plans primarily favor male employees. There may be demand for equivalent value to be paid in the event of death of any employee.

A decade ago, many in business held their breath in anticipation of the onslaught of the value system of the young people then graduating from school. Senior managers expected from the generation raised in the 60s, strong opposition to authority, demands for more leisure, less loyalty to the employer, less patience to wait for advancement, and a strong preference for "now" compensation rather than "later." The outcome was somewhat different. Why?

First, the runaway inflation of the 1970s (as the new higher levels of price increases were then perceived) rendered irrelevant desires to take more gains in the form of leisure time. Workers needed all the pay increases they could get to protect their living standard. Second, there were not enough young people in most businesses to force their value system on an older employee majority that was much more conservative and traditional. But at the start of the 1980s, there are good reasons to think that the changes in the value system of the younger generation will finally erupt in the work place.

Social critics are seeing more "now" and less "later" in the new value system. Perhaps this has resulted partly from the decline of religious influence in modern society. Jerome Rosow of the Work in America Institute has observed that the work ethic has been associated with penitence and expiation since ancient days. Rosow believes: "Many people today are not as prepared to tolerate adverse conditions, hard-unrewarding work, and self-sacrifice for rewards in an after life. This is not an anti-religious view, but is rather supported by increased knowledge and the growing skepticism about the immortality of man. The deferred gratification of pleasure is less acceptable, less rational. Hedonism and Narcissism are more in vogue. The 'now' generation is a self-explanatory slogan."

This emphasis on "now" is accompanied by a marked decline in the satisfaction received from work. Yankelovich, Skelly and White report a tremendous shift of energy and attention to leisure time activities. When work and leisure are compared as sources of satisfaction, the majority of workers (about 60%) feel that, while they enjoy their work, it is not a major source of satisfaction. Only about 15% say that work means more to them than leisure. The remaining 25% or so find work so dull or exhausting that there is neither satisfaction nor fulfillment in it.

Other clues to worker attitudes can be found in the *Quality of Employment Surveys* conducted by the University of Michigan's Institute for Social Research. The most recent study compares worker attitudes today with those reported in studies conducted in 1973 and 1969. The studies show a significant drop in work satisfaction centering on a variety of issues — work schedules, chances for promotion, pay inequities, and adequacy of fringe benefits.

Comparing only the two most recent studies shows significant declines in the "very true" responses of workers to specific dimensions of their jobs. Those who felt "pay was good" declined 33% between 1973 and 1977; those who believed "fringe benefits were good" declined 26%; and those who thought "promotions were handled fairly" declined 38%.

The new value system is not antiwork. True, its proponents seem less willing to accept authority of any kind, but they are not opposed to the proper exercise of authority. They are willing to work hard, but not at boring jobs. They know there must be work in life, but they want more in life than work. To the large numbers of two-worker families, a balancing of work and leisure is important. Indeed, the relationship between the two will be critical in assessing job satisfaction in the 1980s.

The 1980s likely will see the new value system become influential in the work place. The new values will have widespread impact in such areas as how work is organized, the rights of employees, acceptable supervisory practices, work scheduling, pay systems, and incentives.

Work schedules probably will no longer be measured only by the eight-hour day. More variety of work arrangements will develop, primarily for women who cannot work full time or for those who are too old to work 40 hours a week, but prefer not to go into full retirement.

Experiments have already started in combining jobs for older workers so that beginning at or after age sixty-two, the individual receives a combination of retirement benefits (paid from the private plan and from Social Security), and a paycheck. The result of this combination of work and more leisure can be greater satisfaction to the individual and less cost to the employer.

Pressures for more paid time-off are likely to increase. In older manufacturing industries, this may take the form of year-end shutdowns and more four-day weeks to spread the work. In some industries, where growth in the work force is occurring, pressures for increased time-off are likely to take different forms. Granting a specified number of personal days may help the individual meet special needs and help maximize the pressure on employers for adding all sorts of additional holidays.

In general, however, pressures for increased time-off will take second place to demands for greater cash compensation and security benefits *if* inflation continues at a high rate.

CONCLUSION

We have explored here a wide range of areas. What it all boils down to is a period of great change in human resource management. Change usually does not come easily, for every force for something new, there is another valid, good idea that would be replaced or diminished in importance.

We will witness the meeting of employee desires and demands, if you will, with the pressure management faces to contain costs. It will be a time of confrontation which is not necessarily all bad. On the contrary, handled properly, it can be a positive force moving all of us further along on the cutting edge of innovation in human resource management and planning.

Questions for Discussion

1. The staffing process consists of seven elements: determination of needs, selection and recruiting, orientation and training, performance appraisal, compensation, promotion, and termination. For which of these areas does the article seem to have the most impact or importance? Why?

2. Identify the probable impact of the future developments noted in the article on unions and unionization.

EXERCISE

EVALUATION EVALUATION

In July 1979, a personnel evaluation form became the center of a rather substantial controversy. With the presidential election of 1980 imminent, an evaluation of then-President Carter's executive branch personnel was undertaken.

The evaluation form used appears on page 122. Review the form carefully. How would you evaluate it?

1. What is the purpose of an appraisal system *supposed* to be? What do you think the purpose of *this* system is?

2. Circle the questions (or words in the questions) that you think are ambiguous or of dubious value in appraising job performance.

3. Most of the questions require the evaluator to choose a response (usually by selecting a number that represents the extend to which a person possesses some characteristic). How useful (or valid) are the terms used to "anchor" the response?

4. The broad categories evaluated are work habits, personal characteristics, interpersonal relations, and supervision and direction. Which would you eliminate? Why? Which would you add? Why?

5. How well does this form lend itself to decisions regarding a staff member's compensation, promotion, termination, and performance improvement?

EXERCISE

UNION AND STAFFING

The text identifies seven components of the staffing process: determination of needs, selection and recruiting, orientation and training, performance appraisal, compensation, promotion, and termination.

(A) Identify a unionized company located in your region.

   (1) Telephone the company's personnel department to ask for an interview with the personnel officer.

   (2) Find out what procedures the company follows in performing each of the seven staffing components.

   (3) Identify those areas in which the union contract affects the manner in which the company does its staffing process.

   (4) Find out from the personnel officer if the union contract makes the company's staffing efforts less effective than if the company could go about staffing as it wished.

Presidential Staff Evaluation Form

Office: _____

Name of Rater: _____

STAFF EVALUATION

Please answer each of the following questions about this person.

Name: _____

Salary: _____

Position: _____

Duties: _____

Work Habits

1. On the average when does this person:
   arrive at work _____
   leave work _____

2. Place of Work:

1	2	3	4	5	6
slow					fast

3. Level of Effort:

1	2	3	4	5	6
below capacity					full capacity

4. Quality of Work:

1	2	3	4	5	6
poor					good

5. What is he/she best at? (rank 1-5)
   _____ Conceptualizing
   _____ Planning
   _____ Implementing
   _____ Attending to detail
   _____ Controlling quality

6. Does this person have the skills to do the job he/she was hired to do?
   yes _____
   no _____
   ? _____

7. Would the slot filled by this person be better filled by someone else?
   yes _____
   no _____
   ? _____

Personal Characteristics:

8. How confident is this person? (circle one)

x	x	x	x	x	x
self-doubting		confident			cocky

9. How confident are you of this person judgment:

1	2	3	4	5	6
not confident					very confident

10. How mature is this person?

1	2	3	4	5	6
immature					mature

11. How flexible is this person?

1	2	3	4	5	6
rigid					flexible

12. How stable is this person?

1	2	3	4	5	6
erratic					steady

13. How frequently does this person come up with new ideas?

1	2	3	4	5	6
seldom					often

14. How open is this person to new ideas?

1	2	3	4	5	6
closed					open

15. How bright is this person?

1	2	3	4	5	6
average					very bright

16. What are this person's special talents?
    1 _____
    2 _____
    3 _____

17. What is this person's range of information?

1	2	3	4	5	6
narrow					broad

Interpersonal Relations:

18. How would you characterize this person's impact on other people? (for example, hostile, smooth, aggressive, charming, etc.)
    1 _____
    2 _____
    3 _____

19. How well does this person get along with

	1	2	3	4	5	6
Superiors	1	2	3	4	5	6
Peers	1	2	3	4	5	6
Subordinates	1	2	3	4	5	6
Outsiders	1	2	3	4	5	6
	not well				very well	

20. In a public setting, how comfortable would you be having this person represent:

	1	2	3	4	5	6
you or your office	1	2	3	4	5	6
The President	1	2	3	4	5	6
	uncomfortable		comfortable			

21. Rate this person's political skills.

1	2	3	4	5	6
naive					savvy

Supervision and Direction

22. To what extent is this person focused on accomplishing the:
    Administration's goals _____%
    personal goals _____%
    100%

23. How capable is this person at working toward implementing a decision with which he/she may not agree?

1	2	3	4	5	6
reluctant					eager

24. How well does this person take direction?

1	2	3	4	5	6
resists					readily

25. How much supervision does this person need?

1	2	3	4	5	6
a lot					little

26. How readily does this person offer to help out by doing that which is not a part of his/her "job"?

1	2	3	4	5	6
seldom					often

Summary:

27. Can this person assume more responsibility?
    yes _____
    no _____
    ? _____

28. List this person's 3 major strengths and 3 major weaknesses.
    Strengths: 1 _____
    2 _____
    3 _____
    Weaknesses: 1 _____
    2 _____
    3 _____

29. List this person's 3 major accomplishment.
    1 _____
    2 _____
    3 _____

30. List 3 things about this person that have disappointed you.
    1 _____
    2 _____
    3 _____

(B) At a unionized company, preferably the one in "A" here, telephone a union local's president to ask for an interview.

   (1) Find out in the interview why and how the union is concerned with the manner in which the company goes about the staffing process.
   (2) Identify what staffing-related provisions exist in the union contract.

CASE

BY THE NUMBERS

Southern Electex (SET) is an electronics firm that has grown from its proverbial "garage" and "basement" beginnings to a multiplant corporation employing 10,000 persons. SET's growth pattern parallels the growth of the electronics business since 1930; this includes the various progressions associated with radio, radar, television, transistors, and semiconductors. Until 1970, SET was primarily a supplier of vacuum tubes, diodes, capacitors, resistors, and transistors. Since then SET has expanded its activities to include the manufacture and sale of high-quality electronic equipment such as pH meters, highway radar detection devices, calculators, and microwave ovens. It has been singularly successful.

By 1977, SET operated ten plants at seven locations. Production operations were performing smoothly, but during the last six months of 1976, two production managers left the company. Ted had been asked to resign because of unsatisfactory performance after five years as a manager. The other, John, left to take a more "suitable" position with a competitor at a lower salary. He had been promoted to production manager a year earlier.

Ralph May, the personnel director, was disturbed by these terminations. He believed that Ted and John were competent and that SET had lost two valuable managers because these men were mismatched with their new jobs as managers. In fact, Ted and John's terminations tended to confirm Ralph's conviction that SET needed to revise its management personnel evaluation system.

The present management personnel-evaluation system consisted solely of those records that department heads chose to maintain. Periodic evaluations and interviews with management personnel were not required. Merit increases were granted, as funds permitted, based on a written request from an employee's department head; these requests were usually cursorily prepared.

In the past, when SET was a one- or two-plant operation, the informal management personnel system worked satisfactorily, because there were very few promotions and transfers occurring. As SET began to expand to its present size, Ralph realized that the present system was inadequate because no reliable or consistent pattern of records was available for guiding transfers and promotions.

Ralph had been devising a new management personnel-evaluation system and was about to submit his proposal to the president. He felt that the recent terminations would support his contention that a new system was needed. Ralph's formal system consisted of a prescribed annual interview of each management employee by his department head and immediate supervisor (if applicable). Each interview would be followed by completion of an evaluation form, on which the employee would be rated for specified characteristics. (See Exhibit 1.) The form would also have a space for comments.

Exhibit 1

Management Personnel Evaluation Form

Employee's Name _____

Employee's No. _____

Instruction to Department Head/Supervisor: For the characteristics listed below, rate the employee from "1" (very weak) to "10" (very strong).

1. Leadership _____
2. Motivation _____
3. Judgment _____
4. Communications — speaking _____
5. Communications — writing _____
6. Learning ability _____
7. Self-improvement _____

Questions for Discussion

1. In what ways does a performance-appraisal system affect the overall staffing process?

2. Evaluate Ralph's proposed evaluation system.

3. What recommendations would you make to Ralph regarding a new personnel evaluation system?

CASE

UNDERWRITING DEPARTMENT

The underwriting department in the regional office of the Property and Casualty Insurance Company is presently facing an unfavorable manpower situation. The company has been expanding rapidly and projects that its growth will continue. This growth has stretched the existing management staff of the region and of the underwriting department.

Just recently, two of the five supervisors in underwriting were transferred; two underwriters were promoted to fill these slots. Now there is concern that the department's back-up in potential supervisory personnel is very limited. The personnel department agrees that underwriting must recruit new hires who have a high likelihood of success as supervisors. To accomplish this, the underwriting department intends to use the time-honored approach: hire an underwriter and see if (s)he has supervisory potential.

The professional and management staff of the underwriting department consists of 28 employees: 1 department manager, 2 division managers, 5 supervisors, 12 senior account underwriters (most have more than 15 years with the company), 4 account underwriters (most with at least five years with the company), and 4 underwriters (two to three years). In addition, the department employs 13 examiners and 21 full- and part-time clerks.

The normal career development progression is from the new-hire position as underwriter trainee to underwriter, then to account underwriter and to senior account underwriter. Those underwriters who demonstrate potential and desire for supervision are promoted to supervisory positions rather than to account underwriter positions. Supervisors are rotated among the different units to gain exposure to all aspects of underwriting, in order to prepare them for higher management.

The basic function of an underwriter is to evaluate the risk in different lines of insurance and determine the appropriate rate classification for policies. Volume of work produced (files evaluated) is very important. The work is routine and the daily schedule is fairly rigid. Although the underwriters are seated at desks arranged in units, the work is primarily an individual effort. The underwriters have basically a 9-to-5 job. The procedures and guidelines they follow are well established, and they make decisions on individual cases within those guidelines.

In contrast to the underwriter's job, the supervisors organize and control the operations of their units. Although they are required to know the technical aspects of underwriting, their efforts are mainly concerned with directing, controlling, and motivating others. Their jobs involve coordination with other units and departments and demand flexibility and versatility over a wide range of activities. The supervisors usually come to work early and stay late, as the demands of their job require extra hours.

The traditional underwriting approach to hiring new employees has been to interview prospects fresh out of college or preferably with 1-to-3 years of working experience (not necessarily in insurance) for the position of underwriter trainee. New hires go through a three-day orientation program. They gain underwriting skills on the job. Prospects were always told that their underwriting career had two potential paths; one path leads to senior account underwriter, the other to management. They would start out by learning the underwriting function; the rest would be up to them. Fairly early in their careers, it was felt, the path that they had chosen would be apparent both to them and to the company.

During 1980–81 the underwriting department underwent rapid expansion. Ten new underwriter trainees were hired, using the traditional methods. Three of this group have left the company, being generally dissatisfied with their jobs; two have been promoted to supervision; and the remainder have indicated a preference for careers as underwriters. Of these last five, two are slated for transfer to one of the new offices as part of the expansion program.

At the present time [1982] no mass hiring is anticipated, but the underwriting department is actively looking to hire a "superstar" who demonstrates strong potential to move into supervision. They are using the traditional approach.

Questions for Discussion

1. Evaluate the underwriting department's staffing process.

2. What are the major problems faced by the department?

3. What changes in the staffing process would you recommend to solve the department's problems? Explain your recommendations.

ANSWERS TO SELF-REVIEW QUESTIONS, CHAPTER 8

True–False

1-F, 2-F, 3-F, 4-F, 5-T, 6-T, 7-T, 8-F, 9-T, 10-F, 11-T, 12-T, 13-T, 14-T, 15-F.

Multiple Choice

1-B, 2-D. 3-E, 4-A, 5-B, 6-D, 7-E, 8-A.

Completion

1. Likert. 2. Promotion . . . within. 3. Needs. 4. Specifications. 5. Screening. 6. Orientation. 7. Collective bargaining. 8. Management . . . objectives.

Chapter 9

The Question of Authority

CHAPTER OBJECTIVES

1. To show that authority is the seldom-noticed "cement" of the organization

2. To indicate the nature of organizational conflicts that center on improper use of authority

3. To differentiate between different types of authority that affect a manager's ability to do the job

SELF-REVIEW QUESTIONS

True–False

T F 1. Authority is the key to the manager's job, because authority gives the right to influence the actions of others in pursuit of the manager's goals.

T F 2. When joining an organization, one implicity agrees to accept and obey the authority of the manager.

T F 3. For authority to be fully effective, the manager's subordinates must accept the manager's *right* to influence what they do.

T F 4. The authority-acceptance theory asserts that obedience or compliance in a given situation is a natural consequence of authority arising out of a superior situation that is enjoyed because of a position of ownership.

T F 5. Competence authority is a form of acceptance authority.

T F 6. In line authority relationships, the line manager's task is to assist, advise, and facilitate his or her boss's work in every way but by direct command.

T F 7. Functional relationships between line and staff divisions of an organization exist whenever one position is given authority to cut across normal organizational lines.

T F 8. When functional authority is used, employees in other divisions are required to obey two different bosses, instead of just one boss.

T F 9. One of the major benefits of the line and staff concept is the clear-cut delineation of their different responsibilities; this allows line and staff to work together with little friction or difficulty.

T F 10. An important difference between line and staff is that the staff are not responsible for accomplishing primary objectives.

T F 11. Estimating manpower needs for line activities is much easier than for staff activities.

T F 12. The competence theory of authority states that a person gains authority through expertise.

T F 13. Characterizing "line" jobs as necessities and "staff" jobs as non-essential is an accurate way of describing them.

T F 14. A staff manager may give out many requests but few orders outside his or her own department.

T F 15. Functional authority is unlimited for a limited length of time.

Multiple Choice

1. The immediate source of the manager's authority is the position and responsibility held in the company: This statement would derive from the

   (a) formal authority theory, (b) acceptance theory of authority, (c) competence theory of authority, (d) de facto theory of authority.

2. The willingness of an individual to accept the opinion of an expert in a particular field is an illustration of

   (a) formal authority theory, (b) acceptance theory of authority, (c) competence theory of authority, (d) de facto theory of authority.

3. Which of the following is *not* a type of authority relationship within organizational patterns?

   (a) authoritarian, (b) line, (c) staff, (d) functional

4. Staff managers

   (a) never give orders, (b) have had authority delegated by their boss to give orders affecting the activities involved in their superior's job, (c) deal with the basic processes of the business, (d) are links in the chain of command, (e) none of the above.

5. The development of the _____ approach can probably be traced simply to the use of assistants to handle details of a managerial job.

   (a) line, (b) staff, (c) functional, (d) management

6. "A slice of line authority delimited" is

   (a) functional authority, (b) acceptance authority, (c) competence authority, (d) formal authority, (e) none of the above.

7. The idea of increasing functional complexity in a growing enterprise is

   (a) Parkinson's Law, (b) the law of functional growth, (c) thermodynamically sound, (d) attributed to functional authority.

8. Any interpersonal transaction that has psychological or behavioral effects is

   (a) influence, (b) power, (c) competence, (d) authority.

9. Which does *not* belong as a means for influencing behavior?

   (a) emulation, (b) coercion, (c) activation, (d) suggestion, (e) none of the above

10. Which of the following is a source of line-staff conflict?

    (a) line's rejection of staff advice, (b) staff's undermining line authority, (c) unrealistic staff recommendations, (d) all of the above

READING

A BOSS'S MOST CRUCIAL DECISION OFTEN IS TO LET OTHERS DECIDE

Sanford L. Jacobs

The organization of many small businesses is simple: The owner is the boss and makes all the decisions. But if the company grows, that style of management usually won't work; the owner will have to share authority.

Entrepreneurs seldom do that easily. "Surrendering some control is probably the most difficult step for an owner," says Calvin Kent, director of the Baylor University Center for Private Enterprise.

Paul McClinton resisted delegating authority for years. He had to do it eventually for the sake of his business. "It got to the point where I couldn't do it all," he says. "The business couldn't grow unless I let my managers make decisions on their own."

Mr. McClinton owns two Waco, Texas, firms. Automatic Chef Co. is a vending-machine and mass-feeding company with plants in three Texas towns. Texas Cattle Co. is a barbecued-meat processor that Mr. McClinton believes has unlimited potential. Combined sales of the enterprises exceeded $10 million last year.

Reprinted by permission from the July 27, 1981, issue of *The Wall Street Journal*, p. 19.

The forty-two-year-old entrepreneur had been in business 17 years before he began releasing some of the reins three years ago. Today, managers of the three Automatic Chef plants make most management decisions on their own. "It's worked excellently," Mr. McClinton says. "We get a lot more productivity now."

The person who starts the business may be the worst of managers when it begins to grow. "Sometimes the kind of behavior that enables a person to start a company is the kind of behavior that makes it fail later on," says Dan Ciampa, vice president of Rath & Strong, Lexington, Mass., management consultants. Entrepreneurial personalities, he says, often can't share authority with others.

Wayne Swearingen knows about that. He was a founder eight years ago of Swearingen Co., a Dallas real estate firm that now has 160 employes. Two months ago, he finally relinquished the chief executive's chair. "The thing is, I know the place won't run the way it would if I was in charge," he says.

Success forced the family owners of Dierckx Equipment Co. to bring in professional managers. The 41-year-old Long Island City, N.Y., company had grown beyond the owners' managerial skills. "We had built a strong sales company, but we needed better financial controls," says Stephen Gutman, president and thirty-eight-year-old son of the founder. The company sells and services materials-handling equipment, including forklift trucks and conveyors. Annual sales are about $20 million.

Dierckx hired a certified public accountant from a big accounting firm four years ago and made him financial vice president with a starting salary of $50,000 plus bonuses based on performance. An industrial engineer was lured from Phelps Dodge Corp. to be production vice-president.

These executives, Mr. Gutman says, "brought us professional management. Now we have a complete budgeting process. We are concentrating on areas with the greatest profit potentials. Our return on sales is higher."

Mr. Ciampa, the consultant, had been working with Mr. Gutman to improve the company's management. With the new executives came a change in style. "We have open management," Mr. Gutman says. "We get a lot of input into major decisions."

A reorganization of management at Nimrod Press Inc. gave the Boston printing firm a setup like few other printing concerns. Nimrod Press has 150 employes; sales last year were about $11.5 million. In 1972, when Walter T. Tower Jr. acquired the firm, he was an outstanding printing salesman. With the help of consultants, he has learned to be an executive. "When we were small," he says, "we had a system of communications that was just holler. People just did their jobs."

Now things are much more formal. There are a treasurer and manufacturing, production and marketing vice presidents. Printing jobs are carefully orchestrated among the production people.

The new structure ended the practice in which decisions concerning work in progress would go up to a manager for approval, than back down for further processing then up again for another approval. "Work going through our old organization looked like the teeth of a saw," Mr. Tower says. "Now everything is done where it should be done without going up and down for approvals."

A sign of organizational problems, consultants say, is a pattern in which routine decisions go to the top people. A good executive will let subordinates make day-to-day decisions and will free himself for weightier problems.

Another trouble signal: when volume expands and some part of the operation falters. In manufacturing companies, quality drops and more output ends up in the reject bin. Then schedules aren't met, costs escalate and customers are perturbed because of late deliveries. "That's a sign that there isn't a good control system," says Robert Frick, president of Case & Co., consultants.

Still another indication that managerial assistance is needed can come straight from the mouth of the entrepreneur, says Leon Danco, president of the Center for Family Business.

"When you hear talk about controlled growth, or the need to limit the size of the firm," he says, "you know the guy is in over his head and needs to get good managers."

Questions for Discussion

1. Delegation of authority is necessary when creating new executive positions — but why?

2. From the examples cited in the article, what effects do restructuring and delegating have on formal, acceptance, and competence authority?

INCIDENT

THE NEW FOREMAN

One approach to authority is that "The boss may not always be right, but he is always the boss"; certainly this reflects the fact that managers have been given the formal right to influence the activities of their subordinates. But to what extent? Is authority enough? Or do managers have to combine other elements with their managerial prerogatives to achieve their goals through the activities of their subordinates? The following situation points out some interesting facets of the question of authority and the way in which it is used in accomplishing the managerial job.

Tom Hancock was unhappy. You'd think this strange if you had known him two years ago, though. Then Tom had been a real "mover" (some might have called him a rate-buster, that is, a worker who consistently and deliberately produces more than his work group has determined is "fair" to produce).

Sure, he'd been given a hard time by the rest of the guys in the machine shop; he'd known, though, that his efforts would eventually be recognized and rewarded by the company. And sure enough, just six months ago he'd gotten that long-sought promotion. So why was he unhappy?

Maybe it had something to do with the promotion itself and the circumstances surrounding it. Remember that he had been a rate-buster? You probably know that, to many a worker, the only thing lower than a rate-buster is a snake's stomach; Tom's coworkers were not different in their feelings than most workers. They didn't like him showing them up, making them look bad; more importantly they didn't like what his production record reflected on Swede. They reasoned (pretty shrewdly, too) that Swede, the shop foreman, would have to do some tall explaining to the front office about why one guy day after day produced 40 per cent *more* than quota while everyone else was clipping along between 90 per cent and 97 per cent of quota.

One afternoon Swede came into the shop with a worried frown on his face; he explained to the guys that the production manager had just had him on the carpet because of Tom's production record. "He say why you not get the otters to do same," Swede reported apologetically.

The shop crew, without as much as another word being said, picked up; within a week the production rate average was between 20 per cent and 30 per cent above quota. It was the least they could do for Swede, the shop workers said to each other, 'cause a greater guy there couldn't be found anywhere.

The production manager must not have forgotten the incident, though, for he kept giving Swede a hard time — and about the pickiest things. Like the crew's using the safety rails on the equipment or wearing safety glasses. Something about a government agency called OSHA.

Maybe it was just a coincidence, but Swede's health began to slip about that time, and it wasn't too long before he petitioned for early retirement. He's on pension now.

And that's how Tom came to be promoted. You ask, then why's he unhappy? Because he's now the machine shop foreman, over his former coworkers. The production average is around 85 per cent of quota now, and still dropping. Tom's worried as he can be; he puts on his best air of authority and brusquely informs his people that they *will* shape up.

They just laugh.

Tom is not a happy person.

Questions for Discussion

1. What type of authority did Swede have? Tom?

2. Why is Tom having the kind of trouble he is experiencing with his men?

CASE

HIRT CONSULTING COMPANY

Mr. Derr was puzzled. During his first year as Mr. Derr's assistant, Jim Page had been extremely capable and helpful. During his second year, though, for reasons unknown to Mr. Derr, Jim's work wasn't up to par, and Mr. Derr was now thinking that perhaps he should get a new assistant.

BACKGROUND

Hirt Consulting provides advising services for businesses in a metropolitan area. For a fee, usually dependent on the individual business's sales, Hirt will assign a group of specialists to analyze and help implement solutions to the particular firm's problems.

Heading the company is the president, Mike Hirt. Mr. Hirt is responsible for soliciting businesses that are in need of the company's services. Beneath him is Don Derr, executive vice-president, and Steve Mazalin and Dave Loudy, both vice-presidents. Derr, Mazalin, and Loudy each supervise a group of specialists with expertise in management, finance and accounting, marketing, and production. Once a firm requests the company's services, Mr. Derr then assigns it to Mazalin, Loudy, or himself; each then decides how many specialists to allocate for a job.

Because of the large volume of business the company was receiving, Mr. Derr decided to hire a part-time assistant to help coordinate the work of the specialists and the vice-presidents. The person selected for the position was Jim Page, a graduate student at a local college, who was bright, energetic, and highly achievement motivated. His intial duties were to make sure that the specialists' reports were properly prepared and filed upon completion; provide assistance to the specialists when needed, such as doing research at the college library; and to work closely with Derr, Mazalin, and Loudy, keeping them better informed of each other's activities and problems that occurred.

Jim was given a desk in an office located approximately 75 feet down the hall from Mr. Derr's and the vice-presidents' offices. This allowed Jim to work quietly and alone, without the distractions of people moving in and out of other offices. Also, Jim didn't have to worry about the boss looking over his shoulder, and could read or catch up on his studying if there wasn't any work to be done right away. Because he was paid a modest salary and was only required to put in approximately 20 hours per week, Jim was free to set his office hours around his class schedule.

The first year showed Jim to be a very competent assistant. He quickly learned the company's functions and earned the respect and praise of Mazalin and Loudy. Mr. Derr in particular was quick to commend the way he performed his duties and solved problems for the specialists or the vice-presidents. As a reward for his good work, Mr. Derr gave him more challenging tasks with greater responsibility, such as assigning firms to the vice-presidents, as well as deciding which specialists would be used for the consulting. Jim was happy to accept the extra work because he obtained a great deal of satisfaction for doing more meaningful work, even though he didn't receive any additional pay.

During his second year, though, Jim ran into some difficulties. As the result of a recession in the economy, Mr. Hirt was having a harder time getting new customers, which meant fewer good firms for Jim to distribute. It appeared to Jim that Mazalin and Loudy each had different ideas about to whom the bussinesses should be assigned. Mr. Loudy wanted large businesses that would provide a challenge for his specialists and increase their rate of development, not some "rinky-dink operation." Mr. Mazalin felt the same way and thought that he should be getting more of the large firms.

Because the vice-presidents each had the authority to refuse or accept a business for consulting, Jim was occasionally left with unassigned firms that nobody wanted. Sometimes it would take two or three months, if at all, before he could persuade Mazalin or Loudy to accept them. This was frustrating for Jim because it created a lot of unnecessary work for him. He also felt that it fostered poor relations with the business community, where Mr. Hirt functioned.

Jim didn't complain about this problem, although he did mention the situation to Mr. Derr a couple of times, because he was only a staff person and had no real authority to carry out his additional responsibilities. Mr. Derr assured him the problem would be taken care of, but things remained as usual.

Early in the year Mr. Derr decided that he wanted Jim closer to his office so that he could quickly talk to Jim if he needed something done, because Jim didn't have a telephone at his present location. The spot chosen was a desk in the reception area that served Derr, Mazalin, and Loudy's offices. There were two desks in the area that were presently shared by three part-time secretaries. Jim was to have priority at one of the desks and he told Mr. Derr that he could schedule most of his hours around those of the secretaries, so as to minimize any conflict with them.

Almost immediately things began to go bad. Because of the near-constant traffic going through the area, Jim had trouble concentrating on his work and couldn't talk privately with the specialists when they needed some assistance. He was frequently asked by Mazalin or Loudy to allow a secretary to finish her work. Also, on one occasion when Jim was reading a magazine after he had finished his work, Mr. Mazalin came through the area and told him he wasn't to be reading magazines on company time.

After the change was made, Mr. Derr noticed that Jim's work was becoming a bit shoddy. Reports were being turned in incomplete and filed erroneously. Jim seemed to spend less and less time at work and was harder to get hold of than when his office was down the hall. When he was at his desk, he often spent more time talking with the secretaries than actually working. In addition, Jim was bringing problems and questions to Mr. Derr that he normally took care of himself. Mr. Derr was puzzled. . . .

Questions for Discussion

1. Describe and evaluate Jim's authority. Were the nature and extent of his authority appropriate for the accomplishment of the tasks he had been assigned?

2. Why do you think that his performance has fallen off lately?

3. How would you solve this problem?

CASE

SUPER WHEEL

Super Wheel, Inc., is a large producer of all types of wheel rims, used on vehicles ranging from earthmovers to small trailers. The growth of the firm has been steady even in uncertain economic periods. Such success has been largely due to aggressive marketing, innovative sales techniques, and a quality product. Last March, the sales department finally signed a large order with Standard Motors for original-equipment large-truck rims; Standard is one of the largest and most respected manufacturers of semitruck rigs. Sales had been pursuing an order from Standard for three years and finally succeeded in wrestling it away from Super Wheel's largest competitor.

The contract called for the first rims to be delivered from Super Wheel's Pittsburgh plant to Standard's Philadelphia plant by August. The delivery was established after consulting with John Evans, vice-president of production, responsible for the six plants. Michael Swain, plant manager of the Pittsburgh plant, was not involved in the decision.

For three months after receiving the order, the sales, production, purchasing, accounting, and personnel departments were involved in preparing to fulfill the contract. Production finally started in late June. By mid-July it became apparent that it would be difficult to make the first required installment on time unless everything went smoothly.

Also in mid-July, Jerry Butcher, a quality-control inspector at the final inspection point, noted that the rim holes were drilled 1/16 of an inch smaller than required in the contract specifications. He rejected a half-day's worth of rims and shut down the production line until the machine settings were corrected.

The production supervisor immediately called the plant manager, who sent for Jerry. Mr. Swain said, "Jerry, I see you rejected a whole shipment of rims because of the rim hole size and shut down production. Do you know how much it's going to cost to rework those rims? Do you know how much you've cost us already in downtime and how much overtime will be required to catch up on production because you got carried away? We could end up shipping those rims late to our new customer, and lose money on the order! How do you think that'll make the plant, me, and you look?"

Jerry reminded Mr. Swain that the rim-holes were too small according to the customer's specs; therefore, the rims should be reworked to meet the customer's needs. Swain responded that 1/16 of an inch was close enough, because most specs overengineered on tolerances; the rims most likely would still fit, even if more snugly than requested.

Jerry was ordered to release the rejected rims and restart production immediately. While this bothered Jerry, there was nothing else to do but follow instructions, even though insufficient time had passed to correct the settings.

When the first shipment of rims reached Standard in August, they did not fit the trucks. Fortunately, Standard had a small stock of rims left in inventory that had been supplied by their former vendor, so they did not have to shut down the production line. However, shut-down was imminent unless the rims were corrected in three weeks.

When Standard's plant manager called Swain, his reply was, "You should be able to rework those rims so they can fit at your plant. If you're so picky, put one of your people on it; you accepted the shipment. It's out of our hands now."

Within the hour Standard's director of purchasing was on the phone to Super Wheel's corporate headquarters. By the end of the day the executive staffs of both firms were aware of the problem. Super Wheel was close to losing the contract. At best, Super Wheel would take a large loss on the first year of the contract because of incurring the extra costs of shipping the rims back to Pittsburgh, labor overtime to rework them, and shipping them back within two weeks.

Questions for Discussion

1. Identify how the use of functional authority was illustrated in the case.

2. Identify how the use of line authority was illustrated in the case.

3. Evaluate Jerry's reaction to Swain's directive from the perspective of formal, acceptance, and competence theories of authority.

4. Is Swain's position line or staff? Jerry Butcher's position?

5. What does this case reveal about some sources of line-staff conflict?

6. In what ways is the misuse of authority the central problem in this case?

ANSWERS TO SELF-REVIEW QUESTIONS, CHAPTER 9

True–False

1-T, 2-T, 3-T, 4-F, 5-T, 6-F, 7-T, 8-T, 9-F, 10-T, 11-T, 12-T, 13-F, 14-T, 15-F.

Multiple Choice

1-A, 2-C, 3-A, 4-E, 5-B, 6-A, 7-B, 8-A, 9-C, 10-D.

Chapter 10

Know Thyself-The Most Difficult Lesson

CHAPTER OBJECTIVES

1. To review the major philosophies concerned with divining the nature of human beings

2. To introduce major psychological theories of human motivation, including characteristics of the self-actualizing person

3. To provide students with the basic tools to investigate their self-awareness, motivations, and needs and what makes them who they are (and will be)

4. To show that understanding others by classifying or generalizing about people is an old exercise as well as one that is open to many approaches

SELF-REVIEW QUESTIONS

Matching

A. Added to the humanistic theory by developing nondirective counseling.

_____ 1. William H. Sheldon

B. A way for the counselor to reflect ideas to a patient without handing out answers or oversimplifying.

_____ 2. B. F. Skinner

C. In *Beyond Freedom and Dignity* he presented the behaviorist theory that our entire culture ought to be conditioned to behave in such a manner as to allow us to survive.

_____ 3. Erich Fromm

D. Human motives are basically good and
oriented toward happiness and
accomplishment _____ 4. Nondirective
counseling

E. Physical characteristics and temperament are related. _____ 5. Carl Rogers

F. His theory of productive orientation
stated that most people do not achieve
their true potential, or self-actualization, because they don't make an effort
to cultivate themselves. _____ 6. Abraham Maslow

True–False

T F 1. The most basic need on the stepladder of needs is security.

T F 2. Everyone possesses all six of the needs classified on the stepladder or hierarchy of needs.

T F 3. Erich Fromm developed the nondirective approach to psychological counseling.

T F 4. More people in the world today feel secure from threat or de-
privation than feel that their social needs are satisfied.

T F 5. Most people in our society are motivated by the need to fulfill
their potential.

T F 6. After fulling one's potential, satisfaction of the need for self-
esteem typically is desired.

T F 7. Relatively few people in our society are motivated by self-
actualization needs.

T F 8. Your self-image is important because it can affect your behavior
and motivation.

T F 9. J. B. Watson started the behaviorist school of thought with his
theory that human behavior is essentially the results of input
through the five senses, much like a computer.

T F 10. Because mentally healthy people can accurately judge situations,
they tend to get more done and spend less time spinning their
wheels by relying on inappropriate judgments.

T F 11. People who do not like themselves have more difficulty solving
problems and dealing with ambiguous or complex situations.

T F 13. Physiognomy is based on the belief that personality traits and
physical types are highly interrelated.

T F 14. An ectomorph is a bulky, but beloved, jolly-old-Saint-Nick type.

T F 15. When we stereotype, we jump to the conclusion that a person has a specific *set* of traits because of exhibiting *one* certain trait or characteristic.

Multiple Choice

1. The psychoanalytic view of the motives of human beings is that

   (a) our motives are basically rational, (b) we are goal-oriented, (c) sex drives our decision-making processes, (d) unconscious or hidden motives form the basis for much of our behavior.

2. Which of the following are rungs on the hierarchy of needs stepladder?

   (a) pride and self-confidence, (b) accomplishment and power, (c) security and self-esteem, (d) physiological needs and achievement

3. In our society, how many of the rungs on the needs stepladder are widely satisfied?

   (a) two, (b) three, (c) five, (d) none of the above

4. In his classification scheme, Hippocrates felt that all people were either

   (a) extroverts or introverts, (b) optimistic, sluggish, melancholy, or grouchy, (c) endomorphic, mesomorphic, or ectomorphic, (d) masters or slaves.

5. An extrovert is a person who is

   (a) thoughtful, rigid, self-centered, (b) active, flexible, interested in his or her immediate surroundings, (c) strong, tough, athletic, with a good physique, (d) none of the above.

6. The _____ is said to be intellectual, shy, inhibited, tall, and skinny.

   (a) ectomorph, (b) introvert, (c) phlegmatic, (d) none of the above

7. A test that tries to measure your traits or tendencies relating to physical characteristics, fears, concerns, or attitudes is called

   (a) an opinion poll, (b) a psychoanalytical delineator, (c) a personality questionnaire, (d) a psychosomatic extrapolation.

8. The psychologically healthy individuals that Maslow investigated can be characterized as usually residing on which rung of the needs stepladder?

   (a) love and belonging, (b) self-actualization, (c) security, (d) self-esteem

9. Which of the following do *not* characterize the psychologically healthy persons Maslow investigated?

   (a) They are self-satisfied and content with the way things are around them. (b) They value their privacy and are secure in not exhibiting their deeply personal feelings. (c) They tend to be more generous in their evaluations of others than might be required by the facts. (d) They tend to need more and different kinds of stimulations because their greater mental abilities become bored with the usual. (e) All of the above.

Completion

1. Emphasis on the end result of what one does, rather than the causes of action, is the trademark of the school of thought known as _____ .

2. The person associated with the classification of the needs of human beings on a "stepladder" is _____ .

3. A common emphasis in theories of mental health is the basic need to accept one's _____ .

READING

TAKE-CHARGE GUY

He Likes Setting Goals, and His Next Big Goal is Two Billion Dollars

Harlan S. Byrne

MINNEAPOLIS — Curt Carlson seems obsessed with setting higher goals for himself.

When he started working, more than 40 years ago, he would write his next goal on a piece of paper and put it in his wallet. Once he reached the goal, he would replace the slip of paper with another one.

Well, Mr. Carlson is so rich now that he isn't bothering anymore with the paper-in-the-wallet routine. But he is still lifting the sights up and up for the Carlson Cos., his solely owned enterprise that operates a wide range of businesses. Among them: trading stamps, catalog showrooms, restaurants, hotels, candy and tobacco wholesaling and the importing of optical and tennis equipment.

He created a stir here three years ago by announcing that the company was aiming for $1 billion in annual sales by 1981, more than double the sales figure at the time. As things are turning out, Carlson Cos., skeptics notwithstanding, is well ahead of schedule; it will hit the $1 billion mark this year. Not one to allow his executives to relax, 63-year-old Curtis LeRoy Carlson is dangling a new target to shoot at — $2 billion by 1982.

That may seem heady for a company that had sales of $120 million 10 years ago and for a one-time soap salesman whose first goal was to earn $100 a week, yet Mr. Carlson fully expects to attain the objective. And by then, he will have his eye on a new sales peak.

"I believe that you should never be content with reaching a goal," he says. And to sustain a company's success, he feels, the chief executive has to set higher goals for his subordinates than they set for themselves.

PUSHING FOR MORE

To illustrate the point, he recounts a recent management meeting at which the head of one of the company's two restaurant chains was outlining plans for opening 50 new units this year. Mr. Carlson says, "I kept asking, If the

Reprinted by permission from the May 16, 1978, issue of *The Wall Street Journal*, pp. 1, 18.

chain could open 50 new units, why not 100? And he finally agreed. Now he's more enthusiastic than ever.''

Such prodding has had a lot to do with making Carlson Cos. one of the nation's largest privately owned businesses. Observers figure that it will be in the top 20 or so this year, with at least $1 billion in sales. Last year, Mr. Carlson says, sales totaled $755 million and profits were "the best ever." Today the company has more than 70 subsidiaries and divisions and it employs more than 10,000 people.

Mr. Carlson, who is chairman and president, concedes that much of the company's growth in recent years has come through acquisitions, and he expects acquisitions to be a big part of the drive to $2 billion of sales. But he believes that sustained growth requires keen management, and one of his criteria for acquisitions is that the companies should have capable executives willing to stay at their jobs. "I could never run any of these businesses we acquire," he says.

He prefers to keep his company privately owned for the usual reasons. There are no stockholders to criticize management or clamor for dividends; privileges such as use of the company's plush lodge in northern Wisconsin aren't subject to the scrutiny they might receive if the company were publicly owned; and Mr. Carlson can wheel and deal without worrying about reactions of directors or stockholders.

BUYING BY PHONE

"Several years ago I reached an agreement to acquire a company in a few hours of phone-calling after I learned it was for sale," he recalls. "Usually I can convene a meeting of a few executives here on a moment's notice if I need advice. If we were a public company, it might take weeks to make a deal, or we might lose one by not moving fast enough."

The rapid buildup of his company has enabled Curt Carlson to achieve a net worth that outside sources estimate at well over $100 million. This has brought him a commensurate style of living. He has a family compound of three large homes near Minneapolis, two of which are occupied by the families of his two children, married daughters Marilyn and Barbara. Mr. Carlson and his wife, Arleen, play tennis on their private court and take daily dips in a heated indoor pool at their home. Another luxury is a television set that is recessed in the ceiling above his bed and descends to viewing height with the touch of a button.

Mr. Carlson travels a lot, much of the time in the company's jet plane, and he takes cruises on an 85-foot yacht that he keeps based in Florida. For socializing, his preference seems to be get-togethers with his family, particularly his eight grandchildren. One ritual of recent years has been a Christmas-week gathering of about 50 Carlson clan members at the company lodge, which is called Minnesuing Acres. Minnesuing is an old Indian word that means land surrounded by water.

Getting where he is today didn't come easy for Curt Carlson. After working part of his way through the University of Minnesota, he got a job with Procter & Gamble Co. in 1937 selling soap to stores for $85 a month. While working for P&G, he soon noticed that a Minneapolis department store had considerably increased its sales by offering trading stamps. He also observed that few grocery stores in the area offered such stamps, and he decided there might be room for another trading-stamp company, one that concentrated on lining up grocers.

A trading-stamp company makes its money by selling stamps to merchants, who give them away to customers — so many stamps per so many dollars in purchases. When they have collected a bunch of them, customers turn them in for merchandise at a redemption center run by the stamp company.

With $50 in borrowed capital, Mr. Carlson set up such a company, which he occasionally had to subsidize by persuading his landlord to wait for his rent. On evenings and weekends, he made the rounds, persuading one and then another small grocery store to try trading stamps. It was strictly a small-scale operation.

By 1939, the outlook was promising enough that Mr. Carlson quit P&G and went into business for himself full time. He formed the Gold Bond Stamp Co., which had tough going for more than a decade, including the World War II years when most stores, because of shortages, had little reason to stimulate sales. Gradually the business expanded out of Minneapolis to become a regional operation and then, in the early 1950s, a national company.

A breakthrough came in 1952 when Mr. Carlson signed up his first large grocery chain, Super Valu. Many others followed suit, and Mr. Carlson soon had made his first million.

In the mid-1960s, trading stamps began losing favor among supermarkets, something that generally happens when consumers worry about inflation and think that stores might be able to hold their prices down if they dropped stamps. With the stamp business declining, Mr. Carlson saw need to diversify. He entered the hotel business in 1962 by acquiring the Radisson Hotel here and building it into a 20-unit chain. Then followed other acquisitions.

SOME ACQUIREES

Among his other large units today are Ardan Wholesale Inc., which specializes in jewelry; Premium Corp. (sales incentive programs); Indian Wells Co. (tobacco and candy wholesaling); Jason/Empire Inc. (importer); the two restaurant chains, Country Kitchen International Inc. and TGI Friday's Inc.; and Naum Bros. Inc., a catalog-showroom retailer.

Like most salesmen, Mr. Carlson seems like an affable optimist, a practitioner of positive thinking. But to hear some present and former underlings tell it, he isn't easy to work for.

"I'm not used to being screamed at," says the president of one subsidiary whose company was acquired by Carlson Cos. Mr. Carlson's methods of motivating executives are more than he had bargained for. But this officer figures he can put up with a short-tempered chief executive because selling out to Carlson Cos. has proved profitable for himself.

A former Carlson Cos. executive says, "Curt has a computer mind and is probably the smartest businessman I've known, but I couldn't handle the way he treated some of his people." He recalls how he and other executives were grilled for hours by Mr. Carlson as they made presentations at company conferences. He says that it didn't bother him too much but that some of his colleagues wilted under the constant needling.

Having heard about Mr. Carlson's volatility, an executive recruiter says he offers a piece of advice to Carlson Cos. job candidates: "I tell them to pay attention to what Curt has to say, not the way he says it."

CINNAMON CARS

Mr. Carlson brushes aside talk about his outbursts in meetings with executives. Even if he does find it necessary to push his executives, he says, it is obviously worth it to them. He says that their pay and benefits are competitive with those of most major companies in this area.

Also, he widely dispenses one lavish perquisite: He gives each of his top 20 executives the use of a new luxury car. The cars are all the same model and color, and you can see them lined up in a row outside the company's headquarters. This year Mr. Carlson selected cinnamon-gold Lincoln Continentals for his executives; last year he chose maroon Cadillacs. "If they like those cars as well as they say they do," he says, "you can see I'm not so hard to get along with."

Mr. Carlson invites a reporter to sit in on a company conference to observe his style. He obviously holds back on fireworks, but exhibits a flair for showmanship. Donning a yellow hard hat along with the other executives (at another recent conference, they all wore railway engineers' caps), he mixes in some ribbing of subordinates with announcements of new goals for them. He soaks up applause as he reveals a plan to take his executives on a round-the-world trip to reward them for reaching $1 billion in sales. Then he brings out the stick to go with the carrot:

"Of course, some of you may get left at home if you don't meet your targets."

He saves the big moment for near the end. He points to a giant wall chart that lays out company goals by years, then walks over to the chart and begins chalking up a new set of higher figures. As he comes to 1982, a well-rehearsed aide rushes to the front with a big new sign: "Billions — TWO in '82." More applause and a big smile from Mr. Carlson. Finally, a group picture is taken. Mr. Carlson is still very much in charge, directing this person to move here and that person to squeeze in there.

DELEGATING AUTHORITY

While the company seems like a one-man show, Mr. Carlson says he has turned to professional managers for such specialties as financial planning, acquisition and legal affairs. He also says he has learned to delegate more authority as the company has grown. "But I'll never delegate goal-setting," he says.

Mr. Carlson has a reputation for being a work addict, and can frequently be found at his office on evenings and Saturdays. He doesn't seem to ease up much when he is on vacations, which tend to be brief anyway. "I call in every day when I'm away," he says, "and usually do it early in the morning so I'll feel better about taking the rest of the day off."

Success enables Curt Carlson to cut a wide swath in Minneapolis, but some people say he is looked down upon as nouveau riche by older wealthy families. "Until recently at least, Curt may have been a little too brash and brassy for some rich types," one executive says. This executive tells a story, which may be apocryphal, that a leading businessman said there were at least 50 people in town who would like to see Curt Carlson fall on his face in business.

Raymond O. Mithun, an advertising executive who has known Mr. Carlson for years, tends to dismiss that. "There are always some people jealous of a fast-rising businessman," he says. Mr. Mithun believes that Mr. Carlson has gained wide acceptance in Minneapolis for his work in civic affairs and generous donations to the arts and to charity. He is now heading, along with Irving S. Shapiro, chairman of Du Pont Co., a $20 million drive to finance the Hubert H. Humphrey Institute of Public Affairs at the University of Minnesota. Mr. Carlson has helped the cause with a $1 million donation.

As in any private company, succession weighs heavily in the future of Carlson Cos. Lack of an heir, or lack of interest among heirs, often leads to the sale of family-owned companies. Mr. Carlson says Arleen and his daughters would inherit the business, and if that should happen soon, he has a plan, contained in a sealed envelope, for continuity of management. His wife and daughters would go on the board of directors, and one of his present officers would become chief executive.

In time, he expects thirty-seven-year-old Edwin C. Gage, who is married to his daughter Barbara, to head the company. He thinks his older daughter, Marilyn, who is married to Dr. Glen D. Nelson of Minneapolis, may eventually assume a key role in management. Then, some day, he would like to see one of his four young grandsons take charge, "so he can feel the thrill I've felt as an entrepreneur." Mr. Carlson concedes that that is one goal that can't be reached well ahead of schedule.

Questions for Discussion

1. From the article, what can you conclude about where on Maslow's hierarchy of needs Mr. Carlson is operating? Why?

2. From the article, what can you conclude about Mr. Carlson's possible self-image? Why?

3. How does Mr. Carlson — because of who and what he is and because of how he behaves — affect other people?

EXERCISE

SELF-EVALUATION AND DEVELOPMENT

The following exercises are intended to provide the opportunity for you to "know thyself" more fully. There are, therefore, no "right" or "wrong" answers.

As pointed out in the text, often we blind ourselves to our own natures and goals; other times we don't take the time to examine ourselves.

Take the time *now*. By applying yourself honestly and conscientiously to these exercises, you should have a unique chance to see yourself and your motivations.

After you clearly see and understand yourself and the forces that make you what you are (and will be), you can make more realistic personal and career plans and decisions.

What Do I Need?

List below activities or events in which you are now (or have been recently) voluntarily involved.

1. _____
2. _____
3. _____
4. _____
5. _____
6. _____
7. _____
8. _____
9. _____
10. _____

Activity Classification

Rewrite this list of activities in order of importance to you. Number one is most important. Now write a noun that summarizes what you wish to accomplish *in* or *through* each of these activities (ask yourself, "Why am I involved in each activity? What do I hope to gain?") under "Goal."

Review the textbook section on Maslow's hierarchy of needs (Chapter section entitled, "The Humanistic Approach"). Then, under "Level," write the need you feel best describes each goal and activity.

	Activity or Event:	Goal:	Level:
1.			
2.			
3.			
4.			
5.			
6.			
7.			
8.			
9.			
10.			

Level Identification

Now, because human behavior is usually directed toward fulfilling some need or reaching some goal, we should be able to draw some conclusions about what is motivating *you* — what your needs are, where you probably stand on Maslow's stepladder.

Beside the appropriate need level below, place the number of activities that you classified as belonging to each need.

Self-actualization   _____

Self-esteem   _____

Love and belonging   _____

Safety and security   _____

Stimulation   _____

Physiological   _____

Toward what level of need do you seem to be directing the bulk of your activities?

EXERCISE

PERSONAL DEVELOPMENT PROGRAM

Life Inventory

1. Make a list of times when you really felt good.

   _____

   _____

   _____

   _____

   _____

2. Make a list of the things you do well.

   _____

   _____

   _____

   _____

   _____

3. Make a list of things you would like to stop doing.

   _____

   _____

   _____

   _____

4. Make a list of the experiences you would like to have.

_____

_____

_____

_____

5. Make a list of values that you would like to realize.

_____

_____

_____

_____

6. Make a list of things you'd like to start doing now.

_____

_____

_____

_____

_____

7. In which of your past experiences have you received the greatest sense of accomplishment?

_____

_____

_____

_____

8. In which of your past experiences have you received the least sense of accomplishment?

_____

_____

_____

_____

_____

EXERCISE

WHO'S WHO

You have been advised that you are elegible for listing in _Who's Who_.

Prepare a paragraph that would describe you today.

Prepare the paragraph that you would like to have appear 10 years from today.

Today:

_____

_____

_____

_____

_____

_____

_____

_____

Ten Years from Today:

_____

_____

_____

_____

_____

_____

_____

Review the exercises which you have just completed for Chapter 10.

Based on a thoughtful appraisal of these materials, answer the question below.

Who will I be? and How?

_____

_____

_____

_____

_____

_____

_____

_____

_____

_____

_____

CASE

LANA DOURMAN

"This is the last time," Lana Dourman thought to herself as she left the factory gate. She climbed into her car, and felt as if an oppressive weight had been lifted from her shoulders. For the first time in several years she felt some promise in her future.

Seven years earlier, Lana had been a sophomore at City High School, trying to decide what kind of work she might want to do. She was a pretty good student with a solid "B" average. Her teachers considered her to be conscientious and hardworking. Her guidance counselor and parents had tried to persuade her to enter one of several challenging careers or attend college.

Her best friends, however, were moving in another direction. They were tired of schoolwork and wanted to get out into the world, make some money, and enjoy themselves. Her two closest friends saw secretarial work as a way to make a living without exerting themselves too much and had already decided to pursue this alternative.

Lana had been caught in the middle. Should she stay with her friends and work in a secretarial position or should she pursue the career possibilities that her parents and counselor recommended?

The decision was difficult, but she finally decided to try the world of work as a secretary. After all, she thought, it would be very difficult to leave her friends and make new ones; besides, secretarial work sounded fairly interesting. She'd gotten good marks in typing and bookkeeping.

So Lana took the other secretarial courses offered at City High in order to be ready for that type of work. She found that some of the courses were interesting; she enjoyed the challenge of learning the material and completing the work.

Two years later, Lana graduated from City High in the top 10 per cent of her class. She applied for and got a job at the Downs Manufacturing Company. She and several of her friends started as members of the steno pool. As in her previous school work, she jumped in and worked tirelessly. At the same time, she enjoyed being with her friends at work, having an enjoyable time during coffee breaks and lunch. She also found that she could make friends with many of the other secretaries and company staff quite easily. As these new friendships developed, they became as satisfying as the friendships with her old classmates.

Lana's supervisors noticed her hard work with approval. Soon she was promoted to secretary and was transferred into a section of five salespeople.

At first the new job excited Lana; she had the responsibility of taking care of the secretarial-clerical needs of the five salespeople. There was a lot of work, for each needed three or four letters typed a day, many sales documents catalogued and filed, and numerous forms filled out, among many other activities. Lana was extremely busy most of the time, although she still found time to see her friends during the regular coffee breaks and lunch.

About two years after leaving steno, Lana started having second thoughts about how happy she was. With her daily contact with the five salespeople, she could see how much these college-trained individuals really enjoyed their work. Their jobs were challenging, with something new and different happening every day. She could also see their excitement and satisfaction when one of them made a big sale. Her own job began to seem very narrow and boring. Typing letters became almost automatic, as she didn't even read what was being typed any more; the rest of her clerical duties had become downright monotonous. During the same period, her contact with her old classmates no longer was as much fun as it used to be. They always wanted to talk about the same things they had talked about back at school, whereas she was more interested in talking about the new things that were attracting her interest. They talked about the next high school football game or someone's engagement, but she wanted to talk about some of the things the salespeople were doing or about something she had heard on the news.

One day while shopping, Lana bumped into one of her ex-teachers who asked how she was doing. Upon hearing of Lana's disillusionment, the teacher mentioned the virtues of attending college. This discussion rekindled many of the possibilities her high school counselor and parents had talked about several years earlier. This time the decision was different. The day after she was accepted for admission to the Community College she handed in her resignation.

Questions for Discussion

1. Explain Lana's choice of pursuing a secretarial career according to Maslow's hierarchy of needs.

2. Explain Lana's growing dissatisfaction with her secretarial job and eventual resignation according to Maslow's heirarchy of needs.

CASE

NATIONAL ARTCARD

"Ted, you're too good an artist! You can't quit!" said Dell Arns, creative director of National Artcard Company. "You've been here a good while, your work is good, and you've accumulated fine pension benefits. You just can't chuck all that! What would you do?"

Ted Roberts is an artist for National Artcard. It's the only job he's ever had. Ted graduated from Mid-City Art School as one of their top students. Soon after graduation he married. A three-month job search had resulted in three job opportunities. One was an assistant manager position in an art supply and framing store. The store was part of a growing retail chain. The district manager told Ted that he'd probably have his own store to manage within a year. Ted might possibly become regional manager within four or five years; from there, "the sky is the limit."

Ted had declined the offer even though the job seemed secure enough and chances for promotion seemed good. He felt that the job would not permit him to do what he liked — to be actively involved in art as an artist; he would only be on the fringes of the art world. The job would involve waiting on customers; Ted wanted to be an artist, not be "in sales."

The second job he considered was with a newly formed advertising agency, Ad-World, Inc., which was established by several key executives who had resigned from an established agency. They liked Ted's portfolio and wanted him to join them as staff artist. This would permit him active involvement in art. He would be producing in all art media in a variety of situations. He'd have a fair amount of freedom to design, and his work would be seen by the public.

There was a problem, however. Because the agency was new, Ted's salary would be small. Quarters were cramped, and his office was dingy. The founders told him that this situation wasn't likely to last long. They had good contacts in the city and felt sure they would soon have a stable full of clients. They assured Ted that as their business grew so would his pay and responsibility. Ted was tempted.

His third job choice was National Artcard Company. National was a major producer and marketer of greeting cards of all kinds. It had been in business for 62 years. The company employed 1,200 people, including 67 artists. The creative department was housed in a modern building that included studios, photo labs, and an extensive library. Ted was impressed with his tour of these facilities. He went to work for them.

Ted spent his first few years with National as an artist-detailer. He drew segments of cards such as flowers, angels, or lettering. Ted knew that this was not creative art, at least as he perceived it, but the pay was good, the surroundings and people were pleasant, and the job was steady. Besides, there were now four children to raise and a mortgage to pay on his suburban home.

National sponsored an annual art show for its employees; Ted was a regular entrant and won several awards. Eventually he was promoted to senior staff artist, which meant that he could then draw entire greeting cards. He could not design them, however. National had a large marketing research staff that had sales statistics on every card and design format they had ever made. These statistics, as interpreted by the marketing department, dictated card design; only minor modifications were allowed. Even with his new duties, Ted still considered himself a captive paint-by-number artist.

He built a studio in his home and, in his spare time, painted large, modern pieces with vivid colors and wide brush slashes. A few were sold. Most were given to friends or stored at home. Ted's wife encouraged him to enter his work in the Art Museum's Spring Show. He was delighted when the museum judges accepted his work as part of the show. Ted displayed at the spring show for several years, at which some of his work was sold. Yet some years his work was not accepted. Ted thought it was because his work was getting in the way of his artistic development.

Ted decided to quit his job, pack up his van with art supplies and family, and move to Mexico to paint.

Questions for Discussion

1. Analyze Ted's initial job-selection decision according to Maslow's hierarchy of needs model and the self-concept theory.

2. Trace and explain Ted's increasing dissatisfaction with his job at National Artcard according to Maslow's hierarchy of needs model and the self-concept theory.

ANSWERS TO SELF-REVIEW QUESTIONS, CHAPTER 10

Matching

A-5, B-4, C-2, D-6, E-1, F-3

True–False

1-F, 2-T, 3-F, 4-T, 5-F, 6-F, 7-T, 8-T, 9-T, 10-T, 11-T, 12-T, 13-T, 14-F, 15-T.

Multiple Choice

1-D, 2-C, 3-B, 4-B, 5-B, 6-A, 7-C, 8-B, 9-E.

Completion

1. Behaviorism. 2. Maslow. 3. Self.

Chapter 11

Working with Others

CHAPTER OBJECTIVES

1. To let you see how groups are and will continue to be a common part of your life

2. To demonstrate the natures of groups — how they behave differently from their individual members

SELF-REVIEW QUESTIONS

True–False

T F 1. The "two-heads-are-better-than-one" idea summarizes the meaning of syntality.

T F 2. One's security needs can be satisfied to some degree by belonging to a group.

T F 3. One's self-actualization needs can be satisfied to some degree by belonging to a group.

T F 4. In order for a group to form and develop, the first thing that must happen is for the members to accept and trust each other.

T F 5. As a group becomes more and more mature, the group members more readily give up the formerly held functions of directing, controlling, and motivating to the manager; in this way they can concentrate on satisfying their higher needs.

T F 6. One common characteristic of a "command group" is a policy manual (or manual of rules and regulations).

T F 7. An "interest group" exists so that its members can readily share a common interest.

T F 8. In a "friendship group" one finds members who associate because they work at the same company.

T F 9. In groups, everyone is just as important as anyone else; all are equals in rank.

T F 10. The appointed authority figure in a group is usually group oriented; that is, the welfare of the group is of utmost concern.

T F 11. In a group, the opinion of the majority can strongly influence the opinions held by dissenters.

T F 12. Labor unions are an example of the esteem-of-one's-peers cause of group formation.

T F 13. Rank and division of responsibility are optional in a group; the group can function just as effectively without them as with them.

T F 14. Group pressure is the application of discipline by methods such as public rebuke or ostracism.

T F 15. A sociogram is a diagram that illustrates the interpersonal relationships existing within a group.

Multiple Choice

1. The combined efforts of a group

   (a) are minimal, (b) can be much greater than the sum total of each individual working separately, (c) usually end in a stalemate as a result of individuals' separate efforts canceling out each other's efforts, (d) should be but rarely used.

2. Groups can form because of

   (a) the locations of members, (b) shared interests, (c) tasks that members have in common, (d) the needs on Maslow's needs ladder, (e) all of the above.

3. During the Korean War, American prisoners of war rarely attempted to escape, but collaborated with their captors. The North Koreans achieved this by not allowing their prisoners' _____ needs to be met.

   (a) self-esteem, (b) social, (c) security, (d) none of the above

4. The forming of professional organizations (and other groups that make communication easier between workers in the same job) can be seen as attempts to satisfy

   (a) social needs, (b) security needs, (c) self-actualization needs, (d) none of the above.

5. Which of the following is *not* one of the steps groups go through in their development?

   (a) decision making, (b) motivation, (c) control, (d) planning

6. The natural leader of a group

(a) will occupy its official leadership position, (b) is the manager in charge, (c) should be immediately transferred, (d) none of the above.

7. The informal leader differs from the formal leader in that the informal leader

(a) always stands for those things the group values most, (b) meets some need of the group, (c) must have the support of the group to continue as leader, (d) all of the above.

8. *Synergy* is a popular term for the concept that

(a) committees create more headaches than they solve, (b) two heads are better than one, (c) committees have become the object of a new cult, (d) success is the reward for individuality.

9. Edgar Schein's study of American prisoners of war in North Korea showed that

(a) the inability to develop organization and mutual trust keeps group accomplishment low, (b) the desire to belong to a group is stronger in some societies than others, (c) part of job satisfaction is in being the only person in the wing of the building who is working on a particular project, (d) people in an upper social class view lower classes differently from the way those classes view themselves.

10. As groups mature they

(a) learn to be motivated by desire for the group's advancement rather than individual goals, (b) learn to become self-directing and self-regulating rather than controlled from outside, (c) learn to agree on all subjects, (d) grow from a task group into an interest group, (e) all of the above.

Completion

1. When the creative output of a group exceeds the separate creative outputs of its members, _____ has occurred.

2. _____ needs are most likely to cause a group to form when individuals lack enough power to bring about a change separately.

3. If the manager recognizes that the various jobs of the work group are seen by the workers to vary in prestige, he or she will probably be in a good position to work with the _____ system of the work group.

4. The application of disciplinary measures by the group to a member who is not adhering to group procedures is called group _____ .

5. A diagram that shows how group members feel about each other is a _____ .

6. _____ is the strength of the forces between group members that keep them deeply involved in the group's activity.

READING

GROUP DECISION MAKING:
WHAT STRATEGIES SHOULD YOU USE?

J. Keith Murnighan

Jay Smithson is about to bite his fingernails. He has just finished reading a report concerning his company's latest project, and it is clear that a decision must be made. Should his division go ahead, despite the obvious risks? Or, after an investment of nearly a million dollars, should the project be scrapped? Even when all the facts are laid out, it's not a clearcut yes or no. Instead of making the decision himself, Jay decides to call a meeting of the people who are involved in the project, and the people who will be most affected by its success or failure.

This is a fairly typical scenario. But group decision making requires greater understanding. What are the different strategies that Jay can choose as the group progresses toward a solution? What about preliminary activities, such as constructing an agenda and selecting the group members, as well as the process that develops within the meeting itself?

From Jay's perspective, making decisions in groups can have several advantages over individual decision making. Bringing several people together increases the sum total of knowledge, information, and perspectives that can be brought to bear on the problem. Another advantage is the increased acceptance that should follow a group decision, especially compared to individually made decisions. In addition, there tends to be greater understanding of the final decision when people have seen the reasoning that contributed to it: They realize *why* a particular course of action is better than others.

Now that Jay has decided on group decision making, he must design and prepare for the first meeting. He should consider four distinct steps that can contribute to an effective, efficient decision: (1) he must identify the "type" of problem to be solved; (2) he must carefully select the group members; (3) he must compose and distribute the meeting's agenda to each group member; and (4) he must choose the single most effective decision process to employ.

IDENTIFYING THE PROBLEM

If, as in our example, Jay needs to decide whether to continue a project, the problem is easily identified. Other problems are not always so easy to specify. For instance, one may observe a number of symptoms that are indicative of a problem without actually knowing what is at the root of things. If sales are declining even though the market is improving, if absenteeism is increasing, or if important personnel are leaving for other jobs, a problem exists somewhere in the organization. And there can be a multitude of causes for each of these particular problems. Group decision making can be used to try and identify the underlying causes of a problem — even before it is used again to solve it.

The chairman should, at a minimum, be able to formulate an agenda that identifies the topic for discussion. This should be done in as much detail as possible, without implicitly suggesting a final solution or even what set of alternatives might be considered as solutions. If the meeting is going to draw as much as possible from the individuals assembled, it is critical that the chairman divorce his or her ideas from the statement of the agenda. The issues should stand by themselves, with no evaluative comments of any kind.

In addition to identifying the problem, it is important, especially in trying to get the most out of the decision process, to identify the type of problem. After interviewing 72 managers, Richard Guzzo of New York University identified four fairly distinct problem types. The first, emotive decision problems, are highly value-laden issues (possibly having a win-lose character) that lead to emotional responses by group members. An example is budget allocations when funds are tight. The second and most prevalent type, technical/factual decision problems, are more cut-and-dried and may, for instance, include deciding how to accommodate the federal government's most recent changes in income tax regulations. They often have importance for only part of the organization, and solutions typically are more certain than in other types of problems. Jay Smithson's example of determining whether to continue a project is primarily (but not completely) a technical/factual decision problem.

The third type, policy/planning decision problems, are characterized by a long-term perspective that coincides with little agreement about the goals to be accomplished or even the importance of accomplishing them. Feedback will not be quick, and uncertainty prevails. The often constructed five- or ten-year plans for organizations (or countries) are examples of solutions to policy/planning decision problems. The fourth type, crisis decision problems, are characterized by high importance and critical time constraints. They are the organizational fires that need to be controlled or extinguished immediately. An example is what to do with a perishable commodity when normal storage units are unavailable.

Each of these decision types is distinct; each requires a different kind of group or a different kind of meeting, as we will discuss later.

SELECTING GROUP MEMBERS

Tradition or company policy often dictates, at least to some extent, who will be included. "Any decision that has anything to do with marketing has to include Nancy; any decision involving production must include Joe." But in most cases, an individual has the discretion to invite participants who may not be so obviously necessary.

Years of leadership research have indicated that groups need two kinds of leaders: task-oriented and interpersonally-oriented. Task-oriented leaders tend to be concerned with organizing the work process, and with directing people in their tasks. Interpersonally-oriented leaders tend to be concerned with establishing a warm climate and with promoting trust and respect among fellow workers. Thus, the chairman should include people who can fill both these roles, allowing the group to make a decision without provoking interpersonal conflict.

Of the two types of leaders, the task-oriented individual may not be as necessary as the interpersonally-oriented. This is true only if the decision process structures the situation to such a degree that the group must keep on track; some of the procedures we will discuss almost ensure a fairly strong task orientation.

Internal conflict is more difficult to avoid. Expecially in our competitive society, the announcement of a group decision-making session is often the call to arms for political aggressors. Thus, an interpersonal facilitator can be particularly helpful, especially if he or she recognizes the positive potential that can be harnessed from the presence of conflict over ideas versus the harm that can result from interpersonal conflict.

Another consideration in putting together the members of a group is the right mix to ensure creative discussion. Tapping people who have important information is vital. Experts from outside a department or even the organization can often bring a fresh perspective to the issues at hand and may have less of a personal commitment to a particular course of action. Thus, their biases may be different from those of insiders. They also cause changes in the stable membership structure of the group, which can increase the quality of the decision, particularly for emotive and policy/planning problems. Stable groups can fall into behavior patterns that do not change with the times or the situation. An outsider forces the group to examine and explain why it proceeds as it does. And outsiders may also be able to play the all-important role of devil's advocate — one who questions even the most sensible propositions. The role of devil's advocate, whether held by an insider or an outsider, is particularly important in avoiding "group-think," the problem of too much agreement and solidarity. A questioner or devil's advocate is appropriate for all of the decision problems except crises, where there may be no time for questions.

In selecting the members of the group, one consideration in addition to each of their identities is the size the group should be. Are three people enough? Are ten too many? Groups are frequently overstaffed; people are asked to participate more out of respect than from a concern that they can contribute to the decision. For groups that meet face-to-face, more than seven people can be cumbersome. Groups of fewer than five often sacrifice information and different perspectives. Five to seven members is usually optimal.

THE AGENDA

The third step in preparing for a group decision is the simplest — formulating and distributing an agenda. But even here, there are several factors to keep in mind.

Making sure everyone has a copy of the agenda prior to the meeting merely increases the chances that everyone will be prepared. In the agenda, the chairman should provide both background information concerning the purpose of the meeting and an outline of what stages the meeting will move through and what is to be accomplished. To make the most out of the session, everyone should have an adequate foundation of current information relevant to the problem at hand *without* any hints of possible solutions. Unfortunately, this is an impossible task. Just as biases surface in television news reporting, they are inevitable in constructing an agenda. Blatant slanting of the information can be avoided, however.

Distributing the agenda to all concerned completes this stage of the process. The timing of the distribution is important — for most managers, anything over a week old is ancient history. But the information should probably be on their desk at least a day ahead of the meeting to allow for adequate preparation.

DECISION-MAKING PROCEDURES

There are at least five distinct decision-making procedures: the ordinary group procedure, brainstorming, statistical aggregation, the Delphi technique, and the nominal group technique (NGT). Each is directed toward discovering the best solution for the problem. Each has particular advantages; each also has some disadvantages. Depending on the goals that the decision and the decision procedure are designed to accomplish, one process might be chosen over another, sacrificing some outcomes to obtain others.

The ordinary group procedure entails calling a group together, presenting the problem, and asking for comment and discussion. The meeting is open-ended, and the discussion tends to be free-flowing. The chairman usually controls the speakers so that everyone does not talk at once, and also states the consensus if one is reached. On occasion, Robert's Rules of Order are employed.

The ordinary group procedure is very unstructured. As a result, few alternative solutions are suggested, and groups often choose the first satisfactory solution. Because of a lack of structure, discussions can seem endless. Fatigue sets in; people are anxious to get out of the meeting and move on to other things; the last solution suggested is often seized just so the meeting can be completed. The ordinary group procedure is particularly vulnerable to the problems resulting from social pressure and conflict. It does provide an atmosphere, however, for close interpersonal contact which, if things go well (and occasionally they do), can increase cohesiveness and esprit de corps among group members. If the people involved know and respect each other, and have interacted productively in the past, the ordinary group procedure usually works well. But there are many ways for things to go wrong.

In summarizing the information in the agenda, the chairman may inadvertently communicate personal biases to the group. As the meeting progresses, he is presented with many opportunities to insert personal prejudice; who should get the floor during a heated discussion, when should the discussion be summarized, when is there a consensus, when should the meeting be adjourned so that more outside information can be obtained, and so on. The success of the ordinary group procedure, then, depends to a great extent on the actions of the chairman.

Brainstorming is a well-known technique for generating ideas. It does not deal with the evaluation or selection of one of the ideas; another process is required to complete the decision making. The success of a brainstorming session depends on the group members following a few simple rules. First, people are encouraged to generate as many ideas as possible. Not only are many ideas encouraged, but wild ideas are encouraged. The second, most important rule is: No evaluation of any kind during the brainstorming meeting. The pros and cons of an idea are not allowed — ideas are suggested without additional comment. Finally, people should "piggyback" or build on other people's ideas.

Brainstorming typically results in a very enjoyable meeting: People like to brainstorm. They also leave the meeting with the feeling that they have really accomplished something. Unfortunately, research indicates that brainstorming groups do not generate that many alternatives. Individuals can generate more ideas of higher quality working alone. Thus, from a task accomplishment perspective, brainstorming in groups is not efficient. What is lost with individual brainstorming, however, is the camaraderie that is generated in brainstorming groups.

Statistical aggregation uses the ideas of a group of individuals, but does not ask these people to interact with one another in a group setting. It is limited to quantitative problems. Simply, several people make individual estimates of the best answer to a problem. The estimates are collected, and one of a variety of aggregation procedures is used to determine the final solution.

The mean or average of the responses is one procedure often used. For instance, if Jay Smithson's group decided to continue the project, he might want to project the amount of subsequent expenditures. In problems of this type, the mean estimate is often quite accurate — overestimates and underestimates tend to cancel one another out. But if one of the estimates is extreme, the mean will be swayed in that estimate's direction. The effects of an extreme estimate are even greater with fewer responses. With more estimates, or less extreme estimates, however, the mean is a more reasonable measure of central tendency.

The median can also be used. This is simply the estimate that falls exactly in the middle of a set of estimates that have been rank-ordered from smallest to largest (or vice versa). The median with an even number of estimates typically takes the average of the middle two. Compared to the mean, the median is more reflective of central tendencies when an extreme estimate is present. Very low and/or very high estimates do not affect the median.

If people make quick, thoughtful estimates, statistical aggregation incurs little cost and can be particularly effective. No social pressure can influence the choice; but no group is ever formed, so the social rewards (and potential costs) associated with communal activity are also lost. The major limitation of statistical aggregation procedures is their restriction to quantitative problems. Other types of problems, like which plan to choose, whether an individual deserves promotion, or Jay Smithson's original problem concerning whether to continue the project, cannot be solved using the statistical aggregation technique.

The Delphi technique. Norman Dalkey and his colleagues at the Rand Corporation developed the Delphi procedure, which extends statistical aggregation to include feedback and reestimates. The group does not need to meet face-to-face; indeed, individuals can and have been sampled from almost anywhere in the world. In the Delphi procedure, the chairman acts as the administrator of an estimate-feedback chain. The first of several questionnaires, constructed to state the problem as clearly as possible, is sent to the Delphi panel. Because the group never meets, there is no easy way to clear up any misunderstanding; thus the problem statement must be particularly clear. Potential solutions are returned to the chairman, who summarizes the solutions suggested and feeds them back to the panel in a second questionnaires which also asks for their reactions to this set of suggestions. New solutions can also be suggested. The chairman summarizes the preferences of the panel numbers and feeds back this information. Preferences are again solicited in the third questionnaire/feedback report. Thus, after each questionnaire, the group's responses are fed back to the panel with additional queries. The procedure continues until a clear solution emerges. If the problem is quantitative in nature, aggregation techniques can be used to determine the final solution. If the problems are not quantitative, various voting schemes can be used if a clear consensus does not emerge.

Because both the Delphi technique and statistical aggregation do not require individuals to meet together to make a decision, they avoid the trouble of social pressure but lose the advantages of togetherness. No longer is seven the optimal number of group members; instead, if costs are not a factor, many people can be included. If many interactions are necessary, however, the Delphi technique can be particularly expensive. Thus, the economics of the situation tend to dictate the number of members of a Delphi panel. For most issues, seven seems to be a minimum; only on rare occasions would more than 100 be necessary.

Another problem with the Delphi technique is time. With people responding at different rates, and the necessity of waiting for everyone's response before sending out feedback, the Delphi technique is very slow.

The Delphi and statistical aggregation techniques work particularly well when desired group members are people who hate committees, who work well alone, who are independent. People who feel strongly that group meetings are a waste of time can still contribute their skills to group problem solving. Also, when it is impossible to convene a particular set of individuals, the Delphi technique works very well.

The nominal group technique (NGT), the most recent procedure, was developed by Andre Delbecq and Andrew Van de Ven at the University of Wisconsin. By combining some of the characteristics of the other techniques, it takes advantage of each of their good points. It draws from brainstorming by having people generate potential solutions individually; it draws from the ordinary group procedure by allowing for some group discussion; it draws from statistical aggregation by using a formal, restrictive process for arriving at a solution; and it provides feedback concerning others' suggestions, like the Delphi technique. NGT mixes a fairly structured decision process with the interpersonal characteristics of face-to-face groups.

NGT passes through several stages. After the problem is clearly stated, group members sit together quietly and individually generate as many alternatives as they can. After about 15 minutes, ideas are presented in round-robin fashion. Each individual presents a single idea, taking turns, until all of the group's ideas have been presented. The chairman records them in full view at the front of the room. As in group brainstorming, individuals are encouraged to piggyback on others' ideas. This process psychologically separates the ideas from the individual who has suggested them. Although each of the ideas is not strictly anonymous, as in the Delphi technique, the round-robin recording process may reduce some social pressure.

A brief discussion focusing primarily on the clarification of each idea is next. This discussion may generate additional ideas, which are also recorded. After everyone is clear about the entire set of suggestions, a voting or rating process is used to reach the group decision. Each group member might vote for the five alternatives that he or she feels are best, rank-ordering them from one to five. Alternatively, each of the ideas can be rated on a 10-point scale, from good (1) to bad (10). Votes or ratings are done on private ballots. The chairman tabulates the votes and announces them to the group. In most cases, this first ballot identifies a small set of possible solutions. If the vote should reveal a clear-cut winner, the group is finished. If there is the usual difference of opinion concerning some of the ideas, a discussion of the vote can follow. Voting or rating is repeated, with intermittent discussion, until a solution can be identified. This procedure (like some of the others) provides back-up alternatives should the initially chosen solution fail to produce desired outcomes.

To assess NGT's effectiveness, it can be compared with the closely related Delphi technique. Like the Delphi technique, a large number of specific ideas is typically generated. The major advantages of NGT over Delphi are its reduced costs (in money and especially in time) and an increase in cohesiveness and commitment of group members due to their face-to-face interaction. As always, however, this interpersonal contact leaves a group open for conflict and social pressure. The relatively restricted discussion, however, reduces these effects. Also, NGT often generates a strong feeling of accomplishment in reaching a solution. In two hours, or sometimes less, sticky problems can often be resolved. This can be a really uplifting experience, especially for people who are accustomed to laborious, ineffectual committees.

The role of chairman is always particularly important. Even when no group is meeting, for the Delphi and statistical aggregation groups, the leader must pay strict attention to the procedures to maximize their advantages. Changes can be made in any of the procedures. But it is critical, expecially when groups are going to continue to interact, and the reputation and credibility of the leader hangs in the balance, that certain guidelines be followed. The leader must be particularly concerned about his own behavior. To blatantly advocate a particular position while espousing the participative aspects of group decision making can quickly sabotage any potential an individual has for obtaining the respect of his colleagues. Instead, a style that keeps the group on track, moving toward a solution, without personally interfering, is particularly effective. And requiring a true consensus results in higher-quality decisions.

RESEARCH FINDINGS

Empirical research has attempted to determine which of the techniques yield more accurate solutions (when accuracy of a solution can be determined) and which lead to a greater number of specific ideas being suggested. The findings on accuracy are mixed: With some problems (for example, how many telephones were there in Africa in 1967?) the Delphi technique appears to be more accurate than the ordinary group procedure. With probability estimate problems (for example, what is the probability that an adult 68 inches tall is male?), NGT has done better. In a recent study David Boje and I found that for problems like these two, statistical aggregation was most accurate. At the same time, group members were most confident of their answers in the NGT groups. Aspects of the problem itself seem to affect accuracy while aspects of the decision process seem to influence satisfaction. Consistent findings show that both NGT and the Delphi technique lead to more, and more specific, ideas than the ordinary group procedure. In addition, NGT is enjoyed more than the Delphi or statistical aggregation techniques.

Recent research suggests that, for technical/factual, policy/planning, and crisis decision problems, structured decision procedures resulted in high-quality decisions. For emotive decisions, structured decisions were of poor quality. This suggests that the ordinary group procedure would be best used for emotive decision problems and that the other procedures should be used for all other problems.

Finally, the procedure used to actually select one of the ideas as the group decision also can have an impact. Carl Castore and I recently found that structured majority rule (asking people to vote between pairs of alternatives) led to a higher overall commitment to the group decision, even when the individual group members' own preferences were not similar to that decision. Thus, if an individual participates equally in the decision, and if the decision is reached using a "fair" procedure like majority rule, then he tends to support the decision when implementation becomes necessary. Stressing the participative aspects of a decision process, then, can bear long-run benefits.

MAKING YOUR SELECTION

In deciding which of the decision procedures to use, an individual might consider some of the criteria we have used in discussing each of the processes. Figure 1 lists these criteria, along with each of the decision procedures and what might be expected of each. These expected outcomes are not absolute — it may be that, for a variety of reasons, an NGT or Delphi group will not yield a large number of high-quality ideas.

The ordinary group procedure does not appear to yield particularly positive outcomes. For feelings of accomplishment, its outcome is up in the air — if something *is* accomplished smoothly, feelings of accomplishment will be high. Unfortunately, it's more likely that this will not be the case, thus leading to relatively low feelings of accomplishment. If a solution is reached, commitment to that solution can be very high, as can the cohesiveness within the group. Thus when things get personal, cohesiveness may be all important and the ordinary group procedure is best (if its many problems can be avoided through the efforts of a skillful chairperson).

Figure 1
Evaluating the Decision Processes

Criteria	Ordinary	Brain-storming	Aggre-gation	NGT	Delphi
Number of ideas	Low	Moderate	NA*	High	High
Quality of ideas	Low	Moderate	NA*	High	High
Social pressure	High	Low	None	Moderate	Low
Time/money costs	Moderate	Low	Low	Low	High
Task orientation	Low	High	High	High	High
Potential for inter-personal conflict	High	Low	Low	Moderate	Low
Feelings of accomplishment	High to low	High	Low	High	Moderate
Commitment to solution	High	NA*	Low	Moderate	Low
Builds group cohesiveness	High	High	Low	Moderate	Low

*NA = Not applicable

Brainstorming scores well on several counts — given its popularity, this is not too surprising. If the number and quality of the ideas are not that important, and if no solution is required, it is excellent.

Statistical aggregation is particularly useful for quick, low-cost solutions to quantitative problems. If other criteria become important, or if the problem is not quantitative, this procedure is clearly not the best.

NGT has no severe weaknesses. If one were to assign pluses and minuses to each of the procedures for each of the criteria (and thus ignore the relative importance of one criterion over another), NGT would easily win over the other procedures. In general, it appears to be the most effective group decision making procedure. In specific situations, however, other procedures may be more appropriate.

The results for the Delphi technique are almost as positive. Little potential for conflict and a lack of social pressure are its advantages. It is also useful when group members cannot be present in one place at one time. If the composition of the group is more important than other factors, the Delphi technique might be the best way to accommodate irreconcilable schedules.

Figure 1 can be easily used to select a group decision procedure. To return to Jay Smithson again: First he must list all of the goals that he would like this particular decision to satisfy. This list might include all of Figure 1's criteria. Second, he must determine his priorities. To maximize the possibility of group cohesiveness, for instance, potential interpersonal conflict must be risked. And Jay must determine whether this feeling of cohesiveness is more or less important than generating many alternatives.

After ranking his priorities, Jay can turn to Figure 1 and go through the process of eliminating some procedures in favor of others. If Jay is faced with a sticky problem that has previously resisted solutions, he may set many alternatives of high quality as his top priorities. These may be followed by the need for a quick decision, with all other criteria secondary. In this case, Figure 1 indicates that NGT and the Delphi technique will yield the most high-quality alternatives and that of these two, NGT is much quicker.

A similar, straightforward example is one where Jay has almost no time or money, wants to avoid interpersonal conflict at all costs, and is faced with a quantitative decision. The choices eliminate the ordinary and Delphi techniques due to costs, NGT because of potential conflict, and brainstorming because it doesn't yield a decision. Thus, statistical aggregation is chosen. In some situations, however, the choice is considerably more difficult. If Jay sets commitment to the solution as his top priority, followed by little social pressure, no interpersonal conflict, and high-quality alternatives, his choices are difficult. High commitment to the solution suggests that he should choose the ordinary group procedure; all of the other criteria suggest using the Delphi technique. Where can he turn?

All of the decision processes can be changed and, depending on the situation, simple alterations may have strong effects. For instance, individual plus group brainstorming can be used to generate a large number of individual suggestions and to establish a feeling of togetherness. To combine the two, Jay would merely recommend that individuals brainstorm by themselves, before coming to the group meeting. Ideas could be shared with the group, especially if they were submitted to a coordinator who summarizes them for everyone prior to the meeting. Then group brainstorming, focusing primarily on piggybacking, could add to the list that was generated individually.

Other combinations are also possible. In Jay's last problem, a Delphi group would anonymously generate a large number of ideas. A group discussion with all members present could take advantage of the positive aspects of the ordinary group procedure, such as high commitment to the solution. Thus, the positive aspects of the ordinary group procedure and the Delphi technique could be combined to fulfill all of Jay's important priorities.

So there are a variety of strategies that an individual can select when a group decision is indicated. Portions of different techniques can be combined and/or modified to fine tune the problem-solving procedure. There are hazards along the way; but by identifying the problem (and the type of problem) one is facing, by carefully composing the group, by designing an agenda that comes close to being free of bias, by selecting the best procedure for the situation, and by carefully moderating the process, group decision making can generate fruitful returns.

Question for Discussion

The article identifies a number of group-process factors that affect in important ways how effective the various decision formats are. These factors include need for synergy, potential for intermember conflict, role and influence of the leader, cohesiveness, satisfaction, social pressure, group enforcement, personal values, and communication network. Discuss how — and why — each of the preceding group-process factors affects the quality of group decisions.

INCIDENT

THE SPORTS IN SPORTING GOODS

Groups are a normal part of our lives, both on and off the job; through groups we satisfy our personal needs. By happy coincidence we can sometimes satisfy personal needs at the same time the organization's demands are fulfilled. The wise manager must be aware of the extent that social groups *can* help fulfill the manager's needs by allowing subordinates the opportunity to fulfill theirs. The following incident illustrates such a situation in which group and organizational needs affected each other.

The sporting goods department was one of the real joys of the Realway Department Store. All six of the department's salesmen were consistently way over quota in their sales figures. And it was widely known that salesmen more knowledgeable about their wares — or more willing to help their customers — were not to be found in the greater metropolitan area, if in the entire state.

A more unlikely set of salesmen you'd be hard pressed to find anywhere, however. They ranged from a 6'6" ex-college basketball star to a 5'4" chronic overeater, from twenty-six to thirty-five years old, from bachelor to married with five kids. Only two things could you find in common among them: They loved sports and genuinely liked each other.

These six had comprised the department's sales staff from the beginning. On any given day off, one might easily find most of the salesmen bowling or hunting together or doing whatever the season called for. And when one was a little late getting to the store, the others would cover for him. Why, they even arranged every week for a different salesman to make sure the displays were just so and that the stock on the shelves wasn't getting low.

If, say, Rod waited on you and you wanted a rifle but were anything but an expert, Henry would help Rod out; Henry was sponsor of a boy's club rifle team and was pretty sharp on firearms. Henry would help you decide, but Rod got the commission. Naturally, Rod would return the favor when Henry was confronted with a customer interested in a motor for his fishing boat. This was a typical arrangement among all the salesmen.

As a result, each took pride in his work; customers went away satisfied, told their friends about the service and kept coming back to Realway. Each salesman, consequently, made an extremely good living on a job he really liked.

Just last week the store's sales manager decided to expand the sales force and number of hours of the sporting goods department. Two new salesmen were to report to each of the experienced salesmen. To facilitate the training and to cover the new 10 A.M. to 10 P.M. hours seven days a week, the hours of each of the experienced salesmen were split up. Now, at any given time, usually just one of the "old gang" is on duty in the department.

The sales manager, in looking over the individual commission sheets for the week, is surprised that all six of the original salesmen's commissions are down substantially; he's also noticed that they don't seem as happy on the job as they used to be.

Questions for Discussion

1. Why was this group so successful despite the vast differences among its members?

2. Why was the group's former total commission more than the sum of the individuals' commissions after the change?

3. What satisfactions were the salesmen deriving from their work situation before the change? After it?

EXERCISE

GROUPS AND YOU

Each of us belong to groups of different types; each group returns something to us for our involvement. This return might range from a weekly paycheck to fulfilled social needs.

The text points out that groups may be classified as being a command, task, interest, or friendship group. Each exists for different reasons, and we belong to each for our *own* different reasons.

FOR THE STUDENT

1. Think of two of *each* of the four types of groups (command, task, interest, and friendship) to which you belong or have belonged. Briefly describe each.

2. Give a short description of what each *group's* primary goal is.

3. Which of your sociopsychological needs are you attempting to satisfy by belonging to each group? (Your needs might be physiological, stimulation, safety and security, love and belonging, self-esteem, or self-actualization.) Write the need each group helps you satisfy.

CASE

CHANGING TIMES

The Smalltown Jaycees is a relatively young organization, only four years old. Their predecessors, the Lake Local Jaycees, had disbanded about five years earlier. Lake Local had consisted of men from two communities, Small-town and Uniontown. As a result, when projects had been proposed, great conflict had arisen in the Lake Local organization as to where they should be conducted. Unrest, dissention, and eventually a formal division of the two groups led to the disbanding of the organization.

Gene Frazier, a former member of the Lake Local group, had a strong desire to reorganize a Jaycee chapter, for Smalltown. Gene was quite a dynamic young man who felt that a Smalltown Jaycee chapter would greatly benefit the community. He contacted and worked through state officers and other local chapters to meet the requirements for a new chapter. Then, along with the help of other Jaycee chapter members, Gene set out on a door-to-door membership drive. In order to charter, 25 members were required by the state constitution.

Gene and his friends accomplished their 25 member goal in only four evenings. It seemed that there were many more than just two or three people who were interested in an organization that could benefit the community. No one organization had established itself as the community leader. In fact, most groups were oriented toward the social fulfillment of their individual members. Gene saw the Smalltown Jaycees as a broader-based organization than this.

As with many new organizations, the first year was expected to be the most critical for the new Jaycee chapter. The most difficult aspect would be the community's accepting the new group. Gene had anticipated this, and as a result, already had a detailed program laid out for the first year's activities and for the initial organizational meetings.

Because of his efforts, Gene was elected first president of the organization. The new members were eager to get started when Gene proposed his program. All were impressed with it and overwhelmingly approved it without change. For the most part, the new members were dedicated to bettering the community.

As with young organizations, novelty tends to wear off fairly rapidly. When enthusiasm appeared to drop in the Smalltown Jaycees, Gene was there. Gene's basic (and most successful) tactic was to put pressure on those who appeared to be tapering off. He never took "no" for an answer and would never give up on a slacking member. Furthermore, Gene executed his programs to a "tee." He strongly felt that what he had proposed was best for the community and was only interested in suggestions that would support his program.

The efforts of Gene and the group during the first year of the chapter resulted in achievement of all the major goals established. The Smalltown Jaycees had been overwhelmingly accepted by the community. Membership rose from an initial 25 members to 36. By-laws had been established, as well as an effective administrative structure for carrying out chapter functions and individual development. In fact, the next two years the Smalltown Jaycees were recognized by the state as the number one chapter in its size division. It seemed that the "foundation" year had been extremely effective in laying the ground work and developing leaders to further promote the goal of the chapter.

In the third year, the chapter began to take on a new face. Many of the original members who had put tireless effort into the group the first two years were now relatively content to sit back and watch how things went. This was not uncommon among Jaycee chapters. And although membership recruitment remained high, the attitude of the newer members was different. Many of the newer members who were the most outspoken joined the organization to make friends and acquaintances. Their ideas ran more toward chapter parties than community betterment and individual development. Although existing community programs did not suffer, no significant strides were made in upgrading existing programs or introducing new ideas. Older members began to shy further and further away from the mainstream of the organization. Prior to this time, personal differences and conflicts had been left out of the business aspect of the group; now they began to emerge more and more often. Some members took, personally, criticism (constructive or otherwise) of their ideas and suggestions.

By the fourth year, the "social" clique had gained administrative control of the organization. The older members participated less and less. Prospective members for the organization seemed to better reflect those views of the organization, even though they still lived in the area.

Participation, or lack thereof, on the part of the older members created great concern in the existing board of directors. They could simply not understand why, all of a sudden, motivated individuals were content to sit back and watch the chapter from afar.

Questions for Discussion

1. How does the Smalltown Jaycees currently meet the definition of a group? How does this differ from how well the Jaycees met the definition of a group in its first two years?

2. Discuss the reasons behind the formation of the Jaycees.

3. Groups pass through recognizable stages as they grow. Identify the stages through which the Smalltown Jaycees have passed.

4. How was group control brought about in gaining the compliance of members?

5. How successful is the group in its fourth year? Why are there differences between its initial and current states?

CASE

CRAIG JOHNSON'S FIRST JOB

Craig Johnson was just eighteen years old and fresh out of high school. He had been a rather average student, although he had maintained an overall B average while participating in basketball and track, receiving varsity letters in both sports his senior year. Craig had decided on going to a local university to study mechanical engineering. He was not able to pick up a scholarship of any kind (scholastic or athletic); consequently, the matter of financing his education became a problem. He didn't want to go to his parents for the money, reasoning that they had financial obligations of their own; apparently the only realistic way to finance his education would be to work at night and go to school during the day.

The job market at that time was fairly tight, but Craig heard that his town's only manufacturing plant was taking applications; this would be a good place to work because most of the jobs were based on piecework — the more you produced, the more you were paid! He applied, took the dexterity and math tests administered by the personnel department and was hired four days later. The man in personnel told Craig that his dexterity was excellent and that he had scored a perfect mark on the math test. Because of this, the personnel man was placing him in a department that was based on piecework — washing machine assembly. Johnson was to start on the third shift (11 P.M. to 7 A.M.) for two reasons: (1) he didn't have seniority (experienced men usually chose the first and second shifts), and (2) if he were going to school, this shift would work out just right.

Craig approached his first night of work with apprehension. He had never worked before at a job that paid as much as this one did. The nature of the job also concerned him — he was to be an automatic spot welder. On the way to work that night, he laughed nervously to himself that he didn't know the first thing about welding.

Craig approached the plant guard, as he had been instructed to do by the personnel man, and received directions to the washing machine assembly department. He had arrived a little bit early, but approached the office and introduced himself. His supervisor, John Craddle, was there. Craddle explained what was done in washing machine assembly (WMA). WMA spot-welded all the individual parts of a washing machine and then, in one final operation, combined all the parts together with more spot-welding. Upon questioning Craig and discovering his college desires, Craddle went into a little more detail on how the welding machines operated. Craddle then explained the rules and procedures in the department, such as reporting to work on time, taking breaks, and how to report sick.

As Craddle wrapped up his discussion with Craig, another man entered the office and was introduced as the foreman, Al Piscitelli. Piscitelli then took Craig around the department, showing him all the automatic welding machines, how they worked, and what part they welded. He met all of the men, twelve in total, and noticed that about half looked as if they were in their early twenties. After the tour Piscitelli explained how to fill in his time card and how to call for more materials when he needed them. He also explained how to tell what the piece rates meant. Piscitelli went on to explain that he should not worry about the rate for the first couple of weeks; if a new worker didn't produce at least the standard rate, he would still be paid a day rate. After all the preliminaries had been taken care of, Craig was given his first assignment. He was to weld the base for the washing machine. Piscitelli demonstrated how to take the four separate pieces and spot-weld them together, as well as how to clean the copper tips — this would improve the quality of the weld. In the course of the next four nights of work, Craig also assembled belt guards, various caster assemblies, spin drums, and other parts.

At dinner time, Craig noticed that a group of seven ate together with the foreman, while the other five workers went somewhere else. On his fifth night of work he was approached by one of the seven, Tom Chester. Chester asked if he would like to eat with the other workers, to which Craig replied in the affirmative, and went with Chester. Through discussions with the others during dinner, Craig learned that no one else was going to college; a couple of fellows had tried it, but sooner or later dropped out. Chester asked Craig how he liked his job, and he replied that it was interesting. Chester then casually remarked that it was best if a person stuck right around the day rates instead of busting himself to break the rate. The others in the group nodded in agreement.

Craig's skill increased as time progressed. Within three weeks he could make day rate on all the assemblies to which he had been exposed. He felt this was great because now he could attempt to work harder and faster, making more money to finance his education. Craddle would come by every so often and remark what a good job he was doing, and to keep it up. It wasn't long before he was making one and half times the day rate on all the assemblies, and in some cases, twice the day rate. Some of the workers in the department would come by and jokingly tell Craig he was going to drop over dead from exhaustion if he continued to work at that pace. When paychecks were passed out, the same workers would ask if it were worth it to work real hard and then have the government take away all his earnings. But all of this good-natured ribbing failed to deter him from working his hardest.

One day a time study team came in to watch Craig work on his favorite assembly — caster mountings. This was his favorite because he made at least 240 per cent of day rate on it, obviously the reason that the time study team was there. Their observation, furious stopwatch work, calculations, and writing did not bother Craig that much, but it did irritate Chester and his friends. Chester came over after the time study had been completed, and remarked that "that's what happens to a rate buster." Another worker came over and said that other people besides him [Craig] would be affected by the rate change.

After this incident, he still worked his hardest. But he noticed something peculiar was happening. At the dinner breaks he felt that his co-workers were avoiding him, not talking to him. During one break, there was quite a lengthy discussion by the others of the bad effects that a "rate buster" had on the department as a whole. Craig got the distinct impression they were talking indirectly about him. He didn't like the dinner breaks to go like this because he enjoyed the time away from the machines when he could "shoot the breeze" with the other workers.

Not too long after this, Piscitelli remarked that if he kept getting the rates changed on all the jobs, washing machine assembly would not be a very good department to work in. Craig did not know exactly how to take this statement. He had learned that Piscitelli had been a spot welder and had been promoted about fourteen months ago.

After these culminations of events, his output started to decrease a bit. He no longer produced at twice the standard rate; in fact, his production dropped a bit below one and one-half times that of the standard rate. Mr. Craddle, due to the nature of his job, noticed this decrease in output. He was not concerned at first because he felt that Craig might be physically exhausted, or maybe there were problems at home. But when his output failed to increase again, Mr. Craddle began to wonder what was behind the drop-off.

During the dinner break one night, Mr. Craddle called Piscitelli into his office. The following conversation took place.

> Craddle: Hey, Al, is there anything wrong with that Johnson kid?
>
> Piscitelli: In what way, Mr. Craddle?
>
> Craddle: I've been watching his production output. When he first came here, he was a heckuva worker. He had those time study guys scrambling all over the place. Now his output has kind of tapered off a bit. I wonder why. Doesn't he get along with the other fellows?
>
> Piscitelli: Why sure, look at them now (pointing in the direction where the men were eating). He's one of the guys.
>
> Craddle: (Noticing that Johnson was taking part in the conversation) Well, that doesn't seem to be a problem. Do you have any ideas?
>
> Piscitelli: Well, these young fellows come in here ready to tear up the world. But after a while it gets to them — they just can't handle it anymore. Maybe that's what happened to Johnson.
>
> Craddle: That could be. Well, that's all.

As the bell sounded to end the dinner break, Mr. Craddle could see that the group did not get up immediately to go back to work. They were still talking, and Craig was taking an active part in the conversation.

Questions for Discussion

1. Discuss the reasons for Craig's productivity decline.

2. At the beginning of the case, which of Craig's needs were satisfied through group acceptance and membership? Which were satisfied at the end of the case?

3. What were the specific methods by which Craig was "encouraged" to change his behavior?

ANSWERS TO SELF-REVIEW QUESTIONS, CHAPTER 11

True–False

1-F, 2-T, 3-T, 4-T, 5-F, 6-F, 7-T, 8-F, 9-F, 10-F, 11-T, 12-F, 13-F, 14-F, 15-T.

Multiple Choice

1-B, 2-E, 3-B, 4-C, 5-D, 6-D, 7-D, 8-D, 9-A, 10-E.

Completion

1. Synergy. 2. Security. 3. Status. 4. Enforcement. 5. Sociogram. 6. Cohesiveness.

Chapter 12

Communication-The Idea Transplant

CHAPTER OBJECTIVES

1. To demonstrate the importance of effective communication for the manager

2. To show how communication can become ineffective needlessly

3. To examine styles of communication as necessary extensions of the manager

4. To develop an appreciation of communication styles as management tools that have a profound impact on the job of achieving results through others

SELF-REVIEW QUESTIONS

Matching

A. believes that "two heads are better than one" in communication and seeks new approaches or experimentation

_____ 1. relinquishing communicator

B. interested in maintaining a communication status quo

_____ 2. developmental communicator

C. communicator who believes that others have more to say than he or she does

_____ 3. withdrawn communicator

D. authoritarian or paternalistic communicator who tends to be "one-way" in communication acts

_____ 4. controlling communicator

True—False

T F 1. Most people find the majority of their communication is written communication.

T F 2. Interference, in the communication process, is the trouble the receiver experiences as he or she decodes the message.

T F 3. Encoding occurs when an idea is changed from an abstract concept into some expression of language.

T F 4. Communication is merely the transmittal of meaning between two or more persons.

T F 5. Selective perception is the ability of a select few to communicate effectively.

T F 6. The developmental communicator is apt to use one-way communication.

T F 7. The relinquishing communicator is willing to contribute ideas and suggestions, but he or she strives to build joint understanding of problems or tasks.

T F 8. The withdrawn communicator assumes that nothing can be done to improve the situation and so avoids interaction and contributions.

T F 9. In transactional analysis, feelings of frustration, inadequacy, and helplessness are most likely to be part of the child ego state.

T F 10. If your life position category were that of "I'm not OK — you're OK," you'd probably be a relinquishing communicator.

T F 11. If your life position category were that of "I'm OK — you're not OK," you'd probably be a developmental communicator.

T F 12. The KISS formula is a technique for communicating with others who share your life position category.

T F 13. Most communications activity is handled through single mode channels with simultaneous multiple modes of communication seldom, if ever, employed.

T F 14. There are similarities between the developmental communicator and the adult ego state of transactional analysis.

T F 15. Although the developmental communicator is extremely effective in solving problems, speed and accuracy are sacrificed.

Completion

1. A simple model of the process of communication could be constructed as follows: An individual has an _____ that he or she wishes to share

or communicate. This is transformed or _____ into some communicable form, and the communication is _____ along a channel or circuit. _____ may intervene in the channel providing unwanted distortion and garbling of the message. The message is ultimately _____ , _____ , and re-expressed, one hopes, as the original _____ .

2. _____ _____ is a recently developed theory that helps analyze interindividual communication and behavior patterns. The theory postulates three ego states that affect behavior patterns. The _____ is that body of experiences stored in the brain when the person was small. The _____ develops from early-life observation of "big" people, most generally the parents of the small person. The _____ is the inquisitive, exploring, collect-the-facts-and-analyze-them state of the individual.

3. The _____ communicator uses two-way communication.

4. The _____ communicator is most effective in crisis situations when there is no time for discussion.

5. The _____ communicator has little self-confidence and seldom contributes any ideas of his or her own.

6. The _____ communicator is primarily interested in maintaining the status quo; he or she neither contributes nor solicits contributions from others, in order to keep from confusing the issue.

READING

A PRODUCTIVE WAY TO VENT EMPLOYEE GRIPES

Last year more than 100,000 employees — ranging from production workers to senior managers — minced no words in telling their bosses exactly what they thought of them, the company they work for, and their fellow workers. But instead of being fired, they were encouraged to sound off. Their companies were using a management tool called climate surveys, which not only get employee opinions out in the open but force managers to face up to — and correct — often unpleasant situations.

Giving employees a say, of course, is nothing new. Attitude surveys — which sample employee opinions companywide on such general topics as pay, benefits, and the like — have existed for decades. But climate surveys zero in on individual departments or work units of about 15 or fewer employees, and ask such questions as "Does your boss make assignments clear?" and "Do you get recognition for a job well done?" What is more, they offer a no-holds, two-way feedback process — an interpersonal exchange between managers and subordinates — in which unwarranted employee gripes can be explained away and legitimate ones handled.

For example, Houston-based Geosource Inc., which has used climate surveys for three years, discovered that one unit of welders was extremely dissatisfied with pay levels, even though Geosource paid competitively. In a survey feedback session, the unit manager found that workers had been reading want ads for welders offering pay of "up to $7.84 per hour." When he pointed out to the disgruntled welders that no company hires at the maximum wage because it could not give raises, the grumbling subsided.

EFFECTING CHANGE

Such feedback sessions are the key to making climate surveys work. "[Some] companies conduct surveys, give the information to top management, which says, 'That's interesting,' and doesn't do anything about it," explains Bernard D. Estafen, who develops employee programs for the Southern California region of Kaiser-Permanente Medical Care Program, the country's largest health maintenance organization. "We take survey information back to small teams of employees and ask, 'What do you recommend we do about it?'" Adds Barry D. Leskin, manager of organizational development at Sun Co.: "[Climate surveys] have more value than just taking the pulse of the organization; they can be used to effect change."

After managers tell subordinates what to expect and assure them that responses will remain anonymous, they distribute questionnaires that usually contain 100 or so questions, with some often tailored to the particular group. Anonymity is important. "We don't want bosses using the survey as a billy club," says David G. Bowers, program director of the University of Michigan's Institute for Social Research, which helped pioneer climate survey concepts in the mid-1960s. To protect confidentiality, survey respondents send completed questionnaires directly to either inside personnel or organizational development staffs, or to outside consulting firms that tabulate and analyze results and return them to department managers several weeks later.

Once results are returned, managers hold feedback sessions, or workshops, with subordinates and a person involved in the survey analysis. At Kaiser-Permanente, for example, workshops usually include 5 to 12 persons and last about two or three hours. Participants discuss each question and ask if results point up any problems. Once patterns emerge — a boss is too authoritarian or communication is poor — the group lists proposed changes on chart pads. "After the workshop, you could throw away all the survey data," notes Kaiser-Permanente's Estafen. "What is up on the wall on chart pads is the most valuable part."

What ends up on the chart pads, of course, can point to a host of employee gripes. But, as Geosource discovered, information gaps are often the primary target. Some examples:

General Electric Co.

Last year it surveyed 20,000 employees and expects to top that number in 1978. GE found that more than half the respondents to one survey were unhappy with the information and recognition they received, as well as with their opportunities for advancement. So the unit's manager instituted regular monthly meetings, brought in experts to answer questions, and started a newsletter. A year later, those unhappy with the information they received dropped from 50 per cent to none. And the number unhappy with the opportunities for promotion fell from more than 50 per cent to 20 per cent even though not one person was promoted or changed jobs. "But they understood the situation," points out Thomas D. Holman, manager of personnel research, "and that made the difference."

American Can Co.

It also turned up employee complaints about job opportunities and career advancement in a survey last year. Accordingly, the company set up a job information center — a place where employees can talk about their qualifications, ambitions, and training needs — and a weekly job seminar, a 30-minute session on Wednesdays at which a senior executive talks about career opportunities in his area.

Westinghouse Electric Corp.

The company's Pressurized Water Reactor Systems Div., after a climate survey, began posting job openings, offering a flexible work schedule, and distributing a brochure explaining exactly how salaries are set and raises given. "We spilled our guts on the mystery and mystique," says Robert A. Dannels, director of organization development for the division, "and concern about pay has been reduced."

Still, beefing up traditional corporate news channels rarely provides a quick cure. For example, while a newsletter apparently helped at GE, it can also be used as a management cop-out. Only by face-to-face contact, asserts Sun's Leskin, does management find out what employees really want to know, such as "Will someone tell us if the company is in trouble," or, "Our department head never tells us where we stand," — problems that a newsletter will not solve.

A 1973 survey at Gulf Oil Corp.'s Canadian headquarters in Toronto also proved beefed-up communications was not the answer. When forty-seven per cent cited "the grapevine" as their prime source of information, Gulf installed videotape TV sets to notify employees of company events, policy decisions, and the like. Yet in a second survey conducted last year, fifty-one per cent said they continue to get their information through the grapevine.

COMMITMENT

Even when results are nebulous, employees tend to react favorably to just being asked their opinions. Observes Thornley Wood, human resources director at Samsonite Corp, a division of Beatrice Foods Co.: "Almost any time a company survey is conducted, employee expectations go up."

Consequently, companies are finding that a successful climate survey program must have a firm commitment from senior management. "The keynote is: 'Don't ask if you don't want to hear,'" says D. Keith Sutfin, senior vice-president and personnel director at Pittsburgh National Bank, which recently completed a survey of bank managers. "Don't ask if you're not going to share what you find out with respondents and aren't willing to tell them what you're going to do about it. Many companies haven't the guts to go back and talk."

At the same time, the successful survey is equally dependent on a willingness by managers to open themselves up to subordinate scrutiny. The most successful surveys are requested by managers. Otherwise, they can be "highly threatening to middle and lower level management," points out John R. Stanek, president of International Survey Research Corp. in Chicago, which specializes in organizational surveys. "They often feel they're being put under a microscope or that it's some sort of a scientific witch hunt." Such fears usually arise when senior executives "ramrod [the survey] through the lower ranks," says Stanek. "Then there is no ownership by middle management. They feel it's not that we're doing a climate study, but that a climate study is being done to us."

BOMBSHELLS

Even self-confident managers who like being rated can find survey results devastating. The president of a suburban Pittsburgh bank, for one, thought he had operations well in hand when he returned from a seminar on management by objectives and implemented all kinds of new programs. So he invited an area consulting firm to conduct a climate survey. "We found a lousy climate all over," recalls Raghu Nath, president of the Institute for Development of Organizational & Human Potential, which ran the survey. The president of the bank was flabbergasted by the massive problems, says Nath.

The president of another client company of the institute resigned after a survey found managers at odds with workers and professionals under them. "When we summarized the results for management, we shot them out of their boots," notes Nath. "They were sitting on a bombshell."

COMPARISONS

The impact of survey results, of course, is not usually so overwhelming — findings are neither that grim nor that great. Rather, results tend to indicate strengths and weaknesses in certain areas. Thus, companies are devising ways to compare their own data with norms established not only in other departments within their own companies but with data from other companies. For example, a group of 24 companies — including GE, Ford, Xerox, Prudential Insurance, and Control Data — has put together a standardized survey that asks both attitudinal and climate questions. Called the Mayflower Group, its member companies exchange findings.

Likewise, a growing number of consulting firms are cashing in on climate surveys by providing multicompany data bases of their own. Boston's Forum Corp. of North America, for example, has conducted climate surveys for about 60 clients — including Union Carbide, Ashland Oil, and A. B. Dick. Michigan's Institute for Social Research has worked with more than 100 companies and has surveyed about 40,000 employees since 1970.

EXPANDING USE

Costs for most climate surveys vary widely. Two consultants affiliated with Ohio State University, for instance, are conducting a climate survey at no charge for the Columbus-based Lazarus division of Federated Department

Stores Inc. By contrast, Forum charges about from $3,000 to $16,000 for a package deal involving a computerized analysis.

Rising fees for surveys are being matched by expanding the use of surveys. Springs Mills Inc., for example, which first used the survey five years ago at one plant, this year is surveying 17,000 employees at its 22 textile plants. And next year the company plans to expand the program to 3,000 frozen-food employees.

Climate surveys are "beyond their infancy, somewhere between late teens and maturity," notes Continental Illinois' Becker. "We've learned over the years that you've got to work at managing effectively. If you're investing money, you've got to have reports on the return on your investment. And if you're going to manage effectively, you've got to have reports that help you determine how well you're managing. That's what this does."

But even most staunch supporters are quick to note that climate surveys are just one tool for improving workplace productivity and morale. "It's like an organization taking a physical exam," says Randall Schuler, an assistant professor at Ohio State and one of the two consultants working with Lazarus. "You can't really fail a physical, even if the heartbeat is too fast and the cholesterol is too high. What you have is useful information for improvement."

Questions for Discussion

1. The climate surveys discussed in the article provide a means for ensuring upward communication and feedback to managers. Why is upward communication and feedback to managers important enough to go to all this trouble and expense?

2. The article points out that an essential part of conducting climate surveys is the feedback of survey results to the employees. Why is this so important?

3. People communicate. If this is so, why isn't the "normal" communication process "good enough"? Why use climate surveys? (Hint: consider the elements of the communication process and the pitfalls possible in each stage of communication.)

EXERCISE

NEW TRAINEE

Each communicator usually exhibits a characteristic "style" of communication. The *way* in which each of us communicates, however, can distort the

This and the following short case are adapted from Malcolm E. Shaw's *Developing Communication Skills* (Westport, Conn.: Educational Systems and Designs, Inc., 1968), pp. 111 and 121.

way that the message is received; just as important is the fact that our communications style directly influences how the receiver sees that he or she is to act. Each manager should recognize that he or she must communicate in a fashion that is consistent with both managerial philosophy and the situation in which he or she is communicating. Given this situation, can you see which of the examples of communication styles would result in inappropriate actions?

You're the department manager and are in the process of introducing a trainee to his duties. He is new to the company and inexperienced in the work of your department. You have given him an overview of the department, the nature and purpose of its work, and his key responsibilities during the early stage of his employment. After having discussed his job and his duties, you say to him:

A: "I think you're ready to go to work now and follow all the instructions I gave you. Work slowly and deliberately. I'm sure you'll get good results. I'll be around in an hour or so to check on you and be sure you understand everything."

B: "Okay, I basically outlined the job responsibilities to you. I'm sure the first time around it won't be too clear. I suggest that right now we review and you repeat my instructions as you understand them. We will discuss it as we repeat my instructions as you understand them. We will discuss it as we go along to be sure you understand what's needed. Also you will have an opportunity to ask questions and clarify things as we move through the discussion."

C: "Okay, I've outlined the job to you and, now, it's probably not too clear the first day of the job. It's probably getting pretty confusing. But don't worry if you have trouble. Do the best you can. If you get stuck, maybe one of the guys sitting next to you can help or if I'm around, give me a call and I'll help you out."

D: "Okay, from now on it's up to you."

FOR THE STUDENT

1. Carefully review each of the four statements above. Choose the one you think is best. Find your first choice below and put "1" in the blank beside your choice, under "Rank Number." Put a "2" beside your *second* choice below. Continue in the same fashion with "3" and "4." (Place a "4" beside the statement you like *least*. Only one number per choice, and no ties please!)

Statement	Rank Number	Style
A	_____	_____
B	_____	_____
C	_____	_____
D	_____	_____

2. *After* you have ranked the statements, decide whether each statement is a *developmental, controlling, relinquishing,* or a *withdrawn* style of communication. (You might want to review the text section on "Philosophies of Communication.") Place the name of the communication style for each statement in the blank under "Style."

3. *After* you have classified each statement, look at the statements you ranked "1" and "4." What do you think would result from these two statements; that is, how would each affect the trainee's job performance during his early stage of his employment?

The statement I ranked "1" is _____ . It would affect the trainee in these ways:

_____

_____

_____

_____

_____

The statement I ranked "4" is _____ . It would affect the trainee in these ways:

_____

_____

_____

_____

_____

EXERCISE

HANDLING A PROBLEM

Each communicator usually exhibits a characteristic "style" of communication. The *way* in which each of us communicates, however, can distort the way that the message is received; just as important as the message content is the fact that our communications style directly influences the receiver. Managers should recognize that they must communicate in a fashion that is consistent with their managerial philosophy and the particular situation. Given the following situation, can you see which of the examples of communications styles would result in inappropriate actions?

Late yesterday afternoon, you initiated an emergency call to the director of staff services. An extremely complex and difficult technical problem had just cropped up, threatening the operation you supervise. Costs and waste, as a result, have gotten out of hand; the problem must be dealt with immediately before things get out of control and the operation runs into even more serious difficulty.

First thing this morning, a technical expert reported to you from staff services; the staff man has had, fortunately, extensive experience in the problem area facing you. He has quickly investigated the complicated situation and given you a verbal report advising what to do.

The advice doesn't sound completely "right" to you, and what's more, you don't fully understand it. You say to him:

A: "Well, to tell the truth, I'm not exactly clear on every step you've recommended; but we're under great time pressure, and you have a great deal of experience with this kind of problem so I'm going to follow your recommendations."

B: "I can't go along with your approach. I don't know exactly what should be done, but I'm sure I can work it out. I'm going to go down to this area myself and straighten it out."

C: "Well, you're the expert."

D: "I'm not clear on your plan of action. We're just going to have to take the time to thrash it out until we both understand the best approach."

FOR THE STUDENT

1. Carefully review each of the four statements above. Choose the one you think is best. Find your first choice below and put "1" in the blank beside your choice under "Rank Number." Put a "2" beside your *second* choice below. Continue in the same fashion with "3" and "4." (Place a "4" beside the statement you like least. Only one number per choice and no ties, please!)

Statement	Rank Number	Style
A	_____	_____
B	_____	_____
C	_____	_____
D	_____	_____

2. *After* you have ranked the statements, decide whether each statement is a *developmental, controlling, relinquishing,* or a *withdrawn* style of communication. (You might want to review the text section on "Philosophies of Communication.") Place the name of the communication style for each statement in the blank under "Style."

3. After you have classified each statement, look at the statements you ranked "1" and "4." What do you think would result from these two statements; that is, how would each affect the problem situation?

The statement I ranked "1" is _____ . It would affect the problem situation in these ways:

_____

_____

_____

_____

_____

_____

_____

The statement I ranked "4" is _____ . It would affect the problem situation in these ways:

_____

_____

_____

_____

_____

_____

_____

CASE

COMMUNICATION GAP

Western Companies is a medium-sized private insurance company. Private in this sense means it is not a stock company and is not listed on any of the stock exchanges. Owned by its employees and the many agents who represent it throughout the country, Western has been able over the years to return its profits to the employees in the form of many benefits; one of these is a very good profit-sharing program based on base salary. In addition, Western has constructed a luxurious country club with swimming pool, tennis courts, and now two eighteen-hole golf courses. All are used by the employees and the many agents the company invites in regularly for recreation at the company's expense.

Western began operations in 1890 to provide insurance protection to the agricultural community. Throughout the prosperous years since, the image has been maintained of a small company, run as a close-knit operation that is deeply concerned about the people they represent and the people who represent them. The home office is located in a small rural community. Almost all of the managerial employees reside in this community and take pride in established traditions. The remaining employees reside almost entirely several miles away in various other small rural communities.

All of this had led to the creation of a warm, friendly, family-type atmosphere within the office. The company also sponsors company outings several times during the year to encourage employee interaction, and to facilitate the development of this atmosphere that results as individuals become better acquainted.

Several years ago the company enacted a management by objectives program. A program of having employees write up position descriptions was also begun. Both plans were attempts by management to allow the individuals to become more involved in their work, to set standards and objectives, and to become a part in the planning of the overall direction of the company. The plans seemed successful in their purposes, to make the office a more pleasant place, to eliminate boredom, and to create a situation of meaningful employment — one with which the employee could be satisfied rather than being just a "clock watcher."

Over the years the results of their efforts were fruitful. Western was able to become an efficient operation with a free-flowing system of communication. It was a de-centralized system with several executive vice presidents reporting to the president. The important point is that the communication was a two-way street; top management was willing to listen to ideas presented by others lower in the corporate structure.

The entire operation began to show a turnaround almost a year ago with the retirement of the president. The new chief executive soon let his philosophy be known. Nothing was to occur without his approval. More and more suggestions were turned down, and before long communications came to a standstill. Hardly a day would pass in which you wouldn't hear someone say, "Oh, what's the use of even suggesting it; it will never reach upstairs." Dress codes were established and enforced. No longer were things as secure as before. Departments were having a tough time making plans because they really didn't know what was expected of them. It's hard to imagine that such a rapid change could occur, but it did.

One incident of particular importance was the elimination of the morning cafeteria service. Western operates under a system of flex-time; this allows employees to start work when they want, between the hours of 7:00 and 9:00 A.M., as long as they put in a seven-hour day. This was nice because it enabled employees to get home at a reasonable hour for whatever purpose one might have. However, many people had become dependent on their morning coffee and doughnut from the cafeteria. The cafeteria had become a place where employees could gather and enjoy a pleasant social atmosphere before they began their day's work; it was a nice way to start the day. Also many business decisions were resolved over the morning cup of coffee. All things considered, the morning coffee-time had its benefits. Of primary importance, however, was that it started the day in a relaxed, friendly way. It kept the troops happy. Too, many depended on it for their breakfast.

If there was a problem with the cafeteria operation no one was aware until the day it was announced that it would no longer be operable. (See attached Letter 1.) This came as a surprise to almost everyone. Especially resented were the form and tone of the communication.

Employee "rumblings" were soon heard. After all, this was a rather drastic decision reached without any employee input. Of course some employees did feel it was necessary to respond. The result was an "employee memo." (See Letter 2.)

LETTER 1

To: Home Office Officer and Managers
From: H. Carney, President
re: Coffee Problems
Date: August 19, 1982

Effective Monday, August 23, 1982, the cafeteria will no longer be open for morning coffee for *anyone*. If you think that this is a sudden decision, it isn't. It's the culmination of many problems, only a couple of which will be mentioned.

1. The consumption of doughnuts without paying for them.
2. The loss of cafeteria china and other items.

Although dispensing coffee via the current cart system is working out fairly well, this, too, has presented several problems. One of the problems is spillage due to the failure of some coffee users to use lids. Another problem arises due to sloppiness in filling cups from the jugs on the carts.

Still a third problem has been created by disposing of half empty coffee cups into waste baskets at the workplace.

We ask that you communicate the following items to your employees as soon as possible:

1. Advise that the cafeteria will no longer be open for morning coffee after Friday, August 20, 1982.
2. Ask employees to use more care in filling cups from the jugs on the coffee carts.
3. Insist that lids be used with all cups.
4. Insist that half empty cups should be thrown into the waste baskets located beside the coffee carts.

Since 1955 there has been a policy in existence that prohibits consumption of food at the employee's desk. This policy exists primarily to prevent the attraction of rats and other undesirable species of animal life into this office.

Some exceptions have been made to this policy and these exceptions still exist. Cakes for birthdays, Christmas goodies the day before Christmas, and candy bars at any time have been and are exceptions to the policy. Other than these, there are no other exceptions. Please make sure that your employees are aware of this policy, also.

Either by memo or phone advise me as soon as possible when the contents of this letter have been communicated to your employees.

LETTER 2

To: Home Office Officers and Managers
From: H. Blarney, Honcho
re: Paper Pirating
Date: August 20, 1982

You, no doubt, remember the recent coffee problem in the cafeteria and the well-thought-out solution that corrected the problem *immediately*.

Well, we have another problem involving the misuse of toilet tissue in the rest rooms. It has come to our attention that certain individuals (both male and female) have circumvented the intended use of the toilet tissue in the rest rooms and have utilized it in the following ways:

1. As a substitute for Kleenex to blow noses
2. To shine shoes
3. To wipe up coffee spills resulting from not using coffee lids, etc., etc.
4. To wrap up stolen food from the cafeteria
5. To clean ball point pens
6. To clean eyeglasses
7. Taken to parking lot to clean dirty windshields

There are even more abuses too numerous to mention, but I'm sure you get the idea of the problem we face.

Employing the same logic that resulted in closing the cafeteria to morning coffee drinkers, we announce the following solution to the current dilemma:

Effective Monday, August 23, 1982, we are removing the toilet tissue from all the rest rooms.

Please be sure that all employees are notified of this in advance and please be sure to give warning that the smuggling in of "personal" toilet tissue by employees will be looked upon, at best, as a violation of the spirit of this policy.

Questions for Discussion

1. Evaluate the effectiveness with which Mr. Carney communicated. What "messages" were being received by his employees, and how did these compare with the message Mr. Carney probably intended to send?

2. What meanings can be attributed to the "employee memo"?

3. Evaluate Mr. Carney's memo according to
   a. the four philosophies of communication (developmental, controlling, relinquishing, withdrawn).
   b. Transactional Analysis.

188 / EXPLORING THE NEW MANAGEMENT

ANSWERS TO SELF-REVIEW QUESTIONS, CHAPTER 12

Matching

A-2, B-3, C-1, D-4

True–False

1-F, 2-F, 3-T, 4-F, 5-F, 6-F, 7-F, 8-T, 9-T, 10-T, 11-F, 12-F, 13-F, 14-T, 15-T.

Completion

1. Idea . . . encodes . . . transmitted . . . Interference . . . received . . . decoded . . . idea.
2. Transactional Analysis . . . child . . . parent . . . adult.
3. Developmental. 4. Controlling. 5. Relinquishing. 6. Withdrawn.

Chapter 13

The Mystique of Motivation

CHAPTER OBJECTIVES

1. To examine the effect of various assumptions about the nature of human beings on the way in which the manager relates to subordinates

2. To highlight different approaches to the motivation of people in the organization

3. To show that the management of people demands a deep knowledge about their inner workings

4. To investigate learning theory as it attempts to explain why people behave as they do and what we can do about it

SELF-REVIEW QUESTIONS

Matching

A. developed the classical theory of motivation that said that employees will be highly motivated if their reward is directly connected to their performance

_____ 1. Rensis Likert

B. felt that when basic physiological needs are satisfied, higher order needs become dominant and must be included in motivational plans

_____ 2. Frederick Herzberg

C. feels that the manager is the key factor in motivation, whose responsibility is to make the worker feel personally important — this is known as the human relations theory

_____ 3. Frederick Taylor

D. The motivation of a worker depends
on the extent to which it is expected
to receive those things that are personally important as a reward for
desirable behavior.

_____ 4. preference-expectation
theory

E. felt that working conditions were
never satisfiers and were sometimes dissatisfiers, and that recognition, responsibility, etc., were the
motivating factors to an employee

_____ 5. Abraham Maslow

F. developed the X and Y theories of
human nature

_____ 6. Douglas McGregor

True–False

T   F   1. For each person there is one single factor that is the indisputed
determinant of his or her personality.

T   F   2. Personality results directly from behavior.

T   F   3. Frederick W. Taylor felt that achievement was the most effective
motivator.

T   F   4. Maslow's philosophy of motivation was that some motivations
are of higher orders than others.

T   F   5. Maslow felt that a satisfied motivator is not a requirement of
behavior.

T   F   6. The human-relations theory of motivation is different because it
emphasizes that the manager is the motivator.

T   F   7. Preference-expectation theory recognizes that one is motivated
to prefer what he or she reasonably anticipates.

T   F   8. A Theory Y manager believes that people are responsible and
creative.

T   F   9. Theory Y produces consistently better results than Theory X.

T   F   10. Because the personality is formed in early childhood, after about
the age of seven, one's personality does not change.

T   F   11. A worker who prefers a certain outcome will not be moved to
perform unless there is a certain degree of expectation of
receiving what is preferred.

T   F   12. Both Maslow and Herzberg emphasize the sequential nature of
various motivational forces.

T   F   13. According to Douglas McGregor, the average person dislikes work
and will avoid it as much as possible.

T   F   14. Many aspects of our lives indicate that we are conditioned by outside forces.

T   F   15. It has been found that monetary reward continues to be the best way to elicit improved performance from employees.

Multiple Choice

1. Personality is

    (a) able to be directly observed, (b) a stable thing once a person matures, (c) determined by a person's ability to communicate, (d) none of the above.

2. _____ is considered by many to be the key to behavior.

    (a) personality, (b) motivation, (c) leadership, (d) Theory X

3. Taylor's pay system was unique because

    (a) when an employee produced a given amount, he or she could go home, (b) the employer received no pay for days in which a required amount was not produced, (c) all members of the work group were paid the same amount, (d) the employee received the same pay per piece produced above quota as for each piece up to quota, (e) none of the above.

4. Vroom's preference-expectation theory describes how one's preference and expectation combine to determine

    (a) degree of motivation, (b) morale, (c) management activity, (d) job satisfaction, (e) none of the above.

5. When one responds in specific ways to particular "signals" or stimuli, we may say he or she is

    (a) rational, (b) robotlike, (c) predictable, (d) conditioned.

6. The man recognzied for his theory that any person will act as you wish if you can merely find the appropriate stimulus is

    (a) Machiavelli, (b) Skinner, (c) Jung, (d) Ormsbee.

7. The two factors in Herzberg's two-factor theory are

    (a) preference and expectation, (b) supervision and motivation, (c) job and security, (d) challenge and recognition, (e) none of the above.

8. Which of the following is a maintenance factor, according to Herzberg?

    (a) responsibility, (b) achievement, (c) advancement, (d) recognition, (e) none of the above.

9. Which of the following is a motivational factor, according to Herzberg?

    (a) salary, (b) status, (c) work conditions, (d) technical supervision, (e) none of the above.

10. In _____ conditioning, a reward or a punishment is administered after an activity, and the subject can control which is to be received.
   (a) instrumental, (b) classical, (c) stimulus, (d) expectation, (e) none of the above.

Completion

1. Taylor introduced the _____ — _____ bonus-pay system to encourage production.

2. The classical theory of motivation makes the assumption that _____ is the best motivator.

3. According to the human _____ theory of motivation, motivation operates primarily in the satisfactions of _____ — level needs.

4. Herzberg's _____ factors relate to the items that are necessary for and surround one's work activity but do not affect the actual nature of the job.

5. Herzberg's _____ factors deal with the things that directly affect the content of one's job, bringing satisfaction when they are present.

6. Theory _____ managers believe people must be forced to work and need to be told exactly what to do.

7. Any permanent behavior change (or modification resulting from experience) is called _____ .

8. The famous Russian psychologist associated with "conditioning" was _____ .

9. The concept that all behavior is a direct result of some stimuli is called _____ behavior.

10. The major managerial lesson in behavioral psychology is the fact that, given clear _____ , any problem can be solved.

READING

BURGER BLUES

Low Pay, Bossy Bosses Kill Kids' Enthusiasm For Food-Service Jobs

Jim Montgomery

Wendy Hamburger no longer makes Wendy's Old-Fashioned Hamburgers. After working three months at a Wendy's fast-food shop in suburban Chicago, she got fed up and quit.

Miss Hamburger, a winsome seventeen-year-old, was a press agent's dream come true when she applied for a job last summer at a Wendy's outlet near

Reprinted from the March 15, 1979 issue of *The Wall Street Journal* , by permission.

her Barrington, Ill., home. She hoped to earn some money toward entering art school after she graduates from high school this year.

What she earned mostly was a lot of free publicity for Wendy's hamburger chain in Chicago-area newspapers. And a little attention from R. David Thomas, founder and chairman of Wendy's International Inc., who mailed her an autographed photograph of himself. Until she walked out on a manager who threatened to fire her if she refused to work an extra turn on a holiday, she earned about $40 for 15 hours' work a week. "It seemed," she recalls, "like the job cost me more than I made."

FREQUENT TURNOVER

Low pay, distasteful working conditions and autocratic bosses are hardly a new story to the millions of teen-agers that the fast-food industry depends upon to peddle the billions of hamburgers, fries and shakes it sells every year. But, like Wendy J. Hamburger, few youngsters realize when they apply for a fast-food job that they will be doing better than average if they don't get disgusted and quit within four months.

Some critics, in fact, contend that the fast-food chains, by and large, actually count on frequent turnover. Just about every job in these restaurants changes hands three or four times a year. In most businesses such turnover would be catastrophic. In the fast-food business it means almost everyone is paid the minimum wage and almost no one ever gets a merit raise or joins a union.

"The whole system is designed to have turnover," thus averting pay increases and frustrating organizing efforts, asserts Robert Harbrant, secretary-treasurer of the AFL-CIO Food and Beverage Trades Department in Washinton, D.C.

To be sure, a fast-food job is the first work experience for many youngsters, and some of them have a hard time adjusting to the discipline of getting to work on time or even showing up every day. "You have about an 80 per cent reliability factor," says one restaurant executive whose chief complaint about his teen-age work force is that "about the time you get them trained they take off."

CAUSE. . . OR EFFECT?

However, Harlow F. White, president of Systems for Human Resources Inc., Mill Valley, Calif., a management-consulting firm that recently did a national survey of food-service-employe attitudes, questions whether the 300 per cent annual turnover of fast-food employes is a cause or an effect of the way the industry operates. In any event, he says, "the industry has managed to manufacture a self-fulfilling prophecy: "We're going to have turnover. And, by God, we do.' "

A sudden, sharp decline in employment turnover, Mr. White adds, would plunge the industry into turmoil, a development neither he nor anyone else sees as an imminent possibility. In fact, the survey found that more than one-third of management employes and four-fifths of hourly employes in the food-service industry plan to get out of it.

Operators of fast-food chains acknowledge that teen-age part-timers working for the minimum wage are the backbone of their business. But the operators deny that they purposely encourage turnover or do anything worse than to provide youngsters a chance to earn some spending money.

"Turnover costs us money," says a spokesman for the Burger King unit of Pillsbury Co., even though "it only takes a day or two" to train a new employe to a level of reasonable proficiency. Also, he says, there's "nothing we can do about a lot of the turnover" because employes are students who only want the jobs for the summer or for a school term or two.

UNDERCURRENT OF DISCONTENT

Despite such declarations of good intentions by executives at fast-food home offices, it is quickly evident that out in the field, at the restaurants themselves, there is a strong undercurrent of discontent and a feeling of being exploited among the unsophisticated young workers.

At an Atlanta Steak n Shake, for instance, a black teen-age waitress complains that she has been scheduled to work a two-hour day although it takes her more than two hours of riding time on city buses to get there and back home. (A company official concedes this reflects "mismanagement at that store." He says that if a worker is called in at all, "we have a written policy to pay them for a minimum of three hours.")

In New York's Westchester County, a Burger King keeps a seventeen-year-old applicant waiting expectantly for weeks before telling him it won't have an opening after all, costing him a month of job hunting and $200 in forgone pay. (A Burger King spokesman says, "Unfortunately, things like that do happen." He adds that the chain has installed a "new scheduling technique" that will allow better estimates of their future manpower needs.)

A suburban New York McDonald's orders teen-age part-timers to arrive up to an hour ahead of work time and then "wait in the back room and punch in later when they need you," says one such worker. ("I'll bet it's not a company-owned and operated location," a company official says. "That's something we wouldn't condone. But I can't say it mightn't happen in an isolated case.")

Teenagers usually don't know that the law requires that they be paid for such waiting time and that they be paid for even a few minutes of work that many of them do voluntarily before or after their work turn.

Store managers should know better but often don't. Richard Gilbert, a compliance official in the U.S. Labor Department's wage and hour division, faults the store-manager training programs run by the home offices of franchise chains. He says, "We find in many cases that these twenty-year-old managers are sales–oriented and cleanliness–oriented. But they aren't taught much about employe relations. And the Wage–Hour Law is just another three pages in the operating manual."

There's a lot of agreement on that score from insiders and outsiders alike. "I went through three managers in the short time I was at Wendy's," recalls Miss Hamburger. "They needed managers so badly they hired anyone. They get a lot of young guys in there who think they're Mr. Macho and want to exercise their power. They don't know anything."

"THEY CALL YOU STUPID"

"I quit because I didn't like the way managers treated us," says a seventeen-year-old who was cashier at an Atlanta McDonald's last summer. The managers, she says, "are real snotty. They yell at the workers in front of customers and call you stupid. At the end of August, 15 of us quit because of one manager. Otherwise, most of us would have kept working after school."

The industry deserves much of the criticism, says the Burger King spokesman, for "putting young men or women in their early twenties in charge of a $1 million restaurant with 40 employes under age eighteen and expecting them (the managers) to function" like professionals. As a practical matter, he says, "you can train someone to fix a piece of equipment a lot easier than you can to deal with people." To remedy this situation, he says the company is "formalizing people skills" as part of 10-day training courses for managers at its new $1.6 million Burger King University in Miami.

Steak n Shake Inc. also is instituting reforms aimed at making employes happier. In addition to "refining our training program so it isn't so damn complicated," says Thomas Delph, executive vice president, the company has started "listening" to its employes. One result: automatic pay increases for older employes when the minimum wage goes up. "Really," Mr. Delph says of employe relations in the fast-food industry, "we're all just learning in the past two or three years."

COMPLAINTS ABOUT PAY

The industry still has a lot to learn, if one believes the anonymous remarks scribbled on Mr. White's firm's survey questionnaires, which were filled out by thousands of fast-food employes last summer and fall. A worker in Arizona griped that "management seems very reluctant to employ enough people. We seem to be constantly asked to work a double turn or nights off." An Alabama worker wrote: "We have too many schedule changes. You never know when you will have to work, so it is hard to plan anything else."

Low pay is a constant irritant. A sixteen-year-old who quit an Atlanta Wendy's last fall says he was "doing more work than I was getting paid for" at $2.65 an hour. "Sometimes I'd have to work 12 hours a day. Other times there weren't enough of us for lunch-time crowds. One month we went through five assistant managers. When I get another job it won't be in fast foods."

James Badger, another sixteen-year-old, says in an interview that he learned more than he wanted to know about the fast-food business while working nights as a part-time head cook for a Long John Silver's outlet in Atlanta at $2.60 an hour. One week, he says, "I could have sworn I earned $85. I worked about 32 hours. But I only got a check for $47." Also, he says, "we were supposed to be paid on Fridays, but often we didn't get our checks until Monday or Tuesday."

Another young Southerner said his only gripe was pay: "I receive $2.06 an hour. I would like at least the minimum wage." The national minimum wage was $2.65 in 1978; it increased to $2.90 on Jan. 1 [1979].

While some small fast-food operations are exempt from the minimum-wage and overtime-pay provisions of federal law, most chains are covered and are subject to enforcement actions for failure to comply. Thus, in 1977, Kentucky Fried Chicken of Middlesboro, Ky., had to make up $2,086 in overtime pay to 35 employes. Last summer a Florida operator of Lum's and Ranch House restaurants was ordered by federal court in Miami to reimburse $100,000 to 1,290 employes who weren't paid required minimum and overtime wages. And, in New Jersey, the Department of Labor last December charged 18 Burger King restaurants in that state with systematically underpaying their employes and failing to keep adequate wage reports. Similar cases dot court records in all parts of the country.

To be sure, the survey found a number of fast-food employes who felt well-treated. "I like working here," says an Alabama fast-food worker. "It gives me a chance to meet new people." Another teen-ager, who makes $2.65 an hour as a Burger King food handler, says, "It's a lot of fun. The managers are nice to work for. I work pretty much the time I want to." And a young man working the counter in a Florida store says, "All the hard work is rewarding in the long run because the manager is a friend, parent, counselor, adviser, teacher and boss."

More numerous, however, were comments such as the one from a counter employe in Texas who complained: "Management puts tremendous mental strain on the employes. We have all learned how to successfully steal enough money . . . to make working here with all the bull and pressure worthwhile."

WORKING ROUND THE CLOCK

The manager's job is no bed of roses either. One young woman, who is paid $12,000 a year to run a McDonald's franchise store that grosses more than $750,000 a year, declares, "They don't pay managers enough. I'm on my feet from 6 A.M. to 6 P.M.. Often I don't have time to eat all day, On days off I come in a couple of hours or call in to check on my assistant managers. And I have to take work home, like the weekly scheduling."

McDonald's officials say they can't control everything a licensee does but that managers of company-owned stores are better trained and paid. Stanley Stein, McDonald's assistant vice-president of employe relations, says that "we try to establish mutual respect" with employes. The company must be succeeding, he adds, because "we haven't had a union organizing attempt in four or five years, and we've cut our turnover to maybe a little more than 100 per cent from between 200 per cent and 300 per cent several years back."

Mr. White, the management consultant, says the industry has only itself to blame for employe ill-will. "Most (store) managers are very young and untrained," he says, "insensitive rather than malicious in most cases." In his report on the survey, he observed that "the industry doesn't do the kind of manpower planning a labor-intensive environment demands," and that this is resulting in "higher labor costs."

Nation's Restaurant News, which sponsored the survey, echoes his warnings. "Unless food-service executives move quickly to develop an effective working relationship between top management and all unit employes — from general manager to dishwasher," the trade publication declared recently, "the industry will soon face a labor-management debacle of crisis proportions."

Questions for Discussion

1. Evaluate the motivational states or approaches in the fast-food industry according to
   (a) Theory X, Theory Y
   (b) Maslow's hierarchy of needs
   (c) Taylor's classical theory of motivation
   (d) Herzberg's two-factor theory
   (e) Vroom's preference-expectation theory
   (f) Porter and Lawler's reward-equity model.

2. Which of the above seems most useful in describing and explaining the causes and effects of motivation in the fast-food industry?

INCIDENT

MR. GREEN'S UNDERSTANDABLE DILEMMA

Does the manager actually affect subordinates merely by his or her attitude toward them? How do the manager's feelings and assumptions about subordinates influence how well he or she accomplishes organizational goals through their efforts? This incident illustrates how subtly behavior can be changed by an attitude.

Mr. Green, the manager of a substation of a large post office, was disturbed. He'd tried just about everything he could think of but to no avail. James Martin's unit was still way below their performance goals.

When James had first hired on, he'd been the real hotshot in his duties as a postal clerk. His ambitions and hard work were eventually rewarded with a promotion to supervisor.

James reported directly to Mr. Green, who felt they'd always been able to talk easily about performance goals and their attainment. As a matter of fact, it had been James' idea to set specific output goals for his group of postal clerks. The goals were expressed in terms of numbers of pieces handled per hour, number of minutes per delivery, and so on.

Mr. Green and James had quickly agreed on the original goals they had jointly set for the unit; they were, consequently, surprised when the unit failed to meet the goals. After re-evaluating the work group and the goals, they revised the output goals downward slightly. Even though they both felt that the first target figures were completely reasonable, they were willing to try again for lower targets.

James has just left Mr. Green's office after a discussion on the latest output figures for his unit. Not only were the lower goals still not being met, but output was lower than it was *last* month!

After having stared in disbelief at the output figures, James obviously was more than a little upset.

"I've done everything I can to get my people on the ball . . . I've threatened them, I've hollered at them, I've even tried giving time off to the ones who work best! It's not me to mollycoddle and pamper people . . . what counts is how well they do their jobs and how willing they are to work. The real workers I don't mind, but you know *those* people — they just basically don't want to work."

Mr. Green mulled over for some time what James had said, then thoughtfully looked over an action request from central industrial relations staff. James' unit compared quite unfavorably with the other regional units in number of grievances filed, rate of absenteeism, and turnover rate, as well as in output.

Mr. Green wondered if James' slip about the minority group workers (who comprised a large majority of the unit) meant anything, or perhaps if the output targets themselves had anything to do with the unit's record.

Questions for Discussion

1. Identify and evaluate James's concept of what motivates his employees. Why has his approach apparently been unsuccessful?

2. How has James's perception of his employees affected the way in which he attempts to motivate them? Would you classify his approach as consistent with Theory X or Theory Y?

INCIDENT

STAFF MEETING

One of the major tools available to the manager is the knowledge of what motivates (and what doesn't motivate) subordinates in the course of achieving their goals. Many managers earnestly try to motivate their employees by using the wrong rewards (or punishments). Is this what is happening in this incident?

"What we need around here is a little more motivation and a whole lot less goofing off!" General Finch slammed his fist on the table to emphasize his point. "Gentlemen, the army is only as good as its fighting men, and they're only as good as they want to be. Now let's get down to brass tacks about what we can do about it."

His staff officers shifted uneasily in their chairs and exchanged quick sidelong glances around the mahogany conference table in the general's office. No one said anything.

The silence was becoming unbearable, and the general's neck was beginning to turn beet-red — an ominous sign as world-famous as the temper it preceded.

Major O'Brien, with a hasty look heavenward, charged into the breach, hoping desperately to get the ball rolling on the general's newest kick. "Uh, sir, perhaps, we should first conduct a study of sorts to find out what the men want. . . ."

With a triumphant sneer, Major Henry quickly moved to outflank and decimate his rival. "Balderdash! We know our men, and we know their pride and dedication. We're already making great strides in giving them what they want. As the general suggests, we just need to get tough and keep them on their toes; then they won't have a chance to goof off!"

Rather gently, the general reminded the others, "I didn't necessarily say anything about getting tough. I *did* say we need to find new ways of building an effective team with each man doing his job to the best of his ability. We need to consider motivating them."

"But general," protested Colonel Davis, "We're already doing that. Congress gave us our appropriation for the soldiers' pay hikes; we're renovating and air conditioning barracks and mess halls all over the world; special services runs great entertainment and clubs for them; and all NCOs are going through management development courses. These are most of the things the congressional investigations found the troops were griping about, so we're doing something already about giving them what they want. What more can we do?" Davis sat down abruptly, suddenly aware that he may have overstepped his bounds.

General Finch, however, just nodded slowly; for the first time in memory, the iron man of action seemed uncomfortable . . . almost puzzled. "I know you're right about that, Davis. It just seems to me that those just aren't enough, somehow. We could do everything by the book, send them on forced marches when they're not busy doing something else; we could make them sign time cards telling what they did every hour of every day. We could even reward the best soldiers with bonuses or vacations. Each soldier's job could have a manual written for it, telling him exactly what to do so he'd never make a mistake . . . Would these things (and what you mentioned) make our men *want* to be better soldiers?" The General looked around at his staff officers almost imploringly. "Is that motivation?"

Questions for Discussion

1. Colonel Davis's argument is that the things soldiers had griped about had been removed, so that they should now be motivated. Discuss this reasoning in view of Herzberg's two-factor theory.

2. At what levels in Maslow's hierarchy of needs had previous efforts been directed? To what effect?

3. What should the general do to motivate his soldiers?

CASE

JACK MOORE

In 1976 Jack Moore was looking for a job. He was twenty-five years old and had spent the last two years attending a Detroit vocational school noted for its fine internal combustion engine program. Jack had spent most of his free time working on cars to support his education and hoped to find a job that would relate to this experience; he had developed a good understanding of the fundamentals of engine design and had been told by his instructors that he had a natural ability for troubleshooting.

Prior to Jack's graduation, the personnel manager of Easy Marine Corporation contacted the school, inquiring if they might recommend a graduating student for the position of engine development technician. Jack and two other students were highly recommended. After these three were interviewed, Jack was invited to visit Easy's engineering department to discuss the job in great detail.

When Jack arrived at the plant, he found it to be rather old and small; total employment was just over 450 people, of whom 35 were in the engineering department.

Sam Cline, the program manager who had the job opening, explained to Jack that Easy had decided to develop a new light-weight diesel engine for marine applications. The engine was to be totally new and incorporate several advanced concepts. Sam mentioned that the company's sales had been declining in recent years and top management felt that this new engine, if it met its design objectives, would turn sales around and make the company strong in the marine market once again.

The current program to prove out the design objectives was very small, consisting of only six people: one mechanic, two development technicians (including the current opening), one designer, one project engineer and the program manager. The program was expected to remain at this level for the next two years, at which time (if the prototype engines met the design objectives) the program would be expanded to a full-scale development effort consisting of 15 to 20 people. Sam also emphasized the current opportunity to get in at the start and grow with the program.

By the end of the day Jack had met all the people working on the program. Each person appeared to be friendly and the entire group was very enthusiastic. It was not hard for Jack to accept the position of development technician when it was offered him. The salary offered was comparable to his other offers, but the possibilities for future advancement and the experience he would obtain working in a small group were just what he had been looking for.

When Jack arrived to start work, he found that the project was treated truly as a group program. Each Friday all six members got together and reviewed what had been accomplished and what problems had developed during the week. Each member expressed his opinion as to how to solve the problems and what the next week's course of action should be. In addition, it was not uncommon to find members of the group working a half hour or hour past quitting time to complete a test even though they were not paid overtime. Occasionally the group even worked on Saturday if they felt they were falling behind schedule.

By the end of Jack's first year, he was able to do his job with virtually no direct supervision. He conducted not only the development tests but also analyzed the data and prepared rough draft reports. In addition, when he discovered a design problem, he worked directly with the designers to correct the problem. At his annual performance review, Sam appraised Jack's performance as considerably above average, saying that he was extremely satisfied with Jack's work. Jack received a 10 per cent merit raise effective the first of the month. Jack knew he had made the right choice in coming to work for Easy Marine.

The second year progressed much as had the first. Jack continued to receive increased responsibility and gain valuable experience. Near the end of the second year the group had demonstrated that the new engine did meet all the design objectives; the project was a success. Jack installed the new engines in two twenty-foot boats for use as demonstrators for potential customers.

Jack accompanied Sam and one of the company's sales representatives on calls to several prospective customers, in order to help answer technical questions about the engine's design and performance. Following the third trip, Sam had an auto accident that severely restricted his activities. For the next two months Jack and the sales rep made the calls alone.

Based on the favorable response generated during the demonstration visits, the Easy Marine Corporation decided to implement the second phase of the program, accelerating the development program in anticipation of production. The president of Easy Marine sent each member of the group a memo congratulating them on a fine job; the president wrote that he was certain, with the group members' continued support and enthusiasm, the second phase would also be a great success.

Two weeks after receiving the president's memo, the vice-president of engineering posted a memo on the bulletin board which in part stated ". . . Now that the diesel engine program has proven to be a success, the company is expanding the program effort to finalize development for production. Because of the increase in manpower requirements, the following personnel changes have been made . . . ." The memo had an organizational chart attached that indicated that Jack was now working for the supervisor of experimental testing, Bill Johnson, along with ten other development technicians.

Following the announcement, Jack went in to talk to his new supervisor to find how this change in organization would affect him. Mr. Johnson explained that he would review Jack's work daily and assign him jobs on a daily basis. Jack was to obtain the desired test information but do no analysis of the data nor prepare any reports.

After three months of working for Mr. Johnson, Jack asked when he would be receiving a performance review since it had now been 15 months since his last review. Mr. Johnson said that Jack had not worked in his department for a sufficient time to fully evaluate his work but that his initial reaction was that Jack was satisfactory. Mr. Johnson stated that he did not feel a merit raise was warranted at this time, even though Jack had not received a raise in 15 months because (as Mr. Johnson put it) "considering your relatively short length of employment at Easy Marine, your salary is comparable to other development technicians with comparable work time."

Six weeks later Jack quit.

Questions for Discussion

1. Using Maslow's hierarchy of needs, explain why Jack quit.

2. Using Herzberg's two-factor theory, explain why Jack quit.

3. Why was Jack more satisfied with the first project assignment than with the second?

CASE

THE COLLEGE-EDUCATED BANK TELLER

Paul Wilson sat on his bed and thought about the events that had led to his decision to leave the Savings and Loan Company. Paul had graduated from the local university in June 1981 with a bachelor of science in business administration with specialization in the field of finance.

He had interviewed throughout the spring of his senior year but had no job offers other than to sell life insurance. He was looking for a job in the field of finance close to his home town because he had a steady girlfriend there. He had always thought that with a college degree, good grades, and a neat appearance — all of which he had — it would be easy to find a job.

As the summer wore on, however, Paul found that he was all wrong. Every job opening was for someone with experience. "Well, how am I suppose to get experience if nobody will hire me?" he had thought. He had gone to an employment agency, but all their openings were for jobs out of town. He interviewed with most of the banks in town but got no offers other than to be a teller. "I didn't go to college for four years to take a job as a teller," he had thought. But a few of the bank personnel directors had told him that even their manager trainees started out as tellers.

Finally, in September 1981, with his savings nearly depleted, he accepted a job as a teller with the Savings and Loan. At the same time he had been accepted into graduate school at the local university. Paul remembered the conversation he had had with the S&L personnel director, Mr. Kessler.

Mr. Kessler: "Paul, normally we ask for a two-year commitment from our new tellers. The reason is we spend a lot of time and money training our tellers, and we don't want them quitting after six or eight months."

Paul: "What do you mean by a commitment? Do I have to sign some sort of contract?"

Mr. Kessler: "No, it's merely a verbal agreement."

Paul: "What are my chances of getting into your management training program within the next two years?"

Mr. Kessler: "I can't guarantee you anything. I can only say that we are a company that believes in promoting from within, and with your educational background you would certainly be considered for any openings that come up,

> but I can't say for sure when that'll be." (Pause) "So
> what about it, could you give me a two-year com-
> mitment?"

Paul: "Well, Mr. Kessler, let me put it to you this way: It's
going to take me at least two years to finish my MBA,
but if during that time I decide to get married, I may have
to look for a better job."

Mr. Kessler: "Okay, then, training class starts Monday at 8:00."

So he had taken the job, hoping it wouldn't be long before he could enter management training. He couldn't believe how low the pay was — $550
a month — but it was better than nothing, and he still lived at home so he
didn't really need a whole lot.

He had completed his training and been sent to a branch office. The
people at the branch were a lot of fun to work with, and he developed some
good work relationships with the other tellers as well as the branch manager.

About two months later, he and his girlfriend became engaged and set the
date for August of the following year. His fiancee worked as a secretary.

A few more months went by and Paul began to wonder if he'd been
forgotten. So he called the main office to ask Mr. Kessler if there had been
any openings in the management training program or if he foresaw any in
the near future. Mr. Kessler was out when he called, though, so he asked his
assistant, Mrs. Jarvis. He remembered her reply. "No, Paul, there are no
openings now, nor do I foresee any in the near future. All I can say is that
we are a company that believes in promoting from within, so hang in there."

He wanted to believe that; but one of the women at work, who had been
with the company for 13 years, said she couldn't remember anybody having
been promoted from teller to manager. In addition, he found out that
most of the company's current managers were hired from outside the company.

So he had decided to start looking once again for a better job. Within
a month he had an offer from a bank in a town about twenty-five miles
away to be an assistant branch manager. He had accepted the offer and told
Mr. Kessler he was leaving. Mr. Kessler asked him to come in and talk to
him the next morning. Paul clearly remembered their conversation:

Mr. Kessler: "Good morning, Paul."

Paul: "Good morning, Mr. Kessler. How are you?"

Mr. Kessler: "Frankly, Paul, I'm disappointed."

Paul: "Why?"

Mr. Kessler: "Why! Because I misjudged you. I thought you were the
kind of guy who would live up to a commitment. You
said you would work here two years, and here after five
months you're leaving!"

Paul: "Now wait a minute, Mr. Kessler. I told you when I took
the job that, if I decided to get married, I might have to
look for a better job. You knew I was engaged."

Mr. Kessler: "Well, anyway, it's ironic that you should leave now."

Paul: "What do you mean?"

Mr. Kessler: "Because your file has been pulled for consideration for
a management trainee position here."

Paul: "But I talked to Mrs. Jarvis three weeks ago, and she said there were no openings."

Mr. Kessler: "Why didn't you talk to me?"

Paul: "You weren't here."

Mr. Kessler: "You should have talked to me."

Paul: "How long before you would decide about this new opening?"

Mr. Kessler: "Six to eight weeks. But don't get me wrong. I can't promise you'll be the one to get the job."

So Paul had decided to stay, because (1) he believed Mr. Kessler and thought he had a better than 50-50 chance at the new position, and (2) the other job would have been about a 45–50 minute drive every day.

Six months later he was bitter and frustrated. He had received no word whatsoever about the position Mr. Kessler had said would be filled in six to eight weeks. About that time he received a letter from the placement office of his school informing him of a management position opening with a local bank. He applied, interviewed, and got the job. When he told Mr. Kessler he was leaving, Mr. Kessler again wanted to meet with Paul and talk.

They met for lunch and Mr. Kessler offered him a management training position. Paul politely refused it.

Question for Discussion

Analyze Paul's decision from the perspective of preference-expectation theory.

ANSWERS TO SELF-REVIEW QUESTIONS, CHAPTER 13

Matching

A-3, B-5, C-1, D-4, E-2, F-6.

True–False

1-F, 2-T, 3-F, 4-F, 5-F, 6-T, 7-F, 8-T, 9-F, 10-F, 11-T, 12-T, 13-F, 14-T, 15-F.

Multiple Choice

1-D, 2-B, 3-E, 4-A, 5-D, 6-B, 7-E, 8-E, 9-E, 10-A.

Completion

1. Piece-work. 2. Money. 3. Relations . . . higher. 4. Maintenance.
5. Motivation. 6. X. 7. Learned. 8. Pavlov. 9. Operant. 10. Objectives.

Chapter 14

Learning to Lead

CHAPTER OBJECTIVES

1. To review the role of the leader in reaching group goals
2. To illustrate the importance of leadership to the effective manager
3. To highlight components of successful leadership

SELF-REVIEW QUESTIONS

Matching

A. power based on fear

B. power based on the subordinate's desire for forthcoming rewards

C. power derived from position in an organizational hierarchy

D. power based on skill or knowledge

E. power based on a follower's identification with a leader

F. a powerful and prestigious manager who can be communicated with and yet is able to take prompt actions for activities within his or her jurisdiction

G. This theory states that types of leadership attitudes toward subordinates range from employee centered to job centered.

_____ 1. two-dimensional theory

_____ 2. benevolent autocrat

_____ 3. coercive power

_____ 4. legitimate power

_____ 5. Fiedler's situational theory

_____ 6. expert power

_____ 7. continuum theory

H. This theory places management qualities on two different axes and scores them on a multitude of combinations of initiating structure and consideration.   _____ 8. managerial-grid theory

I. a theory that extended the two-dimensional chart theory and gave descriptions of the kind of manager that might be found at each of the four corners and at the center of the chart   _____ 9. referent power

J. the theory that states that leadership equals the function of the leader's personality, the group's personality, and the situation   _____ 10. reward power

True–False

T   F   1. Leaders possess a common set of characteristics that differentiate them from nonleaders.

T   F   2. Leadership and popularity are generally acknowledged as the same quality.

T   F   3. Fiedler's situational theory of leadership postulates that the ways in which the leader seeks to accomplish objectives are responsible for having been chosen leader.

T   F   4. The Theory X approach to leadership holds that workers are lazy, unreliable, and seek to avoid responsibility.

T   F   5. Laissez-faire styles of management often allow workers to determine their own policies, procedures, or objectives.

T   F   6. Fiedler's situational approach to leadership postulates that leadership is a function of the leader's personality, the group's personality, and the situation.

T   F   7. The best way to appraise the quality of a leader is to look at the followers and see if they are reaching the group's goals.

T   F   8. A democratic leader believes in theory Y, which is that employees have to be told what to do and how to do it.

T   F   9. Leaders generally are free to use the type of leadership style that they feel best suits them.

T   F   10. Strong, healthy organizations may be better able to support democratic leadership activities than weaker organizations.

T   F   11. The individual is the factor that makes the vital difference in all the theories concerning leadership.

T F 12. In a circle in which no leader sits in the middle, there is much more difficulty in choosing a leader, and, therefore, the members of the circle tend to be less happy.

T F 13. Hersey and Blanchard's theory of leadership recognizes that maturity of subordinates affects required leader behavior.

T F 14. According to Hersey and Blanchard, leaders should increase their task behaviors as subordinates increase in competence.

T F 15. Decisions made at the level on which they must be carried out are much less likely to meet with resistance.

Multiple Choice

1. As Katz and Kahn suggest, the real indicator of the extent to which any given person is a leader is the amount of influence he or she wields

   (a) within the hierarchical structure, (b) based on position in the structure, (c) over and above the authority inherent in the office, (d) in spite of organizational resistance.

2. "Benevolent autocracy" is a nice way of describing an all-powerful ruler who

   (a) does not wish to be confused by the facts, having predetermined the decision, (b) listens considerately to employees' opinions and then makes his or her own decision, (c) acts in a participative management fashion, (d) is a generous ruler.

3. In supporting the benevolent autocrat theory, Robert McMurry does *not* offer which of these reasons for the demise of democratic leadership?

   (a) the climate within organizations is favorable, but it is extremely difficult to get the workers to accept responsibility, (b) most organizations must make rapid, difficult decisions and should therefore maintain a centralized power formation, (c) democratic leadership concepts are relatively new and difficult to mesh with already existing bureaucratic structures, (d) the leader is unwilling to delegate authority which he or she has striven to attain

4. Continuum theory postulates

   (a) a theory somewhat like the trait approach to leadership, (b) that leadership styles and attitudes may be charted along a continuum, (c) a theory with opposite extremes between which are a number of possible leadership attitudes, (d) a theory of opposite "centers of concern," (e) all but a.

5. Which of the following is *not* a characteristic of the circle form of group interaction?

   (a) least efficient in communications, (b) no clear choice of leader, (c) members were happier, (d) highest resistance to incorporation of new ideas

6. Which of the following is *not* a leader behavior identified by Hersey and Blanchard?

   (a) delegating, (b) selling, (c) interacting, (d) participating

Completion

1. _____ is the ability to persuade others to seek certain goals and then help them reach these goals.

2. Rather simply stated, congruence of _____ means that everybody in the company is heading the same way.

3. Likert's research at the Institute for Social Research provided statistical data also supporting a continuum of leadership attitudes; the extremes on his continuum depended upon the degree to which the leader was _____ -centered or _____ -centered

4. One of the results of the Ohio State Studies was a two-dimensional theory of leadership behavior, the two dimensions being _____ and _____ _____ . _____ _____ is task oriented and emphasizes the needs of the organization, whereas _____ is more relations oriented and emphasizes the needs of the individuals.

5. According to study results of Zander and Cartwright, all group objectives fall into one of two categories: (1) _____ and (2) _____ .

READING

LEADERSHIP AT WORK

No form of social organization has ever existed without leaders. To have someone in charge is as natural as the birds and the bees, the former with their pecking orders, the latter with their queens. In human affairs, even those who reject traditional leadership structures find a need for leaders themselves; anarchist parties dedicated to the destruction of the state regularly elect slates of officers The Bolsheviks who strove for the dictatorship of the proletariat wound up with the pure and simple dictatorship of one man.

Like cream, it seems, leaders naturally rise to the surface. But unlike cream, they are not necessarily the best part of the whole. The wizardry of popular leadership has been applied at least as much to evil as to good over the course of history. The example of Adolph Hitler springs to mind — a charismatic leader whose ability to muster a mass following for his twisted visions brought immense suffering to mankind.

There are those who would argue, however, that dictators like Hitler and Stalin were not really leaders. They may once have led in a demagogic

From the Royal Bank Letter (September/October 1980), published by the Royal Bank of Canada. Reprinted by permission.

fashion, but they turned into tyrants when the absolute corruption of absolute power took hold. "A leader and a tyrant are polar opposites," wrote James MacGregor Burns, the award-winning American political scientist. In his 1978 book *Leadership*, Burns drew a strict line between those who lead and those who wield blunt power.

This may seem like an overly idealistic view of the question, since so many so-called leaders are demonstrably quick to force people to do their bidding. But it does fit in with the theory, if not always the practice, of democratic rule. The democratic system tries to guard against excessive power and its attendant corruption. In the Watergate affair the world witnessed the system in action when no less a personage than the president of the United States was driven from office for abusing his power.

One of the reasons for the restraints on power is to control ambition. The democratic system recognizes that ambition always has been and always will be a vital force in human affairs. It seeks to harness this force to the best interests of the people. Similarly, the private enterprise economy, with its rewards for performance and risk-taking, pools the efforts generated by personal ambition into a general effort to produce an endowment in which everyone shares.

When viewed in the light of ambition, Burns's distinction between tyrants and leaders stands out vividly. The tyrant's ambition is for himself alone; he may use other people to gain it, but they are no more than his tools. In contrast, the leader is ambitious not only for himself, but for a cause which he shares with his following. Rightly or wrongly, he believes that his followers will be better off when and if they reach their common goal. (Neither leaders nor tyrants are exclusively males, of course; the masculine gender is used throughout in a generic sense.)

It is the presence of a following that compels leaders to act responsibly. They occupy their positions only by others' consent. Responsibility is the lynchpin of leadership in a democratic society. A prime minister is responsible to the electorate; a general to the civil authority; a chief executive officer to the shareholders of his company. And every leader is responsible to those who follow him, no matter how many or how few.

It would be naive to suppose that this system precludes autocratic behaviour. There will always be those who love power for its own sake, and who will short-circuit the system to put their own ambition first. A tyrant refuses to work for a common cause, and is pathologically afraid of rivals. He "suppresses every superiority, does away with good men, forbids education and light, controls the movements of the citizens, and, keeping them in perpetual servitude, wants them to grow accustomed to baseness and cowardice . . ." That was written by Aristotle in the third century B.C., but such tactics linger on today.

Yet if tyrants continue to carve out places for themselves in offices, on shop floors and elsewhere, they are no less vulnerable to overthrow than their counterparts in palaces. They may be mistaken for leaders, which they often believe themselves to be. But they are not because they force people to go along with them instead of *bringing* them along with them. They bully and blackmail and manipulate; they do everything but lead.

Unfortunately, leadership is very often confused with something else, its antithesis included. Burns cited a study in which people attributed 130 different meanings to the word. His own definition was the product of years of research and thinking about the subject. It is that leadership is a symbiotic relationship between those who lead and those who are led.

THE ART OF THE POSSIBLE IN BUSINESS LEADERSHIP

"Leadership is inseparable from the followers' needs and goals," Burn declared. His theory takes on flesh and blood when you think of what happens in democratic politics. Each party leader vies for followers by attempting to create a symbiosis — a feeling that "we need each other." Any intelligent leader will attempt to adjust his needs and goals to those of his potential followers within the limits that principle allows.

"Leaders are essentially politicians and must deal with political forces," wrote psychologist Harry Levinson in his excellent *Levinson Letter*. He was referring to managers in business and other organizations, who, he insists, should think of themselves as leaders ahead of anything else. Apart from having to gain and hold a constituency, manager/leaders must practice the political art of conciliation. They are subject to pressures from above, below, and sometimes on the same level from other departments. It takes political acumen to smooth these pressures out.

No one is exempt. The chief executive officer must be mindful of the disparate interests of directors, other shareholders, employees, consumers, governments, and the general public. "Middle managers" might ruefully conclude that they are in the middle like the ham in a sandwich as they try to cope with demands from on high for more production while the union is insisting on adherence to work rules. The foreman must try to meet his schedule on days when his crew seems to be all thumbs, one of the machines is down for repairs, and the shop steward is raising hell over a grievance. If politics is the art of the possible, it is never more so than in the leadership of a business concern.

USING ROUTINE AS A BLOCK TO STOP NEEDED CHANGES

It should be stressed, though, that the politics of leadership is quite a different thing from what is commonly called "office politics." Political intrigue within the organization is usually counterproductive, and greater productivity is the ultimate goal of a leader with the best interests of the organization at heart.

"Leading does not mean managing," wrote organizational expert Warren G. Bennis in his 1976 book *The Unconscious Conspiracy*. By definition, a leader's mission is to make progress; those who manage but do not lead are mired in the *status quo*. Office politicians generally fall into this category. The routine in which they take such delight may be the wrong routine; it may be outmoded or useless in the first place. But they are adept at using routine to block off needed changes. They also tend to be empire builders, and the bigger the empire, the harder it is to change.

They will sometimes accept change, but only when it suits their own purposes. This clearly makes them non-leaders from Burns's point of view. They are thinking of themselves first, not of the good of the organization or the people who work with them. Their ambition — and it is often intense — is aimed at a personal, not a collective, goal.

But even those who genuinely want to lead frequently find themselves managing the *status quo* against their own wishes. Their schedule is jammed with daily chores, interspersed with trouble-shooting current crises. Very little time is left over for leadership functions such as planning and maintaining staff morale.

A CASE OF RUNNING AS FAST AS YOU CAN TO
STAY WHERE YOU ARE

In a study of the working days of five top U.S. executives, management scientist Henry Mintzberg found that they rarely had time to think about anything except the question immediately before them. Half of the activities they carried out lasted less than nine minutes, and only 10 per cent lasted more than an hour. They "met a steady stream of callers and mail from the moment they arrived in the morning until they left in the evening," Mintzberg recorded. "Coffee breaks and lunches were inevitably work related, and everpresent subordinates seemed to usurp any free moment."

Nor was this frenetic regimen confined to the executive suite. A study of 160 British managers, mostly in the middle ranks, found that they were able to work for a half-hour or more without interruption only once every three days or so. The working lives of foremen were even more fragmented. A study of 56 foremen in the United States showed that they averaged an astonishing 583 activities, or one every 48 seconds, per eight-hour shift.

It would seem to be a case of running as fast as you can to stay where you are. How, in such conditions, can anyone afford to function as a leader? The first answer would seem to be to ask whether you might not be using routine as a subconscious excuse to avoid more difficult, longterm activities. "I think that all of us find that acting on routine problems, just because they are the easiest, often blocks us from getting involved in the bigger ones," Warren Bennis observed.

It may call for a considerable reordering of priorities to pay more attention to leadership, but it rightly should be at or near the top of the priority list for any manager. "Free time is made, not found, in the manager's job; it is forced into the schedule," wrote Mintzberg. Time should be made with determination to plan, to introduce needed changes, to appeal to the motivation of the staff, and to develop people's potentialities if leadership is to be accorded the importance it deserves.

There are various ways of eliminating routine, including the greater employment of specialists to present managers with well-thought-out priorities and alternatives for decision. The way that fits best with good leadership is the delegation of authority and tasks. Delegation often requires forbearance on the part of the superior, who may be able to handle work better and more easily than his deputy. There is always a temptation when watching an inexperienced person go through the trials and errors of an unfamiliar exercise to do or redo it yourself.

But it is foolish to believe that your way is the only way of doing something; the method is less important than getting the work done satisfactorily. When things go wrong with delegated work, a conscientious leader will point out the mistakes in the hope that they will not go wrong the next time around.

Delegation should be used to bring forth new leaders by training them in an everbroadening range of experience and responsibility. Many leaders fail to give sufficient weight to the continuity of leadership in the positions they occupy. In a sense, they should be working themselves out of their present jobs by preparing others to take over. Delegation is a method of doing just that.

Certainly it would seem to be the right approach for dealing with the present and coming generations of working people. They are better educated, more assertive and more sceptical than ever before. Changes in values in the past two decades have brought a variety of fresh forces to bear on the leadership of all types of institutions. In 1958 Robert Tannenbaum and Warren H. Schmidt published a paper in the *Harvard Business Review* entitled "How to Choose a Leadership Pattern." In 1973 they felt called upon to write an addendum to it in the light of the social changes that had taken place in the meantime — the rise of the youth, civil rights, ecology and consumer movements, and concern with the quality of life in the workplace and everywhere else.

They concluded that all this called for more sensitivity and flexibility in management. "Today's manager is more likely to deal with employees who resent being treated as subordinates, who may be highly critical of any organizational system, who expect to be consulted and to exert influence, and who often stand on the edge of alienation from the institution that needs their loyalty and commitment," they explained.

EMPLOYEES TODAY ARE NOT EASILY SCARED OR FOOLED

The social atmosphere has cooled down somewhat since that was written in the early 'seventies, but that does not change the fact that a distinctly new breed of workers has emerged. They have been brought up in their homes and schools to expect a say in decisions that affect them. They are downright suspicious of institutional motives as a result of media muckraking into the sins of the "Establishment," some of it valid, some of it not. They are jealous of their rights, real or perceived. They are forward in making demands for a fair share of rewards and recognition. They demand to be treated as individuals. They are not easily scared or fooled.

Some walk around in T-shirts exhorting: "Question Authority!" Though they stop short of displaying their sentiments on their chests, the majority would subscribe to Arthur Schlesinger, Jr.s', view that "authority is entitled only to the respect it earns, and not a whit more." No longer does a title on a door or a carpet on a floor command automatic deference.

With the rise of the new worker, leadership has become a matter of eliciting co-operation rather than commanding obedience. Co-operation means a willing effort on both sides; the first definition of the word in the Oxford Concise Dictionary is "working together to same end." This brings us back full circle to Burns's definition of leadership as a relationship in which the leader and followers share the same goals and needs. Nowadays, their needs are apt to be similar. Recent studies show that modern workers are highly concerned with personal autonomy, appreciation of their efforts, and a chance to realize their potentialities. If they cannot fulfil at least a portion of these needs at work, the energy generated by the drive to meet them is the organization's loss.

In the present setting, management scholar Douglas McGregor has suggested that "the essential task of management is to arrange organizational conditions and methods of operation so that people can achieve their own goals *best* by directing *their own* efforts toward organization objectives." For the manager, this implies a thorough understanding of the individual personalities of the people he is called upon to lead. It also implies the exercise of some of the finest human values — respect for the individual, justice, consideration and understanding. The old-fashioned boss accustomed to the servant-master system might protest that this approach can only lead to slackness. But given that bosses must get tough at times, it would seem that people will respond to toughness more positively when they know that it is justified by a record of fair play.

In the final analysis, leaders can expect their decent treatment of others to be reciprocated. It is this reciprocation that makes the difference between an outstanding and an adequate job, and inspires people to pitch in with an extra effort when the going gets rough. Lao-Tse was a poet and philosopher, not a management consultant, and he lived almost 2,500 years ago. But he showed that the principles of leadership are timeless when he wrote: "Fail to honour people, and they will fail to honour you; but of a good leader, who talks little, when his work is done, his aim fulfilled, they will say, 'we did this ourselves'."

Questions for Discussion

1. How powerful is a leader? Which of French and Raven's types of power (coercive, reward, legitimate, expert, or referent) is most likely to characterize the effective leader described in the article?

2. What role does congruence-of-goals play in the leadership situation?

3. Why *should* a leader be concerned with the interests of his or her followers?

EXERCISE

LEADERSHIP QUESTIONNAIRE*

The following items describe aspects of leadership behavior. Respond to each item according to the way you would be *most likely* to act if you were the leader of a work group.

In the space provided before each statement, place the letter that corresponds to *how often* you would be likely to behave in the described way. Put *A* for Always, *F* for Frequently, *O* for Occasionally, *S* for Seldom, and *N* for Never.

*Adapted from "T—P Leadership Questionnaire," in J. William Pfeiffer and John E. Jones (eds.), *A Handbook of Structured Experiences for Human Relations Training*, Vol. 1 (Iowa City, Iowa: University Associates Press, 1972), pp. 7–11.

If I Were The Leader of a Work Group . . .

_____ 1. I would most likely act as the spokesman of the group.

_____ 2. I would encourage overtime work.

_____ 3. I would allow members complete freedom in their work.

_____ 4. I would encourage the use of uniform procedures.

_____ 5. I would permit the members to use their own judgment in solving problems.

_____ 6. I would stress being ahead of competing groups.

_____ 7. I would speak as a representative of the group.

_____ 8. I would needle members for greater effort.

_____ 9. I would try out my ideas in the group.

_____ 10. I would let the members do their work the way they think best.

_____ 11. I would be working hard for a promotion.

_____ 12. I would be able to tolerate postponement and uncertainty.

_____ 13. I would speak for the group when visitors were present.

_____ 14. I would keep the work moving at a rapid pace.

_____ 15. I would turn the members loose on a job and let them go to it.

_____ 16. I would settle conflicts when they occur in the group.

_____ 17. I would get swamped by details.

_____ 18. I would represent the group at outside meetings.

_____ 19. I would be reluctant to allow the members any freedom of action.

_____ 20. I would decide what shall be done and how it shall be done.

_____ 21. I would push for increased production.

_____ 22. I would let some members have authority which I could keep.

_____ 23. Things would usually turn out as I predict.

_____ 24. I would allow the group a high degree of initiative.

_____ 25. I would assign group members to particular tasks.

_____ 26. I would be willing to make changes.

_____ 27. I would ask the members to work harder.

_____ 28. I would trust the group members to exercise good judgment.

_____ 29. I would schedule the work to be done.

_____ 30. I would refuse to explain my actions.

_____ 31. I would persuade others that my ideas are to their advantage.

_____ 32. I would permit the group to set its own pace.

_____ 33. I would urge the group to beat its previous record.

_____ 34. I would act without consulting the group.

_____ 35. I would ask that group members follow standard rules and regulations.

Your instructor will tell you how to score your Leadership Questionnaire.

T _____   P _____

After your Leadership Questionnaire has been scored, you can indicate your preferred style of leadership. Find your score on the *concern for task* dimension (T) on the left-hand arrow. Next, move to the right-hand arrow and find your score on the *concern for people* dimension (P). Draw a straight line that intersects the P and T score; the point at which that line crosses the *team leadership* arrow indicates your score on that dimension.

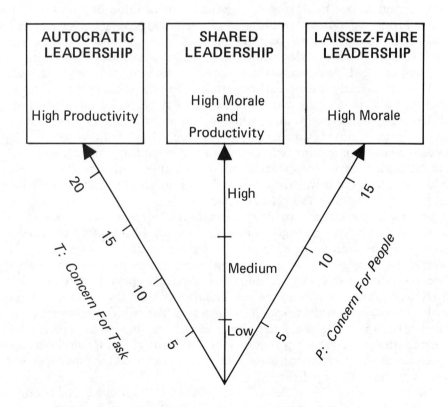

Shared Leadership Resulting from Balancing Concern for Task and Concern for People

CASE

AUTO AND AWNING REFINISHING COMPANY

The Auto and Awning Refinishing Company was established in 1970 to re-finish the painted surfaces of automobiles and awnings. The company was founded by Bob Tudor and Arty Grodenski. Bob handled the administrative and sales functions of the business while Arty managed the refinishing shop.

Arty had five men working under him in the shop. Two men worked on preparing the awnings to be painted, and two men worked on preparing the automobiles. The awnings and automobiles were painted by Arty and his assistant. Work was seasonal, and in the spring, summer, and fall the shop was mainly devoted to refinishing awnings. In the winter the shop concentrated its efforts on automobiles.

The five men in the shop worked well together under Arty's supervision. Arty encouraged a congenial atmosphere, allowing the men to participate in deciding who would do what specific task on a given day. For example, if Arty had to go out on the road and pick up a customer's awnings, he would ask if anyone in particular wanted to go. This would break up the routine of the shop, and no one man would be placed in the position of doing the same job day in and day out. Even though each man was given a choice as to what he was going to do in a given day, the men fell into a pattern of having the same two men go on the road while the other three worked in the shop. The men were satisfied, however, because each was doing what he wanted to do.

Work was usually done on schedule with the men taking pride in the way their work was done. This worked out well for Arty, for often he was not able to closely supervise his men; while he was at the shop, he was usually painting inside a closed painting booth. The only time work would back up was at the height of awning refinishing season, when the company did not have the manpower to keep work going on schedule. This would upset Bob Tudor, who believed it was Arty's lackadaisical method of handling the men that caused the work to fall behind schedule.

During the peak of the awning season, Bob confronted Arty concerning the way in which Arty managed the men. Bob argued that Arty should develop a more organized and efficient method for getting the work done. He also said that Arty should discourage the men from so much talking with each other, because this was only wasting time. Arty disagreed; he felt that he would need more men if business continued to grow at the present rate and that his men were already working to capacity. The heated argument continued until Bob insisted that Arty leave the partnership, to be replaced by someone who could get the job done more efficiently. No longer being able to tolerate Bob's interference, Arty left and was replaced by a manager Bob hired away from a competitor.

The new manager, Tom Terser, was quick to take charge in the shop at Auto and Awning Refinishing Company. His first step was to set up work schedules for the upcoming months for road work and work in the shop. Mr. Terser required that the schedule be followed without question. Mr. Terser's next move was to separate the jobs of preparing the awnings and autos for painting into different sections of the building with the men working alone in each section. Mr. Terser also made a point of constantly inspecting the men's work and making sure his men were working.

With Mr. Terser, Bob Tudor felt certain that more work would be accomplished since less time would be spent on talking and on deciding what each man should be doing. Mr. Tudor also liked the way Mr. Terser took charge of the situation, demanding that the men put forth a greater effort to get more work done while constantly making sure that the men were working.

With an optimistic outlook, Mr. Tudor worked hard to increase sales. At the same time he was facing more customer complaints than ever, especially that the awnings were being returned dented and showing signs of poor-quality workmanship. Also the customers had to wait longer for their awnings to be refinished.

Mr. Tudor returned to the shop to confront Mr. Terser with these problems, only to find one of the men in the shop had quit; Mr. Terser was considering firing one more.

Questions for Discussion

1. Contrast the leadership styles and results of Arty and Mr. Terser.

2. "Leadership is dependent on the voluntary response of those being led." Relate this statement to what happened in the case, both under Arty and Mr. Terser.

3. Compare Arty's and Mr. Terser's leadership from the perspective of Tannenbaum and Schmidt's leadership continuum.

4. Why was Arty a successful leader, while Mr. Terser was not?

CASE

THE BELLBURG NATIONAL BANK

Don Masters sat back in his chair and stared out the window. He thought about his past five years at the Bellburg National Bank and was very satisfied with the job he felt he was doing. He remembered how he came to the bank after getting out of active duty in the army. The personnel manager at the bank, Doug Anderson, was an ex-army officer like Don; they talked about army days and had hit it off from the start.

With his background in accounting, Don's first assignment at the bank was working directly with the bank's comptroller. Don liked the work and changed several procedures to make the work flow more smoothly. The comptroller had complimented Don on his work, to which Don remarked how much business and the army were alike — especially the organization that's needed in people's jobs and their assignments.

Last year, because of the rapid growth of the bank, it was decided to appoint a formal manager of the savings department. After several different people were considered, Don was selected. Don eagerly accepted the job, for he saw an opportunity to get out of the background and into the management stream.

The savings department handled all regular savings accounts, certificates of deposit, all special savings (such as Christmas Club accounts), and all correspondence with customers dealing with any of the savings items. Five employees worked in the department; although no one was currently head of the department, the employees looked to Alice Ferguson for leadership because she knew all of the department's functions and she had been with the bank for twenty years.

The department was efficient, and was considered a nice friendly place for friendly people to work. Each employee handled all of the different functions and savings types of accounts. The employees liked the exposure to the different jobs in the department, for it offered them the opportunity to do different things on different days.

As soon as Don as appointed manager, he went to work to make everyone a specialist. Each employee was assigned very specific duties and was not allowed to perform any other duties. In this way Don felt he could minimize mistakes and keep a close eye on the employees. A detail sheet was given to each employee; it outlined their duties and step-by-step job analysis. One employee handled regular savings, another certificates of deposit and so on. Don felt he needed this close a watch on the employees; his army experience showed him people must have things down in black and white and be led through their duties for them to perform them efficiently.

After three months several people mentioned to Don how the department had quieted down; the employees sat at their desks and rarely talked with any other department members. Don felt this was proof his plan was working and remarked, "Guidance, that's what they needed!"

During the next six months, several of the employees quit the bank and took other jobs. Absenteeism increased, although it had not been a problem in the past. After one year at the helm, only one employee that started with Don remained, Alice.

Doug Anderson mentioned to Don the high turnover ratio. Nothing specific was done to attack the problem, basically because Don said he felt things were fine. This morning, though, Doug called Don and said they'd have to discuss the savings department operation. Alice had quit!

Questions for Discussion

1. Discuss Don's leadership behavior from the perspective of *initiating structure* and *consideration*. What caused the high turnover?

2. Identify and evaluate Don's leadership according to the Managerial Grid.

3. Discuss the basis for the leadership shown by Alice before Don was appointed manager.

4. Does Don's predicament illustrate anything about the requirement that a good manager be a good leader, or *vice versa*?

ANSWERS TO SELF-REVIEW QUESTIONS, CHAPTER 14

Matching

A-3, B-10, C-4, D-6, E-9, F-2, G-7, H-1, I-8, J-5.

True–False

1-F, 2-F, 3-F, 4-T, 5-T, 6-T, 7-T, 8-F, 9-F, 10-T, 11-T, 12-F, 13-T, 14-F, 15-T.

Multiple Choice

1-C, 2-B, 3-A, 4-E, 5-D, 6-C.

Completion

1. Leadership. 2. Goals. 3. Job . . . employee. 4. Consideration . . . initiating-structure . . . initiating structure . . . consideration. 5. Achievement (of goals) . . . maintenance (of the group).

Chapter 15

Training and Development for Tomorrow

CHAPTER OBJECTIVES

1. To point out the never-ceasing requirement for workers *and* managers to increase their professional competence

2. To increase understanding of management's responsibility to take an active part in developing the capabilities of workers and managers alike

3. To introduce common training techniques

SELF-REVIEW QUESTIONS

Matching

A. While learning it, one is doing it.

B. training received in working conditions resembling actual shop or office conditions

C. Traditional in crafts and technical fields, this training entails a relatively long period of instruction by experts.

D. a joint program of training in which schools and businesses cooperate

E. a solution to the problem of certain jobs becoming obsolete and others being newly created

F. a technique by which the young manager receives a definite idea about the path or paths he or she may take to the top

_____ 1. lecture

_____ 2. internship

_____ 3. simulation exercises

_____ 4. planned progression

_____ 5. on-the-job training

_____ 6. role playing

G. a training technique that is useful for
presenting specific information; if
misused, can lead to boredom   _____ 7. apprenticeship

H. a teaching aid that can illustrate a
particular point and confront trainees
with realistic problems   _____ 8. cases

I. attempts to encourage the participants
to get inside the skin of the characters
in an incident — the best way to under-
stand both sides of a problem   _____ 9. retraining

J. attempts to construct a situation or
demonstration that illustrates a procedure or practice in a realistic manner
and teaches or emphasizes a lesson at
the same time.   _____ 10. vestibule training

True–False

T   F   1. Further education after completing college is becoming less
necessary.

T   F   2. The manager's learning is practically complete by the time he or
she shoulders top management responsibility.

T   F   3. Ideally, on the job training should be done by the supervisor.

T   F   4. Vestibule training is especially appropriate for jobs in which
turnover is high or for which there is a steady increase in demand
for workers.

T   F   5. Apprenticeship training is increasingly required because of the
greater complexity and sophistication of jobs.

T   F   6. Methods used in training for management are very similar to
employee indoctrination techniques.

T   F   7. Training in an "assistant-to" position permits trainees to learn
management first-hand, by close ongoing contact with veteran
managers on the job.

T   F   8. Role playing is an example of the approach taken in the junior
board device of management training.

T   F   9. Small firms, especially, should develop or organize their own
complete training program.

T   F   10. Lectures can be used effectively in training.

T   F   11. The training technique that encourages learning from comprehensive descriptions of business situations is role playing.

T F   12. The group-dynamics approach to management training involves group activity that illustrates lecture concepts.

T F   13. A major benefit derived from training with simulations is that mistakes made by the trainee do not have the impact they would if they were made in the *actual* situation.

T F   14. The "in-basket" is a form of simulation.

T F   15. Job rotation is a method of job training that has been very successful.

Multiple Choice

1. Education is changing today because

   (a) tomorrow's needs are changing, (b) fewer people will be needed to produce tomorrow's goods and services, (c) ideas and services are becoming increasingly more important than material goods, (d) job and skill requirements are changing, (e) all of the above.

2. Today's manager should expect to return to a university for _____ years of full-time study during his or her career.

   (a) zero, (b) two, (c) between two and four, (d) five

3. A properly designed and conducted training course can bring about

   (a) greater delegation of authority, (b) improved executive morale, (c) reduced costs, (d) increased executive management skills, (e) all of the above.

4. The most common method of employee indoctrination is

   (a) vestibule training, (b) apprenticeship training, (c) internship training, (d) retraining, (e) none of the above.

5. Which of the following employee indoctrinations do *not* utilize a learning-by-doing approach?

   (a) on-the-job training, (b) vestibule training, (c) apprenticeship training, (d) internship training, (e) none of the above

6. Who should do the training in an on-the-job training program?

   (a) an outside consultant, (b) a representative from the personnel department, (c) the supervisor, (d) a worker

7. If a job entails danger or if large costs result from mistakes, the manager would probably use which of the following to train new employees?

   (a) on-the-job training, (b) vestibule, (c) outside courses, (d) teaching machines

8. Benefits of planned progression include which of the following?

   (a) the worker knows where the completed work goes after it's finished, (b) the manager knows what is expected of him or her, both now and in the future, (c) the manager's experiences and learning are carefully planned in advance, (d) the salary increases are carefully timed and calculated to reinforce the learning desired, (e) b and c

9. The technique that uses dramatic situations in which participants act out different parts so as to change their perception of the problem is

(a) a case, (b) an incident iceberg, (c) group dynamics, (d) a simulation exercise, (e) none of the above.

10. An attempt to construct a situation or demonstration that illustrates a procedure or practice in a realistic manner and teaches or emphasizes a lesson at the same time is

(a) group dynamics, (b) a simulation exercise, (c) a case, (d) a self-development program, (e) none of the above.

Completion

1. In _____ training, employees are taken through a short course under conditions that resemble actual shop or office conditions.

2. Proficiency in fields that require relatively long periods of instruction by experts can be developed through _____ training.

3. Planned _____ is a technique by which the young manager receives a definite idea about the path he may take to the top.

4. Job _____ involves moving from job to job in different parts of the company to learn how the entire business operates.

5. _____ training can lead to increased self-knowledge and insights into interpersonal relationships.

READING

AT&T AND CITICORP: PROTOTYPES IN JOB TRAINING AMONG LARGE CORPORATIONS

Stan Luxenberg

Hundreds of businesses, large and small, are now engaged in activities once reserved for schools and universities. Corporations, pressed to maintain skilled work forces, have been providing more and more of their own education and training. It was once possible for a bright college graduate to learn skills entirely on the job. But in the computer age where whole industries change in a matter of months, new employees must be trained and then constantly retrained. To meet this need, companies now design courses and develop teaching techniques. The Conference Board, a business research group, estimates that 45,000 people are employed full time by corporations

Reprinted by permission from the January 1980 issue of the *Phi Delta Kappan*, pp. 314–317. © 1980. Phi Delta Kappan, Inc.

to provide education and training. The number of this new breed of teachers is growing.

Two of the most sophisticated programs are those of the American Telephone and Telegraph Company and Citicorp, parent company of Citibank. The corporations invest heavily to insure that their employees can handle their responsibilities. AT&T, the biggest private company in the world, offers the largest education program in the U.S., spending about $1 billion a year in order to prepare its nearly one million employees. It has hundreds of classrooms ranging from spare rooms in local Bell System offices to campus-style facilities. AT&T trains its computer programmers, engineers, accountants, operators, and the thousands of managers needed to oversee the army of employees. Citicorp, with only 40,000 employees, has a much less extensive program but one whose quality rivals that of the best business schools. The bank teaches basic clerical and accounting skills and trains officers how to determine whether to grant loans.

Neither company is much interested in experimentation. They seek education that produces results, enabling the businesses to provide their services more efficiently and profitably.

Though the two training programs are similar, they reflect the different natures of the parent corporations. Ma Bell's employees are engaged in the exacting task of using the latest in electronic wizardry in order to make billions of phone calls possible. The bankers, while relying heavily on computers, must make more subjective judgments — e.g., who should be loaned how much.

TRAINING AT AT&T

At the phone company most jobs are standardized and everyone's performance is carefully assessed. There is only one correct way to install a phone and one way to bill a customer. Service representatives, who answer customers' questions, should reply with the company's standard responses. If a customer calls to complain about an error in a bill, the representative must apologize about the problem, ask permission to check the file, and reply within 77 seconds. If a problem is not covered in the regulations, the representative must notify a supervisor.

All employees are monitored; their performance is observed and rated. Supervisors listen in on directory assistance operators and record proper handling of calls as well as the number of incorrect responses given. Repair personnel are watched closely to determine whether they are working fast and accurately enough. AT&T says that this rigid operation is necessary in order to provide uniform and efficient service. "We want the customer who deals with us to have very little difference in service, whether he is in New York or San Francisco," explains H. W. Clarke, vice president for human resources.

To prepare people for such tightly structured jobs, AT&T has, in the past 20 years, developed highly focused training programs. Phone installers — whether they work in Phoenix or in Miami — are given nearly identical instruction. And all courses emphasize effiency. AT&T is a carefully regulated utility answerable to state and federal regulatory bodies and to consumers who are increasingly impatient with rising phone bills. Training classes are designed to teach employees only the specific information they need to do their jobs. To accomplish this, courses are designed around job studies and test criteria. There is little room for free-ranging discussions or student creativity.

AT&T has had some form of training for decades, of course. Operators were once trained on mock switchboards. Supervisors attended (and still attend) brief classes on personnel management. When executives thought a course was needed, one was put together in a "seat-of-the-pants" fashion. But beginning in the early 1960s, as the new discipline of training technology was developed, AT&T began to systematize its training methods. "We have professionalized the development and delivery of training," says Ed Sutton, AT&T director of training and education. "If you have to train thousands of people, you have to devise a systematic approach."

Many Bell System classes are taught in local company offices or at locations near employees' homes. But for training that requires specialized equipment or is very complex or that is only necessary for a few people, many of the Bell operations maintain corporate learning centers throughout the United States. In addition, AT&T operates several such centers. At the company's major site for technical training of managers, the Bell System Center for Technical Education at Lisle, Illinois, courses must be proven to be effective before they are offered to Bell engineers and executives. It may take as much as a year to develop a course. The techniques employed at Lisle are similar to those used at other Bell schools. Whether the course is aimed at thousands of installers or a few dozen engineers, it is designed in the same fashion.

The Center for Technical Education is divided into four departments corresponding to the broad areas of work done by the phone company: forecasting, engineering, business services, and network operations (circuitry, operator services). Each department is headed by a board comprising some half dozen company managers. The departmental boards oversee curriculum councils that cover more specific areas such as transmission engineering and accounting. The councils solicit ideas for courses from company personnel. Managers and lower-level employees may suggest areas where courses are needed. The departmental boards review suggestions and make final decisions.

The curriculum councils begin reviewing ideas for courses by assigning training technologists to investigate. The Lisle school employs about 80 technologists, most of them trained at the center in the young discipline of developing education and training programs. The technologists interview people with problems, people who might benefit from new courses. For example, workers may complain that they are undertrained, or they may say they need better equipment. Often the demand for a course originates from operating difficulties: Callers in certain areas may be kept waiting for dial tones; workers may be taking too long to install new equipment. Or courses may be suggested as a means of introducing workers to new equipment or techniques. In less than half the cases they investigate, the technologists recommend training. Whenever possible, the company avoids providing training, because training costs a lot of money. The center will try other solutions

— redesigning jobs or changing computer programs, for instance — before recommending the creation of a course.

When the departmental board decides to offer a course, a development team designs it. The team consists of a training technologist and a specialist in the subject; typically, specialists are taken off the job for several years to serve at the school. The training technologist has two concerns: the quality of the course design and the quantity of material offered (no more than the minimum required). The subject specialist makes certain the material is of immediate practical value. "You try to prepare people for the kinds of trouble they'll have to face on a weekly basis," says Pat Slagley, a course developer.

The first step in designing a course is to write the final exam. The course will only be considered successful if students pass the test. The test may consist of a student's being required to fix an artfully broken or fouled-up piece of equipment, or to solve a difficult engineering problem. After devising the test, the course developers construct lesson plans, always aiming the class-work toward the final exam. The completed course is tried out on a pilot group of students. Following the final exam, students fill out a questionnaire on the value or utility of the course. The developers take the responses very seriously, since the students are employees who generally have good ideas on what they need to know for their jobs. If the pilot course receives passing marks, a detailed daily lesson plan will be printed and instructors will begin using it.

The courses emphasize solving real day-to-day problems. In a course on business phone systems, students break into groups of four to answer an imaginary customer's query. In the exercise a company seeking a phone system turns to Bell. The students must decide what system is best for the customer and provide a cost estimate that will match those of Bell's competitors.

For some jobs at Bell — switchboard operation, for example — new employees learn necessary skills on the job, working under supervisors as well as in classes. Managers and engineers are offered regular courses as well as electives. Because of the rapidity of change in the communications field, almost all Bell employees receive training and retraining on a continuing basis throughout their careers.

Mel West, a schedule engineer, took his third course at Lisle last year. West, whose job involves determining the equipment needs for the San Antonio area, had been a switching engineer, responsible for the machinery that makes it possible for calls to connect quickly. "You get a new job and you need training to keep up," explained West, whose latest course at Lisle dealt with a new electronic switching system. "I feel more comfortable knowing I have more training."

TRAINING BY CITICORP

In contrast to AT&T's methodical approach, Citicorp's smaller operation is run more loosely. The bank's training program is decentralized. The various divisions, such as the consumer services group and the world corporate group serving multinationals, are responsible for training their own people. As at AT&T, employees may recommend classes, but there are no systematic studies to determine whether courses are needed. Division training coordinators and senior bank executives make these decisions.

However, unlike AT&T, the bank does have standard training programs for many of its newly hired executives. Citicorp's national banking group, the division that handles business with large U.S. corporations such as General Motors, has devised a nine-month training program. Future loan officers begin training after three months on the job, working under a supervisor, to learn about the bank's operations. Then they go to a training center in Long Island City, New York. Those with a bachelor's degree and little accounting knowledge begin with a four-week course in basic accounting. Accountants and trainees with MBAs review material on their own. Then there is a three-week segment on corporate finance taken by all trainees, including MBAs. This is followed by six weeks of advanced accounting. The students are taught by officers of the bank as well as outside consultants, who in some cases are business school professors. The trainees learn to determine what risk is involved in lending to a particular company. After determining the risk, the officer must decide how to structure the loan, then persuade the customer and the bank to accept those terms. Much of this is taught by lecture and case study, as in business school. But the perspective is different from that presented in business schools. "In business schools the question is: How should a company borrow?" said Edward S. Munday, an assistant vice-president who formerly worked in the real estate division and is serving a tour as a supervisor in the training program. "We look at it from the bank's standpoint and decide whether we should lend."

In the case study method, students are given real cases, some taken from business school materials, others from bank cases, and are required to analyze the situation. Students work at problems in different areas such as manufacturing, real estate, and small-company loans.

The training program is more accelerated than college courses. Classes last about half a day, and then the students spend much of the rest of their time studying. No grades are given, but students tend to work hard because they are anxious to start their careers on a good footing. Admission to the training program is competitive; most of the students come from Ivy League schools or prestigious institutions such as Stanford. About 100 students come through the training center each year.

After the classroom work, the trainees are assigned to real cases the bank is handling. Working with account managers, the trainees analyze the material and supplement the account managers' data. In some instances the account manager will use the trainee's analysis as the basis for deciding the loan. In other instances it will be of marginal use.

After the fledgling executives finish their trainee period and become regular employees, there is no regular course of study. But managers are encouraged to continue their training, and in some instances a supervisor may strongly urge an employee to take a certain course. The national banking group offers about a dozen different courses a year, some of them repeated several times to accommodate the volume of requests. Each officer takes an average of seven days' training a year, which is paid time taken away from the job.

Last year Citicorp's national banking group offered courses in such subjects as managing problem loans, persuasive selling skills, and multinational business. Most courses last only a few days and are generally taught by outside consultants who specialize in teaching courses for corporations. This is different from AT&T, which generally relies on its own staff to teach most courses, although the use of outside consultants and college faculty is growing in the area of executive development.

A group executive vice president of Citicorp recently asked Elaine Adler, head of the national banking group's training program, to develop a course to teach supervisors how to make salary decisions and present them to employees. The company has guidelines on compensation that managers must follow, and strict budget limits. Managers must determine how to compensate employees adequately enough to keep them content and to present the salary decisions in a manner that avoids hard feelings. In some cases supervisors had been sending memos informing employees of salary decisions, making no attempt to explain how the figures were reached.

Adler and her staff began to design the course by interviewing potential students and personnel managers responsible for salary matters. From those discussions Adler developed a two-day course. It is described in a 20-page pamphlet that will be used by consultants hired to teach it. On the first day a class of about 24 will listen to lectures on salary problems and discuss the situation. The second day will include case studies and role playing. Students are given profiles of a dozen employees — their performance, salary history, and potential. Then the participants must devise a salary plan for the next year for the unit. The group breaks into teams, each of which must reach a collective decision. Each team presents its verdict to the instructor, who challenges it. When this exercise has been completed the instructor announces that the budget has been cut and new salary scales must be developed. After this there is role playing in which the managers act out how they would inform an employee of the salary decision. "The program gives them an opportunity to learn to discuss an area that is highly charged with emotional hostility," says Adler.

Each newly designed course is given to a pilot group. If Adler is satisfied with it, she announces that it is available to employees. If the course works well, demand for it may grow enough that it will be offered several times a year. If there is no demand, the course may be redesigned or dropped. While some courses are developed by the bank's staff, others are created by outside consultants. In some cases consultants develop the courses especially for Citicorp, but in other instances they have "off-the-shelf" courses that they offer to a number of businesses.

Citicorp makes little effort to assess the effects of its classes. AT&T, on the other hand, does extensive follow-up to determine the value of a course. As noted, students submit written evaluations of AT&T courses at the time of the final exam, and a year later both the employee and his supervisor are carefully questioned to see whether the course contributed to improved job performance.

Like many companies, AT&T and Citicorp have tuition reimbursement programs. Employees may take courses at accredited colleges and be reimbursed for tuition after completing them. Citibank spends $1 million a year on tuition reimbursement; last year 4,000 employees took advantage of the program. Thirty thousand AT&T employees took courses in 1978. But AT&T and Citicorp insist that their employees take courses leading to degrees that are related to their work. For instance, a Citicorp employee could be reinbursed for a history course if that were necessary for a degree in business administration, but the employee could not receive funds for a degree in history.

To make it easier for employees to pursue business studies, Citicorp sponsors programs for associate degrees in business and the MBA. The programs are given on bank property so that employees can easily come straight from work for evening classes or take classes on their lunch hours. The associate degree program is run by the College of Staten Island, a unit of the City University of New York. St. John's University of New York offers the MBA program.

The degree programs are given at Citicorp's learning center, located in Citibank's Park Avenue headquarters. The spacious modern center holds classes that are not necessarily connected with the job but are considered a benefit to the worker. There are classes in French and Chinese, using the center's language laboratories. There are classes in basic math, in preparation for the high school equivalency exam, and in subjects such as assertiveness training and accent correction for people who are not native speakers of English.

AT&T and Citicorp say they have not built extensive training programs because of failings on the part of educational institutions. Neither do they suggest that colleges should begin giving courses in telephone engineering or bank credit analysis. Rather, they argue that the role of schools is to provide a broad general education to help students *learn how to learn*, so that they can come into the business world and easily master the specific skills necessarily taught by companies.

AT&T has, over the years, experimented with supporting liberal arts courses, hoping to make its managers more "well rounded." Managers were sent to such colleges as Dartmouth, Carleton, and the University of Pennsylvania in the 1950s and early 1960s, where such courses were run for Bell System managers exclusively. Today selected Bell managers attend similar programs run by colleges but open to people from all companies as well as the public sector. In-house programs are designed to develop better understanding of specific business, social, political, and human resources issues affecting the organization as well as to examine specific solutions to such problems.

At a time when many students are demanding assurances that their educa- will help them earn a living, it is unlikely that AT&T and other major corporations, under heavy pressure from shareholders to squeeze out maximum profits, will shift their in-house educational offerings to include more humanities courses. Still, it seems likely that these companies will spend more and more on educational programs in the future. They have little choice. Education as a business tool is becoming increasingly important, a necessary way for companies to maintain their competitive position.

Questions for Discussion

1. What are the differences in the purposes for training at AT&T and Citicorp?

2. What types of training techniques are used at AT&T? Citicorp? Which others do you think might be useful at AT&T? Citicorp?

3. Is it useful to evaluate the effectiveness of training efforts? Why or why not?

INCIDENT

THE SKY'S THE LIMIT

An important part of the manager's job is training; he or she must encourage employees to develop their capabilities to the highest degree. And this must be done constantly, so that subordinates are allowed to learn more and more at their own pace. In this way, the manager can maintain highly qualified and motivated people who are available for whatever challenging role is offered them.

Mr. Smith leaned back in his swivel chair, folding his hands across an ample expanse of vest. "Yes, Smithson, it is a rare privilege for one of our younger people to be sent into international operations. A real glamour field, with plenty of opportunities. We've had our eyes on you for some time now." He chuckled merrily. "Didn't you wonder why I'd asked about how you liked traveling and seeing new places?"

"To tell you the truth, Mr. Smith, I didn't really think much about it! My wife and I do travel a good bit on our vacations, of course; we've been all over Canada and even down to Mexico City. The promotion and reassignment do come as a bit of a surprise. . . . I mean, after all, all I've been is a financial technician on our corporate information systems. . . . I really don't think of myself as a manager. . . ."

Mr. Smith leaned forward and shook a semistern finger at Smithson. "Nonsense! We figure you for a lot of potential, a real fine manager. The sky's the limit, my boy. . . . and (ha ha) that's just where you're going — the sky, I mean. You're to report in Riyadh, Saudi Arabia, in three weeks to take over our Middle East office. We need someone to take charge, get things settled down and straightened up out there, and do some good for us."

Smithson paled noticeably and stuttered, "Ri-Ri-Riyadh?! B-B-But that's an office of over 200 people! How am I supposed to know what to do? That's a mighty touchy area over there, both for business *and* politics. What if I goof?"

Mr. Smith snapped, rather irritably, "Goof? I think not. You can pick up the job easily enough. Your staff can brief you as soon as you get there on the technical part of their operations, the political situation, and all the rest." More gently now, he said, "My boy, I know you'll enjoy the challenge. It'll be a great opportunity for you."

As Smithson rose to go, he couldn't help being bewildered, not to mention a little scared. Why did he have to go so soon? He wasn't a manager and had no supervisory experience. How did one go about becoming a manager? Could he train himself while learning a completely new business activity without jeopardizing the company's holdings in the Middle East? Plaintively, he wondered why Smith hadn't prepared him for taking on such an "opportunity."

Questions for Discussion

1. Evaluate the process by which Smithson has been prepared for his new assignment.

2. What do you suggest that Smithson do in the three weeks he has before he reports to his new post? Schedule his training activities for those three weeks.

3. Carefully describe the alternative training activities to which Smithson *should* have been exposed in being prepared for this challenge.

CASE

THE BIONIC ACCOUNTANT

Big Eight Accounting, Incorporated, is one of the largest public accounting firms operating in North America and overseas. As such, it commands a certain amount of respect from the members of the business community. Such respect, coupled with a reputation as being "hard nosed" regarding accounting trends and policies, makes it very easy to recruit the top accounting talent from among the current year's college graduationg class.

Like all public accounting firms, "Big Eight" has experienced a rapid turnover in its staff; turnover is especially high during the first two years of the staff hired. Mr. Burdge, vice-president of personnel, estimated that Big Eight's "first two years" turnover was considerably in excess of the industry norm of approximately 50 per cent.

One of the firm's recruiting points is that the new employee is given more and more responsibility before really being ready to take it on comfortably. Mr. Burdge recognized that, with his turnover rate so high, pretty soon there wouldn't be enough experienced people in the firm's offices to train the new crop of college graduates coming into the firm.

He decided to conduct a study of some of the larger U.S. offices of the firm to determine what could be causing this variation from past experience. What follows is representative of the firm's practice within several of Big Eight's offices.

In one instance an experienced staff member had been with the firm for three years. She was required to observe three different companies while they were counting their stock for year-end closings on three consecutive days. The first observation takes approximately 12 hours, assuming no problems are encountered. What all this meant was that she got about 10 hours of sleep during the 72-hour period covering these three work assignments.

Mr. Burdge also noted from the payroll records that first and second year staff generally worked an inordinate amount of overtime. It was not uncommon to find staff members who had worked over 300 hours of overtime during the six-month period referred to as the "busy season", as well as some with as much as 600 hours. Further information obtained from randomly selected individuals revealed that they worked in excess of 12 hours per day — day in and day out for weeks on end.

The offices Mr. Burdge visited were large both in size, occupying several floors of an office building, and in number of employees, usually two hundred or more. Yet they usually were devoid of people! When he did see some unassigned staff in one of the several large rooms set aside for them to use when they were unassigned, they appeared to be getting ready to start another audit somewhere else. When he mentioned the noticeable emptiness of the offices, the personnel managers would grin and refer to the fact that their office had a very high percentage of time chargeable to the firm's customers, which would be profitable to the firm. Some managers even boasted that some of their employees were 110 percent chargeable.

With another "busy season" fast approaching and his more experienced help leaving at previously unexperienced levels, Mr. Burdge felt that he should initiate some form of remedial action.

Questions for Discussion

1. Because 50 per cent of Big Eight's turnover occurs among the accountants with *over* two years' service, what should Mr. Burdge do to develop a sufficient number of experienced people for training the new staff?

2. What training techniques would you recommend to be used in training the new accounting staff?

ANSWERS TO SELF-REVIEW QUESTIONS, CHAPTER 15

Matching

A-5, B-10, C-7, D-2, E-9, F-4, G-1, H-8, I-6, J-3.

True–False

1-F, 2-F, 3-T, 4-T, 5-F, 6-F, 7-T, 8-F, 9-F, 10-T, 11-F, 12-T, 13-T, 14-T, 15-F.

Multiple Choice

1-E, 2-B, 3-E, 4-C, 5-E, 6-C, 7-B, 8-E, 9-E, 10-B.

Completion

1. Vestibule. 2. Apprenticeship. 3. Progression. 4. Rotation.
5. Sensitivity.

Chapter 16

Coping with the Challenge of Change

CHAPTER OBJECTIVES

1. To emphasize that effective managers, to do their task of getting results through the efforts of others, must plan and put changes into effect

2. To describe the causes of common difficulties that managers have in implementing change

3. To give alternatives open to managers in overcoming resistance to change.

SELF-REVIEW QUESTIONS

Matching

A. any alteration that occurs in the organization of the total environment

B. reduces worker feelings of autonomy and increases worker resistance to change

C. describes the condition in which a change in one variable produces change in a second variable

D. worker inclusion in the decision-making process

E. analysis of the comparative strengths of the positive and negative forces that might be causing resistance to change

_____ 1. cause and effect

_____ 2. participation

_____ 3. control

_____ 4. force-field analysis

_____ 5. future shock

F. baffling confusion that comes from
an overwhelming stream of changes   ____ 6. change

G. change introduced by technology is a
function of   ____ 7. human and technical
problems

True–False

T   F   1. Systems operate in an equilibrium in which the parts are directly and harmoniously related.

T   F   2. One of the major problems facing management today is restraining worker demand and enthusiasm for change.

T   F   3. In spite of all that is said, technology really has little effect on the worker.

T   F   4. The individual evaluates change in personal terms rather than in terms of secondary considerations such as efficient production at the job.

T   F   5. Few workers are open-minded enough to accept change as beneficial when their past experience with change has shown that this is not the case.

T   F   6. On many occasions an appropriate justification for introducing change is the variety that it will provide.

T   F   7. Internalization is a process of trying, adopting, and using new attitudes or techniques.

T   F   8. Time and support are required in the refreezing stage to assure final integration of the desired attitudes into the individual's personality.

T   F   9. In nearly every given situation requiring change, there is one best way to effect that change.

T   F   10. Some fear of change can be overcome by just providing information that will answer questions such as "Who?" or "Where?"

T   F   11. A good manager, because he or she realizes how much resistance to change there is, recognizes the obligations of ritual more than the challenges of current problems.

T   F   12. Just being right is enough to allow management to initiate change easily because human rationality is appealed to.

T   F   13. There is no direct cause-and-effect relationship in change.

T   F   14. One way to make changes more easily in an organization is to make many changes as often as possible to acclimate the workers to change and make them more comfortable with it.

T F 15. Those who are successful find it easier to cope with change than do others.

Multiple Choice

1. Much of the resistance to change encountered in an organization can be best accounted for in terms of

   (a) Maslow's hierarchy of needs concept, (b) economic fears of individuals, (c) threats to an individual's social relationships, (d) uncertainty of what the future holds.

2. That Gilbreth was more successful in his human engineering enterprises than was Taylor is probably attributable to the fact that

   (a) Gilbreth's wife had a Ph.D. in psychology, (b) Taylor failed to recognize the psychological dimension in the workplace, (c) Gilbreth was more successful in combining psychological dimensions with the industrial engineering concepts, (d) all of the above.

3. Which of the following does not provide substantial effect in determining an individual's response to change?

   (a) extent of information about the change, (b) number of top management communications telling workers that the change will be beneficial, (c) worker participation in change decisions, (d) trust in the initiator of change

4. Most of the ways in which we meet situations arising from our environment

   (a) were adopted after long, careful study, (b) are generally the best way of doing things, (c) were originally instituted by accident, compromise, or expediency, (d) are followed without any conscious consideration of the action, (e) c and d.

5. In a change situation, management's objective is all the following except to

   (a) gain acceptance for that change, (b) maintain strict managerial control of the work environment, (c) restore group equilibrium, (d) aid personal adjustment to the new situation.

Completion

1. _____ theory has been one of the significant contributors to the description of interrelationships between parts.

2. The influential factors diagnosed in the Hawthorne studies as complicating simple cause-and-effect relationships in an organization are _____
   _____ .

3. Professor Roethlisberger used an _____ chart to illustrate and identify factors operating in the environment; each change situation, Roethlisberger discovered, is _____ by the individual according to his or her past _____ .

4. _____ - _____ is the term that probably best describes the level at which workers operate when included in decisions affecting their environment and the workplace.

5. A manager, after having proved to be honest and interested in employees, may be accorded a special authority by those employees—the authority of _____ . This authority is _____ , not delegated, and most generally is held by supervisors who have established their reputation with their workers.

6. Management is the creator of the correct balance of _____ and _____ .

7. Edgar H. Schein of MIT has suggested a three-factor theory related to the introduction of change in an organization. _____ is the unlearning of old-attitudes stage, and breaking down resistance is the important process in this stage. _____ , the second stage, is concerned with worker identification with the change elements and internalization of the benefits of change. _____ is the stage in which the change in process or attitude becomes internalized as habit.

READING

CORPORATE CULTURE

The Hard-to-Change Values that Spell Success or Failure

Five years ago the chief executives of two major oil companies determined that they would have to diversify out of oil because their current business could not support long-term growth and it faced serious political threats. Not only did they announce their new long-range strategies to employees and the public, but they established elaborate plans to implement them. Today, after several years of floundering in attempts to acquire and build new businesses, both companies are firmly back in oil, and the two CEOs have been replaced.

Each of the CEOs had been unable to implement his strategy, not because it was theoretically wrong or bad but because neither had understood that his company's culture was so entrenched in the traditions and values of doing business as oilmen that employees resisted — and sabotaged — the radical changes that the CEOs tried to impose. Oil operations require long-term investments for long-term rewards; but the new businesses needed short-term views and an emphasis on current returns. Success had come from hitting it big in wildcatting; but the new success was to be based on such abstractions as market share or numbers growth — all seemingly nebulous concepts to them. Too late did the CEOs realize that strategies can only be implemented with the whole hearted effort and belief of everyone involved. If implementing them violates employees' basic beliefs about their roles in the company, or the traditions that underlie the corporation's culture, they are doomed to fail.

Culture implies values, such as aggressiveness, defensiveness, or nimbleness that set a pattern for a company's activities, opinions, and actions. That pattern is instilled in employees by managers' example and passed down to succeeding generations of workers. The CEO's words alone do not produce culture; rather, his actions and those of his managers do.

A corporation's culture can be its major strength when it is consistent with its strategies. Some of the most successful companies have clearly demonstrated that fact, including:

- International Business Machines Corp., where marketing drives a service philosophy that is almost unparalleled. The company keeps a hot line open 24 hours a day, seven days a week, to service IBM products.

- International Telephone & Telegraph Corp., where financial discipline demands total dedication. To beat out the competition in a merger, an executive once called former Chairman Harold S. Geneen at 3 A.M. to get his approval.

- Digital Equipment Corp., where an emphasis on innovation creates freedom with responsibility. Employees can set their own hours and working style, but they are expected to articulate and support their activities with evidence of progress.

- Delta Air Lines Inc., where a focus on customer service produces a high degree of teamwork. Employees will substitute in other jobs to keep planes flying and baggage moving.

- Atlantic Richfield Co., where an emphasis on entrepreneurship encourages action. Operating men have the autonomy to bid on promising fields without hierarchical approval.

But a culture that prevents a company from meeting competitive threats, or from adapting to changing economic or social environments, can lead to the company's stagnation and ultimate demise unless it makes a conscious effort to change. One that did make this effort is PepsiCo Inc., where the cultural emphasis has been systematically changed over the past two decades from passivity to aggressiveness.

Once the company was content in its number 2 spot, offering Pepsi as a cheaper alternative to Coca-Cola. But today, a new employee at PepsiCo quickly learns that beating the competition, whether outside or inside the company, is the surest path to success. In its soft-drink operation, for example, Pepsi's marketers now take on Coke directly, asking consumers to compare the taste of the two colas. That direct confrontation is reflected inside the company as well. Managers are pitted against each other to grab more market share, to work harder, and to wring more profits out of their businesses. Because winning is the key value at Pepsi, losing has its penalties. Consistent runners-up find their jobs gone. Employees know they must win merely to stay in place — and must devastate the competition to get ahead.

But the aggressive competitor who succeeds at Pepsi would be sorely out of place at J. C. Penney Co., where a quick victory is far less important than building long-term loyalty. Indeed, a Penney store manager once was severely rebuked by the company's president for making too much profit. That was considered unfair to customers, whose trust Penney seeks to win. The business style set by the company's founder — which one competitor describes as avoiding "taking unfair advantage of anyone the company did business with" — still prevails today. Customers know they can return merchandise with no questions asked; suppliers know that Penney will not haggle over terms; and employees are comfortable in their jobs, knowing that Penney will avoid layoffs at all costs and will find easier jobs for those who cannot handle more demanding ones. Not surprisingly, Penney's average executive tenure is 33 years while Pepsi's is 10.

These vastly different methods of doing business are but two examples of corporate culture. People who work at Pepsi and Penney sense that the corporate values are the yardstick by which they will be measured. Just as tribal cultures have totems and taboos that dictate how each member will act toward fellow members and outsiders, so does a corporation's culture influence employees' actions toward customers, competitors, suppliers, and one another. Sometimes the rules are written out. More often they are tacit. Most often, they are laid down by a strong founder and hardened by success into custom.

"Culture gives people a sense of how to behave and what they ought to be doing," explains Howard M. Schwartz, vice-president of Management Analysis Center Inc., a Cambridge (Mass.) consulting firm that just completed a study of corporate culture. Indeed, so firmly are certain values entrenched in a company's behavior that predictable responses can be counted on not only by its employees but by its competitors. "How will our competitors behave?" is a stock question that strategic planners ask when contemplating a new move. The answers come from assessing competitors' time-honored priorities, their reactions to competition, and their ability to change course.

Because a company's culture is so pervasive, changing it becomes one of the most difficult tasks that any chief executive can undertake. Just as a primitive tribe's survival depended on its ability to react to danger, and to alter its way of life when necessary, so must corporations, faced with changing economic, social, and political climates, sometimes radically change their methods of operating. What stands in the way is not only the "relative immutability of culture," as the MAC study points out, but also the fact that few executives consciously recognize what their company's culture is and how it manifests itself. The concept of culture, says Stanley M. Davis, professor of organization behavior at Boston University and a co-author of the MAC study, is hard to understand. "It's like putting your hand in a cloud," he says.

Thomas J. Peters, a principal in McKinsey & Co., cites a client who believed it was imperative to his company's survival to add a marketing effort to his manufacturing-oriented organization. Because the company had no experts in marketing, it wanted to hire some. Consultants pointed out that this strategy would fail because all of the issues raised at company meetings concerned cost-cutting and production — never competition or customers. Rewards were built into achieving efficiencies in the first category, while none were built into understanding the second. Ultimately, the CEO recognized that he had to educate himself and his staff so thoroughly in marketing that he could build his own in-house team.

Similarly, American Telephone & Telegraph Co. is now trying to alter its service-oriented operation to give equal weight to marketing. Past attempts to do so ignored the culture and failed. For example, in 1961, AT&T set up a school to teach managers to coordinate the design and manufacture of data products for customized sales. But when managers completed the course, they found that the traditional way of operating — making noncustomized mass sales — were what counted in the company. They were given neither the time to analyze individual customers' needs nor rewards commensurate with such efforts. The result was that 85 per cent of the graduates quit, and AT&T disbanded the school.

AT&T prides itself on its service operation, and with good reason. It provides the most efficient and broadest telephone system in the world, and it reacts to disaster with a speed unknown anywhere else. In 1975, for example, a fire swept through a switching center in lower Manhattan, knocking out service to 170,000 telephones. AT&T rallied 4,000 employees and shipped in 3,000 tons of equipment to restore full service in just 22 days — a task that could have taken a lesser company more than a year.

But costs for AT&T's service had been readily passed to customers through rate increases granted by public service commissions. Keeping costs down was thus never a major consideration. Now, however, since the Federal Communications Commission has decided to allow other companies to sell products in AT&T's once-captive markets, AT&T must change the orientation of its one million employees. In numbers alone, such a change is unprecedented in corporate history. Still, to survive in its new environment, Bell must alter its plans, strategies, and employee expectations of what the company wants from them, as well as their belief in the security of their jobs and old way of doing business.

To make the changes, Bell has analyzed its new requirements in exquisite detail that fills thousands of pages. It acknowledges its lack of skills in certain crucial areas: marketing, cost control, and administrative ability to deal with change. The company has rewarded managers who administered set policites by the book; today it is promoting innovators with advanced degrees in business administration. Once it measured service representatives by the speed with which they responded to calls; today they are measured by the number of problems they solve.

AT&T'S NEW ROLE MODEL
Instead of its traditional policy of promoting from within, some new role models were hired from outside the company. Archie J. McGill, a former executive of International Business Machines Corp., was made vice-president of business marketing, for example. McGill is described by associates as an innovator who is the antithesis of the traditional "Bell-shaped man" because of his "combative, adversarial style." Just as IBM's slogan, "Think," encouraged its employees to be problem-solvers, McGill is hammering a new

slogan, "I make the difference," into each of his marketers, encouraging them to become entrepreneurs. That idea is reinforced by incentives that pit sales-people against each other for bonuses, a system unknown at Bell before.

Even so, the changes are slow. Learning to become solution-sellers has produced "a tremendous amount of confusion" among Bell marketing people, reports one large corporate customer. For example, AT&T is "absolutely trapped" if a customer requests an extra editing part for its standard teletype system, he says. "If you want something they don't have, they tend to solve the problem by saying, 'Let's go out for a drink'."

Even McGill concedes that "anytime you have an orientation toward consulting [past practices] as opposed to being adaptive to a situation, change doesn't happen overnight." Bell's director of planning, W. Brooke Tunstall, estimates that it will take another three to five years to attain an 85 per cent change in the company's orientation. Still, he insists, there has already been "a definite change in mindset at the upper levels." The arguments heard around the company now concern the pace of change rather than its scope. Says Tunstall, "I haven't run into anyone who doesn't understand why the changes are needed."

The AT&T example clearly demonstrates the need for a company to examine its existing culture in depth and to acknowledge the reasons for revolutionary change, if changes must be made. As AT&T learned from its earlier attempt to sell specialized services, change cannot be implemented merely by sending people to school. Nor can it be made by hiring new staff, by acquiring new businesses, by changing the name of the company, or by redefining its business. Even exhortations by the chief executive to operate differently will not succeed unless they are backed up by a changed structure, new role models, new incentive systems, and new rewards and punishments built into operations.

A chief executive, for example, who demands innovative new products from his staff, but who leaves in place a hierarchy that can smother a good new idea at its first airing, is unlikely to get what he wants. In contrast, an unwritten rule at 3M Co., says one manager, is, "Never be responsible for killing an idea." Similarly, if a CEO's staff knows that his first priority is consistent earnings growth, it will be unlikely to present him with any new product or service idea, no matter how great its potential, if it requires a long incubation period and a drag on earnings before it reaches fruition. At Pillsbury Co., for example, managers are afraid to suggest ideas for products that might require considerable research and development because they know that Chairman William H. Spoor is obsessed with improving short-term financial results, sources say.

THE REAL PRIORITIES
One element is certain: Employees cannot be fooled. They understand the real priorities in the corporation. At the first inconsistency they will become confused, then reluctant to change, and finally intransigent. Indeed, consistency in every aspect of a culture is essential to its success, as PepsiCo's transformation into an archrival of Coke shows.

For decades, Coke's unchallenged position in the market was so complete that the brand name Coke became synonymous with cola drinks. It attained this distinction under Robert W. Woodruff, who served as chief executive for 32 years and is still chairman of the company's finance committe at age ninety. Woodruff has an "almost messianic drive to get Coca-Cola [drunk] all over the world," says Harvey Z. Yazijian, co-author of the forthcoming book, *The Cola Wars*. So successful was Coke in accomplishing this under Woodruff — and later, J. Paul Austin, who will retire in March as CEO — that Coca-Cola became known as "America's second State Dept." Its trademark became a symbol of American life itself.

"A real problem in the past," say Yazijian, "was that they had a lot of deadwood" among employees. Nevertheless, Coke's marketing and advertising were extremely effective in expanding consumption of the product. But the lack of serious competition and the company's relative isolation in its home town of Atlanta allowed it to become "fat, dumb, and happy," according to one consultant. Coke executives are known to be extremely loyal to the company and circumspect to the point of secrecy in their dealings with the outside world.

In the mid-1950s, Pepsi, once a sleepy New York-based bottler with a lame slogan, "Twice as much for a nickel, too," began to develop into a serious threat under the leadership of Chairman Alfred N. Steele. The movement gathered momentum, and by the early 1970s the company had become a ferocious competitor under Chairman Donald M. Kendall and President Andrall E. Pearson, a former director of McKinsey. The culture that these two executives determined to create was based on the goal of becoming the number 1 marketer of soft drinks.

Severe pressure was put on managers to show continual improvement in market share, product volume, and profits. "Careers ride on tenths of a market share point," says John Sculley, vice-president and head of domestic beverage operations. This atmosphere prevades the company's nonbeverage units as well. "Everyone knows that if the results aren't there, you had better have your resume up to date," says a former snack food manager.

To keep everyone on their toes, a "creative tension" is continually nurtured among departments at Pepsi, says another former executive. The staff is kept lean and managers are moved to new jobs constantly, which results in people working long hours and engaging in political maneuvering "just to keep their jobs from being reorganized out from under them," says a headhunter.

Kendall himself sets a constant example. He once resorted to using a snowmobile to get to work in a blizzard, demonstrating the ingenuity and dedication to work he expects from his staff. This type of pressure has pushed many managers out. But a recent company survey shows that others thrive under such conditions. "Most of our guys are having fun," Pearson insists. They are the kind of people, elaborates Sculley, who "would rather be in the Marines than in the Army."

Like Marines, Pepsi executives are expected to be physically fit as well as mentally alert: Pepsi employs four physical-fitness instructors at its headquarters, and a former executive says it is an unwritten rule that to get ahead in the company a manager must stay in shape. The company encourages one-on-one sports as well as interdepartmental competition in such games as soccer and basketball. In company team contests or business dealings, says Sculley, "the more competitive it becomes, the more we enjoy it." In such a culture, less competitive managers are deliberately weeded out. Even suppliers notice a difference today. "They are smart, sharp negotiators who take advantage of all opportunities," says one.

While Pepsi steadily gained market share in the 1970s, Coke was reluctant to admit that a threat existed, Yazijian says. Pepsi now has bested Coke in the domestic take-home market, and it is mounting a challenge overseas. At the moment odds are in favor of Coke, which sells one-third of the world's soft drinks and has had Western Europe locked up for years. But Pepsi has been making inroads: Besides monopolizing the Soviet market, it has dominated the Arab Middle East every since Coke was ousted in 1967, when it granted a bottling franchise in Israel. Still, Coke showed that it was not giving up. It cornered a potentially vast new market — China.

With Pepsi gaining domestic market share faster than Coke — last year it gained 7.5 per cent vs. Coke's 5 per cent — observers believe that Coke will turn more to foreign sales or food sales for growth. Roberto C. Goizueta, who will be Coke's next chairman, will not reveal Coke's strategy. But one tactic the company has already used is hiring away some of Pepsi's "tigers." Coke has lured Donald Breen Jr., who played a major role in developing the "Pepsi Challenge" — the consumer taste test — as well as five other marketing and sales executives associated with Pepsi. Pepsi won its court battle to prevent Breen from revealing confidential information over the next 12 months. But the company's current culture is unlikely to build loyalty. Pepsi may well have to examine the dangers of cultivating ruthlessness in its managers, say former executives.

Quite a different problem faces J.C. Penney today. Its well-entrenched culture, laid down by founder James Cash Penney in a seven-point codification of the company's guiding principles, called "The Penney Idea," (see page 245) has brought it tremendous loyalty from its staff but lower profits recently. Its introduction of fashionable apparel has been only partially successful, because customers identify it with nonfashionable staples, such as children's clothes, work clothes, and hardware. It has also been outpaced in the low end of the market by aggressive discounters, such as K mart Corp., which knocked Penney out of the number 2 retailer's spot in 1976 and which has been gaining market share at Penney's expense ever since.

Penney's is proud that two national magazines cited it as one of the 10 best places to work in the nation, a claim that is borne out by employees. "Everyone is treated as an individual," notes one former executive. Another praises the company's "bona fide participative" decision-making process, and adds that Penney has "an openness in the organization that many large companies don't seem to achieve."

But Penney's paternalistic attitude toward its work force has meant that it always tries to find new jobs for marginally competent employees rather than firing them, says Stephen Temlock, manager of human resource strategy development. He concedes that some workers "expect us to be papa and mama, and aren't motivated enough to help themselves." The corollary of that, he admits, is that the company sometimes fails to reward outstanding performers enough.

Penney's entrenched culture makes any change slow, Temlock adds, but he insists that this solidity helps to maintain a balance between "an out-and-out aggressive environment and a human environment." Penney Chairman Donald V. Seibert believes that the company's problems have more to do with the retailing industry's endemic cyclicality than with company culture. Although he admits that he worries sometimes that the company is too in-bred, he notes that it has brought in different types of people in the last several years as it entered new businesses, such as catalog sales and insurance.

Seibert adds that the company firmly believes that the principles of "The Penney Idea" will be relevant no matter how much the economic environment changes. "You can't say that there's a good way to modernize integrity," he emphasizes.

Seibert may be right. One competitor notes that the aggressive new-comers in retailing have profited from older retailers' mistakes, and thus have found shortcuts to growth. But, says this source, "the shortcuts are limited, and the newcomers' staying power has yet to be proven." Still, if the new threat continues, Penney's pace must speed up, and it must soon act more flexibly to protect itself; it may even have to abandon some of the customs that have grown up around its humanistic principles.

Another gentlemanly company found that it had to do just that to re-gain its leading position in banking. Chase Manhattan Bank had cruised along comfortably for years, leaning on the aristocratic image of its chairman, David Rockefeller. In the mid-1970s, however, Chase was jolted out of its lethargy by a sharp skid in earnings and a return on assets that plunged as low as 0.24 per cent in 1976. Its real estate portfolio was loaded with questionable and sour loans, and its commercial lending department's reputation had been severely tarnished because high turnover of its lending officers and the re-sulting inexperience of those who replaced them made the bank less respon-sive to customers. Some embarrassing questions about Chase's basic manage-ment practices began to be raised.

Rockefeller and a group of top executives, including Willard C. Butcher, now chief executive and chairman-elect, decided that the fault lay with a culture that rewarded people more for appearance than performance and that produced inbreeding and a smugness that made the bank loath to grapple with competitors. The typical Chase executive in those days was a well-groomed functionary who did not drive himself hard or set high stan-dards for his own performance, banking analysts remember.

The first step toward change, Chase executives felt, was for the bank to define what it wanted to be. Early in 1977 it drew up a three-page mission statement that outlined the company's business mix. "We will only do those things we can do extremely well and with the highest level of integrity," the statement said. For Chase, this meant taking a hard look at some un-profitable parts of its business. Subsequently, it closed some 50 low-volume

Evidence of Cultural Change in a Better Bottom Line

	1978	1979
	Millions of dollars	
Assets	$45,638	$64,708
Deposits	33,808	44,725
Loans	30,683	40,170
Interest income	2,711	5,638
Net chargeoffs for bad loans	269	93
Net Income	116	303

Data Chase Manhattan Corp. annual report

Every store has its rules, so do we. We call it The Penney Idea.

Adopted 1913

▶◀ **1** ▶◀
To serve the public, as nearly as we can, to its complete satisfaction.

▶◀ **2** ▶◀
To expect for the service we render a fair remuneration and not all the profit the traffic will bear.

▶◀ **3** ▶◀
To do all in our power to pack the customer's dollar full of value, quality and satisfaction.

▶◀ **4** ▶◀
To continue to train ourselves and our associates so that the service we give will be more and more intelligently performed.

▶◀ **5** ▶◀
To improve constantly the human factor in our business.

▶◀ **6** ▶◀
To reward men and women in our organization through participation in what the business produces.

▶◀ **7** ▶◀
To test our every policy, method and act in this wise: "Does it square with what is right and just?"

75 years ago, we decided that the only way we'd run our business was by doing what's right. For our customers. And for the communities we live in. In our stores it means offering the best merchandise and services at the fairest possible prices. In our home towns, it means giving what we can, when we can, on both corporate and personal levels. Ever since the first JCPenney opened in 1902, we've believed that doing what's right is good business.

domestic branches in New York, and it began to turn away questionable loan business that it had accepted before.

The mission statement also spelled out specific targets for financial goals, such as return on equity and assets and debt-to-capital ratio. At the start employees doubted that the company could meet these goals; one, for example, was a return on assets of 0.55 per cent to 0.65 per cent, more than double the 1976 figure.

Chase began a major effort to step up communications between top management and the rest of the staff. This was a departure from the old days, when decisions were simply handed down from the seventeenth-floor executive suite, says one former manager. The participation of all employees created a sense of "ownership" of the program by all, something consultant Robert F. Allen, president of the Human Resources Institute in Morristown, N.J., believes is essential to any long-lasting change.

Like AT&T, Chase promoted new role models, such as Richard J. Boyle, now a senior vice-president, who took over the bank's troubled real estate operations at age thirty-two. Boyle, described as a "workaholic" with strong opinions and a willingness to make hard decisions, such as writing off floundering projects rather than carrying them on the company's books, is the antithesis of the old-style Chase banker, analysts say. To run commercial lending, the bank lured back James H. Carey, who had left Chase for Hambros Bank. "They put absolutely brilliant people in problem areas," remarks John J. Mason, banking analyst at Shearson Loeb Rhoades Inc.

REWARDS FOR PERFORMERS

But tradition suffered: One third of the bank's top executives were replaced by outsiders. Salaries and incentive payments were overhauled to provide greater rewards for top performers. And an advanced management course was started for promising young managers. The culture has been altered from its emphasis on style to a focus on performance. And now that employees' expectations of the company have changed, the new order is likely to prevail. But even Butcher, although pleased with the improvement, warns, "The danger is always that you become complacent."

Chase was able to effect the change in its culture under the aegis of its reigning leaders, Rockefeller and Butcher. But some companies find that the only way to solve problems is to bring in a new chief who can implement sweeping change. Yet even a new strongman can run up against a wall unless he understands the company's existing culture.

Dennis C. Stanfill, a corporate finance specialist, ran into just such problems when he took over as chief executive in 1971 at Twentieth Century-Fox Film Corp. Stanfill's aim was to balance the risks of the motion picture business with steady earnings from other leisure-time businesses, which he began acquiring. But he also insisted on running all of Fox's businesses, including the film operation, on an equal basis by keeping the corporate purse strings pulled tight — and in his hands.

What Stanfill overlooked was that creative people require a different kind of managing than do typical business employees. While the latter group can usually be motivated by using the carrot-and-stick approach, creative people are self-motivated. They will work as hard as needed to perform as perfectly as they can, because they identify their work not with the company but with themselves. What they want from their patron-managers, however, is applause and rewards for a good job, and protection when they bomb.

Stanfill violated those expectations when he refused to give Alan Ladd, Jr., president of the film group, control over bonuses for his staff, which had produced such hits as *Star Wars*. From Stanfill's point of view, the decision was sound: In just three years he had erased a $125 million bank debt and brought the company into the black after it had been in default on its loans. He believed the traditional extravagances of the film company would keep the corporation on a shaky foundation. Indeed, he says, he wants "to keep the balance between show and business."

NOT A 'BROKERAGE'

But the film company's response was predictable. Ladd quit to start his own operation, taking several key people with him. "In my opinion, Stanfill doesn't understand what motivates creative people," says Ladd. "You don't run a film business like a brokerage house."

Fox's directors quickly stepped in and demanded that Stanfill find a "name" replacement for Ladd. Stanfill has since picked Alan J. Hirschfield, who had been laid off by Columbia Pictures Industries Inc. and who has been praised by the industry for adding a creative spark to Fox this past year. But Stanfill now must make financial decisions jointly with Hirschfield.

Whether Stanfill will ever be comfortable in such a high-risk business remains questionable. One film industry analyst thinks not. He says: "Stanfill has never felt comfortable running an entertainment company. He is down-side-risk-oriented on motion pictures, and didn't know why Ladd was so successful." If that is true, Stanfill could be on a collision course with Fox's implicit culture.

Stanfill may have recognized that the strategy he was imposing on Fox's film business, which produces 63 per cent of the corporation's pretax operating earnings, violated its culture. But he obviously believed that it was necessary for the company's survival. He has not, however, changed Fox's culture. As more and more chief executives recognize the need for long-range strategies, they will have to consider the effects of these strategies on their companies. It may well be that CEOs must then decide whether their strategies must change to fit their companies' culture or the cultures must change to assure survival.

Questions for Discussion

1. The article points out the difficulties experienced by several companies in implementing major changes deemed necessary by top management. What were some of the apparent sources of resistance to these changes?

2. In the instances where the major change efforts were successful, how were the various sets of resistance factors overcome?

3. Why is the term *culture* used to describe the complex sets of factors and values by which an organization runs?

INCIDENT

ENGINEERING CHANGE

One element common to each manager's functions is that, in doing his or her job, decisions must be made constantly. And any decision typically means a change. Because change is usually threatening to those directly affected, the manager must recognize the problems involved in implementing changes if unpleasant surprises are not to occur. A manager must be able to analyze and prepare for change. This exercise shows what can happen when the effects of change aren't taken into account.

"I just don't understand it," Harry shook his head slowly, bewildered. "My micromotion studies and work analyses were all conclusive that production would increase by better than 20 per cent. . . . instead it went *down* by 12 per cent. . . . Most of all, though, I'm sorry that I let you down, Charlie. After all, you gave me the opportunity to try my hand on a project. It's not often that a brand-new industrial engineer can do that and I blew it."

Charlie patted Harry on the shoulder soothingly. "Don't sweat it, kid. Look, the only real way to learn practical stuff is by trying it out and seeing if it works. Theory's fine, but a lot of the time what the textbooks tell you just doesn't work." Harry looked up in surprise, and Charlie continued, "Don't get me wrong, now . . . the big thing is just that things are never as simple in real life as they are in books. Take your production project, for example. Tell me how you went about it."

"Well, you know about my analysis; it's all in the report I turned in to you before you gave the go-ahead." Charlie nodded. "Then I took my stop watch and data sheets and went into the production area. All five of the three-man teams were at work — if you call it work, laughing and talking and carrying on. I asked the foreman to pull one of the teams off duty to test out my ideas; I took them over into the empty shed and told them that they were to learn a new production setup that would be easier and less fatiguing and that would increase production and, therefore, their pay. (As you know, they're paid on the basis of the team's production.)

"I showed them the new procedures and workplace layouts, then let them get used to it before timing them. You know, they should have been happy as larks — here they worked less hard than before but were able to make more money. I timed them in their new procedures for two weeks. Do you know that the *best* they did was a production rate 12 per cent lower than the old way? I couldn't believe it. My figures all checked, though.

"Paying each worker for his own production should have encouraged each one to put out more. And getting them out of each other's way by spacing their work stations five feet apart and connecting them with a conveyor belt should have increased efficiency, too. So why didn't it?"

"Hmmmm," said Charlie.

Questions for Discussion

1. Why didn't Harry's proposal seem to work out in practice?

2. If you think resistance to change occurred in this incident, identify the causes of such resistance.

3. With a force-field analysis, identify the forces operating on Harry's situation with his proposal.

4. What should have Harry done?

EXERCISE

EVERYBODY INTO THE POOL?

The effective manager soon learns to evaluate the impact of any proposed change on all interested parties. The manager knows that planned results and the actual results are sometimes quite far apart. This exercise presents a situation in which you are to analyze the proposed change and make a recommendation.

You are a director of management services for a rapidly expanding corporation. Your duties, generally, are involved with providing and managing facilities and support for the corporate headquarters.

The company has grown over the past few years; more and more executives have been added to oversee or provide technical (staff) assistance for the company's wide diversity of operations.

On several of your recent tours of the headquarters, it has come to your attention that the secretaries seem to have less and less to do; at least, they are actively working relatively rarely. This is, you feel, probably due to the increased specialization that has taken place among the new executives; each is responsible for much narrower activities and therefore has less to keep a secretary busy all the time. Of course, each executive (and his or her secretary) still has a few peaks of frantic activity that occur randomly throughout the year.

After more study, you conclude that — on the average — each secretary is actually working only 40 per cent of the time. It occurs to you that the secretaries would be much more efficiently used if they were assigned to a central secretarial pool. Any executive who had secretarial work could merely call for a secretary who, after completing the task, would return to the pool for reassignment. On other tasks, like typing of reports, the work could be routed to report typists (much cheaper than multiskilled secretaries).

The personnel savings, you figure, could be as much as 50 per cent.

FOR THE STUDENT
1. Evaluate the impact of this proposed change on secretaries and on executives. (A force-field analysis may be helpful.)

2. Based on your analysis in (1), would you recommend making the change from personal to pool assignment of secretaries? Discuss your answer.

CASE

MOON'S MARKETS

After months of hearing rumors and speculating on their validity, the announcement had finally been made. Moon's Markets, a local five-store grocery chain, had been bought out by a national food chain.

Al Bossler, the manager of store 1, had called all of the personnel together and informed them of the sale. To soften the blow, a representative of the national chain was on hand to explain the immediate implications of the change. He told them of an expansion of the store's area, an addition of an in-store bakery, and the replacement of the old cash registers with electronic check-out equipment that would save time and facilitate inventory control.

Then came the shocker. The manager, Al, was being replaced immediately. He would go off to another store in the national chain while another person would come in to supervise the changeover.

John, Howard, and Paul, the members of the store's stock crew, listened to the announcements in stunned silence. Despite the rumors, none of them had actually believed that there would be a sale. After all, what did a large national chain want with five small, neighborhood-oriented stores?

Immediately following the announcement, the trio retired to Shaft's, the corner bar, to discuss what they'd heard.

"You know," John started, "I didn't really believe they'd do it, much as I like the idea. Maybe now we'll move into the twentieth century around here."

"Shut up, will you?" replied Paul. "You act as if you believed all that stuff. Pay a little more attention to what you see and believe a little less the lines people feed you."

"What the heck are you talking about?"

"Look, he said a lot of nice things about expanding and improving the place, didn't he? But what's the only change that's going to take place immediately? They're going to ship Al out and bring in a new manager; a 'company man.' And you better believe before they sink all kinds of money into new equipment and building costs, they're going to trim all the fat they can!"

"So what? We don't have anything to worry about. The three of us are the only stockmen that place has. We're the ones that know the merchandise, the customers, and the setup. They're not about to get rid of us. As for transferring Al, that's the best move they could've made. If they're really going to modernize the place, the last thing we need is some wishy-washy, old-fashioned manager fumbling around trying to figure out which way's up. Besides, the new guy is going to need some help getting to know the new store. Maybe this is our chance to finally get some things straightened out."

"Hey, come on! We haven't done so bad under Al. He doesn't hassle us much, and we don't exactly kill ourselves getting the work done. This new guy is going to clamp down soon and hard and you know it. Suppose they do expand and add on that bakery, and we're still the only three stockmen. We're going to have to work our cans off just to keep even, and you know our new 'company man' isn't going to fall for the same old lines Al used to."

"Wait a minute, both of you," Howard said. "I've been around a lot longer than either of you, and I'll probably still be here when you've gone. Al has been the third manager I've worked for in that store and they've all had their own way of running things. None of them have been any better or any worse than any other, they've all just been different. The only way to survive in that place is to adjust to what each man wants. Just make him happy. Maybe he'll be a nice guy; maybe he'll be a real problem. Either way we're going to have to live with it. We'll just take it easy and do our jobs and see what happens. Speaking of which, tomorrow morning is going to come awful early. Come on, let's finish our beers and get out of here."

Question for Discussion

Discuss the reasons for the different reactions shown to the change.

CASE

_____

INTRODUCING CHANGE REGIMENTALLY

FRANCE, 1806

Colonel Daubigny laid the dispatch on the table. "Merci, Lieutenant D'Haut-pol, tell the general that I shall forward my plan to him within a fortnight."

As the lieutenant saluted and left the room, Daubigny looked out through the sunlit window and considered the situation. He had been expecting this ever since his arrival a week ago, but he had been hoping that he would not be forced to act quite so soon. He picked up the dispatch and read the message again:

17 Juli, 1806

Mon Colonel,

As you know, the recent performance of your new command, the 13me Regiment de Ligne, has been very upsetting to the Emperor. The failure of the regiment to arrive at the bridge at Saalfeld in support of the 3rd Corps was very costly to that unit, and was the cause of your being appointed to the command of the regiment. The Emperor insists that the regiment's continued use of the old revolutionary drill and supply techniques is in part responsible and desires you to adopt the new methods being standardized throughout the Grand Armèe. Because the effective performance of the regiment is very important to the Emperor's plans, he desires you to submit your plan for bringing about these changes by the end of the month.

Signed,

La Houssaye
General de la division

Daubigny was fully aware of the regiment's recent performance, but he also knew that a major cause of the problem was the regiment's current physical condition. It had been campaigning steadily since the earliest days of spring, had taken a severe beating in a couple of engagements, and was now physically and mentally worn down. The regiment was well understrength, morale was low, and it had lost confidence in itself. In this condition, the use of the old methods only compounded the problems because the rest of the army say them as "different."

He was concerned that the standard army remedy of more and tighter discipline in order to improve performance would actually have the opposite effect. Although it was clear that something had to be done — and quickly — any major changes might be resisted so much and be so disruptive that the unit would lose all effectiveness.

Ever since the moment of his arrival he had been taking the measure of the regiment, attempting to get a feel for the true state of affairs and to assess the impact that any changes he might make would have. He had talked to many of the men and had observed their activities. He felt that they were aware of their problems and that the methods they used were outmoded and not used in the rest of the army. There was also a general feeling of apprehensiveness throughout the regiment over what might happen as a result of recent events. They thought that they might be punished for events over which they had no control.

Daubigny had also talked to each of the senior officers and evaluated them as follows:

Major Boudet

The major had risen to his rank very quickly. He was the son of a peasant farmer and served as an example to many of the younger officers, who were not of the nobility and who also aspired to higher ranks. He had performed well while he had been with the regiment and displayed no strong interest in matters of administration or drill. He seemed sure of his abilities and was anxious to get back to effective campaigning.

Chef de bataillon Dumonceau

From the old nobility, Dumonceau had been with the army for 35 years, somehow surviving all of the political upheavals during that time. He had been with the regiment a long time and was an influential figure within the unit's informal structure. He had been the operations and training officer for several years. He was very conservative, still wearing his hair braided in the old revolutionary fashion. His dislike of the "Bonapartists" was known, and he deplored the way Napoleon's armies "lived off the land" as they traveled, instead of maintaining proper supply trains and depots.

Chef de bataillon Champeaux

Champeaux had only joined the regiment a month previously as a replacement for his predecessor who was killed in one of the early engagements of the campaign. He felt no stigma from the recent events, being too new to the regiment to have had much influence on its recent activities. He had served with Napoleon in Italy and typified the dashing young officer who found glory and ready promotion in Napoleon's armies.

Chef de bataillon Monnier

Like Dumonceau, Monnier had been with the regiment a long time. Although his service record was excellent, he seemed to have reached a dead end several years ago. He showed no interest in advancing, even though he had held his present rank for nearly 10 years. He seemed to be very satisfied with his role and function within the unit. Daubigny thought that he seemed tense and anxious, as though he feared that the recent events would reflect unfavorably on him and bring some change to his standing within the regiment.

APPENDIX

Rank equivalents

French	*English*
Colonel	Colonel
Major	Lieutenant Colonel
Chef de bataillon	Major
Capitaine	Captain
Lieutenant	Lieutenant
Sergent-major	Sergeant-Major
Sergent	Sergeant

Questions for Discussion

1. How could Colonel Daubigny's carring out the changes required affect each of his officers? Would each welcome — or resist — the change?

2. How would you recommend that Daubigny implement the change?

ANSWERS TO SELF-REVIEW QUESTIONS, CHAPTER 16

Matching

A-6, B-3, C-1, D-2, E-4, F-5, G-8

True–False

1-T, 2-F, 3-F, 4-T, 5-T, 6-F, 7-T, 8-T, 9-F, 10-T, 11-F, 12-F, 13-T, 14-F, 15-F.

Multiple Choice

1-B, 2-D, 3-B, 4-E, 5-B.

Completion

1. Systems. 2. Attitudes. 3. X . . . interpreted (perceived) . . . experiences. 4. Self-actualization. 5. Trust . . . earned. 6. Order . . . originality. 7. Unfreezing . . . changing . . . Refreezing.

Chapter 17

Managing Production and Operations

CHAPTER OBJECTIVES

1. To examine the stages by which production and operations processes are refined and improved

2. To show how managerial expertise is an important element in creating utility and value

SELF-REVIEW QUESTIONS

Matching

A. breaking down a raw material into one or more usable products

_____ 1. analysis

B. making something of value that did not exist before

_____ 2. assembling

C. the product moves constantly from one production stage to another

_____ 3. continuous process

D. charting the various phases of the project through the required preparations and assemblies

_____ 4. fabricating

E. method most often used to provide relative assurance that products meet quality standards

_____ 5. form utility

F. changing new materials to create something that did not exist before

_____ 6. sampling

G. creating utility by putting together things to form a product

_____ 7. scheduling

True–False

T F 1. Successful production and operations managers can save consumers money.

T F 2. Mass production volume has led to emphasis on continual production refinements no matter how small.

T F 3. The successful operations manager is able to create the best possible working manufacturing process before the expense of setting it up is incurred.

T F 4. The most vital information for improving the production process can come from production workers.

T F 5. Every successful business creates utility.

T F 6. Very few people in our society have had the opportunity to have a production experience.

T F 7. Most companies are initially located in the vicinity where the founder lived.

T F 8. The first step in determining where to build a plant is to consider the tax incentives offered by a proposed location.

T F 9. The wise operations manager does not let community attitudes affect the economics of the decision to locate a plant in a particular place.

T F 10. A good rule-of-thumb for plant location is to avoid building in an area in which a competitor is located.

T F 11. The attractiveness of the proposed plant area is a minor consideration in the location decision process, especially in comparison to availability of transportation, power, and water.

T F 12. Actual performance of the work is far less critical and demanding than designing the best possible layout of the work.

T F 13. The "continuous process" plant requires three eight-hour work shifts per workday.

T F 14. Products made under the continuous process are identical to each other, a major benefit of this process.

T F 15. The predominant consideration in plant design is esthetics and architectural integrity.

Multiple Choice

1. Production and operations managers are rewarded for

   (a) managing to come to work on time, (b) devising ways for the firm to operate at a profit, (c) reducing the costs of producing a product, (d) supervising assembly line workers.

2. Successful production and operations managers can provide consumers
_____ .

(a) with fancier products that become obsolete more quickly, (b) superior products at top prices, (c) with products they didn't know they wanted, (d) better products at the same cost

3. In our society, for a firm to _____ it must _____ something people want at a suitable _____ .

(a) prosper . . . monopolize . . . profit, (b) survive . . . provide . . . price, (c) grow . . . create . . . location, (d) avoid prosecution . . . manufacture . . . savings

4. The elements in the production process are _____ .

(a) materials, people, machines, and money, (b) skill, management, and consumer feedback, (c) quality, promotion, and utility, (d) analysis, synthesis, fabrication, and assembly

5. Which of the following is a characteristic related to enjoyment of the production management job?

(a) attention to how the steps in a process are interrelated, (b) attention to process components, (c) attention to details, (d) all of the above

6. The factor that helps determine where to build a factory or plant is
_____ .

(a) product characteristics, (b) raw materials, (c) required worker characteristics, (d) product-customer closeness, (e) all of the above

7. In transportation, one of the least predictable and most important factors is _____ .

(a) energy costs, (b) government regulation, (c) labor supply, (d) profit margins

8. An example of continuous process production is _____ .

(a) auto assembly line, (b) bread making, (c) ship building, (d) none of the above

9. A continuous process may be laid out in the form of a _____ .

(a) U, (b) S, (c) O, (d) I, (e) all of the above

10. What are the functions of operations management?

(a) maximize, exploit, and supercede, (b) plan, route, and schedule, (c) innovate, complete, and distribute, (d) administer, make decisions, and delegate, (e) none of the above

Completion

1. _____ utility is created when materials are changed or combined in the process of making a product customers want.

2. The process of determining where to build a factory or plant is called _____ .

3. The production process in which the product moves to a certain state of completion and then must hesitate before moving into the next stage is the _____ process.

4. In _____ , the manager establishes the sequence in which events ought to happen and the flow of work.

5. The _____ chart depicts the sequence in which work must happen and the time each task is expected to take.

READING

BUSINESS REFOCUSES ON THE FACTORY FLOOR

John F. Budd Jr., an Emhart Corp. vice-president, calls it a "new pragmatism." David W. Wallace, chairman and president of Bangor Punta Corp., terms it the beginning of the "era of the manufacturing executive." Whatever the label, companies across the country are refocusing on one of the basics of business: making a better product faster and cheaper. They are recognizing that the best-conceived strategic plans or marketing analyses are useless if products are too costly to produce or too shoddy to sell. And they are putting in corporatewide programs aimed at spotting every quick and lucrative fix available to increase manufacturing productivity at the lowest cost.

Of course, cost-cutting programs are not new to well-managed companies. Indeed, most of the money-saving techniques being adopted at plants today represent concepts that have been used with success at other companies — and in some instances, at other plants within the same company. The difference, however, is that top management is pulling out all stops in its attempts to make sure that anything that works in one plant is being implemented in others and that plant managers who have reduced costs by, say, 5% do not rest on their laurels when an additional 10% in savings might be readily available.

Through the Cracks
Although the push is apparent in almost every industry, it is most dramatic in batch manufacturing, where setup times, materials flow, and the like require far more control than in continuous manufacturing. The batch plants are seeking techniques and concepts that may have slipped through the cracks in their own operations.

For example, it was not until last year that Harris Corp.'s management categorized the type of work that was needed on the 5,000-odd parts that one of its plants uses in the manufacture of newspaper presses. The categorization has allowed the company to rearrange the placement of machine tools so that whole families of parts can flow consecutively from one machine to the next. The tool realignment — a process called group technology — reduced handling time on many parts to less than 10 days from as much as 10 weeks and also enabled the plant to cut its finished-parts inventory by more than 10%.

Similarly, although electronics technology has cut costs for numerous companies, it was not until 1977 that Chesebrough-Pond's Inc. started developing in-house electronics expertise. Today it employs 20 electronics specialists, and its corporate technology group has developed specialty items such as a $160 knitted-textile scanner that can alert an operator to easily corrected but potentially troublesome defects without unnecessarily shutting down the knitting machine. The group also installed a home-grown $200 thread saver on each of the company's 2,000 sewing machines. This device, which turns a machine off when material is not in position, is saving $1,000 annually per machine.

Clearly, top managers have realized that the nuts and bolts of business afford the best opportunities for savings. They are eliciting factory workers' ideas to increase quality and efficiency. And in companies as diverse as Emhart, TRW, Kellogg, Phillips Petroleum, and Westinghouse, they are hiring corporate vice-presidents for productivity to pull all the ideas together.

New Stress

The executive suite itself is changing. According to Heidrick & Struggles Inc., executive recruiters, in 1977 only 16.5% of the chief executives of the 800 largest U.S. companies had come up mainly through manufacturing. By 1980, a look at the 1,300 largest companies showed that 27.2% of their CEOs were manufacturing men. Sums of Steven C. Wheelwright, an associate professor of manufacturing policy at Stanford University's Graduate School of Business: "Companies are saying that operations have been neglected for too long."

The neglect of the past decade not only resulted in waste but also tended to institutionalize inefficiency. For example, Pitney Bowes Inc., a nonunion company, had been basing incentive pay for its workers on their performance against some 150,000 shop-floor standards that were set just after the Korean War. By 1977 incentive payments equaled nearly 100% of payroll. PB finally decided to spend $500,000 to update the standards, with the result that incentives are down to 20% of payroll and overall productivity is up 20%.

Tales of missed opportunities because of the lack of focus on the mundane aspects of day-to-day operations are just as prevalent. For example, one General Refractories Corp. plant was using a homegrown nozzle for packaging products that cost one-third of conventional nozzles. Yet the plant manager had never told the division's other five plants about it. In late 1978 the company instituted a corporate wide productivity improvement program to make sure such ideas are disseminated. In just 14 months it has saved $15 million by applying existing cost-cutting methods to labor, materials, selling, and administration. "We had a wealth of specific ideas at all levels that had never been communicated up nor forced down from the top and thus had never been implemented," recalls John E. Hartshorn, president.

Production First

The new emphasis on cost-cutting is sometimes perceived as a threat by executives in staff functions, particularly marketing. But marketing need not be downgraded when manufacturing operations are improved. For example, Harris, which ran five plants to make newspaper presses of all sizes, now produces small presses, whatever their market, in two plants and large presses in the other three. "It was the first time we put manufacturing considerations ahead of marketing considerations," says James E. Pruitt Jr., vice-president and general manager of one of Harris' two pressmaking subsidiaries. But while the switch has involved some reorganization of reporting responsibilities, it did not change transportation costs, salesmen's duties, or any other customer related function. It simply allows Harris to select machine tools more efficiently, which Pruitt predicts will lower manufacturing costs by some 5% to 10%.

It is clearly easiest for someone from the vantage point of corporate headquarters to spot opportunities for interdivisional economies. But most top managers recognize that efficiency improvements cannot be achieved by the top staff alone. Phillips Petroleum Co., for one, has kept its new corporate productivity staff to just two people, and their main role is ensuring that line managers measure and improve productivity. "Management makes it clear through letters, bulletins, and quarterly reviews of the company's productivity status that this is important to us, but we still feel that actual improvements are the responsibility of line managers," states B. B. McDonald, corporate productivity administrator.

At General Refractories, responsibility for coordinating productivity improvement falls to Charles E. Dyer, director of operations planning and control. He, in turn, assigns responsibilities for cost improvement to managers at the plant level and sees that their ideas are disseminated from plant to plant. "If a project has a big cost savings, it comes to light pretty fast, but if savings are marginal, it is not so obvious," he explains. Because even marginal savings can mount up, "a formalized program helps," he says.

Standard Parts

Perhaps the most formal productivity-improvement program is at Westinghouse Electric Corp., which in September started staffing a new productivity center. Its main goal, according to L. J. Hudspeth, vice-president for productivity, is to standardize as many productivity improvement tools as possible across the company's 37 business units. Hudspeth is pushing for a "common data-base system" — already working in two transformer plants — that would force design engineers and manufacturing people to work with the same production criteria. Too often, manufacturing managers must waste time persuading designers to review their specifications to make them conform with the availability of parts and other manufacturing realities.

Hudspeth is also excited about the potential of a Japanese system called *kanban*, which represents a total reversal of U.S. conventional wisdom on production runs. Most U.S. plants aim for the longest, fastest run on parts, even though it may mean increasing inventory carrying costs. They pay comparatively little attention to the time costs of tooling up. *Kanban* concentrates on the other side of the equation, stressing short setup times, regardless of run length. Hudspeth notes that one Japanese auto company has designated 10 minutes as the maximum setup time. It concentrates on short production runs and has been able to cut its parts inventory to one hour. "We think in terms of weeks of inventory," Hudspeth admits.

The Westinghouse center cost $10 million. It will eventually employ 250 people and operate with an annual budget of $30 million. Much of its focus will be on potential cost savings from avant-garde technology such as robotics. But in the area of streamlining existing operations alone, it hopes to increase productivity by 50%, although Westinghouse has not targeted a specific savings figure.

Few companies are willing to mount such extensive internal efforts, and they are turning to consultants and universities for assistance. Emhart, for one, is about to announce a joint program with Worcester Polytechnic Institute to study microelectronics and robotics.

Model Building

The role of most universities, however, will be larger than simply supplying consultants. After a decade in which their focus was primarily on management science or business policy, business schools are again starting to stress nuts-and-bolts courses. "In the '60s courses tended to be descriptive, not analytical, including things like plant tours," recalls Richard R. West, dean of Dartmouth's Amos Tuck School of Business Administration. "Then the technicians took over. While the old guys would show how a company made scheduling decisions, the new approach was to build models." West is hoping to expand Tuck's operations faculty from two to four, and he notes that he is not "running into competition" from other schools for the few "practical" professors that are available.

Apparently, companies are showing enthusiasm for a new generation of "practical" MBAS. Stanford's Wheelwright notes that he has a list of 80 large companies interested in hiring graduates directly into operations, rather than into staff positions. And numerous corporate leaders agree that the "practical" side of business will probably turn into a viable route to the corporate top.

"The people who play the key roles in the 1980s and 1990s are going to be executives who have a strong manufacturing background," insists Bangor Punta's Wallace. Adds Marion S. Kellogg, vice-president for corporate consulting services at General Electric Co.: "The person who goes into either manufacturing or a combination of engineering and manufacturing is probably the person with the most exciting future."

Questions for Discussion

1. How are operations management and productivity improvement related?

2. Why is there such high interest in operations management by business today?

3. What types of skills should the operations manager possess?

EXERCISE

LOCATION

The text points out that site selection requires evaluating several alternatives on a number of important criteria. How would you evaluate the location of your college? The building in which you attend class? Evaluate the location of (A) your college, (B) your building.

(1) First identify at least six factors or criteria important to your location problem. (2) Then assign weights to each criterion based on importance. (3) Identify at least one other alternative site. (4) Evaluate the actual site and the alternative site on your criteria. (5) Which is better? Why? (6) Is there anything that could be done to improve the location of your actual site on your criteria? What?

CASE

HOME-CONSTRUCTION OPERATION*

Mass-production technology and home construction might seem to be an unlikely combination, but one major developer has found a way to link them successfully. Fox & Jacobs Construction Company, based in Dallas, Texas, is one of the nation's five largest builders and one of the fastest-growing. Its president, David Fox, Jr., took over the company in 1965 when it had built only 200 houses; for the 1978 fiscal year Fox expects to produce 8,000 houses. The company has already built a total of 26,000 houses.

The company sells well-designed, average-sized homes at prices well below the average national price and about one third the price per square foot of its competitors. While concentrating on the booming Dallas, Fort Worth, and Houston markets and relying on nonunion labor helps, a unique operational strategy distinguishes Fox & Jacobs from its competitors. The strategy Mr. Fox chose recognizes the boom-or-bust nature of the volatile housing industry and seeks a manner of operating with predictable continuity.

The company focuses on first-time buyers and young, moderate-income families. Three product lines are offered, each with about twenty different floor plans; standard features include two baths, three or four bedrooms, air conditioning, carpeting, fireplace, kitchen appliances, brick veneer, and landscaping.

*Based on Robert L. Simison, "Mass-Output Methods Help Fox & Jacobs Gain Leadership in Housing," *Wall Street Journal*, March 29, 1978, p. 1.

Cutting costs is the key to Fox & Jacobs's success. Land costs are low because undeveloped farmland is acquired that lies just outside the metropolitan markets. Quantity discounts on large orders of materials, placed well in advance of delivery dates, contribute to lower materials costs.

The single most important component in Fox & Jacobs's operational strategy is the use of mass-production technology. The usual approach is to subcontract the labor and use craft skills in custom building a house at a time, at the building site. Fox & Jacobs have the wall and roof parts and cabinets built in their own factories and employ teams of unskilled workers who are trained in narrow-scope jobs to put the pieces together to form a house. The tight scheduling of work crews and delivery of housing materials reduce expensive down time.

About 3,000 workers make up 15 crews. At work at 46 building sites, 31½ new houses are built per day. Each crew averages 44 working days per house, dramatically lower than the 90 to 120 days typical in production building.

Questions for Discussion

1. Discuss the reasons for the higher productivity gained with the Fox & Jacobs operations methods over "traditional" methods.

2. In the text, Figure 17.1 illustrates the central role of the transformation process. From the point of view of Fox & Jacobs, what are their inputs? Elements in the transformation process? Outputs? Feedback?

3. If you worked for Fox & Jacobs, what are the factors you would evaluate in selecting the next multihome building site?

4. What types of techniques would you use to chart progress on a multi-home Fox & Jacobs project? Why?

5. Discuss the role of quality control in the Fox & Jacobs system. How would you maintain quality in their system?

CASE

AN OPERATIONAL OVERSIGHT

George Montgomery threw down his pencil in disgust and cast a withering glare at his calculator. He had been going over the income statement projections made by his controller. The new two-year union contract, fuel and utility-rate increases, equipment maintenance and replacement, special local tax levies, state unemployment and worker compensation insurance payments — he just didn't see how his company could make a profit next year (or in the years after that, the thought came to him).

He smiled grimly. His business administration professors would probably have recommended raising his prices or motivating his workers or using zero-based budgeting. Something easy to raise revenues while keeping costs the same, or decreasing costs while keeping revenues up. "But it's not that simple!" he reminded himself for the tenth time. "With my marketing background and experience in finance, plus these seven years running my own company, you'd think the answer would be obvious to me. I've had my vice-presidents report on profit-improving suggestions in their areas of sales and distribution, finance and administration, production scheduling, inventory management, sales orders' contribution to profit and overhead, optimal reordering quantity and timing, and all the rest — including that study on the company's salary structure and the review of our organizational setup. It seems that we're doing about as well as we can; with our past success, we've added staff and production capacity haphazardly at best — our plant and offices look like a rabbit warren. Sometimes I need a map to find my way around! And yet the things we can improve on won't make the kind of difference that'll change red ink to black! And our competitors are breathing hard down our backs, keeping the pressure on. The union hems us in, too, so what can we do?"

He must have spoken these last words out loud, for he heard a quiet, "Anything I can help with, George?" from the open doorway to his office. Embarassed, George sat down and laughed bitterly. "I wish you could, Joan. I've tried about everything."

Joan Harrison came in and sat opposite George. George thought absently, "She's taken hold of her job a lot faster than even I'd hoped. And being plant manager is no simple task!" He cleared his head and summarized the problem as he saw it — the profit picture and an apparent lack of options to change what looked like a dismal future.

When he'd finished, Joan continued to sit there, staring at the ceiling. Finally, she said, "So that's what all the flap's been about! I've had my hands full these past few months so I didn't get the full picture. I guess you've done about everything you can do . . ." George's spirits dove. ". . . but get to the crux of the situation." George's raised eyebrows threatened his hairline.

"As I see it," she continued, "there are several things you've overlooked. No reason why you should have picked them up, because you're neither an engineer nor an operations manager. You know my training and experience in operations management, so it's fairly obvious to me that you've missed some fundamental productivity-related and cost-based considerations."

Questions for Discussion

1. What alternatives can you think of, related to operations management, that George might have missed?

2. What would you recommend George do? Lay out a plan of action for him, including criteria that may help his decision processes.

ANSWERS TO SELF-REVIEW QUESTIONS, CHAPTER 17

Matching

A-1, B-5, C-3, D-7, E-6, F-4, G-2.

True–False

1-T, 2-T, 3-F, 4-T, 5-T, 6-F, 7-T, 8-F, 9-F, 10-F, 11-F, 12-T, 13-F, 14-F, 15-F.

Multiple Choice

1-C, 2-D, 3-B, 4-D, 5-D, 6-E, 7-A, 8-A, 9-E, 10-E.

Completion

1. Form. 2. Site selection. 3. Intermittent. 4. Routing 10. Gantt.

Chapter 18

The Modern Manager's Quantitative Tool Kit

CHAPTER OBJECTIVES

1. To consider some of the newer quantitative tools of management
2. To show the ways in which quantitative tools can be applied effectively

SELF-REVIEW QUESTIONS

Matching

A. the bases of ZBB

B. insurance, interest, management salaries

C. amounts paid to produce and distribute the product

D. the steps taken by the company in trying to accomplish its goals

E. the excess of revenue over variable costs, used to defray fixed costs

F. amounts received from the sale of the product

G. packaging, delivery, sales commissions

H. the volume level where revenues equal costs

_____ 1. break-even

_____ 2. contribution to margin

_____ 3. costs

_____ 4. decision packets

_____ 5. fixed costs

_____ 6. revenues

_____ 7. strategies

_____ 8. variable costs

True–False

T F 1. Break-even analysis is comprised of five basic elements: revenues, costs, break-even point, contribution margin, and probability of earning a profit.

T F 2. Profit is the difference between variable costs and fixed costs.

T F 3. Since fixed costs are constant, they do not affect profit calculations.

T F 4. Under ZBB, various budgetary alternatives for particular tasks are compared by their effects on productivity.

T F 5. A "state of nature" must fall under the control of the manager to be included in the payoff matrix.

T F 6. A decision situation is termed "uncertain" when the manager finds the possible states of nature outside his or her control.

T F 7. A decision situation is termed risky when the expected values of all feasible alternatives are less than zero.

T F 8. A process chart uses various symbols to represent the movement of a product through various operations.

T F 9. One desirable outcome of the development of the network analysis approach to planning is that the individual employee can better understand the importance of his or her own job when it can be seen graphically as a part of the whole project.

T F 10. Using a decision tree allows the decision maker to consider the anticipated results of various alternatives before choosing one.

T F 11. A decision tree is most effective when one wishes to examine a series of decisions.

T F 12. PERT is usually more accurate than CPM on time factors.

T F 13. PERT and CPM reach their highest utilization and give the greatest benefits when used by management to monitor the production process.

T F 14. In constructing a CPM chart, three possible estimators are made for the time required to complete each activity.

T F 15. Transportation method is used to balance the costs and benefits of transporting items between various geographic locations.

Multiple Choice

1. The purpose of having a budget is to

(a) eliminate undesirable flexibility from the organization's planning, (b) harass employees, (c) eliminate undesirable inflexibility from the organization's planning, (d) give accountants something to do.

2. To reflect the impact of production volume changes on costs that are related to volume, the _____ budget is most appropriate.

   (a) volume-based, (b) deterministic, (c) break-even, (d) zero-based, (e) variable

3. Fixed costs are those costs that

   (a) do not vary, (b) do not vary up to some point, (c) are related directly to production volume, (d) none of the above.

4. ZBB stands for:

   (a) Zone of Basic Balance, (b) Zymic Bonus Basis, (c) Zero Base Budgeting, (d) Zenith of Bilateral Badinage.

5. At every level, ZBB forces managers to

   (a) continuously add to their appropriations base, (b) build an empire, (c) put expenditures in order of priority, (d) confer with their superiors.

6. Techniques of probability theory are particularly useful in

   (a) monitoring activity and decision making, (b) forecasting the future, (c) preparing budgets, (d) creative hindsight.

7. The variables in any decision consist of

   (a) strategy, state of nature, and response from the competition, (b) problem, decision maker, and consequences, (c) givens, assumptions, and alternatives, (d) none of the above.

8. Which of the following is not essential for the planner using network analysis?

   (a) a starting point, (b) a budget, (c) a definitive objective or ending point, (d) knowledge of the length of time to complete each part of the project

9. The parts of a _____ are points, paths, and courses of action.

   (a) dynamic program, (b) payoff matrix, (c) linear program, (d) decision tree

10. PERT stands for

    (a) Probabilistically Educed Ratio Testing, (b) Polaris-Established Readout Time, (c) Partial Estimation of Reduced Time, (d) none of the above.

11. If you were interested primarily in saving time on a project you'd never done before, you'd use

    (a) CPM, (b) PERT, (c) budgeting, (d) none of the above.

12. EOQ stands for

    (a) Equitable Opportunity Quota, (b) Ergonomically Estimated Quality, (c) Excess Obligation Quotient, (d) Economic Order Quantity.

Completion

1. The _____ budget is a tool that can help overcome the problem of inflexibility of budgeting.

2. By using _____ _____ analysis, one can determine the levels of production and sales needed to earn a profit.

3. Under _____ _____ _____ , planning is integrated with the budgeting process, and each manager must justify each proposed expenditure.

4. Decision _____ are formularized approaches to represent the many alternatives in any decision.

5. A _____ matrix is a chart of the relationships among alternative strategies and each of the possible states of nature or competitive responses.

6. The decision situations that occur most often are _____ , _____ , _____ , and _____ .

7. The goal of the _____ decision is to minimize the potential negative outcome.

8. The _____ chart was one of the first successful attempts at graphically portraying the work flow and the interrelationships of the components of a total job.

9. _____ _____ is a tool with which one can determine the exact point of optimum profits from a wide range of possible product and process mixes.

10. The _____ method of project control requires that the project has been done before so that data is available on the amount of time and cost of completing each step in the project.

11. The shortest time possible to complete all the essential phases of the project is given by the _____ path.

12. _____ allows the manager to find the point of balance between storing too much and ordering too much.

READING

USING MANAGEMENT SCIENCE MODELS: A CRITIQUE FOR PLANNERS

Raj Aggarwal and Inder Khera

Management science is not just an assorted set of mathematical techniques. It is much more. Webster's New International Dictionary defines management

Reprinted by permission from the January/February 1980 issue of *Managerial Planning*, pp. 12-15 and 19.

as the "judicious use of means to accomplish ends." Starting from this rather broad definition of management, we can define management science to be an aid to discharging executive responsibility using the methodology of model building based on scientific investigation and the structure of the decision problem. Management science techniques and methods can be applied by all goal seeking-organizations, small or large, profit or non-profit, private or public, local or international. Thus, it is the scientific method applied to decision making that characterizes management science. Since mathematics provides a concise, precise, and convenient language for the scientific method, it is, like in other sciences, used extensively by management scientists to formulate their models of the decision process. Management science is a systematic approach to organizational problem solving and formulation, and has an interdisciplinary focus on organizing data into information for decision making using mathematical, behavioral, and computer skills.

I. SYSTEMS VIEW OF DECISION MAKING

Adaptation in the interest of survival characterizes the activities of all living beings. Even the simplest organism can, and must, adapt to environmental changes. Man's increased effectiveness to do this, as represented by his institutions and technology, largely accounts for his dominant position among terrestrial life forms. Environmental changes cause stress in organisms leading to strains in the organism. Behavior that results in successful strain reduction is essential for the survival of the organism since unrelieved stress can build up to levels that may ultimately cause the systems to collapse. Strain reduction and adaptation are accomplished through random or purposive behavior.

In simple organisms, with little or no memory, the strain reduction takes place mostly through a process of *random* behavior. Organisms that survive over a long period of time have an increased tendency to adapt successfully. Successful adaptive behavior patterns often get coded in the organism's genetic structure and form its evolutionary memory. In more complex organisms, including man, this is supplemented by short-term and explicit neurological functions of memory, learning, and thinking. These capabilities enable man to select the most appropriate course of action, from among the various alternatives, that will enable him to adapt most efficiently. This process of deliberation characterizes the *purposive* behavior of man and his organization(s) as distinguished from the instinctive, random behavior of simpler organisms. Purposive behavior requires explicit decision making in response to environmentally and internally generated stresses. Decision making, thus, forms the very basis of our survival and successful adaptation. It is this process of "deciding upon the appropriate actions" that we are interested in. In terms of the stimulus-response model, we are interested in the act of stimulus processing that leads to a particular response. In other words, "How are decisions made?" Furthermore, the process of decision making is central to the "judicious use of means to achieve ends".

II. MANAGEMENT SCIENCE IN ORGANIZATIONS

The process of management involves making decision in response to external and internal stimuli which are interpreted in the light of the knowledge and experience of the decision maker(s). Results of implementing the decisions are evaluated in the light of the intended objectives of the decision makers. The managerial conceptualization underlying the decision-making process is characterized by the search for alternatives, data gathering, prediction of environmental variables, and value estimation and ranking of the various outcomes. Since decision makers operate within the context of an organization, the goals and objectives of the organization itself would influence the choice of a strategy. Ideally, the organizational context faced by the decision maker should be such that in pursuing his own objectives the decision maker furthers the overall goals of the organization.

The management science approach to decision making is based on the scientific method. Scientific method is based on the use of organized common sense and the powers of reason and logic to the understanding of a phenomenon. The focus of scientific method is on cause-and-effect relationships derived from objective and bias-free conclusions based on representative sampling and careful measurement. These criteria differentiate scientific method from what is normally known as intuitive behavior which is based more on subjective evaluation. Scientific method, in the form of management science, has been applied to many areas of organizational management, such as production, marketing, finance and others, often with spectacular results.

Systematic gathering of information using scientific method to discover cause-and-effect relationships in a field constitutes a theory. Thus, while theory is the body of basic and substantive knowledge in a field, a model is a particular representation, using the theory, that is designed with specific objectives in mind. The objective of management science models is to assist management in optimizing the use of available resources, subject to the human and environmental constraints.

Management science models can be classified according to their purpose or according to the technique used. Based on the purpose of a model, it can be designated as a descriptive or a decision model. Descriptive and decision models have, at various times, also been labeled as positive and normative models; systems and goal models; behavioral and optimization models.

The purpose of descriptive models is to communicate, explain, and predict. Markov process models, queuing models, and simulation models are examples of such models in management science. A unique application of simulation has been the development of management games which help illustrate the decision process via role playing. The purpose of decision models in management science is to help management evaluate the expected outcomes of alternative actions and to determine, if possible, the "most desirable" course of action. Examples of decision models in management science are pricing models, optimal allocation models, capital budgeting models, inventory level models, and others.

Based on the techniques used, management science models may be classified as verbal models, graphical models, or mathematical models.

Verbal models explain the relationships of variables in descriptive terms. Such models have been the most extensively used means of describing complex phenomena in many fields. Theories of Marx, Darwin, Freud, Weber and Adam Smith are good examples of verbal model building. Verbal models represent a minimum degree of abstraction and can, therefore, convey particular nuances and connotations that may be lost in more abstract models. Graphic models use pictorial representation of the logic or structures and processes. Such models are usually more abstract than the verbal models, and require greater clarification of the underlying concepts. However, the communicative efficiency and clarity of such models can be much greater than that of the less abstract verbal models leading to a more generalized understanding. The old adage, "A picture is worth a thousand words," amply illustrates this advantage. Management science examples of such models are logical flow diagrams illustrating the sequential steps of a computer program, network planning diagrams for project management, causal-analysis diagrams depicting cause-and-effect relationships, decision-tree diagrams and functional relationship diagrams such as the consumption function, and others.

Mathematical models represent an even higher level of abstraction and precision. Such models use the language of mathematics to describe the relationships among the selected variables. When the relationships between variables can be expressed as straight lines, the mathematical model is termed linear. Although many real life relationships are non-linear, the assumption of linearity is commonly used as a first approximation for mathematical convenience. Additionally, while most real-life decision situations involve multi-period considerations, for mathematical convenience, only single-period static models are often used. Development of multiperiod, dynamic models is, however, essential to depict many real-life phenomena more accurately. Mathematical models that account for chance or random variables are known as *stochastic* models, whereas *deterministic* models consider only exact relationships in which chance plays no role. Management science models often begin as verbal models which then evolve successively into graphic models and, ultimately, into mathematical models. This process is guided by the fact that descriptive and decision models are interdependent and complementary, in that the development of better decision models depends on more accurate descriptive models and vice versa.

While descriptive models do not involve any form of value analysis, the use of decision models necessitates a ranking of the desirability of various outcomes based on a particular set of utility functions. All decisions involve both factual analysis and value analysis. For example, the decision process underlying management science models can be depicted as follows:

1. Course of action A leads to result 1.

2. Course of action B leads to result 2.

3. Result 1 is better than 2.

4. Therefore, choose action A.

The first two statements are dependent on factual analysis, while the third statement is dependent on the decision maker's value analysis which determines his utility function. If the decision maker is behaving rationally to maximize his utility, the fourth statement follows logically from the third.

III. LIMITATIONS OF MANAGEMENT SCIENCE MODELS

Management science models are based essentially on the above decision process. However, their application to real-life situations is not without limitations. First, factual analysis is hardly ever that simple. We often talk of a specific cause having a specific effect. However, cause-and-effect relationships are usually much more complicated. A cause can have multiple effects, and an effect can be caused by multiple causes. Sometimes it is difficult even to identify causes and effects. Even if all causes and effects could be identified, it is not always possible to measure them, and sometimes only effects can be observed or measured. Thus, each course of action can have multiple results. Rational decision making would involve accounting for all of these, intended as well as unintended consequences or results.

Second, value analysis is also more complicated in practice since each of the *unintended consequences* have some utility (positive or negative) to the decision maker that would modify the utility of the intended consequence or the desired result. Actions can be compared only if the overall desirability of *all* their consequences can be measured on a single scale. Thus, the value statement can be made only if all results or consequences of our actions can be placed on a *unidimensional* and *cardinal* utility scale. This may not be possible in actual practice for all consequences of an action. Third, if the utility of more than one person has to be consulted, a way must be devised to add the utility of each consequence for each person. This can be accomplished only if we have a *universal* cardinal measure of utility. In an attempt to overcome this problem we sometimes try to measure all utility in terms of money. This is never completely possible, and our decision models, thus, must remain incomplete. In another attempt to overcome this problem, the condition of "pareto optimality" can be investigated. An action is pareto optimal if it increases at least one person's utility without decreasing anybody else's utility. Again, this condition can only rarely be found in actual practice.

Fourth, consequences and results can be compared only if all of them refer to, or occur in, a single temporal span. In other words, the temporal problem arises because the decision maker cannot completely compare consequences occurring in different time periods. To do so would involve devising appropriate trade-off functions for inter-temporal comparisons such as the concept of discount rate in capital budgeting. However, no scientific procedures have yet been developed for universally applicable functions for inter-temporal comparisons of different types of consequences. The inter-temporal trade-off functions may differ not only from one individual to the next, but also for the same individual from one time period to another. Fifth, all the consequences have been assumed to be known with certainty. This, again, is seldom the case in reality, especially when future time periods are involved since uncertainty can never be completely overcome even by using prediction models. Consequently, methods must be devised to estimate and compare the uncertainties of various consequences, and the functions

Figure 1
SOME COMMON GRAPHIC MODELS

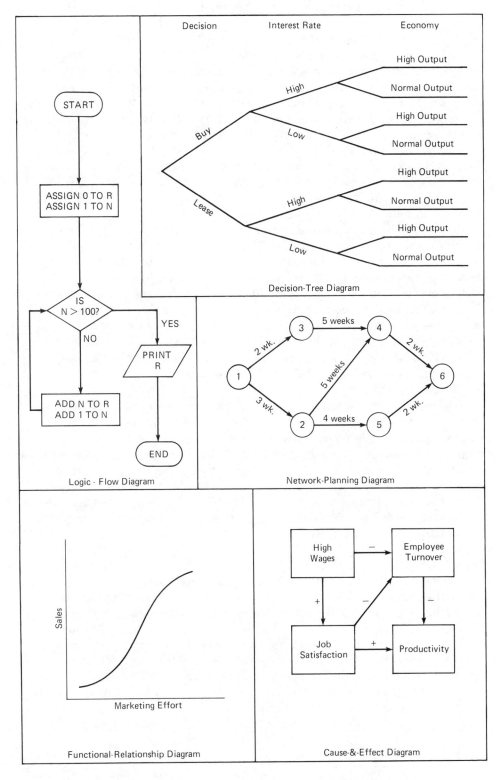

governing the trade-off between a certain and an uncertain outcome must be developed. This function may also differ from individual to individual, and may vary from time to time for each individual.

IV. IMPLICATIONS FOR MANAGEMENT SCIENCE MODELING

These factors suggest that applying models of rational decision making in human organizations may have significant limitations in practice. However, for the foreseeable future, humans with *bounded rationality* will continue to be the principal developers and users of such models. Each action will have a large number of variables affecting it. In such a case, it is unlikely that the human brain, with its bounded rationality, will be able to grasp the full significance of an interaction between all of these variables. Additionally, the number of available choices for action may be simply too large to be analyzed in the reasonable amount of time. While these are some reasons why computer-based models have unique strengths, for many realistic situations the problems and limitations outlined above remain.

In perspective then, management science has developed as an effective means for solving tedious but limited problems. *Algorithms*, or exact procedures for optimum solutions, are developed only for problems that are well defined or repetitious, and where a unidimensional cardinal scale of utility, such as money, can reasonably be used as a measure of the desired outcome. Complex real world problems are sometimes recognized, and in such cases, only generalized rules of action known as *heuristics* are developed to aid the intuition and judgment of the decision maker. Besides, in most cases, because of the large number of goals and sub-goals in an organization, *satisficing*, or "good enough" approach, may be taken instead of the more comprehensive process of *optimization*.

The use of management science, thus, requires the ability to judge not only how, but where and when it can be used; and to be able to modify the results obtained to correct for some of the assumptions made while constructing the model. The management scientist should not only have a research orientation towards organizational decision making, but since decisions are made ultimately not only by people but for them, his success will depend on documentation on how the actions recommended by his model will contribute toward the objectives of the organizations, and in increasing the welfare of those involved.

CONCLUSIONS

The paper started with a definition of management science and next explored its function and role in an organization. Some limitations of the use of management science-based models because of the complexity of decision making in human organizations is detailed in the next section. In the last section, some of the implications of these limitations for the practice of management science were developed. While computer-based management science models have some strengths and can complement the abilities of the human brain, they also have significant limits that are important to keep in mind when using them in human organizations.

References

1. Aggarwal, Raj and Inder Khera, *Applications in Management Science: Cases* (San Francisco, California: Holden-Day, 1977 forthcoming).

2. Aggarwal, Raj, "The First Course in Quantitative Methods for Business Programs: A Pareto-Optimal Approach," Chapter 7 of Delmar M. Goode (ed.) *Improving College and University Teaching Yearbook* (Corvallis, Oregon: Oregon State University Press, 1976).

3. Miller, David W. and Martin K. Starr, *Executive Decisions and Operations Research*, 2nd edition (Englewood Cliffs, New Jersey: Prentice-Hall, 1969) Chapters 1-9 and 13-15.

4. Morris, William T., *Management Science, A Bayesian Introduction* (Englewood Cliffs, New Jersey: Prentice-Hall. 1968) Chapters 1-4 and 12-15.

5. Kotler, Philip, *Marketing Management*, 2nd edition (Englewood Cliffs, New Jersey: Prentice-Hall, 1972) Chapter 10.

6. Thompson, Victor A., *Decision Theory, Pure and Applied* (New York, New York: General Learning Press, 1971).

Questions for Discussion

1. What are the differences between descriptive and decision models? How would their uses differ?

2. What is the purpose of management science models? Why are they necessary? What do they do that cannot be done as well by other approaches?

3. What are some of the limitations of management science models?

EXERCISE

PLANNING A CONFERENCE

Congratulations! You've just been elected to chair the program for a major regional professional conference. At the conference will be colleagues from the geographic region, gathered to listen to papers selected from those submitted by their authors. They will also renew old acquaintances as well as seek to develop their professional competence.

The conference site has already been selected, but you still must be responsible for the efficient discharge of numerous activities that make any conference successful. Among these are the preparation of mailings, establishing the program format, setting up program evaluation procedures and committees, registering participants, and so on.

It's up to you to initiate all the activities as well as coordinate them while they are underway and make sure that everything is going smoothly.

Adapted with permission from Herbert G. Zollitsch and Richard A. Kaimann, "A Systems Approach to Planning Professional Conferences," *Collegiate News and Views*, Winter 1973-74, pp. 5-8.

It's a big job, with high stakes. Many professional rewards are available to one who performs this task successfully, while unsuccessful performance results in a poor conference, dissatisfied participants, and possibly your arrested professional development.

Over the weekend you jot down the things that you know make up the activities necessary for the conference. It strikes you that this activity should lend itself very well to network analysis techniques after looking over your notes.

Notes: Listing of Conference Activities

Activity description	Approximate time needed
Determine conference goals.	1 day
Get master mailing list ready.	1–2 weeks
Order materials for mailings.	1 hour
Prepare first call for papers.	1 week
Secure a Paper Evaluation Committee.	1–2 weeks
Mail first call for papers.	1 day
Prepare conference inquiry letter.	1 day
Host institution prepares materials for conference mailout.	2 weeks
Prepare second call for papers.	2 days
Mail second call for papers.	1 day
Prepare third call for papers.	2 days
Prepare tentative program format.	2 weeks
Mail third call for papers.	1 day
Prepare instructions for Evaluation Committee.	1 week
Prepare tally forms for evaluating papers.	1 day
Receipt of papers submitted for program consideration.	1 month
Prepare papers for mailing to committee.	2 days
Mail papers and materials to Evaluation Committee.	1 day
Prepare acceptance and rejection letters.	1 week
Committee judge papers and return to Program Chairperson.	4 weeks
Notify authors if paper is selected or rejected.	1 week
Establish order of topics and speakers for program.	3 days
Line up session chairperson.	2 weeks
Finalize program format.	2 weeks
Prepare instructions for Session Chairpersons and speakers.	2 days
Mail instructions and papers to Session Chairpersons and speakers.	1 day
Send final program draft to all concerned.	2 weeks
Select printer from three bids.	1 week

Notes: Listing of Conference Activities (cont'd)

Activity description	Approximate time needed
Select publisher for Conference proceedings.	1 week
Send final copy of program to printer.	2 weeks
Prepare program mailing.	1 week
Mail out program.	3 days
Conference registration.	½ day
Conference takes place.	1½ days
Conference critique.	½ day
Prepare and edit conference proceedings.	2 weeks
Send conference proceedings to publisher.	1 week
Prepare final report for executive committee.	3 weeks
Publisher prints conference proceedings.	3 months
Conference proceedings mailed to conferees.	3 days

The conference will be held on April 4 and 5, beginning at 8 A.M. on the fourth and ending at noon on the fifth. Set up an appropriate network by which to plan and control your preparations for the conference through milestone dates and the most efficient time-path.

EXERCISE

ANDY'S DILEMMA

Decisions are something managers make, right? And analytical techniques are fine if you're a businessperson and paid to use these techniques. Right? Well, Andy is faced with a not uncommon problem. Your problem is to help him solve *his* problem. You'll probably find, after going through the exercise, that many decisions that face you every day are just as open to sound analysis. Which technique should you use though? You may find yourself unable to see the forest for the "trees."

Andy had just gotten back to the dormitory from supper and was locating his books and notes. Tomorrow was final exam day — make or break in his classes. He figured that, given enough coffee, he could just catch up in time for the tests and then be able to graduate.

A note taped to his desk lamp caught his eye: "Andy — Cheryl called while you were out. Asked what time you'll pick her up tonight. Call her. Happy finals. Ha ha. Yr ob't Roomie."

He'd met Cheryl at a fraternity party just last week; he'd gone out of his way to impress her and had promised her a great night on the town. In his eagerness, he'd forgotten about exams. What could he do? Cheryl's dad was president of Bigtown Industrials; if he made a big hit with Cheryl, he figured that the odds were in his favor (about 60–40) he'd be offered a job with the company averaging $30,000 a year for the decade. Even if her dad didn't offer him a job, he should be able to meet other executives through Cheryl and thereby land a job earning $10,000 a year anyway.

Of course, if he struck out with Cheryl (he coolly figured this to be no more than an even chance), the job would not be forthcoming *and* he'd have blown the finals and *any* decent job. He'd then have to be content to get a $500 per month job as a clerk.

He could, on the other hand, forget about Cheryl and tonight in order to study for his finals. He knew that Cheryl would never forgive this but figured this studying would give him an 80 per cent chance to excel on the exams; there was close to a zero chance for him without studying. If he did well, he felt sure that he stood at least a 70 per cent chance of receiving one or more job offers from the corporations he'd already interviewed, probably averaging $15,000 a year for 10 years. But Uncle Bernie had promised him a $10,000 a year job if he did well on the finals.

While he was most confident about his chances of doing well with study, Andy still knew that sometimes his profs would really throw some curves on the finals; if this should happen, and he flunked, he'd welcome a clerk's job at $500 a month.

Being a business major, he had already determined to guide all his actions in order to maximize his earning power over the next 10 years.

What should he do: have a good time with Cheryl or hit the books?

EXERCISE

CPM, 2600 B.C.

Critical Path Methods allow the manager to control the operations he or she has planned. They further give the opportunity to adjust to problems not planned on. The chief engineer is faced with a control problem, but he can discover new ways to get around the problem he faces and still obtain his objective by using CPM. How can he use CPM, and what does the technique suggest that he do? (Evidently he was a wise manager: If he hadn't used CPM and corrected for the problem, the pyramid wouldn't be there now!)

In early Egypt, as soon as a new king (or pharaoh) came to the throne he selected a site for his tomb, his "house of eternity," and began work on it. This long lead-time was necessary because building a pyramid usually took most of the pharaoh's life.

During the Fourth Dynasty, King Cheops instructed his chief engineer to construct his royal tomb near Giza on the Nile River. The king mentioned that he would be rewarded handsomely if he finished the tomb in a reasonable time but punished quite severely if he didn't. The chief engineer (who came from a long line of chief engineers) estimated that it would take 30 years with the help of 100,000 laborers. The nearest stone quarry was 700 miles down the Nile River.

For simplicity, the chief engineer divided the construction project into three major phases and estimated the approximate time period for each major phase, as well as for the projects which compose the construction phases:

1. The cutting of the stone, 10 years
   a. cutting and shaping of foundation stones, 3 years
   b. cutting and shaping of pyramid stones, 6 years
   c. cutting and shaping of capstone, 1 year.

2. Transportation of stones to the pyramid site, 5 years
   a. moving foundation stones, 2 years
   b. moving pyramid stones, 2½ years
   c. moving capstone, ½ year.

3. Erection of the pyramid, 15 years
   a. preparation of base for foundation stones, 1 year
   b. placement of foundation stones, 3 years
   c. placement of pyramid stones, 6 years
   d. preparation of tomb in foundation and lower pyramid, $3\frac{3}{4}$ years
   e. placement of capstone, ¼ year
   f. cleanup and minor housekeeping, 1 year.

Then the chief engineer began the first phase, the cutting of the stone; after two years, the chief engineer realized that the project was beginning to fall behind his timetable, primarily because of an epidemic of chiselitis to which stonecutters are particularly susceptible.

Is there any way he can bring in the project before the 30-year deadline, considering he now estimates the cutting of stone to require a total of 16 years (3 additional years for the foundation stones *and* 3 additional years for the pyramid stones)?

EXERCISE

PROCESS CHART

Text Figure 18.5 shows the symbols used in process charts. Such charts are used widely as the basis by which to analyze some complex process that consists of a number of steps or activities.

Identify some process either with which you have some familiarity or to which you have access. Possible choices are your college course registration system, checking out a book at the library, taking food orders at a restaurant, and so on. Chart the process, using the process chart symbols. Analyze the process for efficiency. What would you recommend changing, based on your process analysis?

EXERCISE

BOTTLE BLUES

"I got it!" Excitedly waving a piece of paper, Rob burst into the dormitory room. His roommate Eduardo glanced up with amusement. "Will a shot get rid of it?"

"No, silly! I got the answer to my money problem. I answered this ad in the paper today, went downtown and everything, and found out all about this *neat* job I can handle around my class schedule. And I can make money like a bandit, too!"

Eduardo seemed skeptical. "Tell me about this once-in-a-lifetime proposition," he said.

"Well, it's a job as a-a 'field marketing representative' and it's got a commission basis and a great territory and . . ."

"Hold on," soothed Eduardo. "Take it one step at a time. Exactly *what* are you supposed to do?"

Rob made a visible effort to control his excitement. "I'll have a sales route, and call on a number of stores. Once in a store, I'll check their stock level of the product — a fancy cologne — replace those sold since the last week, and invoice the store owner. And for that I get a dollar a bottle! Great, eh?"

"Sounds interesting. Think you'll make a bundle?"

"That's not the point," retorted Rob. "I just need a little extra money to make it a bit easier each month. And Hobson City isn't far. Nor is Lilburn. Nor Manleyton. And best of all, I can make my rounds any time of the week, just so I call on each store every week."

"How far will you have to travel each week? Any idea of what you can expect to make?" prodded the pragmatic Eduardo.

"Oh," started Rob irritably, "it must be 40 miles to Hobson City, and 75 to Lilburn. Manleyton's about 80, I guess." Then, slowly, " 'course, they're about as far separated from each other as you could get. I'll have to visit each town on a different day — but with my class schedule, that's no problem."

"You planning to take your old rattletrap? What kind of mileage are you getting? And your tires . . . ."

"Yeah, those tires. The way I drive around town, they'd do me another year, at least. But driving on the road's another matter. A set of recapped tires would set me back $120. Mileage? Oh, I should be able to get about 18 miles per gallon. And gas is . . . what? . . . $1.35 per gallon?"

Eduardo was scribbling furiously. "These tires should last 12 months, which is all you have left in school. Now for the big question. How much of this stuff do you figure to sell?"

Rob grinned happily. "They told me I could count on selling a steady 30 bottles every week! I even went over their route sheets. Can you believe it? Thirty bottles a week, at a dollar a bottle!"

Looking up from his calculations, Eduardo softly said, "Old chum, I think you'd better sit down. There's someting I want to show you."

Questions for Discussion

1. What does Eduardo want to show Rob?

2. Calculate the number of bottles per week Rob must sell to break even.

3. Should Rob take the job?

ANSWERS TO SELF-REVIEW QUESTIONS, CHAPTER 18

Matching

A-4, B-5, C-3, D-7, E-2, F-6, G-8, H-1.

True–False

1-F, 2-F, 3-F, 4-T, 5-F, 6-F, 7-F, 8-T, 9-T, 10-T, 11-T, 12-F, 13-F, 14-F, 15-T.

Multiple Choice

1-A, 2-E, 3-B, 4-C, 5-C, 6-A, 7-A, 8-B, 9-D, 10-D, 11-B, 12-D.

Completion

1. Variable. 2. Break-even. 3. Zero based budgeting. 4. Models.
5. Payoff. 6. Certainty, risk, uncertainty, conflict. 7. Minimax. 8. Gantt.
9. Linear programming. 10. CPM. 11. Critical. 12. EOQ.

Chapter 19

Systems for Effective Management

CHAPTER OBJECTIVES

1. To show the interrelationships among managerial activities, through a systems view
2. To consider the nature of organizations as complex systems

SELF-REVIEW QUESTIONS

Matching

A. total picture

B. simple dynamic system with predetermined necessary motions

C. a good example of the use of a goal system

D. a state of dynamic equilibrium

E. recognizes the existence and influence of external factors on operations

_____ 1. homeostasis

_____ 2. clockworks

_____ 3. gestalt

_____ 4. open system

_____ 5. zero-based budget

True–False

T   F   1. The machine age was characterized by an emphasis on mechanization and specialization.

T   F   2. Ecology is a systems-based discipline.

T   F   3. The "open" system is characterized by its ability to maintain equilibrium through self-regulation.

T F   4. All managers manage systems.

T F   5. The manager's task is to make sure that all goals are clearly separated from, and uncontaminated by, each other.

T F   6. Almost every aspect of our relationships with other people involves information systems.

T F   7. Managerial decision making may be equated with an information system.

T F   8. With training, the manager can process every bit of information that passes through his or her area of responsibility.

T F   9. An organization is a system.

T F 10. The operating system is relatively more important than the authority system.

Multiple Choice

1. The systems age is characterized by emphasis on _____ instead of on just _____ .

   (a) specialization . . . general training, (b) electric power . . . mechanical power, (c) procedures . . . inputs, (d) the whole . . . the parts

2. The systems age began around

   (a) World War I, (b) World War II, (c) Korean War, (d) Viet Nam War.

3. Every organization, every society has sets of individual _____ that are related versions of each other.

   (a) goals, (b) authority, (c) constraints, (d) troublemakers

4. In accurately explaining and predicting human behavior, _____ systems have gradually shown themselves to be essential.

   (a) open, (b) closed, (c) interactive, (d) iterative

5. Managers have commonly given greater attention to _____ systems because they are tangible and relatively easily dealt with.

   (a) production, (b) open, (c) authority, (d) operating

Completion

1. The ecological approach takes the perspective that things are _____ and mutually related.

2. The most complex type of system in Boulding's list is that of the _____ system.

3. The _____ should be able to relate all the tools of communications to each other and to the goals of the organization.

4. One of the most ineffectively applied activities of management is that of
_____ .

5. _____ is the obligation incurred by the manager for the activities
of subordinates.

READING

MASTERING MANAGEMENT IN CREATIVE INDUSTRIES

In Gulf & Western Industries Inc.'s modern New York City offices, Martin S.
Davis, a conservatively clad executive vice-president, rides up in an elevator
with a man wearing jeans, a sweater, and a big political button. Davis,
pointedly, says nothing. "He was a Paramount Pictures executive," Davis
explains. Would he have commented about the strange attire if the man had
been, say, a corporate financial officer? "Probably," Davis says.

Managing people in the so-called creative industries — moviemaking,
recording, mass-market publishing, and the like — simply calls for different
rules, not the least of which is making people in the creative end of the
business feel that Big Brother is not watching. These are industries where
computerized market research does little good, where an idea session in someone's living room takes the place of a research and development laboratory,
and where long-term growth and sales projections are often little better than
a shot in the dark. Whether the company is an independent, free-wheeling
studio or part of a giant conglomerate such as G&W or Transamerica Corp.,
B-school training simply falls short of what is needed. Some prerequisites
for the successful manager:

■ The courage to act on gut feeling and a nebulous sense of the public's
tastes when assigning top dollar to film production or book promotion.

■ The ability to stroke people whose egos are outsized, and whose work
habits are peculiar at best.

■ A willingness to bury any latent Napoleonic instincts and persuade,
rather than order, creative staffers and artists to follow a profitable path.

■ A strong business sense that can attend to details such as keeping warehousing costs down, improving distribution, and holding budgets in line without interfering with the creative process.

The odds against success are sobering. Hundreds of books are published
for every one that hits the best-seller list, only one of five movies ever turns a
profit, and probably less than 5% of all single records and only 20% or so of
all record albums ever break even. Unfortunately, there is no surefire formula or discernible pattern. *The Godfather* pulled in $129 million on an
initial cost of $6.8 million for Paramount, while *The Great Gatsby*, an $8
million endeavor for which the movie company had similarly high hopes,
netted only $24 million.

Even in hindsight, most of the more truthful heads of creative companies admit that many of their biggest successes were surprises to them. "Who could have really predicted that *Bubbles* [Beverly Sills' autobiography] would sell 130,000 copies?" asks Stanley Sills, who, in addition to being Beverly's brother, is group general manager of ITT Publishing, an International Telephone & Telegraph Corp. group that includes Bobbs-Merrill Co. among its holdings. "I told my sister that if she sold 25,000 copies, she'd be an institution."

Keeping Protected

Sills recalls that about the same time Bobbs-Merrill put out *Bubbles*, it also published a book by Aleksandr Solzhenitsyn's wife, giving an inside view of what the world-famous Russian author was really like. "This was something we felt certain that people would want to read," Sills says. "I think we sold all of 8,000 copies, and we would have had to sell at least 15,000 just to break even. I guess to some extent, this business is a gamble in which you throw the dice and hope."

Of course, most of these companies have found ways to hedge their bets, at least partially. Publishing houses have sizable backlists of books that bring in respectable incomes each year — how-to books, textbooks, and the like. Film studios have lucrative incomes from their film libraries, which bring a pretty penny from television networks, as well as from their made-for-TV series and movies. And in the case of those companies that are part of conglomerates, a corporate financial cushion helps them keep at least the semblance of an even keel. "This is a cyclical industry where you can't predict your upsides, and having a company like G&W behind you lets you protect your rear end in case of a downside," explains Barry Diller, chairman of Paramount Pictures Corp.

Diller's comment might surprise anyone who caught the full-page advertisement that ran in *Variety* magazine earlier this year condemning conglomerates as the ruination of all things creative. The ad ran shortly after the much-publicized defection of five high-level executives at Transamerica's United Artists subsidiary. Although neither Transamerica nor UA would discuss that debacle with BUSINESS WEEK, Diller and other G&W creative executives quickly came forward to cry foul for the record.

"There is zero corporate participation in deciding which books we buy," notes Richard E. Snyder, the flamboyant and feisty head of G&W's Simon & Schuster Inc. publishing subsidiary, who adds that the editorial board at S&S serves to make sure that individual editors do not get carried away on bad acquisition decisions. "I retain 99.9% of decision-making authority," Snyder says.

Diller claims an equal degree of freedom at Paramount. "We'll tell G&W we expect to put, say, $60 million on the line for film production and plan to distribute maybe 16 films this year, but we aren't expected to get more specific than that," he explains.

Turning Around

As long as their creative instincts are left unfettered, such executives seem to welcome corporate "meddling" into their businesses. Prior to G&W's

purchase of Simon & Schuster in 1975, "we didn't even have a purchasing department," Snyder recalls. "We had inefficient warehousing and dingy little offices all over the city," he says. Now G&W has moved S&S into plush offices in New York's Rockefeller Center, where it is paying less total rent than it did three years ago and has slashed its accounts payable tally for supplies.

G&W gave similar help to Paramount, recalls Davis, who was with the foundering movie studio for eight years prior to its purchase by G&W in 1966. He claims that the conglomerate modernized the film distribution system, systematized methods for deciding how many prints of each movie were needed, and formed a huge and efficient foreign distribution network as a joint effort with MCA Inc., the consistently profitable entertainment conglomerate that recently made it big with *Jaws*.

Possibly most important, G&W had the foresight to cut Paramount's excess staff and take a $29 million early write-off on money-losing films. It was also G&W's influence that got the film company into the lucrative television business, helping it acquire Desilu Studios. "We had one red year, in 1969 — a bad year for the entire industry. But we've been in the black ever since," Davis claims.

The Talent Search

Still, even Paramount's Diller concedes that "financial controls are not going to make our picture choices any better." So the quest for managers who feel equally at home with creative decisions and with balance sheets continues fast and furious in these industries. Most of these managers grew up in the business. "I'd never buy bringing a guy from a lumber company into the entertainment business," notes Sidney S. Sheinberg, president and chief operating officer of MCA. Although an attorney by education, Sheinberg points to his work as a radio announcer in his youth, his marriage to actress Lorraine Gray, and his 19-year tenure with MCA as proof that he has paid his dues as far as sensitivity to the creative process goes. Similarly, most heads of record companies have been in the music industry since they were teenagers, and most chief editors in book and magazine companies rose through the editorial ranks.

Companies have been putting out fewer movies and books over the last few years, however, and the supply of potential managers may be slowly drying up. Raiding among rival companies for top people is increasingly common. "The musical chairs in the movie industry are incredible," notes G&W's Davis. "In the days of second features you could build up a stable of talent, but now we just don't have a training ground." Adds Simon & Schuster's Snyder: "I spend at least 30% of my time looking for people to bring into S&S who are disciplined, almost compulsive workers and who can deal with intangibles."

Not surprisingly, money is a prime motivator for keeping top managers. Two of the three best-paid executives in the U.S. last year were with American Broadcasting Cos., with both of them grossing more than $1 million in total compensation. And industry scuttlebutt has it that the defecting United Artists executives left as much because of discontent over compensation as they did over disagreements with parent Transamerica on UA's artistic freedom.

Art for Money's Sake

But nowhere is the importance of money more apparent than with the salaries and advances paid to big names in these industries. "Creative artists" may be nonconformist, but apparently they are as interested in their own bottom line as any businessman. "I used to think artists signed contracts based on personal relationships they have with the company, but I've concluded that it almost always comes down to money," notes Arthur Mogull, president of United Artists Records Co. Companies are willing to pay top dollar because it usually comes back in higher profits, Snyder at S&S explains. "Our safest bet is the book that we pay a $1 million advance for, because the author has a brand-name image and we can be pretty sure he'll sell."

But money, while definitely necessary, is nonetheless not sufficient. All of the industry executives BUSINESS WEEK spoke with say they spend inordinate amounts of time coddling, nurturing, and otherwise "managing" creative people. "Employees may be out until 2 A.M. and not make it to work until 11, but you just have to accept certain eccentricities," notes UA's Mogull, who adds that as much as 90% of his time goes to personnel relations. "When someone hits a writing block, you have to be almost like a therapist to get him out of it," notes the manager of a five-person department of magazine writers. "You simply cannot separate being sensitive to the people from being sensitive to their work."

Artists' Relations

Handholding and persuasion are important in bringing together the artist's conception of his own best interest and the executive's gut feel for what the public wants. Dee Anthony, whose Bandana Enterprises Inc. manages such rock stars as Peter Frampton, notes that he deliberately shied from talk about record sales when he persuaded one of his singers to team up with a new band recently. "I had to convince him that there would be a chemistry that could work," he says. Anthony notes that many recording companies are beefing up artists-relations departments to shape subtly performers' careers toward salable records.

The recording companies seem to have the mix of good business sense and good personal relations down pat. Superficially, they are as informal as the offices of an underground newspaper. At RSO Records Inc., for example, the blue-jean-clad receptionist yells questions to executives in neighboring offices, a vice-president interrupts a meeting to look for a pen that turns up in his own pocket, and Albert E. Coury, the slender 43-year-old president, who sports frayed blue jeans, a football jersey, and scruffy suede cowboy boots, looks more like a disc jockey than the head of a company that projects sales of $130 million to $150 million this year. Yet he obviously knows what he is doing: RSO, with a relatively small stable of 14 acts under contract, boasts 4 of the top 10 single record hits in the country as well as 4 of the top 50 albums. "I help the artists pick their songs, but I'm aware of their temperaments, so I don't offend them," Coury says. "They like to feel like they're the only act on the label."

Even the staunchest supporters of the "business is business" theory of managing creative industries admit that flexibility and a bit of psychology are absolute necessities. "It is very important for creative types to be as informed as possible about business, and vice versa," says MCA's Shein-berg. "But you'd better not try to run by a set of hard and fast rules, be-cause by definition you would squeeze out the very elements of creativity that make it work." And Dennis C. Stanfill, chairman and president of Twentieth Century-Fox Film Corp. but also a veteran of such "noncreative" posts as corporate finance specialist with Lehman Bros., adds that even he will let a film go over budget when artistic demands are justified. "We have strict financial controls but administer them with a degree of flexibility," he says. "You have to give quality creative people your confidence."

A Delicate Balance

That does not necessarily mean letting them run the show, of course. RSO's Coury recalls a time when he was with Capitol Records Inc. and had to persuade Paul McCartney of Beatles fame to change the song mix on a new album. "He accepted my argument," Coury says. Result, according to Coury: The album took off in the U.S., but in Britain, where it went with McCartney's original choices, sales were substantially lower.

Similarly, studio chiefs adhere to common-sense rules of thumb — hold-ing off release of a potential big hit until Christmas or Easter, or until a cur-rent blockbuster has peaked. Still, they will grant directors and other cre-ators consultation privileges on ad campaigns and distribution decisions, if for no other reason than to assuage insecure artistic egos. "The narcissus factor is much bigger than in other businesses," sums up Samuel Z. Arkoff, chairman and president of American International Pictures Inc., a small in-dependent studio known both for its willingness to take chances on new talents and for Arkoff's somewhat autocratic managerial style. "Committee decisions haven't worked in this field, and I'm not particularly renowned as a handholder," he says. "But even I have to be more tolerant than if I were in some other business."

Questions for Discussion

1. Which of the management activities (planning, organizing, staffing, di-recting, controlling, coordinating) are likely to be most beneficial in managing a creative enterprise? Least beneficial?

2. In what ways important to management practice are creative enterprises likely to differ significantly from "normal" businesses in their goal, in-formation, human, authority, and operating systems?

EXERCISE

SYSTEM IDENTIFICATION

The text points out that any system usually is a part of another, larger sys-tem. (1) Choose a system (perhaps this course) and identify the higher levels of systems of which it is a part. Does the system you chose consist of smaller systems? Identify them. (2) For each system, show how it meets the characteristics of a system by identifying (a) the common elements that comprise the system, (b) the whole that is formed by these elements, (c) the existing relationships that tie the parts together, (d) the interchanges with its environment, and (e) its boundaries.

CASE

MOLSON'S BONUS BONER

Molson Labs is an old-line regional firm that makes and sells various hygiene and cleaning products. Until three years ago Molson's sales were concentrated in only two products, hand soap and hair shampoo. Both products carried the company's name and were leaders in the market region.

At that time a proposal was developed by the marketing division to capitalize on what marketing felt were excellent opportunities for expansion in a number of fields closely related to Molson's current product lines. After a year of additional research, the company put into action a major expansion plan. The decision to expand was based not only on the favorable market situation but also on the need to reduce the firm's dependence on just two products, which were accounting for 67 per cent of the company's sales and 82 per cent of its profits.

A requirement was to develop sufficient new products by which to compete in the new fields of consumer and industrial cleaners. To do this, the firm had to expand greatly the size of its research and development department. Put in charge of the research efforts on the three product lines were Ray Smith, industrial cleaners; Paul Taylor, consumer cleaners; and Linda Forster, the expanded consumer hygiene line.

A new reward system for R&D was initiated to spur quick development for the new products. This entailed paying a bonus of 4 per cent of current salary for each new product developed, as well as a salary increase based on the total number of new products each unit developed in the past year. The salary increase worked as follows: Four new products or less earned an 8 per cent increase; five or six new products, 10 per cent; seven or eight, 12 per cent; and nine or more, 15 per cent. In addition, the chief of the unit that produced the most new products was to be named departmental superintendent.

In the first year, a remarkable total of 23 new products was made ready for production. Nine of these were industrial cleaners; the others were split evenly between the other two product lines. This netted a 36 per cent bonus, plus a 15 per cent pay raise for the workers in the industrial cleaners unit, and a 28 per cent bonus plus a 12 per cent raise for the workers in the other two units.

In the first three months of this year, the productivity of the three units has been about the same as the first year of the plan. Market data on the results of the first-year effort have just become available. Only four of the products have reached or exceeded their initial expected market share of about 5 per cent, three products had been discontinued, and the remaining 16 had not been in the market long enough to judge accurately.

About the same time the market data were available, the Food and Drug Administration (FDA) publicly reprimanded the company for faulty labeling on one product and misleading advertising claims for two others. All three products were industrial cleaners; all carried the company's brand name. About three months later, three more products were criticized by the FDA for similar faults. Two were industrial cleaners and one was a consumer cleaning product.

Sales data for the second quarter show the FDA criticisms to have had a disastrous effect on market share. Almost all of the company's products have lost some share of their markets. Of the total of 33 new products created by the expansion program, only 3 have attained their market share target; 11 have been discontinued.

As a result, bitter animosity has erupted in the department. Smith had been given the superintendent's job; Forster has expressed outrage that the company has not disciplined Smith and his former unit members for having approved five products for production without thoroughly testing them first. Meanwhile, Smith staunchly defended his unit, terming the pronouncements of the FDA "pure hogwash."

Since the FDA press releases, productivity in all three units has dropped off. Lew Molson, president of the company, called a mandatory-attendance departmental meeting. His most recent market data indicate an almost complete failure of the three new product lines to accomplish their objectives. At the meeting Molson not only revealed this but also his anger with the effects the FDA criticisms have had. Molson informed the department members that he was contemplating a major shakeup of the entire department; he encouraged written suggestions to be submitted to him.

After a week, Molson listed the important suggestions he had received and circulated them to all R&D departmental employees for comment:

1. Return the department to a single work group.

2. Pay bonuses and award pay increases on the basis of successful projects only.

3. Change the departmental superintendents.

4. Eliminate interunit competition.

5. Develop a different merit basis for awarding bonuses and pay increases.

6. Assign to a different department the task of evaluating projects for production and marketing.

Questions for Discussion

1. Identify which of the five management systems (goal, information, human, authority, and operating systems) are important in the creating of Molson's problem. How have they affected the problem?

2. To solve the problem, what would you change in these five management systems?

3. Which of Molson's alternatives will be the most appropriate, in view of your response to Question 2, to solve the problem situation?

CASE

AJAX ENGINE COMPANY

The Ajax Engine Company is a small manufacturer of gasoline and diesel engines. For the past five years Ajax has had an annual production volume of approximately 40,000 engines, of which 75 per cent were purchased by the military. All engine models currently manufactured by Ajax have been in production for at least 10 years and were designed and developed for the military by someone other than Ajax.

The approach followed by Ajax's management has been to concentrate on manufacturing completely and to eliminate all new engine design and development activity. New-product development has been limited to adapting current engines to new applications. This has significantly reduced Ajax's overhead and made the company relatively profitable during the last few years.

Ajax obtains most of its business by bidding on military contracts for which the annual production rate has dropped to such a low level that the original producer no longer wants to tie up production facilities by continuing to build the engines for the military. At these low production levels the original producers must significantly increase the cost per engine to recoup higher manufacturing costs and overhead allocation. Because Ajax is a small company set up for smaller production runs, it can underbid the original producers and win the low-volume production contracts.

In 1975 the military informed Ajax that after 1981 Ajax's current model L-175 gasoline engine would no longer be purchased because of the upcoming emission requirements. The military representative indicated that there was a plan to develop a diesel engine that would be interchangeable with the current L-175 engine for emission and logistic reasons. The new diesel engine was scheduled for production starting in 1982.

In 1975 Ajax's L-175 engine production consisted of 12,000 units for the military and 5,000 units commercially. Ajax knew that without the military portion's offset to manufacturing cost, it would not be able to competitively price its commercial L-175 engine. Therefore, Ajax was faced with the possibility of losing more than 40 per cent of its current production by 1981.

Fearing the loss of L-175 engine production and having no engine with which to replace it in the foreseeable future, Ajax's management decided to submit a proposal to design and develop the diesel version of the L-175 for the military. The vice-president of engineering was assigned the responsibility for preparing the cost estimate. Should the proposal be successful, he was to be responsible also for directing the new program.

A meeting was set up among the managers of design, testing, purchasing, industrial engineering, and manufacturing to discuss the program and to prepare a cost estimate. Within a month a detailed cost summary had been prepared. Because this was the first cost estimate the vice-president of engineering had submitted for a complete engine design and development program, he had no previous experience to rely on and thus increased the group's estimate by 15 per cent. When the company controller prepared the bid package, he added another 10 per cent to the cost for miscellaneous expenses.

Yet Ajax was the low bidder and was awarded the contract. The contract called for Ajax to develop and deliver prototype engines for evaluation by the military within three years. Once the contract had been awarded, the following areas of responsibility were established: the vice-president of engineering was responsible for the design, development, and testing of the new engine as well as being assigned overall responsibility for the program; the vice-president of purchasing was responsible for procuring prototype patterns, tooling, and engine components; the vice-president of manufacturing was responsible for designing the required prototype tooling and fabricating prototype material.

During the first 12 months of the contract, the major activity consisted of designing the new engine. As the design for each component was completed, a copy of its blueprint was forwarded to the purchasing department for procurement and another to the industrial engineering department so that any required special tooling could be designed.

At the end of the twelfth month a detailed review of the program's progress was conducted, as was required by the contract. The originally submitted schedule called for the design activity to be completed within 12 months and the testing of prototype engines being completed by the fifteenth month.

The review pointed out several problem areas. First, even though all the engine parts had been designed, only about two thirds of them had actually been ordered. Some items had been in the purchasing department for three months before purchase invoices had been released; the new parts were ordered on an as-time-permitted basis, with production parts taking priority. Second, Purchasing had several questions concerning some of the new parts and had requested additional information from the engineering department before initiating procurement procedures. Those parts about which they had questions and had received no information from engineering had not been ordered. Third, virtually no prototype tooling had been designed or ordered. The industrial engineering (IE) department's manufacturing group was busy keeping production equipment running and had neither time nor personnel to design a lot of new tooling. In addition, IE had requested a detailed list from the purchasing department outlining which items were to be made or machined by Ajax and which items would be purchased from outside sources in the final state. As of the review date no such list had been received. Fourth, the test and evaluation department had made no arrangements to obtain the special test equipment required to conduct the engine development tests.

Questions for Discussion

1. The text identifies five management-related, interlocking systems: goal, information, human, authority, and operating systems. Identify each as they apply to the Ajax case.

2. Systems affect each other. Show how the five systems in Question 1 affected each other. What were the results of the ways in which they affected each other?

3. Is Ajax an open or a closed system? Why?

ANSWERS TO SELF-REVIEW QUESTIONS, CHAPTER 19

Matching

A-3, B-2, C-5, D-1, E-4.

True–False

1-T, 2-T, 3-F, 4-T, 5-F, 6-T, 7-T, 8-F, 9-T, 10-F.

Multiple Choice

1-D, 2-B, 3-A, 4-A, 5-D.

Completion

1. Interdependent. 2. Transcendental. 3. Manager. 4. Authority.
5. Responsibility.

Chapter 20

The Challenging Environment of the Manager

CHAPTER OBJECTIVES

1. To identify ethics as the filter through which the manager screens alternative actions before taking action

2. To investigate the extent to which the businessperson is responsible to others outside his or her business

3. To consider the impetus for and impact on management practice from the internationalizing of operations

SELF-REVIEW QUESTIONS

True–False

T F 1. Ethics no longer exist because the greatly increased complexity of daily life prohibits knowledge of absolute "good" and "bad."

T F 2. A social audit consists of a consumer-advocate-sponsored accountant's review of a company's finances.

T F 3. By establishing foreign operations a company usually is assured of new sources of capital.

T F 4. When operating in a foreign country, the general need for careful planning is even greater than usual.

T F 5. The moral tradition of the United States is unique in that it developed largely on its own.

T F 6. The traditional corporation represents the vast majority of businesses in the United States today.

T F 7. The metrocorporation is greatly more concerned with fulfilling its social responsibility than is the traditional corporation.

T F 8. According to Baumhart, younger and less-experienced executives have higher ethical standards and opinions than older executives and those with longer business experience.

T F 9. Several studies of business ethics reported cause for concern over the widespread lack of ethics among future and present business leaders.

T F 10. A well-defined code of ethics is essential for a vocational specialization to become a full-fledged and legitimate profession.

T F 11. As indicated in studies, there is little chance that the situation will ever arise in which a businessperson must face a conflict between what is expected of him or her as an efficient, profit-conscious businessperson and what is expected as an ethical person.

T F 12. Studies show no indication that future managers will be any less cynical or any more ethical than their predecessors, though they may be less hypocritical.

T F 13. According to a model developed by the Chamber of Commerce of the United States, the highest level of social responsibility for the businessperson is that of obeying the law.

T F 14. Self-regulation can often prevent external controls.

T F 15. It is unethical to get ideas for a code of ethics from the code of another organization.

T F 16. Although final decisions will be made by top management, representatives of all segments within an organization should be asked to approve both the procedure and the content of a code of ethics.

Multiple Choice

1. Ethics are important to the managers because

   (a) they dictate his or her actions, (b) they represent his or her personal beliefs, (c) they represent the values he or she holds, (d) a and c (e) all of the above.

2. Ethics may be considered to be

   (a) rules, (b) standards, (c) moral principles, (d) b and c, (e) all of the above.

3. Which of the following is *not* a major reason to establish foreign operations?

   (a) access to foreign sources of capital, (b) access to raw materials, (c) access to new markets, (d) access to cheaper labor

4. Which is the most significant problem facing multinational corporations?

   (a) the need to bribe foreign officials, (b) distance of foreign operations from headquarters, (c) shortage of qualified management personnel, (d) currency fluctuations

5. In the traditional corporation shareholders are _____ and maximum profits are _____ .

(a) ignored . . . required, (b) few . . . sacrificed, (c) responsible . . . denied, (d) kings . . . the objective

6. The metrocorporation

(a) is exemplified by IBM, (b) purposely attempts to maximize profits, (c) is in the service industry, (d) does not fully meet the needs of society.

7. Which of the following is *not* true?

(a) a code of ethics can provide evidence of a firm's ethical concern, (b) a code of ethics can force abandonment of an apathetic attitude toward ethics, (c) a code of ethics can strengthen the resolve of employees to be ethical, (d) all of the above, (e) none of the above

Completion

1. The notion that business must render a distinct service while pursuing profit, thus insuring against operating against the community's best interests, is called _____ _____ .

2. Professor Levitt, in decrying that he feels is overemphasis on social responsibility, states that "the business of business is _____ ."

3. Creation of a _____ of ethics helps an employee avoid the confusion of trying to determine just what is ethical.

4. The method by which an organization evaluates the extent to which it has performed in areas of social responsibility is called the _____ .

5. The rules or standards governing the moral conduct of the members of the organization or management profession are _____ .

6. A company with plant operations, managerial personnel, and ownership interests in a mix of foreign countries is called a _____ _____ .

READING

OVERDRIVEN EXECS

George Getschow

To hear some middle managers there tell it, the "pressure-cooker" atmosphere at Pittsburgh's H. J. Heinz Co. wasn't confined to the concern's steamy food-processing plants.

"When we didn't meet our growth targets, the top brass really came down on us," recalls a former marketing official at the company's huge Heinz U.S.A. division. "And everybody knew that if you missed the targets enough, you were out on your ear."

In this environment, some harried managers apparently resorted to deceptive bookkeeping when they couldn't otherwise meet profit goals set by the company's top executives. Invoices were misdated and payments to suppliers were made in advance — sometimes to be returned later in cash — all with the aim, insiders say, of showing the sort of smooth profit growth that would please top management and impress securities analysts.

ANNUAL MEETING DELAYED

Today, Heinz officials won't comment on the profit-juggling practices or on what led to them until an investigation is completed by the board of directors' audit committee. However, what began as an attempt to satisfy demanding superiors undoubtedly has tarnished the image of one of the country's corporate stalwarts: The Heinz annual meeting has been delayed and the outside auditors' opinion of the company's fiscal-1979 report has been withheld until the juggling scheme's precise effect — currently estimated at a cumulative $8.5 million — on previously reported Heinz earnings is determined.

Whether at Heinz or at any of thousands of other U.S. companies, pressure to achieve goals is, of course, an everyday fact of life. Properly applied — through threat of punishment or promise of reward — such pressure can motivate employes to turn in their maximum performance. Sometimes, though, corporate goals are set too high or are simply unreasonable. Then, an employe often confronts a hard choice — to risk being branded incompetent by telling superiors that they ask too much, or to begin taking unethical or illegal shortcuts.

"A certain amount of tension is desirable," explains Paul Lawrence, Professor of organizational behavior at the Harvard Business School. "But at many companies the pressures to perform are so intense and the goals so unreasonable that some middle managers feel the only way out is to bend the rules, even if it means compromising personal ethics."

PAINFUL RESULTS

Bent rules or broken laws, in turn, can lead to painful problems for companies. At some, as in the case of Heinz, the result is public embarrassment. But at others, pressure-induced managerial misconduct has brought product-liability and shareholder lawsuits, union troubles, government investigations and even criminal charges. Still other companies, worried that they might become involved in such problems, are devising codes of conduct for employes.

Middle managers, experts say, are the most likely members of the corporate hierarchy to confront the ethical dilemmas that can arise when the dictum goes out to meet company objectives. Unlike top executives, these managers often have little say in how such goals are set; yet unlike production-line workers, whose unions protect them from retribution for occasional shortcomings, a middle manager's future rides almost solely on his ability to serve up whatever the boss demands.

What's more, many experts predict that if the economy slides into a recession, the pressure on middle managers to meet increasingly tough goals will intensify, as will the probability of legal and ethical conflicts. "When a manager feels his job or his division's survival is at stake," Harvard's Prof. Lawrence observes, "the corporation's standards of business conduct are apt to be sacrificed."

Consider the incident at Dorsey Corp.'s glass-container plant in Gulfport, Miss. Manager William Tate, aware that the aging facility's output was falling behind that of the other company plants, began to fear that Dorsey would close his plant and throw him and 300 other employes out of work. According to the company, Mr. Tate secretly started altering records and eventually inflated the value of the plant's production by about 33 per cent.

JANITOR BLOWS WHISTLE

The overreporting was discovered when a janitor, ignoring Mr. Tate's order to burn the actual records, instead hid the documents behind a chicken coop and showed them to company auditors visiting on an inspection tour. Mr. Tate was fired, and Dorsey Corp. was forced to restate downward its 1977 and 1978 earnings to reflect the production discrepancy.

Mr. Tate refuses to discuss the matter. But his wife, Gayle, says her husband was under "constant pressure" to raise the plant's production. "Bill knew that as long as he kept production up, he and his men had a job. But when it fell, that was it," she says.

John Pollock, Dorsey's president and chairman, doesn't disagree that managers such as Mr. Tate are under pressure to turn in a better performance each year "because our stockholders expect and deserve continuing improvement." But he does deny that the company routinely fires managers who don't meet production goals. Ironically, Mr. Pollock adds that Dorsey never had any intention of closing the plant or of dismissing Mr. Tate.

"He was a hard-working guy, and his production was good," Mr. Pollock says of his former plant manager. "There's really no logical explanation for his behavior. Perhaps he felt he was the only guy who could save the plant and the jobs of his workers. But if that's the case, he was a false messiah, because he was under no more pressure than other managers except in his own mind."

While pressure to increase profit is as old as the business world itself, that pressure nowadays is often intensified by government regulations. Sometimes, in fact, middle managers discover that compliance with new laws means falling short of other corporate goals. What can happen next is illustrated by a Ford Motor Co. incident that, although it occurred more than seven years ago, is still a textbook example of a manager's dilemma.

Then, certain Ford managers, worried that many of the company's 1973-model cars would flunk the government's emission standards that year, performed unauthorized "maintenance" on engines undergoing federal certification tests. The tinkering was discovered after a computer analyst noticed that some unscheduled maintenance had been jotted down in company records submitted to the Environmental Protection Agency. Although Ford maintained that its top management wasn't aware of the test tampering, the company did agree to pay $7 million in criminal and civil penalties to settle the matter.

Harvey Copp, a former Ford official who was then in charge of emission testing and who brought the tampering incident to the company's attention, today contends that senior Ford officers were pressuring middle managers to get the engines certified. "If they failed," Mr. Copp explains, "it would have been impossible for Ford to meet its ambitious production and earnings goals that year."

While Mr. Copp emphasizes that top Ford executives didn't condone the test tampering, he does think that they "created the environment" for it to occur. "When senior management puts the squeeze on, it encourages short-cuts," he says.

NOT ENOUGH QUESTIONS?

Others agree that top executives must share some of the blame for middle managers' illegal or unethical behavior. "There's a tendency for top manage-ment at many companies to keep pushing for the numbers without bothering to ask their managers how they got them," says Harry Levinson, a manage-ment counsultant in Cambridge, Mass. "And when top management doesn't ask, lower management figures anything goes as long as they're meeting their targets."

Such thinking apparently sparked discord at a big Chevrolet truck plant in Flint, Mich., where three plant managers installed a secret control box in a supervisor's office last year to override the control panel that governs the speed of the assembly line. With the secret box, they were able to speed up the assembly line — a serious violation of the General Motors Corp. con-tract with the United Auto Workers — and thus increase production. One of the managers explains how the hidden box originated.

"At Chevrolet, we're given a production goal each week that's predicated on the assumption that everything will go perfectly. The problem is that on an assembly line, nothing ever does. There's always a conveyor breakdown or high absenteeism or something. As a result, we were constantly missing our targets, and the bosses were putting pressure on us to do something about it.

"We tried to explain our problems to higher-ups in the company, but we were told, 'I don't care how you do it — just do it.' Given our predicament, we felt the control panel was the only way we could make up for the exces-sive downtime we were experiencing."

DOWNTIME DISAPPEARED

With the aid of the hidden controls, the managers soon began meeting their production goals — and winning praise from their superiors. Says the man-ager: "They had to know we were speeding up the line, because they could see in their reports that we suddenly didn't have any downtime. But they never asked questions, so while we knew what we were doing was wrong ethically, we figured it must have been okay in the eyes of the company."

GM denies this and says its top mangement wasn't aware of the secret box. Beyond that, the company declines comment. However, the UAW workers who discovered the secret speedup and later won $1 million in back pay from GM say they won't soon forget the matter. "It created considerable ill will toward GM managers that will probably linger for years," says Samuel Duncan, a local UAW official in Flint. The three supervisors were temporarily suspended and later transferred to other GM production plants.

Reacting to publicity given corporate payoffs here and abroad and the stricter laws that followed, many companies have introduced in the past decade detailed codes of conduct for employes. Though aimed mostly at proscribing illegal payments to politicians or insider-trading violations of securities laws, many of these codes also spell out what is and isn't ethical in the normal course of business. Thus, middle managers presumably have less reason to step over the line.

But some companies, stung by the consequences of middle managers' wrongdoing, now are going further. They are trying to make sure that in motivating people, they don't create an atmosphere conducive to unethical behavior.

One such company is Mead Corp., which in 1976 found itself among 23 folding-box companies indicted on charges of price fixing. The charges, to which Mead pleaded no contest, stemmed from activities among some of the company's middle managers and came as "a shocker" to top management, a spokesman says.

Since then, Mead has reevaluated the way it motivates its managers. Among other things, it has begun involving middle managers in developing corporate goals. Moreover, Mead's senior executives, in reviewing middle managers' performance, now are asking how results are obtained, not just what they were. Two years ago, an official says, "we didn't bother to ask the 'how' part of the question."

Questions for Discussion

1. What are some of the pressures that encourage the compromise of ethics?

2. What are some of the methods by which you, as a manager, could resist such pressures successfully without jeopardizing your career or job performance?

EXERCISE

BEHAVIOR, IMPACT, AND ETHICS*

Below are 10 statements, each of which describes an action of a business person. You are likely to encounter opportunities for these action to occur in almost any organized situation, if you haven't already. Glance over the list, then follow the Instructions that follow.

*The behavior items are based on some of these used in John W. Newstorm and William A. Ruch, "The Ethics of Management and the Management of Ethics," *MSU Business Topics*, Winter 1975, pp. 29-37.

| | | You | | Peers |
	Impact	Ethical	Frequency	Frequency

1. You've made a mistake in your work, which you blame on an innocent co-worker.

2. As part of your job you must fill out a form for your boss, in which you report your time spent, work quality, or productivity. You falsify the report to reflect more favorably on you.

3. You're on an expense account. You "pad" your claims, for which you will be reimbursed by the company, by amounts over 10 per cent above your actual expenses.

4. A supplier or subordinate gives you a gift worth over $50; you're in a position to assist the other, and you do in fact thereafter give the donor preferential treatment.

5. You give a client or boss a gift worth over $50; he or she is in a position to help you. Your gift will, you hope, "encourage" that help.

6. You're on an expense account. You "pad" your claims for which you will be reimbursed by the company, by amounts less than 10 per cent above your actual expenses.

7. It's a beautiful day, and you just don't feel like going in to the office. You're saving up vacation days, so you call in sick.

8. During your normal work hours you make personal telephone calls, duck out unnoticed for a dental appointment, and in general do personal business on company time.

9. During your normal workday you take longer than allowed for lunch or breaks or leave early for personal business.

10. You observe co-workers violating various company policies and rules, some of which are quite valid. You do not report those violations.

INSTRUCTIONS

A. Under the column headed "Impact," indicate how serious the implications are for each action. Use *1* for "no impact," *2* for "minor impact," *3* for "moderate or not particularly serious impact," *4* for "rather serious or potentially harmful," or *5* for "very serious, or harmful."

B. Under the column headed "You," indicate under the "Ethical" heading the extent to which *you* believe each action is ethical or unethical. Use *1* for "very unethical," *2* for "basically unethical," *3* for "somewhat unethical," *4* for "not particularly unethical," or *5* for "not at all unethical."

Still under the column headed "You," indicate under the "Frequency" heading the frequency with which you engage (or would engage) in each behavior. Use *1* for "never," *2* for "seldom," *3* for "about half the time," *4* for "often," or *5* for "at almost every opportunity."

C. Under the column headed "Peers Frequency," indicate how frequently your co-workers (or those you expect to work with, if you're not working now) engage in (or would engage in) each behavior. Use *1* for "never," *2* for "seldom," *3* for "about half the time," *4* "often," or *5* for "at almost every opportunity."

CASE

THE FREE FLOW HOSE ACQUISITION

In 1938, a small plastics and chemical manufacturer known as Kerbson & Sons merged with Free Flow Hose, Inc., a slightly larger manufacturer and distributor of polysynthetic industrial and commercial hose products. Free Flow Hose bought the majority of its batch stock raw material from Kerbson & Sons; it was felt that such a vertical integration would benefit both companies, Free Flow having the manufacturing and distribution abilities and Kerbson supplying the raw material needs. The new company was to retain the name of Free Flow Hose, which had built up a substantial reputation in the hose products industry.

In the war years that followed, Free Flow Hose become a large producer of hose products, second only to Flexi-Hose, Inc. The next twenty years (1945 to 1965) saw Free Flow retain its relative industry position within this three-to-four-competitor oligopolistic industry, with its sales increasing over 95 per cent to almost $200 million. In the late 1960s, Free Flow management realized that to surpass the industry-leading Flexi-Hose, it would have to establish its name outside the already saturated U.S. market by penetrating the virtually untouched Western European market.

Source: This case was prepared by Robert F. Green under the supervision of Theodore T. Herbert. The case is not intended to reflect either effective or ineffective administrative or technical practices; it was prepared as a basis for class discussion.

The Euro-Hose market was composed primarily of several small manufacturers and a limited import effort from several American and Japanese firms. In an effort to strike quickly and capture a large share of this Euro-market, Free Flow acquired Con Systems B.V., a medium-sized multidivisional holding company. Con Systems consisted of ten hose and hose-related producers and 35 distribution and sales outlets located in the major cities of Holland, Germany, France, England, Belgium, Italy, and Norway. Free Flow acted quickly in an attempt to snatch up what was described as "a deal it couldn't refuse" — so quickly that much of the financial data of the new acquisition remained in the dark for the next several years.

Free Flow's new European plants (excluding the Birmingham, England, plant) employed a high percentage of imported labor from Turkey and Greece, a common practice in high-wage Europe because imported workers were willing to work for lower-than-normal wages and benefits. Free Flow made no attempt to increase these wages or change the practice; as one Free Flow executive stated, "Better for us that we are able to continue to squeeze as much cheap labor as we can from these heathen illiterates [referring to the Turks and Greeks] because the greedy Socialist Dutch and Germans will certainly take more than they deserve." Free Flow management personnel, involved in World War II as they had been, still retained much resentment toward Germans and Italians. Bert Sanderson, a vice-president involved with the overseas operations, had been a prisoner of war in Germany for 3½ years. He was known to have made statements like "These filthy Naxis are all alike and will never change . . . and those Socialist Hollanders will never quit begging for more handouts." Several other high company officials held similar opinions with respect to the Dutch and Germans.

Over the next few years, profits of the new subsidiary eroded. Free Flow management in the United States decided that, to bail itself out of the dilemma, it should take immediate action to isolate and solve the problem situations. Free Flow analysts first focused their attention on the problems of anti-Americanism and employee dissatisfaction.

In various situations, Free Flow discovered incidents of anti-American sentiment. Although now operating in seven different nations, the possibility of anti-Americanism affecting the merged operations had never been contemplated. Two of the hose production plants, Doorwerth and Leiden in Holland, were sites of much discontent since the acquisition. There were growing rates of employee turnover and absenteeism, as well as flagrant sabotage to company property. Each plant, with 905 and 1050 employees, respectively, was located in the older, rundown northern sections of Holland.

When Free Flow acquired Con Systems B.V., they had immediately sent in American managers to run the plants. Before the acquisition, each of the ten plants had been operated in an autonomous fashion by local managers who reported only on a quarterly basis to their parent, Con Systems. Several of Free Flow's overseas American managers took the view that, unlike Americans, Europeans inherently dislike work and will avoid it at all costs. Thus, Free Flow managers instituted a system of close supervision and stiff penalties for any worker found "goofing off." Free Flow's American management retained the philosophy that the only way to motivate their workers was through firing, threats, and peripheral incentives such as plant air-conditioning and brightly painted walls. Under Free Flow American managers, factory employees were characteristically never allowed to interact with management or supervisors, and no system of gathering employee suggestions was ever instituted. Free Flow had reportedly used this management-isolation system with its United States operations and it seemed to have worked effectively. In addition, there was usually nowhere for factory employees to advance and new supervisory and management personnel were hired from the outside.

Free Flow had recently expanded several of its Dutch operations to include the manufacture of polyvinyl chloride (PVC), a substance which was outlawed in the Free Flow United States plants. In a major strategic move, Free Flow decided to restructure its subsidiary by closing five of the seven plants and building two new plants, consolidating all the manufacturing processes of the five closed plants in more modern, growing, and centrally located areas of Europe. The news of the closings were not directly made to employees and consequently rumors sprang up, resulting in additional employee dissatisfaction. Humor among employees was precipitated, such as the following which was found on a factory bulletin board: "Dear colleagues, we wouldn't know what to do without you, nevertheless we will try as of Monday."

As the restructuring news was made public, there were frequent attacks by the news media on the American ability to manage; the works council broke off relations with Free Flow's management. No attempt had been made by Free Flow to find new jobs for the employees of the closed operations. In addition, the Dutch government threatened to exile Free Flow from Dutch industry altogether if it continued to close plants and lay off workers. Factory employees began to rebel through strikes. Others began seeking employment elsewhere with a more secure and stable employer and one concerned with the safety and intrinsic needs of its employees.

Free Flow had discovered that the Euromarket economy and its inhabitants are totally unlike those in the United States. Europeans had a diverse view of industry competitiveness and marketing strategies. As was found out, the structure of trade unionism and the seemingly limitless power granted to unions under governmental control was unlike anything Free Flow had ever encountered in the United States. The buying habits of dealers were completely different from practices in the United States. In addition, there was the effect of long-term alienation of Eurotrade relations, most probably caused by American-managed plants.

Questions for Discussion

1. Discuss the reasons for which the foreign expansion was undertaken.

2. What deficiencies in planning and preparing for foreign operations do you notice in the case?

3. Assuming the necessity of foreign operations, outline a plan for the successful expansion, operation, and growth of Free-Flow overseas.

CASE

OVERTIME

Jack Handle was skimming through the want ads when he saw an ad for a retail store management trainee. Further investigation revealed what seemed to be an attractive situation; he applied for and was given the job. Almost immediately he was sent to another city for an intensive six-week training course. Upon his return he was assigned to one of the smaller stores. Having set his sights on becoming a store manager, he attacked his assigned duties vigorously. His performance was duly noticed.

It wasn't long before Jack was promoted to credit manager and retail sales manager of a larger and more profitable store. The new store's credit accounts were not in very good shape, and the store had incurred highly unsatisfactory levels of expenses through the company's bad-debt accounting procedures in its credit operations for the past two years. Jack viewed this as his first big break. If he could get the store's credit accounts in the black he felt certain he had a chance of being sent to the store-manager training program. Within his first six months he had reduced bad debt loss by 40 per cent; the store actually realized a profit from the credit operation in the sixth month. Not content, he set a goal of realizing a profit for the year on the credit line; this would, in addition, increase the total annual store profit, upon which his year-end bonus was based.

In the second week of the seventh month, however, Jack's store manager, Mr. Barton, was stricken with a heart attack. He was expected to be disabled from four to six months. Jack was told by Mr. Daniels, the assistant district manager, that he would have to handle things until Barton's return.

The company was experiencing a personnel shortage at the time of Barton's illness. Jack viewed his circumstances as an opportunity to show his competence. He and the service manager, Mr. Wrigley, decided they would work whatever number of hours it took to accomplish their sales goals. As a result, their administrative and daily paperwork duties were performed in the hours before the store opened and after the store closed in the evenings; they were thus able to devote business hours to sales activities.

In the first two months after Barton's illness, profits had increased over the same month in the previous year. Jack had continued to barely break even on the credit line by staying late at night and making collection calls. During this period Jack and Wrigley both worked an average of 60 hours per week.

In the third month of Barton's absence, Daniels informed Jack that a new policy forbad any employee from working more than 48 hours per week — for any reason. Jack replied that if there were to be no exceptions, he would have to request approval to hire another person to work in the service department. Daniels granted approval, on condition that wages of no more than minimum wage plus fifty cents per hour be paid, depending on the experience and quality of work of the new person.

After his conversation with Daniels, Jack and Wrigley talked about the new policy. Both were upset, for they knew that a general service employee would relieve neither of them of very much work. They seemed to be faced with the alternatives of allowing the store to slip into a unprofitable position by working only 48 hours per week, or working however long their jobs required without extra compensation for the additional hours. Neither alternative was acceptable to them, so they agreed to find a way around the policy.

Jack was paid at a base rate of $5.50 per hour. Wrigley, who had spent more time with the company, made about $6 per hour. Both were entitled to time-and-a-half for all hours worked over 40 hours per week up to the 48 allowable.

The plan they came up with was to "hire" a fictitious employee at the maximum allowable rate of $4.15 per hour. The employee was to "work" enough hours per week to earn their unpaid overtime. They would divide this pay between them in proportion to the number of hours worked by each and in proportion to their pay rates, which they computed at time and a half. The result was that each was paid for overtime while, on paper at least, complying with the new policy on allowable working hours. They gave the fictitious employee the social security number of Wrigley's son, filled out an application in the fictitious name and in all possible respects tried to conceal the truth from all the company representatives who visited the store during Barton's absence. They "fired" the fictitious employee when Barton gave them notice of his return. Their ploy was never discovered — or if it was, no one ever challenged the arrangement.

Questions for Discussion

1. Is the fictitious employee plan harmful? Fair?

2. Is the restriction on paid overtime harmful? Fair?

3. Was what John and Wrigley did ethical? Why or why not?

ANSWERS TO SELF-REVIEW QUESTIONS, CHAPTER 20

True–False

1-F, 2-F, 3-F, 4-T, 5-F, 6-F, 7-T, 8-F, 9-F, 10-T, 11-F, 12-T, 13-F, 14-T, 15-F, 16-T

Multiple Choice

1-E, 2-E, 3-A, 4-C, 5-D, 6-A, 7-E.

Completion

1. Social responsibility. 2. Profits. 3. Code. 4. Social audit. 5. Ethics. 6. Multinational corporation.

Chapter 21

The Changing Environment of Management

CHAPTER OBJECTIVES

1. To discuss the major changes expected in our society and their impacts on business

2. To identify the changing framework within which management operates and makes the required dynamic responses.

3. To give a perspective on the future and thus allow the student to face it more confidently

SELF-REVIEW QUESTIONS

True–False

T   F   1. The quaternary sector is, for the most part, characterized by smaller and less-centralized units.

T   F   2. The concept of hard work will once again become popular as work weeks become shorter and there are fewer hours in which to get the same amount of work done.

T   F   3. It is predicted that there will be more attention paid to individual output in compensation plans.

T   F   4. The postindustrial society is characterized by the relative decline of industry as a prime force.

T   F   5. U.S. population between 1980 and 1990 is expected to increase by less than 1 per cent.

T   F   6. During the decade of the 1980s, the average age of the U.S. population will decrease from 30 to 28.3.

308

T F 7. The financial value of a college education has never been higher than at present.

T F 8. Between 1970 and 1990, the metropolitan population growth rate will be at least double that experienced in the 20 years before 1970.

T F 9. Because the U.S. labor force will not grow as rapidly in the 1980s as it did in the 1960s and 1970s, productivity is expected to decline because of the higher average age of workers.

T F 10. About half the current labor force is made up of women.

T F 11. Less than one fourth of the current labor force are union members, the lowest ratio in recent history.

T F 12. Slightly more than 60 per cent of all U.S. workers find their jobs more important to them than their lesiure-time activities.

T F 13. Traditional incentives are especially important to young, highly educated middle managers and professionals.

T F 14. Poorly educated, low-income blue-collar workers are motivated strongly by traditional incentives.

T F 15. It is expected that the "cottage office" concept, in which individuals contract with an organization to perform specific types of work at home (rather than at the office), will increase in popularity.

Multiple Choice

1. The term *postindustrial* indicates

   (a) the anticipated dominance of our society by industrial powers, (b) the relative decline of industry as a determinant of our values and way of life, (c) the advent of new manufacturing techniques, (d) a general lack of willingness on the part of the people to be meaningfully employed or to work hard.

2. An industry that processes raw products from farming, forestry, fishing, or mining is a _____ industry.

   (a) primary, (b) secondary, (c) tertiary, (d) quaternary

3. In which of the following is the manpower requirement declining?

   (a) primary industries, (b) tertiary industries, (c) quaternary industries, (d) none of the above

4. In which of the following is the manpower requirement increasing?

   (a) primary industries, (b) secondary industries, (c) quaternary industries, (d) none of the above

5. Which of the following is a major example of a quaternary industry?

   (a) forestry, (b) education, (c) canning, (d) public accounting firms, (e) none of the above

6. What ratio of the U.S. labor force is employed in producing goods (rather than services)?

   (a) about three fourths, (b) more than three fourths, (c) about two thirds, (d) between one half and two thirds, (e) less than one half

7. The key element in the total compensation package will be

   (a) higher salary, (b) improved fringe benefits, (c) challenging work, (d) status symbols.

8. Which of the following is pointed out in the text as factors likely to change people's attitudes toward the value of work?

   (a) increasing affluence, (b) increasing education, (c) continuing automation, (d) a vastly changed future environment, (e) all of the above.

9. "Traditional" incentives consist of which of the following?

   (a) money, (b) economic fear, (c) productivity measurements, (d) a and b, (e) all of the above

10. Which of the following is *not* one of the major challenges for management in the 1980s identified in the text?

   (a) public demands and governmental regulation, (b) weakening of industrial discipline and of support for the work ethic, (c) identification and isolation of major contingent determinants of managerial effectiveness, (d) slow economic growth, (e) high political turbulence and uncertainty

READING

EIGHT PARADOXES FOR THE 1980s

Robert M. Fulmer

In his classic *A Tale of Two Cities*, Charles Dickens described his age and ours:

> It was the best of times, it was the worst of times, it was the age of wisdom, it was the age of foolishness, it was the epoch of belief, it was the epoch of incredulity, it was the season of Light, it was the season of Darkness, it was the winter of despair

An astute observer of life around him as well as a gifted writer, Dickens saw the marked contrasts that surrounded the early days of the Industrial

Reprinted by permission of the author, to whom all rights are reserved. This article is based on an article in the May/June 1981 issue of *Management Focus*, also by Dr. Fulmer.

Revolution. Today, as we near the end of the Industrial Revolution, we find our world marked by contrasts equally as dramatic. An assessment of the probabilities associated with this decade reveals that it is indeed both the best of times and the worst of times.

Futurists come in varying degrees of optimism and pessimism. One group, known as the "Neo-Malthusians," anticipate a world that is growing dirtier, drier, more crowded and more quarrelsome. They see the stark realities of famine, poverty, totalitarianism and terrorism becoming a daily reality for billions of people.

On the other hand, the "Super Optimists" see astonishing advances in medicine, agriculture, information technology, and space exploration that may be able to delay the aging process, forestall death, overcome cancer, provide food from the oceans and transport large loads of passengers and space vehicles to all corners of the earth . . . and beyond.

As the world grows in size and complexity, it becomes more and more difficult for a single individual to assimilate all of the changes that are confronting us. A natural reaction is to focus on one single mind-set and use that as a reference point for the changes that occur. The focus of this article is to suggest that managers assess both sides of contrasting trends that seem to be emerging. With particular emphasis on changes that will be affecting the world of work and workers, we will identify and discuss eight paradoxes for the 1980's.

PARADOX I. THE DECLINE OF TRADITIONAL INCENTIVES, WITH INCREASED POPULARITY OF FINANCIALLY-REWARDED CAREERS

"People just aren't willing to work as hard as they used to. The work ethic no longer exists." In reality, the incentives that have traditionally encouraged people to work hard have become less effective. These inducements include money, fear, and other techniques that don't depend on motivation for productivity. According to Daniel Yankelovich, these traditional incentives still work for 56 per cent of the work force. They mean nothing, however, to the other, primarily younger 44 per cent of contemporary workers. Basically, the work force can be divided into the following groups:

19% — Older dedicated workers who want to make a contribution;

22% — habitual workers who are older, in lower-level jobs and who want job security;

15% — young, ambitious go-getters who are motivated by money and the opportunity to get ahead;

17% — young, middle-managers, highly educated professionals who are more interested in challenge and responsibility than traditional incentives;

21% — alienated, turned-off, poorly educated low-income workers who are not motivated at all. Unfortunately this group seems to be growing.

While traditional incentives seem to be losing some of their clout, financially-oriented professions are increasing in popularity. College enrollments in liberal arts and humanities are declining dramatically. Concurrently, enrollment in business, engineering and preprofessional programs are experiencing record growth. Since 1964, the number of MBA graduates produced annually has risen by 900%. Since 1971, the number of individuals taking the Test for Advanced Study in Management has risen from 83,915 to 212,500.

Clearly, the prospect of a financially rewarding career is a stimulus to many individuals who are currently enrolled in colleges. In some instances, these "practically-minded" students would have preferred to major in English, history, or sociology, but their assessment of the market place indicates that this could be a pleasant, but unproductive choice. This may also suggest that the value systems of the emerging college graduate may allow for more flexibility than was true in the past. Idealism is tempered with a sense of practical reality. Challenge and responsibility will continue to be key watch words, but money is important too. These "new workers" will be dissatisfied if financial rewards are not forthcoming; however, they will probably not stay in a dead-end job or accept arbitrary transfers unless there is more than money to lure them to new assignments.

PARADOX II. INCREASED COMPETITION FOR PROMOTIONS, BUT MORE FLEXIBILITY IN WORK POSITIONS

By 1990, more than half of the labor force will be between the ages of 25 and 44. This means increased competition for available promotions. In the 1960s, there were about ten workers who competed for each middle management position. By the end of this decade, the ratio will have doubled.

The reasons for this promotion crunch are quite simple. First and foremost is the maturing of the baby boom group (born between 1945 and 1965) as candidates for management positions. This will be compounded by deferred retirement of present managers who will stay on their jobs longer because of a persistent inflation problem. These two factors will be further aggravated by a generally slow economic growth rate throughout this decade (probably 2–3 per cent per year) which will limit the creation of new management positions. Roy Amara, president of the Institute for the Future, predicts that new management structures will be required to accommodate this unprecedented number of potential managers. "A flattening of organizational pyramids, creation of smaller, autonomous work groups, development of 'working manager' positions, job design and restructuring. . . . these are some of the ways to ease the expected crunch."

With this kind of competition for advancement, we might conclude that organizations will be less accommodating of special employee interests or demands than has been true in the past. Just the opposite will actually occur. At the lower end of the organizational pyramid, there will be a shrinking supply of entry-level workers. This group will grow during the 1980's at less than one-half the rate of the 1970's.

The impact of a rapid decline in fertility rates since the mid 1960's will be the major contributing factor. Because so many women are already working, the growth of labor force participation among female workers will continue to grow as dramatically. Finally, the rising expectations of entry-level workers will contribute to the need for greater flexibility. In order to meet the demand for entry-level positions, organizations will allow more workers to schedule their own hours under flex-time. Many workers will probably hold two jobs or go to college on a part-time basis. Already the need for life-time learning is a generally accepted principle. Moreover, the number of moonlighters increased about 20% during the 1970's, and the number of women holding multiple jobs doubled.

In *The Third Wave* Alvin Toffler describes the emerging trend of the "cottage office." Increasing numbers of people will be contracting with organizations to complete work in their own homes. It could be art work for an advertising campaign, instructional materials for a training program, or software packages. The worker gains the advantage of flexibility and reduced commuting expenses while the company eliminates the overhead commitment, fringe benefits, and additional "extras" associated with full-time employees.

This work "decentralization" will continue to pick up momentum throughout the decade. The growth of portable computers which can be hooked up to telephone lines and television sets to retrieve data and file reports will hasten this move. Demand for at home "office space" in future houses and apartments will experience significant growth. Corporations will not eliminate their headquarters locations, but the need for them to "warehouse" large groups of workers in a single building will decline.

Over all, companies will become even more accommodating to eliminate the regimentation and boredom associated with entry-level positions. At the same time, increased competition for managerial promotions will be quite intense. Although these jobs will be more demanding than those at the lower levels of an organization, they will be in great demand because of their scarcity and the economic regards associated with promotions.

PARADOX III. INCREASED FINANCIAL PRESSURES, YET MORE SUPERAFFLUENT FAMILIES

In the 1970's energy prices rose 165%, shelter 106%, medical care 111%, and food 115%. During the same period, median family income grew only 107%. The Labor Department recently reported that real hourly compensation for 1980 was at the same level as in the third quarter of 1972. The price of the average house on today's market is $77,600. If 10% inflation continues, the average will be $121,000 by late 1985. By 1995, the average house could cost $314,000.

Coping with inflation has become a national pastime. The four major strategies that have been used to meet the challenge are:

A. *More workers:* The average family today has 1.7 workers in it. Almost half of the families making the average median income do so only because two members of the family work.

B. *Lower savings:* The U.S. savings rate is only 4.5% of personal disposable income. This is the lowest level in more than thirty years and far below the savings rate in countries such as Japan, West Germany, France and England.

C. *Increasing debt:* Record-breaking interest rates have only slightly reduced the level of consumer installment debt which, in 1979, was 18.5% of personal disposable income.

D. *Home equity:* People who bought homes at a relatively low cost and with modest interest rates have been able to cope with inflation because of the tremendous increase in their home values. This equity has been used to obtain loans for everything from college tuition to vacation travel expenses.

Moonlighting, exhaustion, persistent worry, and fighting over money share the spotlight that shines through the picture window of many middle-American homes. Workers dream of upper mobility, affluence and getting ahead, but in reality, find themselves skipping their annual physical check-up, cashing in insurance policies and quibbling with children about allow-ances. Epidemic advances in alcoholism, drug addiction, divorce and early heart attack are not unrelated to financial pressures created by this des-perate race to hold on to the good life.

Yet, the picture is not totally bleak. Every thirty minutes, another dozen people will enter the 50% tax bracket. In 1980, over 2.3 million Americans will discover the good news and the bad news associated with qualifying for this painful honor. As suggested above, the two-income household, along with an emphasis on fewer children, has been one of the most effective ways of preserving living standards. Demand is still high for luxury items such as expensive cars, European vacations, and costly jewelry. Yet, personal bankruptcy rose to 25,000 in mid-1980, a level higher than experienced even during the severe recession year of 1974.

In addition to the extremes of large groups of individuals struggling to make ends meet, and a rapid growth of the super-affluents, there may also be an acceleration of the "rags-to riches rollercoaster." The same individual may go through several stages of relative poverty and affluence.

For example, young people today typically come from families that are wealthier than was true a generation ago. When they leave home and es-tablish their own independence, the high cost of housing and energy often force them into a period of relative poverty. When they join forces to create a two-income family, both living standards rise dramatically. If that re-lationship fails to survive (which is the case with about 40 per cent), both partners are reduced to another round of struggle. This struggle can also come about merely because of the high cost of educating and caring for children. Eventually, however, most people will rear their children, work out living arrangements, and enjoy advanced middle-age with a re-discovered joy of discretionary income.

PARADOX IV: THE INCREASED IMPORTANCE OF FAMILY, YET MORE MARRIAGE FAILURE

The trends that will mark the change in the family emphasis are already apparent. During the past decade, the number of marriages performed in-creased 7.3%. The number of divorces granted increased 65.3% and the number of unmarried couples living together increased 157.4%. The num-ber of children living with one parent grew by 40.1%.

As has already been indicated, families are assuming greater importance as far as financial security is concerned. Sociologist Charles Westoff pre-dicts an expansion of communal living as unrelated people of all age levels band together to reduce housing costs. By the year 2,000, almost 75% of married couples will have both parties working. By the end of this decade, woman will contribute 40% of family incomes. This compares with 26.1% today.

Families also play a greater role in the pressure to create more flexible working hours, and working relationships, as well as day-care facilities. The impact is just beginning to surface as more individuals decline promotion opportunities because it would involve relocating a working spouse. In a 1980 survey, Merrill Lynch Relocation Management Inc. found that 30% of responding companies are providing job-finding assistance for spouses of transferring managers — almost double the number one year ago.

While families are making themselves heard as an active constituency in job-related decisions, they are also being subjected to an increasing number of pressures. Most individuals who are currently in management positions have not totally resolved their ambivalence about the changing sterotypes of sex roles. Despite the increased representation of women in the work force, most two-income families report that women are expected to assume more responsibility for meal preparation and housekeeping. Clearly, if the two-career family is to succeed, men must take a more active role in child-rearing as well as household tasks.

No one yet knows the long-range impact of the "latch-key children" approach to parenting. The Work in America Institute, Inc., a research organization based in Scarsdale, New York, estimates that more than 30 million American children have working mothers. They further estimate that at least 5 million of these children may be receiving inadequate care during their parents' working hours. The Urban Institute predicts that by 1990 there will be a 64% jump in the number of working mothers with children under 6.

The divorce rate currently runs around 40% of the number of marriages performed in a given year. This will probably remain high but not increase dramatically. People will wait longer before remarrying. Still, almost half of the children in the country will spend part of their childhood in a single-family situation.

PARADOX V. MORE ABILITY AND NEED TO CENTRALIZE DECISIONS, BUT MORE PRESSURE TO DECENTRALIZE

Computers, television and satellites are already cutting down on the need for travel, allowing people access to information and communication from their homes or offices. By 1990, many experts believe that home computers will be in 80% of U.S. dwellings and will offer assistance with everything from office and school work to balancing the family check book.

A more direct involvement in the democratic process will shortly be possible via electronic referendums. Within five years, Japan will initiate voting and census taking through video centers within the home. Unfortunately, access to tremendous amounts of data does not necessarily create more information or knowledge. Electronics may be able to bring in a vast variety of entertainment and data into homes, but it will be increasingly difficult for people to comprehend what it all means. The increasing sophistication of electronics in the home will also discourage them from moving out of their "hybernated existence" at home.

Just as technology is making it possible for more individuals to have access to information and to participate in decision making, the same kind of high-quality information is making it possible for centralized decisions to be made with more efficiency. Despite the sad record of government planning, the future offers the potential of much more efficient, intelligent approaches to predicting and controlling the future. Even the optimistic head of the Hudson Institute, Herman Kahn, admits that progress during the last fifth of this century is dependent upon a combination of "good luck and good management." It might appear that there is a greater need for efficiency in decision making than participation. At present, the economic decisions that need to be made are extremely difficult because of political implications. Would it not be more reasonable for someone to make the decisions based on more input and better analysis than the average citizen can muster?

Regardless of the efficiency of centralized decision making, SRI International (formerly Stanford Research Institute) has concluded that the move for more participation in decision making will affect all aspects of life during this decade. Many of the decisions made in this manner may not be optimal, but they will benefit from the motivation associated from taking part in the process.

PARADOX VI: MORE PEOPLE WORKING,
YET HIGHER UNEMPLOYMENT
One of the complex issues of the 1980 presidential election was the convincing argument of the incumbent president that more Americans were at work and earning more money than had been true at any other point in the history of this country. Conversely, the challenging candidate was citing impressive figures to prove that there were more people unemployed than had ever been out of work in the past. Despite the apparent contradiction, both sets of facts were absolutely true. Moreover, both of these trends will probably continue.

Labor economists will remember the 1970's for its unprecedented growth in workers primarily fueled by the maturation of babies born after World War II and the rapid influx of women. During the same period, "acceptable" unemployment increased from about 4% to 6%. In the early 1980's unemployment will probably reach 8.2%. A severe recession could increase that percentage.

While the workforce will not continue to grow at the same rate as has been true in the past, there will probably be 16.4 million more people at work in 1990 than now. A severe recession could increase that percentage. Technical areas such as computers and electronics will create increased employment opportunities along with such professions as accounting, nursing, and engineering. Certain industries such as aerospace, communications, electronics, broadcasting, health care, and energy will experience dramatic increases.

The Center for the Study of Social Policy in Menlo Park, California, portrays chronic unemployment and under-employment as fundamental concerns of the Post Industrial Society. This concern rests on the proposition that economic growth may not continue to generate enough jobs to accomodate even a slowly expanding work force and the quality of available jobs may not be compatible with the rising expectations associated with the higher educational levels of our people. The U.S. Chamber of Commerce believes that the reason for rising unemployment can be explained by the following three trends:

A. Increased benefits offered by employment compensation, welfare and food stamp programs provide less incentive for people to find jobs.

B. Dramatic increases in the number of women and teenagers in the work force lead to higher unemployment since these two groups tend to quit or change jobs more often than other workers.

C. Because of the existence of two full-time workers in families, if one person becomes temporarily unemployed, the other affords a buffer against hardship that was not available before.

In addition to unemployment, Herbert Greenberg, President of Marketing Survey and Research Corporation, believes that 80% of American workers are doing jobs for which they are not suited. This figure applies to "every job category . . . every educational group . . . every part of the country." It, of course, involves people who have stumbled into jobs for which they had little training or aptitude as well as individuals who were highly trained but unable to find employment in their own fields.

Of course, unemployment figures only reflect those individuals who are currently actively seeking employment. When those who no longer seek work, those who are in featherbedding or make-work situations, drop-outs or those in holding institutions such as reform schools and mental institutions are taken into account, real unemployment may be 20 to 25% of the potential workforce. We will probably have to learn to live with a large number of under and unemployed workers even when there will be a tight labor market for entry-level jobs.

PARADOX VII. DRAMATIC PROGRESS FOR WOMEN BUT CONTINUED INEQUALITY.

According to the National Commission on Working Wome, 80% of the working women in the United States are concentrated in the low-paying, low-status jobs. Most are in "pink-collar" jobs such as waitress, beauticians, and clerical positions. Another large concentration of working women may be found in blue-collar jobs (skilled and union trades).

Surprisingly, there has been little progress in closing the gap between earnings for men and women. Since 1967, women have consistently earned about two-thirds of what their male counterparts do. Even in the female ghetto of clerical work where salaries are extremely low, women's wages are only 63% of those paid for the few men in this field. The Labor Department reports that women who support their families earn less than half (46.9%) the amount earned by male breadwinners. According to the Bureau of Labor Statistics, husbands who are the sole family wage earners average $322 per week ($16,744 per year), while women who are sole wage earners for a family average only $151 per week ($7,852 per year).

There have been important areas of the progress during the past twenty years. Women banking and financial officers have increased from 2,100 to 122,000. Female sales management positions have increased from 200 to 12,000. According to the *U.S. News Washington Letter*, the 80's will see dramatic strides made by women in obtaining more equality in the U.S. work force. Within the next twenty years, females may hold the top spots in 10% of the nation's 500 largest companies. That's progress, but hardly equality.

SRI International predicts that one of the most significant changes of the 80's will be the impact of women making key management decisions. The backhanded compliment that "You think like a man" will give way to women making decisions as women. In other words, instead of being forced into a masculine mode, women will gain more freedom to make decisions in their own way. Women do make decisions differently from men. They generally utilize the right hemisphere of their brain in thinking more than men. This means that they are more likely to be creative or intuitive than relying totally upon logic. Your reaction to the foregoing statement may be a test of your own adapability. Some readers will view the statement that "women make decisions differently" as a sexist comment. There are obvious, important differences between men and women (Sexists might say, "viva la differences!"). Women will have achieved a degree of progress when they are not forced to compete with men by duplicating the male behavior pattern. When they can approach problems and challenges in their own individual manner, there may be some surprising, but productive approaches to organizational lives. In summary, there will be more progress than equality.

PARADOX VIII. THE TRIUMPH OF WORKER PARTICIPATION, YET A REVIVAL OF SCIENTIFIC MANAGEMENT.

I've already documented the move toward greater decentralization of decision making. This trend will be particularly important in organizations. In business, it will be accentuated by the results of a quarter century of research in the field of human relations, as well as the example of Japanese management and the successes of a few US pioneers. We can anticipate that industrial workers will be involved in autonomous work teams where they make many of their own production decisions. This "uni-management" is already occurring in a few companies as a result of agreements between the UAW in such firms as Dana Corporation, Rockwell, and Harman. At the Edgerton, Wisconsin Dana factory, production committees of workers and supervisors elect a union-management screening committee which sifts suggestions as to how the factors of production should be organized. At Harmon Industries in Boliver, Tennessee, Worker-Supervisor Core Committees plan production within each department. Their decisions are subject to review by a plant wide union-management work committee.

In Europe, co-determination has made rapid strides. Swedish law puts union representatives on corporate boards. In 1976, West Germany gave workers the right to elect half of the directors of firms employing over 2,000 people. Andre Thiria, international secretary of the Swedish Confederation of Trade Unions, explains, "Demands are being raised for better work environment and more satisfaction on the job, while at the same time mechanization and streamlining of production makes it more difficult to meet these demands." Joint efforts by workers and management is one attempt to solve this dilemma.

Because of the widespread recognition of America's problem of productivity, there will be a concurrent return to some of the basics of scientific management and production efficiency. Unlike the scientific management movement that emerged around the turn of the century, workers will no longer be viewed as minor cogs in the production process. Productivity and efficiency are two themes that will increase dramatically in their popularity during the 1980's. In the last two year, US productivity has been less than one percent per year. This compares unfavorably to countries like Japan (6.8%), West Germany (5.3%), and even Great Britian (2.5%). The factors that will work toward greater productivity include improved production technology (with greater emphasis on computer-assisted manufacturing and robots), an older and more experienced work force, economic pressures on workers, *and* greater involvement of workers in decisions that affect them.

CONCLUSION

The phrase "We live in an age of transition" may have been first spoken by Adam as he escorted Eve from the Garden of Eden. It certainly is an appropriate description of the decade that lies before us. In the midst of dramatic, and sometimes conflicting trends, the astute manager must be able to read the ebb and flow of tides that affect his or her operation. Ralph Waldo Emerson once said, "A foolish consistency is the hobgobblin of little minds." The challenge of the 80's is to unravel the inconsistencies and to understand the paradoxes that confront us. It will not be a time for "little minds."

Questions for Discussion

1. Given the types of changes predicted in the article, identify at least five practices or techniques of management that will have to change dramatically.

2. Which of the changes predicted will have the *most* significant impact on management practice? *Least* significant?

EXERCISE

YOU AND YOUR FUTURE

The text discusses the future and its possible demands and requirements. To be prepared for the future, we should base our personal and professional plans on the best information available, thinking through what we wish to do and what we can (or should) do. This exercise should allow you to develop some broad-gauge directions for your future and your career.

Given the work, industry, economic, and political trends discussed in the text,

1. in which sector — goods or services — do you think you should seek a career? Why?

2. in which *type* of business in the sector you chose in (1) do you think you should seek a career? Why?

3. what types of business skills do you think you should develop? Why?

4. what types of management skills do you think you should develop? Why?

EXERCISE

CHANGES AND MANAGING

The test points out a number of changes expected to occur in the near future. These will affect you in a number of ways, not the least of which will be in the nature of your job and career.

1. Identify the implications of changes in the following areas, as outlined in the text, for management practice.

2. Identify some ways you as a manager would handle these changes, showing the methods you would use.

    a. Changing nature of the work force.

    b. Changing attitudes toward business and work.

ANSWERS TO SELF-REVIEW QUESTIONS, CHAPTER 21

True–False

1-T, 2-F, 3-F, 4-T, 5-F, 6-F, 7-F, 8-F, 9-F, 10-T, 11-T, 12-F, 13-F, 14-F, 15-T.

Multiple Choice

1-B, 2-B, 3-A, 4-C, 5-B, 6-E, 7-C, 8-E, 9-E, 10-C.

Chapter 22

The Changing Practice of Management

CHAPTER OBJECTIVES

1. To investigate future possible changes that are pertinent to management
2. To give insights into how these potential changes will affect the manager's job
3. To consider managerial alternatives available from Japanese business practices

SELF-REVIEW QUESTIONS

True–False

T F 1. The pyramid approach to organizational planning was first used to provide central control over large numbers of activities.

T F 2. One major advantage of the pyramid is the relative ease with which the communication of group goals is accomplished.

T F 3. Group decision making is becoming rather widely accepted by businesspeople.

T F 4. The computer is very likely to take over or replace many of the jobs on the bottom half of the organization chart.

T F 5. Fringe benefits provided for employees by companies are likely to decrease, especially in view of expanding national social welfare programs.

T F 6. The inability of a single chief executive to cope with the sheer volume of work and the required broad range of critical skills suggests the need for a plural executive for top-level decision making.

T F   7. The chief advantage of the pyramid is that each worker need only be concerned with one job and one supervisor.

T F   8. The greatest disadvantage of the pyramid system is that each worker is only concerned with one job and one supervisor.

T F   9. One structural alternative to the traditional pyramid is described in the text as looking like a dandelion on top of a football.

T F 10. Management experts have been found to agree that the pyramid-shaped structure will continue to dominate, with only one fourth of organizations using some other form by the year 2000.

T F 11. In the past decade there was a significant retreat from division of responsibility through the device of plural executives or CEO-COO combinations.

T F 12. Those who believe the organization of the future to be shaped like an hourglass think the traditional roles of middle managers will be taken over by computers.

T F 13. In comparison with Japanese managers, American managers seek more widespread participation in decision making, more consensus about decisions reached, and more widespread responsibility for the success of the decision.

T F 14. Japanese managers are more interested in the employee as a complete individual than are American managers.

T F 15. Although interesting, Japanese management practices are mostly unsuitable for application by American managers, primarily because of the differences between Japanese and American present and future situations.

Multiple Choice

1. Planning for the uncertain future

    (a) is foolish because our efforts may turn out to have been wasted when the future gets here, (b) is wise because through planning we can exert some control over our own prospects, (c) will cease to be a function of management as computers take over, (d) all of the above.

2. For 5,000 years, activities that involved large numbers of people have been charted in the _____ form.

    (a) tactical, (b) mass, (c) pyramid, (d) bipolar

3. The effect that computers will have upon decentralization or centralization of decision making is

    (a) definitely in favor of centralization, (b) definitely in favor of decentralization, (c) not clear.

4. Upper management will retain which of the following, unaffected by the computer?

   (a) creativity, (b) innovation, (c) solving unstructured problems, (d) a and c, (e) all of the above.

5. Which of the following is a reason for managers' becoming more concerned with the future?

   (a) it is fashionable, (b) decreased rate of change of environmental factors allows more successful prediction, (c) increased rate of change and technological development, (d) futurism is becoming a common element in managerial job descriptions

6. An alternative to the bureaucratic form of organization is the _____ _____ form, in which temporary systems of diverse specialists work together on a specific problem.

   (a) project, (b) wheel, (c) plural, (d) diversification, (e) mainframe-and-spoke

7. Which of the following is *not* identified in the text as being a probable cause for the gradual erosion in the use of the organizational pyramid?

   (a) higher educational and aspiration levels, (b) changing challenges of business environment, (c) impact of the computer, (d) attitude of people toward authority

8. Which of the following is identified in the text as an element in the traditional American management model?

   (a) short-term employment, (b) committee decision making, (c) subjective, informal control, (d) generalist-oriented career paths, (e) all of the above

9. Which of the following is *not* identified in the text as a characteristics in the Japanese management system?

   (a) slow evaluation and promotion, (b) elaborate procedures for determining individual responsibility, (c) generalist-oriented career path, (d) consensus decision procedures

10. Which of the following seems the most reasonable perspective on the potential role of Japanese management practices in the American system?

    (a) the two systems are not compatible, (b) the Japanese system is likely to replace the American system, (c) the more task-oriented American system will replace the Japanese system, even in Japan, (d) elements in the American system will be modified to incorporate relevant aspects of the Japanese system

READING

THE TYPE Z ORGANIZATION

A Corporate Alternative to Village Life

William G. Ouchi

Productivity per labor hour in the United States has increased by an average of 2.7 per cent each year since 1960. Within that same time frame, the Japanese have made productivity gains averaging a much more impressive 9.7 per cent.

Why does this tremendous gap exist, and how can it be narrowed?

One reason for the difference may be a technology differential. Following World War II, Japan was forced to rebuild completely its bombed-out factories and industries, replacing them with the most up-to-date equipment and technologies. Meanwhile, the United States continued to rely on its older plants and processes.

However, a far more likely reason for at least part of the difference is found in the fundamentally different labor attitudes and management styles employed by the major industrial corporations operating in the United States and Japan — styles that also reflect elemental differences in their cultures.

These differing management philosophies can best be explained by taking a closer look at the countries involved. Americans have always prided themselves on their rugged individualism. In sharp contrast to this American tradition of individuality, open spaces, and far-flung cities, the Japanese heritage has been built around the positive aspects of closely knit group life. For example, as a chain of volcanic islands, Japan's geographic configuration has forced its people to live much closer together. In addition, the deliberate isolation of the country, coupled with its remarkable ethnic homogeneity, has created a group spirit that has spilled over into the workplace in some extraordinary and obviously productive ways.

At the same time, in America, the traditional social interactions built specifically around group activities related to family, the church, and neighborhoods have diminished or disappeared altogether. Yet, except for a few exceptions, we remain steadfastly predisposed to reject the need for some new binding forces or new group interactions to replace those we have lost. The most obvious replacement is one that the Japanese have long since recognized and exploited successfully and profitable: the cohesion of the work organization.

TYPE J: THE JAPANESE MODEL

The Japanese model or the Type J organization has evolved in a society in which individual mobility has historically been low and norms of collectivism have been strongly supported.

Reprinted by permission from the Spring 1980 issue of *Outlook*, a quarterly publication of Booz-Allen & Hamilton, for the international business community, pp. 12-16. Copyright © 1980.

The typical large Japanese corporation offers its workers lifetime employment. Competition is therefore fierce in a male work force seeking to be employed by the "major companies" that make up the core of many business consortia. University graduates neither have nor need any specialized business experience; they supply the kind of "uncluttered" mind that can easily be geared toward the philosophy of their new employer. For the first 10 years of employment, all workers receive similar wages and the same promotions. Therefore, they naturally think long term, are cooperative within their firms, talk openly, and work as a group.

Career paths tend to be nonspecialized, making each employee an expert in his organization rather than merely an expert in specific functions of that organization. Their particular skills and knowledge are valuable only to the one firm that employs them, producing increased loyalty and decreasing the chances of mobility or disorientation.

Decisions within this cohesive unit are naturally not made by any one person, but by consensus, with as many as eighty persons taking part in the process. While this may initially slow decision making, once a decision is made, implementation is faster and more efficient because so many key managers have already participated in the planning stages of an enterprise.

This mode of consensual decision making spills over into a philosophy peculiar to Japanese business: collective responsibility. Because individuals spend a lifetime working together, they have an interest in maintaining harmonious relationships, not only by consensual decision making, but also by taking responsibility collectively. The larger culture, of course, strongly supports these norms of organizational collectivism. With collective responsibility, no individual receives credit or blame for actions, since organizational actions are, by their very nature, the joint product of many individuals.

One consequence: the biggest error American firms make in Japan is trying to single out and reward individual effort. At one U.S.-owned manufacturing plant in Japan, an American manager made the mistake of setting up a piece-rate system as an incentive for individual assembly workers. The result was not increased productivity, but instead, the threat of a work stoppage. The American manager was told that the assembly workers wanted to be paid in the same way as other workers in large companies in Japan were, and that they did not want to be singled out from the collective effort of all plant workers.

By knowing a company thoroughly, by living a lifetime with a company and within a company, the worker can be accepted by the organization as a permanent member of its family. Two other related characteristics of the Type J organization result.

First, a system of informal and implicit control is created in which performance objectives, such as increases in production or sales, are broadly accepted by employees. In the Japanese model, if a worker knows his company as he should and vice versa, the objectives for all workers become implicitly obvious to, and shared by, all employees.

Second, this informal view results in an organization that takes a "holistic" view of its workers; a company is totally interested in its employees. Records of one Japanese company studied showed that 65 per cent of its women employees over a 10-year period had married males of the same company. The company actually had a sizeable fulltime matchmaking staff. Supervisors became more like mentors than bosses, creating a familial atmosphere and less competition and strain in employee relations.

Such corporate holism has its dangers as well as benefits, of course. If an organization does not maintain a democratic and egalitarian attitude, the holistic approach can become paternalistic and, in extreme cases, totalitarian.

TYPE A: THE AMERICAN/EUROPEAN MODEL

We are all more or less familiar with the other end of the organization spectrum, the Type A organization, commonly found in America and in many Western European countries.

The Type A organization developed and thrived in a society characterized by high rates of mobility and supported by norms of individual independence, self-reliance and individual responsibility. Mobility in the American business system is a given, and employees generally stay in any one organization for a short period of time. Individual decision making and individual responsibility become established patterns of managing organizations in order to cope with the rapid changes in personnel. The holistic approach towards employees takes a decidedly segmented turn.

With interfirm mobility so high, it is difficult to integrate new employees completely into the style of a company (unlike the Type J organization). The employee therefore has only limited and contractual ties to the organization and cannot possibly internalize its values. He or she is dealt with in a relationship that is much more explicit, objective-oriented, and formal.

Specialization becomes increasingly important in this kind of structure. With increased employee mobility and turnover, learning must occur rapidly, so that the most return can be gained from the necessary investment in each individual in the shortest amount of time.

Promotion must also be rapid, because of the rapid turnover of managers. Evaluation occurs quickly, with greater burdens placed on the individual's superior to provide that assessment. Along with the kind of burden — to evaluate and promote quickly — come the more formal boss-subordinate relationships that have developed in most Type A organizations.

These two approaches (A and J) have succeeded in their natural settings. To transplant either to the other's culture would probably be unsuccessful. However, some of the key features of the Type J are not culture-bound and can be transported successfully to western settings, with some significant benefits.

THE "Z": A BLEND OF TYPES A AND J

The Type Z organization is a term used to describe those U.S. firms in which features resembling the Japanese managerial approach have evolved. Typically, these U.S. firms have developed their own form of management, and it is one that achieves a high degree of cooperative effort.

Which American corporations seem to fit the Type Z Model? In a recent series of interviews with managers from a wide range of industries, the same companies were named again and again. Among them were: General Motors, IBM, Hewlett-Packard, Procter & Gamble, Cummins Engine and Eastman Kodak. One noncorporation, the U.S. Military, was also frequently cited.

These organizations, for a variety of reasons, (see page 328) have chosen to manage themselves in a unique and distinctive way, and one which closely resembles the Japanese management style. What features do they seem to have in common?

In a Type Z organization, although performance goals are clearly set, no one, it seems, is promoted solely on the basis of such objective performance criteria. Judging employees is more subjective than in the Type A organization. Career paths are moderately specialized. And once again, the slowness of evaluation and the stability of the organization's membership combine to promote a holistic concern for people, particularly between superiors and subordinates.

In the Z organization, this holism actively includes both the employee and his or her family. In Japan, the family is virtually abandoned (in terms of the company's interest) since wives and children have their own stable social groups to provide order in their lives, allowing them to adjust to a husband who is absorbed in his organization. In America, where wives and children (or their friends) move so frequently, support groups just for them are not as common. The Type Z organization seeks to fill that void without intruding into the private lifes of employees, typically an issue of importance at such firms.

WHY ADOPT A TYPE Z APPROACH?

Why can the Type Z organization, created by combining the A and J types in a unique pattern, be so useful — and profitable — a model? After all, isn't the Type A a natural outgrowth of our society? Perhaps. But the social structures and social conditions that first created the A organization have changed dramatically, and Americans must find ways to adapt to those changes. Some of these adaptions can be provided by a new type of organization — the Z.

Here, the argument moves from the business arena into a somewhat larger context; its thrust is the ability of the American social environment to provide stable affiliations for individuals. Emile Durkheim, one of the first modern sociologists writing at the turn of the century, found that each person needs to have certain "primary bonds" established in his social relationships; otherwise he suffers from "anomie." An anomic society is one without any restraints or supports for individuals. Such anomie results in personal disorientation and anxiety, experienced primarily by those separated from their home towns, families and friends, without new work or personal ties to replace essential bonds. Overcoming anomie may in fact be a vital key to successfully increasing worker productivity.

In American society, families are becoming smaller and are separated by greater and greater distances. There has been a steady decline in clubs, and friendships become more and more transitory as mobility increases.

The traditional supports around which the Type A organization evolved have deteriorated or vanished completely. Coming at a time when our

The Type Z Organization

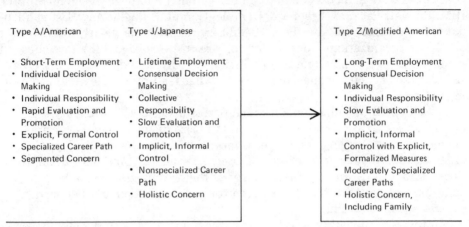

Type A/American	Type J/Japanese	Type Z/Modified American
• Short-Term Employment	• Lifetime Employment	• Long-Term Employment
• Individual Decision Making	• Consensual Decision Making	• Consensual Decision Making
• Individual Responsibility	• Collective Responsibility	• Individual Responsibility
• Rapid Evaluation and Promotion	• Slow Evaluation and Promotion	• Slow Evaluation and Promotion
• Explicit, Formal Control	• Implicit, Informal Control	• Implicit, Informal Control with Explicit, Formalized Measures
• Specialized Career Path	• Nonspecialized Career Path	• Moderately Specialized Career Paths
• Segmented Concern	• Holistic Concern	• Holistic Concern, Including Family

society is more and more unwilling or unable to provide needed affiliations, serious dislocations can develop.

Durkheim predicted that the place where primary bonds could be re-established in an industrial society would be an occupational group — either a labor union or a company. Indeed, no other institution plays as central a role in the lives of Americans as does their place of work.

It follows, then, that no other institution has the same ability, opportunity, and incentive to restore the spirit of community and belonging that is essential to the productivity and the social and psychological stability of any society.

Of course, work organizations cannot, by themselves, replace or compete with other national institutions. Nor should they. But by providing a strong basic stability in people's lives, by following some of the approaches of the Type J organization adapted to a Type Z mode, more traditional forms of group interaction can actually flourish in a corporate setting.

Not all American companies or executives will find the Type Z management approach applicable to their industries. But the model is a provocative one for many managers and may become even more appealing in the future.

The professional manager, increasingly, will be asked to take on a new role — that of social intermediary. Instead of simply bringing together providers of capital with users of capital (as a financial intermediary), every manager will have to bring together people who are simultaneously givers of support and needers of support.

Companies that can successfully build such a culture will attract and hold talented employees, create good will among their workers and, in essence, provide the primary bonds of affiliation and support that are necessary for worker stability and increased and useful productivity.

Our society has reached a critical point in its maturation; at a time when Americans are clearly expressing their needs for stability and structure, both are fast diminishing. Current social institutions seem unable to provide this stability or to foster positive, productive group affiliations. And with most corporations in America clearly not organized to provide such support and affiliations, the Type Z model begins to take on an even more attractive and more critical role as we enter the 1980s.

Questions for Discussion

1. What are the benefits of using the Type Z approach? Disadvantages?

2. What impact would a type Z organization style have on organization structure? Decentralization? Automation and information technology? Labor relations? Fringe benefits? Authority? Staffing? Directing?

EXERCISE

THE OLD SHELL GAME

How will the world of the future affect the manager and his or her job? Will new industries and knowledge yield new managerial challenges? In this incident, you can develop an idea of new managerial techniques as they are used in an unfamiliar setting.

Your name is Buck Rogers III, and you have been called out of retirement by the Chairman of the Galactic Federation. Your talents are needed for a special mission, so important that your retirement has been suspended until you reach age twenty-eight or carry out the job, whichever comes later. (Your first reaction to the Videowarp from the chairman was that you'd already done your duty to the Federation: five years — the maximum allowed, you remember with pride — as starship commander and Federation liaison in the strategic XIV Sector.)

Your experience in XIV Sector, however, made you the choice for this job; Earth astrophysicists discovered (in A.D. 2674) a minor star's instability in the sector and predicted it to go nova within three years, with disastrous results for the civilization in that part of the galaxy's spiral.

The assignment given you was to warn the Sector of the impending disaster and take command of the necessary steps to ensure minimal casualty to the population *and* culture.

Thanks to your contacts and your long-famous charm, warning the proper authorities required little time. The next step, however, has you tied in knots. It would be relatively simple to herd all 500 million Sector inhabitants into transport starships and whisk them to safety, but that would doom their culture by destroying their social relationships and uprooting them from the homelands they so deeply revere. And cause incredible relocation problems; most suitable planets are already rather heavily populated — where would they go?

Ah, but there is a way! Simply move the major five planets from the affected area and relocate them in another, uninhabited system! Available technology can be readily extended and adapted, you note with relish. Atmospheric Life Support, Ltd., specializes in atmosphere-generating and support; they can design and build huge spheres to encompass each of the five planets. Astrodyne, Inc., makes huge propulsion systems. General Electric (a venerable institution) furnishes energy and light sources. And Temporary Personpower could provide navigators, pilots, etc.

But how could this gigantic task be coordinated? If Atmospheric Life Support designed and built the spheres, then Astrodyne would have to modify them for their propulsion systems, not to mention needing engineering information to design the thrusters, their power and physical requirements. And then GE would have to do some redesign, as well as design their energy sources around the existing designs supplied them! Besides, while each phase is easy to assemble in space, the spheres would have to be built near Earth to allow the companies access to their resources when each is finally given the data it needs for its part of the overall job.

Now you're worried. Because, in addition to the time those companies would eat up, you know of no zipper maker on Earth that could install an opening big enough to open (to let a planet *in*), close (to maintain an atmosphere during the trip), then reopen (when the trip ends). And how can *you* make the myriads of technical decisions on your project?

FOR THE STUDENT

1. How would you go about coordinating the requirements of the various companies involved to minimize modifications and overall time?

2. How would you organize the activities to move the planets and their occupants to safety?

EXERCISE

ORIENTALIZATION ORIENTATION

The consultant was just concluding his briefing. Jo Harrison's mind had leaped far ahead, considering the implications of the report for the company she headed. She turned again to the page in the consultant's report, in which the summary of company management practices was given.

She focused on the part that said:

"... the not unusual practices of management employed by Magnetometrics, Inc., which have helped the company succeed and lead the industry. Characteristic of this approach are the following:

• Short-term employment

• Individual decision making

• Individual responsibility

• Rapid evaluation and promotion

• Explicit, formal control

• Specialized career paths

• Segmented concern

Although highly effective in the past, changing conditions and international competitive pressures have led to the possibility of adapting newer, different management practices. They promise unique benefits to company and employee alike. Illustrative of newer practices are those of the Japanese."

Jo's head nodded as her brain whirled with the excitement of using some of the Japanese methods she'd heard so much about.

Questions for Discussion

1. Review the text material on Japanese management methods. Go to the library and review two recent articles on Japanese management. Summarize the major characteristics of Japanese management methods.

2. Compare and contrast Japanese management methods with the list of American Management methods in this exercise.

3. Which Japanese methods should Jo adopt? Why?

CASE

MULTIMECH

"This is going to take a little getting used to!" Tim Burton closed his briefcase abruptly, shutting off his view of the plexite videoscreen centered over the palm-sized area of pushbuttons.

The device was an electronic marvel; it fit easily inside his briefcase, yet left enough room for file folders, an old-fashioned programmable hand-held calculator, and an equally quaint dictating unit. "Those'll have to go," mused Jim, "but not yet . . . not 'til I get comfortable with that gadget."

"That gadget" was the latest edition in a string of increasingly sophisticated technical aids to management. In the late 1960s and early 1970s, hand-held calculators were laughably primitive and narrow in function — yet rather expensive. Then came one new version after another, each lighter, smaller, more powerful, more sophisticated — and cheaper — than before. It was probably inevitable that the craze of the late 1970s and 1980s, the so-called home computer, would combine its power and other advantages with the practical convenience of the small calculators.

The triad, as Burton and his presidential-level peers (a "plural executive," was the old term) were called, had wrestled with the decision of whether to "decisionize" at Multimech for years. No small decision, but no small company; Multimech was an old (critics said that its operating style reflected its age) manufacturing service firm. Some called it stodgy; Burton preferred to think of it as conservative, cautious. Even after having gone to the plural executive concept five years ago, several upstart competitors had eroded Multimech's market share and captured some old customers with their new methods.

The plural executive had been formed to allow more focused attention on Multimech's three main divisions and their unique characteristics. Sometimes the members of the triad fought bitterly with each other over strategy and resource allocations, but all-in-all the divisions' performances had prospered under a better-informed management.

Burton's division, too, had grown and improved. That seemed a mixed blessing, though, for Jim could hardly keep up with the requirements of new markets and the advanced technologies his government applications division developed. R&D had bought a small fleet of surplus space shuttles to function as research platforms from which to test new zero-gravity crystal-growth and imperfection-free casting methods. Multimech technologies were adapted to the particular requirements of their clients, with Multimech division's engineers designing manufacturing and support facilities, supervising the building of the plant (through the deep-space, Terra, and off-world project systems divisions), and then turning over plant operations to the client.

Keeping up with R&D, project progress, client development (another term for what was once called sales — although much more than sales, because a project had to be individually developed and tailored) — major governments' funding trends and economic priorities, and so on, required rapid and accurate information and decisions. By the time a report was prepared or a specialist made recommendations from data gathered hastily from several operating units, a problem could become a crisis and an opportunity disappear.

And that's why a third of his briefcase was occupied by the decisionizer. It was only ("Only!" thought Burton wryly) a portable computer terminal with a videoscreen for output and a keyboard for interacting with the main computer via instantaneous hyperdysraxial communication.

Data that had normally gone into reports from the thousands of operating units such as project teams were input directly to the computer. The "reports" were analyzed automatically against common performance standards, summarized, and remained ready for scanning — and all instantly. Proper queries would give Burton detailed analyses on off-world project costs versus progress, effects on cash-flow projections estimated because of intergovernmental trade disruptions, evaluations through time-series calculations and multivariate analyses of various new applications, and instant data on any division activity anywhere.

Jim knew the decisionizer would help his job of running the division by giving him instantaneous access to information. Yet he was uneasy with the concept — and not with just the new technique.

He knew a more fundamental question had been raised by the new gadget. The way the system was set up, he was the only person with unrestricted access to the data bank. Each unit had access only to its own data, although its own historical data patterns were available to the unit. Because only he had such divisionwide data, he knew that only he could make the thousands of decisions by which the division operated. Before, the report system had been cumbersome and time consuming, but it also forced authority to be delegated and decisions to be decentralized. How could those operating teams handle their own business when he would be swamped with details? Who would have the time to do the strategic planning? Could he substitute his judgment for the experience and closeness to the firing line of the team leaders?

And yet, if others had decisionizers, who should have access to what information? What about security and industrial espionage? Wasn't there risk in the abuse of such information?

He knew such questions related to the very structure of the division. He would have to call a special meeting of the triad to consider them.

Questions for Discussion

1. How would the decisionizer affect the use of the plural executive concept?

2. How would the decisionizer affect the centralization/decentralization of decision making at Multimech?

3. How would the decisionizer affect the organization structure's shape at Multimech?

4. What do you think Multimech should do to accommodate the benefits of the decisionizer? How? Why?

ANSWERS TO SELF-REVIEW QUESTIONS, CHAPTER 22

True–False

1-T, 2-F, 3-T, 4-T, 5-F, 6-T, 7-T, 8-T, 9-F, 10-T, 11-F, 12-T, 13-F, 14-T, 15-F.

Multiple Choice

1-B, 2-C, 3-C, 4-E, 5-C, 6-A, 7-A, 8-A, 9-B, 10-D.

Chapter 23

So Manage!

CHAPTER OBJECTIVES

1. To point out that managing *is* the *attaining* of results — which requires the would-be manager to start managing *now*

2. To develop some insights into the characteristics of the "now" manager

SELF-REVIEW QUESTIONS

Matching

A. based on the premise that contented workers would show their appreciation

_____ 1. contingency coordinator

B. management was more frequently destructive than developmental

_____ 2. machiavellian manipulator

C. this manager saw his or her area as merely a subsystem of the corporate totality

_____ 3. prewar jungle juggernaut

D. this manager was seen as a generalist and the kind of person who made things happen

_____ 4. profits persuader

E. this manager was evaluated on results achieved

_____ 5. situational specialist

F. this manager recognized that every situation is somewhat unique

_____ 6. systems synchronizer

334

True–False

T F 1. Since antiquity the primary purpose of management has been to accomplish goals efficiently through the creative efforts of managers.

T F 2. A successful manager will simply never find that it is possible to stop learning or, for that matter, to end formal education.

T F 3. Around the turn of the century, management was more frequently destructive than developmental.

T F 4. The manager of tomorrow will be more concerned with productivity than with profitability or people.

T F 5. The theory that contented workers would produce more gave rise to what was known as "country club management."

T F 6. The pressures of the Depression contributed to the decline of the hard-nosed concept of management.

T F 7. Since the primary purpose of management has not changed since antiquity, the model manager of the 1950s would still be effective in the modern executive suite.

T F 8. The characteristics that made one a leader in Napoleon's day can have meaning for our leadership thinking today.

T F 9. Every day, you are in a management position regardless of your age or status in life.

T F 10. Styles change in management as well as in automobiles, architecture, and clothes.

T F 11. The model manager of the 1970s was a decision maker rather than a delegator.

T F 12. To the Jungle Juggernaut, labor was a critically important factor of production.

T F 13. Immediately after World War II, managers became more concerned with the welfare of their employees than with production.

T F 14. The Situational Specialist, Odiorne suggested, would be judged primarily by his or her own actions.

T F 15. The key activities of the Contingency Coordinator are anticipating, adapting, and asserting.

Multiple Choice

1. The Jungle Juggernaut model was rather common

   (a) throughout the history of management, (b) until the 1940s, (c) especially during pioneer, rustic times, (d) in times of powerful unions.

2. During the 1950s managers emphasized which of the following?

   (a) revenues, (b) costs, (c) intrigue, (d) results

3. To which of the following does the quotation, "No manager can be an island," relate?

   (a) Machiavellian Manipulator, (b) Profits Persuader, (c) Systems Synchronizer, (d) Situational Specialist

4. Which of the following is *not* a major concern of the Systems Synchronizer?

   (a) stability, (b) people, (c) profits, (d) productivity

5. The manager with the most critical need for adaptability is the

   (a) Systems Synchronizer, (b) Contingency Coordinator, (c) Situational Specialist, (d) none of the above.

READING

IMPROVING YOUR MANAGEMENT SKILLS STARTS WITH YOU

Joseph G. Mason

FACE IT: ONLY YOU CAN MAKE YOURSELF A BETTER MANAGER Training, development programs, and continued study definitely do have a place in the making of a manager. Through making it possible to share in the experiences of others, they can add to knowledge. By providing distilled principles of action, they give guidance. Through the stimulation of new intellectual exposures, they provide a necessary background of confidence that is of inestimable value to the man with the responsibility for making decisions. But academic study can go only so far. One instructor of a creative management course makes this point strongly to his students in the last session. "Don't consider your course completion Certificates to mean you are 'Graduate Creative Thinkers,' " he warns. "Accept them; keep them; display them prominently some place where you will see them every day. But use them as reminders that you have invested some time, energy, and mental anguish to complete this course as a beginning to what is now expected of you. But from here on out, it is up to you whether or not you will make this course pay off for yourself and your company."

And this, of course, is the crux of management development of any kind. All personal development is just that — personal. As Emerson put it, "Self-trust is the first secret of success." It is up to the manager to trust his own capabilities to make a success of the training he has been given and to develop the attitudes and experience that must be truly self-developed because they cannot be taught.

From *How to Build Your Management Skills*, by Joseph G. Mason (New York: McGraw-Hill Book Company, 1965), pp. 219–233. Reprinted by permission of McGraw-Hill Book Company.

REALIZE THAT YOU ARE YOU — AND MAKE THE MOST OF IT

One of the most common misconceptions about being an executive in any organization is that there is some mystical pattern or mold that the aspiring manager should cast himself in if he wants to make the grade. And this is certainly the first attitude that an aspirant should divest himself of. You cannot make the most of your own inborn talents if you try to develop along the lines of any set or ideal or specified pattern of personality characteristics, because the reality of the situation is that there are no set patterns for success.

Consider the most common example of "regimented personalities"; the military. Certainly if any group, as a group, has an image of inflexible sameness, it is a military organization. Yet in *The Professional Soldier*, Morris Janowitz points out that most distinguished commanders were men who deviated from the image. General MacArthur, for example, is cited as having a "career based on a flouting of authority." The Marine Corps' General Holland Smith is quoted in his own description of himself: "I was a bad boy. I always have been a bad boy in interservice arguments and I often am amazed that I lasted so long. . . ." And the description of Marquis Childs of Dwight Eisenhower may come as a shock to anyone whose image of him is that of the conservative he became in later years. As a West Point cadet, according to Childs, "Eisenhower was a roughneck. He broke the rules just as often as he dared. Law-abiding classmates were shocked at his daring. . . . His conduct was that of the tough boy from the wrong side of the tracks, defying the code, and yet managing by his resourcefulness to live with it."

Certainly if such individualistic personalities can succeed in a military organization, they should also do well in even the most image-conscious business and commercial enterprises.

One industrialist who expressed himself on this point is Alfred C. Fuller, founder of the Fuller Brush Company. "Of the first two hundred men who achieved executive position in the Fuller Brush Company," he relates, "only three had previously earned as much as fifty dollars a week in other employment. They were without exception little men of no previous attainment, or inadequate background, and almost no training for their jobs. Neither they nor I could 'think big'; we just knew how to work hard."

Albert Einstein, noted for his individualism, stressed his feelings of the importance of individuality just before he died, with his statement that one of the few things he felt sure of is that no person is just like any other person — "the individual is unique."

The late Moorhead Wright, of the General Electric Company, not only supported the feeling that the best service a company can give its managers is to allow them to be their own men, but also raised some interesting questions regarding theoretical images for managers:

"If you are going to work toward any sort of ideal 'personality pattern,'" he asked, "what, in the face of such a pattern, are you going to say to the managers now in place? Shall we say that they must conform to this ideal pattern or be fired? How," he continued, "do we account for the fact that we now have some managers — good managers — who are tough and rugged personalities, others who are quiet and thoughtful men, others who are aggressive-salesmen types, and others just as widely assorted — all good managers? The truth is," he concludes, "there just isn't any standard pattern of personality traits that make a good manager."

GO AFTER EXPERIENCE RIGHT WHERE YOU ARE

A research project in General Electric involved interviews with three hundred men who had reached positions where they had managerial responsibilities. An outside research group was utilized, and individuals were guaranteed anonymity. In response to the question "What do you consider the thing that was most important in your development?" Ninety per cent of the managers replied that it was the day-to-day work they were involved in. Only 10 per cent attributed major developmental importance to educational background, special courses, job rotation, etc. The outstanding factors were the manner in which the man himself was managed in his daily work, the climate in which he worked, and his relationships with others — particularly his immediate managers.

Amron H. Katz, in commenting on the value of his own past experience as a designer as a guide to work he is now doing in aeronautical engineering states the case this way: "Experience is not always a good teacher, nor is past experience necessarily and universally relevant to the future. On the other hand, it would indeed be strange if, after two decades of studies, experiments, and participation with the military in design, test evaluation, and use of equipment in the air as well as on the ground, in observations on the use of equipment in the field, under a full spectrum of conditions from primitive to plush — if at the end of all this I didn't have some firmly held views on what kind of developments are likely to succeed, what kind of developments are likely to fail — and why."

George Bunker, chairman and chief executive officer of the Martin Company, pointed up one of the real values of first-hand experience in commenting on reorganizations following the troubles that company had in its development work on the Titan missile: "If you burn your fingers lighting a match," he said, "You're going to be more careful next time."

And Joyce Clyde Hall, founder and president of Hallmark Greeting Cards, is famous for his reliance on what he calls "the vapor of experience" in reaching his decisions.

The prime cautionary note to be sounded regarding the principle of going after new experience in your present job is that you must be sure your assigned work is being done. Many eager junior executives realize that even limited management authority brings opportunities to develop themselves through sharing different experiences, but they then make the mistake of working so hard to broaden their horizons that they forget to cover the daily bases they are paid to cover. So while your present job offers you the base for future growth, you probably won't prosper to any great extent if the company's work that is assigned to you isn't being done.

But opportunities to take on new responsibilities and gain the experience that comes from solving the problems connected with them are all around any person in an executive job. They exist in the improved utilization of people; better control of dollars; more efficient and effective use of time; and maximum utilization of company facilities. Few companies, or even divisions, departments, or sections of companies can claim that they are doing the absolute best that can be expected in all of these areas, and anyone looking for opportunities will find plenty of them without having to carry the search very far.

HELP YOUR PEOPLE GROW

Industrialist Henry Kaiser states, "I make progress by having people around me who are smarter than I am — and listening to them. And I assume that everyone is smarter about something than I am."

This is really the secret of effective development and maximum utilization of subordinates' talents: determine what the best qualities are of each of your people, and then give them the opportunities to maximize those qualities for the benefit of the company. This means, of course, that every one in an organization will then have opportunities to grow. This requires a consciousness by the executive of the potential that lies within every man to develop new capabilities and capacities when the climate is right.

One company that makes a deliberate policy of allowing their people to maximize whatever potentials they may have as individuals is Aerojet-General Corporation. Although called highly unorthodox for their organization and operating methods, the company has achieved some startling successes in the highly competitive aerospace industry by following such far-out procedures as allowing the scientists who develop new devices to trot out and attempt to sell them to prospective customers themselves. So far the policy has paid off with more successes than failures, and has come to be the way things are expected to happen all through the company.

Furthermore, no executive can expect subordinates to be ready to take over new responsibilities as suddenly as can be demanded in a situation of rapid growth or unexpected emergency if those subordinates have not previously had the opportunity to practice handling responsibilities on a smaller scale and under noncritical conditions. Even if we were to discount by 50 per cent the predictions of future shortages in executive talent to be available for business, the importance of developing new talents through offering the opportunities to juniors to grow is still an apparent one. As the late J. H. Kindelberger, former chairman of North American Aviation, once said, "Nobody ever pulled a rabbit out of a hat without carefully putting it there in the first place."

The kind of delegation that builds the character of the subordinate, and equips him with the confidence to step out and achieve, is masterfully described by General Matthew B. Ridgway in his biography, *Soldier*. He tells of being assigned the command of the Eighth Army in Korea at the time when the situation was far from encouraging for the UN forces.

"At nine," recalls General Ridgway, "I saw General MacArthur. In a masterful briefing, he covered all the points I had in mind to ask him. As I rose to go, I asked one question. 'General,' I said, 'If I get over there and find the situation warrants it, do I have your permission to attack?'

"A broad grin broke out on the old gentleman's face. 'Do what you think best, Matt,' he said, 'The Eighth Army is yours.'

"That," says Ridgway, "is the sort of orders that puts heart into a soldier."

An example of a similar order in business is one credited to Donald Power, chairman and chief executive of General Telephone & Electronics Corporation. In instructing a newly promoted head of one of the company's areas, he is reported to have said, "I want only three things: high morale, good earnings, and good public relations. If you achieve these, you don't have to bother to send me any other reports."

Mr. Power thereby demonstrated another cardinal principle of good delegation: He knew what he wanted and was able to communicate it.

AIM FOR PROFESSIONALISM

"I like pros," said one manager. "I like to listen to them; watch them in action; work with them; know I have one on the job when there is a major commitment to be met. I don't care how snobbish it sounds, I always prefer to deal with a pro."

You will, of course, find pros in other than management jobs, too: the salesman who never gets flustered or never makes a mistake, no matter how difficult the customer makes the interview.

Or the soft-talking engineer who quietly moves in on a test bench where an instrument that is supposed to take an American to the moon and back is being tested — and not working. This pro listens to all the explanations of why it won't work and then softly asks the one question no one else had thought of asking — and gets the project moving again.

What's more, it isn't just in business that you can find the pros: you'll see waitresses in restaurants who seem able to handle twice the number of customers with half the effort of the other girls on the floor; bus drivers who never get rattled in the heaviest rush-hour traffic, but manage with quiet good humor to keep both their passengers at ease and their tightly drawn schedules; and shoe shine boys who always take the time to give the extra slap of the cloth that puts the highest gloss on the leather — and who always say "thank you" with a smile that says they mean it.

Certainly being a professional in a job is more than just a matter of being paid for it. There are people in jobs they are paid for doing who never seem to shine as brightly as others in similar positions. Professionalism is more a matter of the attitudes that manifest themselves in a man's general approach to his work.

One such characteristic is often the man's willingness to stick his neck out to a greater degree than his colleagues when a new proposition is presented. As Admiral Rickover states: "The first thing a man has to do is to realize that he is going to get his head chopped off ultimately. If he has that feeling, perhaps he can accomplish something."

Another characteristic of the pro is his complete mastery of his job, no matter how complex the problem. Ben Mills, an associate of Robert McNamara in his Ford Motor Company days, tells of McNamara's intellectual abilities in problem-solving sessions. After listening to arguments and propositions from his staff on highly complex problems, McNamara would then take over. "It was incredible," says Mills. "He would rattle off a dozen or more points, often without having taken any notes. If you challenged him, he was likely to defeat you with figures and judgments you yourself had given him several months earlier. It takes a certain amount of genius to be able to absorb and make sense of tough problems as quickly as Bob does. But, more than that, it takes a lot of intense study, a lot of damned hard work."

Another easily observed quality in the real professional is his personal sense of responsibility. The real pro seldom waits for problems to come to him — he goes out looking for problems, and when he finds one he can get his teeth into, he makes it his own personal problem and doesn't sit or quit until that problem has been licked. Frank Fisher, of the management consulting firm of Cresap, McCormick, and Paget, cites the opposite of this attitude as the symptom of a "stale climate" in a company. In the stale climate organization, according to Fisher, executives tend to be acquiescent — they don't develop strong feelings about anything and never bother to disagree over issues. Such men, he points out, tend to play "follow the leader"; they lack a feeling of urgency and therefore tend to postpone decisions. And this, indicates Fisher, is when the businesses begin to run down.

Still another manifestation of the sense of responsibility that makes a pro is when the man realizes he is living in a world greater than just his job. Charles Percy, president of Bell & Howell, may typify the new breed of executive with a sense of both national and international responsibilities in addition to his duties to his company. He is a member of the board of the University of Chicago; chairman of the Ford Foundation's Fund for Adult Education; and chairman of the Republican Party's Policy Committee on Programs and Progress. Says Percy, "If all of us in industry learned better the world in which we live, we'd all be better individuals."

Another readily observable characteristic of a pro is that he goes at his work with the realization that temperament is never a substitute for ability — he know that it is always better to *be* right than to sound right. He measures his own performance by his own standards — and these are usually higher than anyone else would dream of setting for him. Finally, it is never an accident, or a lucky break, when a pro does an outstanding job. He planned it that way, and wouldn't let it happen otherwise.

GUARD YOUR MORAL VALUES

Few men in any field ever reach the ultimate top without a strong sense of moral values. The occasional man who does gain a position of prestige or power with a character not completely honest will soon be uncovered for the weakness. Power or authority demands integrity of the highest type, for without it the occupant of the position will sooner or later give in to the temptation to abuse his authority. And even in lesser positions, a strong and sincere sense of morality is a requisite for winning and holding the respect and confidence of others in the face of the everyday temptations to deal and contrive as being easier alternatives to thinking and planning.

To say that a man can be a little dishonest in business is comparable to saying that a woman can be a little bit pregnant. A man is either honest or he is not; he either has integrity or he does not. And it is not required that he be a psalm-singing Bible thumper for him to be a moralist. As a matter of fact, unless he does have true and deep religious convictions, for him to adopt a superreligious pose merely for the sake of appearances would indicate a lack of integrity.

The practice of honesty has, in many industries, become a way of life — as it should for all businesses. Advertising agencies, for example, despite all the public abuse that is occasionally heaped upon them by critics of one sort or another, are noted for the "word is his bond" nature of their relationships with media representatives and suppliers. An agency executive will bargain like a longshoreman's union chieftain to get favorable arrangements for his clients, and may get into bitter and even recriminatory arguments with the media representative or supplier of the moment. But once agreement is reached, everyone knows that the contract can follow whenever it is convenient. Its main purpose will be a record of the transaction.

Corporate reputations for honesty often pay off in dramatic ways. Donald Douglas built such a reputation for his aircraft company and worked to preserve it despite the strongest temptations. One such was deliberately put in his way by Captain Eddie Rickenbacker at the time Douglas was competing against Boeing to sell Eastern Airlines its first big jets. During the negotiations, Rickenbacker is said to have told Douglas that his specifications and offers for the DC-8 were close to Boeing on everything but noise suppression. He then gave Douglas one last chance to out-promise Boeing on this feature.

After consulting with his engineers, Douglas reported back to Rickenbacker with the news that he did not feel he could make the promise. Rickenbacker is said to have replied, "I know you can't. I wanted to see if you were still honest. You just got yourself an order for $165 million. Now go home and silence those damn jets!"

Another Douglas, Senator Paul, demonstrates the force of integrity against the pressures of group conformity. Senator Douglas has the reputation of always walking alone, often in the face of what is usually referred to as party discipline. He explains his policy in easily understood terms: "One rule I make," he says, "is that if procedure does not vitally affect substance, I will follow my party on procedural grounds. But when substance is involved, I will follow my conscience."

A demonstration of reliance on personal integrity in dealing with others was given by Edgar Kaiser in settling with the United Steelworkers in the face of solid industry opposition to settlement. Kaiser, relying on his own judgment of the situation, explained his decision: "We do not believe it's right to put people back to work under a court injunction," he said. "When you force things upon human beings, you simply make more trouble for yourself in the long run. We think a showdown with labor, an attempt to turn the clock back, will merely result in more government control."

Such views are becoming more and more recognized as the hallmarks of enlightened management today. The blinding glare of publicity resulting from a well-intentioned, if somewhat overzealous, government policy of suspecting everything and everyone in business, is serving the purpose of lighting up the shadows where the big-riggers, the overfriendly noncompeting competitors, and the influence peddlers once did their business. And the only men who will survive with the freedom to pursue truly free enterprise are those whose moral standards are, like Caesar's wife, above suspicion.

To sum up, then, it is apparent that individual improvement must be largely an individual matter. While outside-induced education and academic experience do have much to offer a manager for his own personal development, only the man himself can supply or develop the inner qualities that transcend methods, techniques, procedures, and systems. You start where you are with what you have to work with now and build on it.

And only you can make yourself a better manager.

Questions for Discussion

1. Is there some pattern the would-be effective manager must strive to be like? Explain your answer.

2. What part does experience play in the development of the effective manager?

3. What part does personal integrity play in effective management?

EXERCISE: THE MANAGEMENT CROSSWORD PUZZLE

ACROSS

1. Third level of Maslow's Hierarchy
3. Field site for Coch & French study reported in, "Overcoming Resistance to Change"
8. Two letter abbreviation (singular) for product produced at #3 above
9. First university to offer a course in "Human Relations" (1936)
10. Popular teaching method developed at university referenced in #9 above
12. Country in which the Tavistock Institute is located (abbr.)

Reprinted with permission from the *Academy of Management Newsletter*, Vol. 7 (March 1977), p. 4. Prepared by Arthur G. Bedeian, Auburn University.

13. Consists of the Parent-Adult-Child states (abbr.)
14. Complement to Lawrence & Lorsch's Differentiation
17. Three letters used to designate a popular theory of motivation (1st 2 letters transposed)
18. "Pater Familae et Magister" (last name)
20. An adult male human being
21. First level (non-thesis) graduate degree in Business
23. First name of the originator of Force Field Analysis
24. Last name of the first Managing Director of the Taylor Society
26. Parametric statistical test used to determine if a significant difference exists between 2 means
27. Lowest passing grade in an undergraduate course
28. Letter used to denote sample size
30. Tax collecting arm of the Federal Government (abbr.)
32. School of business accrediting body (abbr.)
34. Research unit that developed the "Survey of Organizations Questionnaire" (abbr.)
35. Organization founded in 1947, located in Bethel, ME (abbr.)
36. Last name of person who popularized MBO
38. Percentage return on investment (abbr.)
39. Measure of satisfaction developed at Cornell University (abbr.)
45. Application of scientific methods to provide for optimum solutions to problems (abbr.)
47. Same as 45 across
48. Last name of person who is associated with the conceptualization of the "Rabble Hypothesis"
49. University located on the Charles River (abbr.)
50. Last name of the individual who developed the concept of sociometry
52. Nickname of the author of the "Management Theory Jungle"
53. First name of Lillian's (the First Lady of Management) husband

DOWN

1. Last name of person associated with "System 4"
2. Swedish automobile manufacturer pioneering in new work methods
4. Percentage return on investment (abbr.)
5. University which held the 1st Scientific Management Conference in the U.S. (1911)
6. Those support units that contribute indirectly to the achievement of an organization's objectives
7. A terminal degree in business (abbr.)
8. First initial and last name of the first editor of the Academy *Journal*
10. A popular contemporary theory of leadership
11. Initials used to designate a professional accomplishment of accountants
15. Corporation reorganized by Alfred P. Sloan, Jr., in late 1920's (abbr.)
16. Last name of the author of *The Art of Leadership*
18. First initial and last name of a former President of Antioch College
19. Developed the concepts of "acceptance theory of authority" & "zone of indifference"
22. Popular social science computer package (abbr.)

25. Letter used to designate Coefficient of Determination
29. Last name of the "Father of Scientific Management"
31. Originator of the MBO concept: former GE executive; 17th President of the Academy
33. Last name of the person associated with the "fusion process"
37. Last name of individual noted for non-directive counseling techniques, esp. "Client-Centered Therapy"
38. Last name of the author of the 1960 *Human Organization* article, "Banana Time: . . ."
39. A leading empirically-based journal in the behavioral sciences (abbr.)
40. Noted British management consultant presently living in Australia
45. Division 11 of the Academy (abbr.)
48. First name of the person associated with the "law of the situation"
51. Letter used to denote sample size
53. Parametric statistical test used to determine if a significant difference exists between two or more means
54. Abbreviation for Input-Output

EXERCISE

PUTTING MANAGEMENT INTO ACTION

The text and this workbook have consistently stressed the application of individual ideas and skills of management. Exercises and incidents have given you the opportunity to analyze situations or to try things out for yourself.

Now comes the acid test. We've tried to get you into the habit of thinking critically and acting decisively in a relatively artificial environment, the classroom and this course.

Can you accept the challenge of the most rewarding activity of all? Put the ideas and skills of management to work *for you*! There's a large gap between theory and practice — try putting your hard-won knowledge to use, day by day.

At first it'll seem hard and uncomfortable when you try to think through the best ways of accomplishing something. But after a short while, it'll come naturally. Continuing your management activities will give you a definite edge when it comes to performing on the job. And it'll help you keep things in perspective and under control, both on and off the job.

It's up to *you* — only you can make that first step that means putting management skills and ideas to work for you.

So manage!

FOR THE STUDENT

Briefly describe two situations in which you are now or will be shortly. Put down enough facts to represent the situation without getting into too many details. Then analyze them as we've been analyzing the incidents.

This will help get you into the practice of thinking analytically about what you want to do (goals), how to do it (planning), what is involved in doing it (organizing), whom you need to do it (staffing), and how well you did what you wanted to do (controlling).

Write on!

CASE

MINOR MANAGEMENT MIRACLES

Tom flipped his management text casually onto his desk. "Ah, nuts! This management stuff is just common sense — why do they have to try and make it complicated?"

Sebastian looked up from his textbook, amused. "Common sense? What's that got to do with you?" And ducked as an eraser whizzed past his head.

"Let me tell you what I mean," began Tom. "Here we go through this whole textbook about management. We have tests, and I do pretty well. The stuff's easy to read and not bad to study, y'know, but it's not like it's something heavy like . . . like calculus or accounting — y'know, where you learn to *do* something and work problems and all! This management is just stuff I must have known something about all along, 'cause I don't see any huge revelations in some new chapter."

Sebastian nodded knowingly. "*Si*, I know what you mean. I thought the same thing until something hit me. What hit me was that most people probably *do* management in their lives, yet don't know they're doing management. So when we study it, it doesn't seem completely foreign to us. I learned some stuff, though. Remember last term when I was in charge of the big fraternity party?"

Tom nodded, "Yeah. Everybody said it was the best one ever!"

Sebastian continued, "Sure, but that was because it was well-organized, well-planned, well-coordinated — well-managed! Long before the party I sat down and drew up a PERT chart, wrote down who was supposed to do what by when, y'know, the whole bit."

Impatiently, Tom snapped, "So what's that got to do with anything? You did a good job — is that what you want to hear? I could've, too! This messing around with activities takes too much time — you need a high grade-point average to get a good job. Minor management miracles are peanuts when we're talking *real* jobs! I'd rather work hard on my studies, 'cause that's what'll get me a good job!"

"But what after that?" asked Sebastian softly. "Will your textbook help you learn how to *do* management when your job depends on it? My 'minor management miracles,' as you call them, are my way of practicing. Do the football players create their plays during the game? No, they get the play right in practice so it'll go as planned in the game; they can't take a chance during the game when a single play can win — or lose — it!

"That's me, too. When I get my first management job, I want to be familiar with the tools-of-the-trade; I don't want to take a chance that a new skill — that *must* work — *will* work when I've not done it before. Pros need practice. I intend to be a professional manager!

"You think my extracurricular activities are just fun and games? Let me tell you something; it's serious stuff to me. These activities are all case problems, practice for the real thing. I even keep a notebook of problems and accomplishments, techniques that worked right, and others that needed a special 'push.' I look it over every once in a while, too, to review what I've learned from my experiences and how they compare with what the textbook says. On my résumé, at least I can say I've been a *practicing* manager!

"And what about you, Tom? You know the theories pretty well, but so do I. You've had accounting, but you still have trouble balancing your checkbook. You've had marketing, but a 'product' as important as your résumé is 'packaged' poorly — looks sloppy — and doesn't 'sell' you. You've had finance, but every month you run short of money, although you start with a good bit. Don't you think your management needs a little 'practice.?'"

Questions for Discussion

1. Do management skills need practice? Why or why not?

2. What activities, in which you are (or will be) engaged, could furnish opportunities for practicing management? How?

3. Prepare a plan by which to develop your management skills through practice.

ANSWERS TO SELF-REVIEW QUESTIONS, CHAPTER 23

Matching

A-2, B-3, C-6, D-5, E-4, F-1.

True–False

1-F, 2-T, 3-T, 4-F, 5-T, 6-F, 7-F, 8-T, 9-T, 10-T, 11-T, 12-F, 13-F, 14-F, 15-T.

Multiple Choice

1-B, 2-D, 3-C, 4-A, 5-B.